Jesus
at the Movies

Jesus at the Movies

A GUIDE TO THE FIRST HUNDRED YEARS

Revised and Expanded

W. Barnes Tatum

 POLEBRIDGE PRESS

Library of Congress Cataloging-in-Publication Data

Tatum, W. Barnes.
    Jesus at the movies : a guide to the first hundred years : revised and expanded / W. Barnes Tatum.
      p. cm.
    Filmography:
    Includes bibliographical references and index.
    ISBN 0-944344-67-4
    1. Jesus Christ--in motion pictures. I. Title.

PN1995.9.J4T37 2004
791.43'651--dc22

                                                  2004057332

TABLE OF CONTENTS

Jesus at the Movies: A Guide to the First Hundred Years first appeared in print seven years ago. As the title suggests, this volume's initial publication coincided with the centennial of commercial cinema and the centennial of Jesus' initial appearance on the screen, both of which occurred in the 1890s.

This year, 2004, during the first decade of the twenty-first century, Mel Gibson's *The Passion of the Christ* was projected publicly onto theater screens around the world and subsequently reflected on television screens in more private settings, thanks to VHS and DVD technologies. The release of Gibson's film serves as the immediate occasion for a revised and expanded edition of *Jesus at the Movies* at the outset of the second hundred years of Jesus cinema.

However, other Jesus films have already contributed to this everlengthening cinematic tradition. *Lux Vide*, the Italian media company, oversaw the made-for-television film called simply *Jesus*. Another film, *The Miracle Maker*, which was produced in Wales and Russia, also for television, brought the Jesus story to the screen using 3D animation. Both films received their premier telecasts in the United States, on network television in the spring of 2000. Last fall, 2003, there appeared *The Gospel of John*, a Visual Bible release which follows the text and translation of the American Bible Society's Good News Bible. After its theatrical debut at the Toronto Film Festival, the film was booked into selected theaters in Canada and the United States. A recent stage revival of *Jesus Christ Superstar*, in London and in New York City, has also been filmed and—like the movies just mentioned—has been made available in VHS and DVD formats.

This second edition of *Jesus at the Movies* represents a revision of the original edition, where appropriate. This edition also represents an enlargement from twelve chapters to fourteen, with each new chapter devoted to a particular film. Chapter fourteen focuses on Mel Gibson's *The Passion of the Christ* (2004). What has become chapter ten features *Monty Python's Life of Brian* (1979). Seven years ago I was not completely convinced that the latter movie was a Jesus film, although I made passing mention of it in the first edition.

What convinced me otherwise was the forum at the annual meeting of the Society of Biblical Literature in Nashville, Tennessee, in

November, 2000. Sponsored by the Bible in Ancient and Modern Media (BAMM) Section, the session on "Jesus Movies" involved formal critiques and responses by the authors of *Jesus at the Movies* and *Savior on the Silver Screen*. Arthur Dewey presided, Adele Reinhartz, Russell Dalton, and Richard Walsh provided the critiques, and Richard C. Stern, Clayton N. Jefford, and Gueric DeBona, joined me as respondents.

Since the beginnings of my study of films based—in some sense—on the gospel accounts of Jesus as the Christ, I have made a formal distinction between two kinds of films. On the one hand, *Jesus-story films* narrate the life and ministry of Jesus, usually within a first century Palestinian setting. An actor plays the part of Jesus, customarily with a beard and a flowing gown. Thus these films have earned the nickname, "bathrobe dramas." By contrast, *Christ-figure films* tell a more contemporary story in which characters, events, and details recall the gospel story of Jesus. Whatever the message of these films, an actor plays a figure who often experiences great suffering and possibly sacrificial death.

In the midst of the give-and-take at the SBL forum, I realized I could apply this distinction and its line of reasoning to *Monty Python's Life of Brian*. Jesus-story films usually feature a character named Jesus in a bathrobe in a first Palestinian century setting. In the Python film, a character named Jesus, in a bathrobe, does appear, in Judea, in the year A. D. 33, on Sunday afternoon, about teatime. Ergo, I acclaimed this to be a Jesus-story film. But, of course, Brian is not Jesus. He is anachronistically, in his own peculiar way, a Christ-figure. So whereas most of the films reviewed in this volume represent Jesus-story films, *Monty Python's Life of Brian* (1979) joins *Jesus of Montreal* (1989, 1990) as a film with both a Jesus-figure and a Christ-figure. I am certain that the Python troupe would have smiled at the setting of our discussion and my epiphany—the Opryland Hotel.

This fall marks the thirtieth anniversary of my co-teaching for the first time at Greensboro College a course called "A Cinematic Quest for Jesus." On the opening evening, Henry Ingram and I projected, in 16 mm, David Greene's adaptation of the musical *Godspell*. (He possessed the expertise in film.) Since then I have periodically continued to teach similar courses with other colleagues, with Ray Martin, an artist and teacher of the visual arts, and with Rhonda Burnette-Bletsch, a teacher of religion and biblical scholar. She also read the new chapters for this edition and applied her considerable editing skills.

Other colleagues at Greensboro College, in various ways, also provided assistance, solicited and unsolicited, during the revision process. These included Jennie Hunt, reference librarian, Richard Crane, of the history faculty, and Cynthia Hanson, in marketing. My class in *koinē* Greek spent much of the spring semester reading and studying the gospel passion narratives—and discussing *The Passion*, after the film opened at a local multiplex. Barney Baggett, Josh Bair, Kat Elkins, David Jones, and Hutch Stull enlivened the course with their insights and good humor.

Greensboro College has continued to provide financial support for my scholarly interest in matters related to Jesus, in history and on the screen. Funds have been provided through several sources, including the Royce and Jane Reynolds Endowment Fund for Faculty Development. I have been enabled to participate in the collaborative work of the Jesus Seminar under the leadership of Robert W. Funk. Over the years, I have come to know fellow participant and film-maker Paul Verhoeven who continues to test ideas for his own cine-matic Jesus project. I would also like to thank Tamme de Leur, a producer and director with EO-TV in the Netherlands, whose guests Linda and I were for an advance screening of *The Passion* in Charlotte, North Carolina.

As with the first edition of this book, Linda—my wife—has been a conversation partner both in the evaluation of the films mentioned herein and in the preparation of the revised manuscript for publica-tion. Recognition must also be given to our friend Carol DeVries, an assiduous consumer of newspapers from around the country, who, for two years, has regularly passed on to me under wrap clippings about the public debate surrounding the Gibson film.

W. Barnes Tatum
Greensboro College
Greensboro, NC
August 15, 2004

How to Use This Guide

This revised and expanded of *Jesus at the Movies* follows the design of its predecessor. Like the previous edition, this volume is intended to accompany the actual viewing of the films included for detailed analysis. As a viewer's guide, the book is written for anyone interested in film, in religion, or both. The guide falls into three main parts.

"The Promise and Problem of the Cinematic Jesus," the first part, introduces the subsequent consideration of individual films by exploring the possibilities and difficulties inherent in bringing the story of Jesus to the screen.

"Jesus-story Films and the Cinematic Jesus," the second and most important part of the guide, consists of fourteen chapters. Each chapter focuses on one or more films selected for analysis. The films chosen span the history of cinema: Sidney Olcott's *From the Manger to the Cross* (1912); D. W. Griffith's *Intolerance* (1916); Cecil B. DeMille's *The King of Kings* (1927); Mervyn LeRoy's *Quo Vadis* (1951); Henry Koster's *The Robe* (1953); William Wyler's *Ben-Hur* (1959); Samuel Bronston's *King of Kings* (1961); Dino De Laurentiis' *Barabbas* (1962); George Stevens' *The Greatest Story Ever Told* (1965); Pier Paolo Pasolini's *The Gospel According to St. Matthew* (1964 in Italian; 1966 with English subtitles or dubbing); Norman Jewison's *Jesus Christ Superstar* (1973); David Greene's *Godspell* (also 1973); Franco Zeffirelli's *Jesus of Nazareth* (1977); *Monty Python's Life of Brian* (1979); John Heyman's *Jesus* (1979); Martin Scorsese's *The Last Temptation of Christ* (1988); Denys Arcand's *Jesus of Montreal* (1989 in French, 1990 with English subtitles); and Mel Gibson's *The Passion of the Christ* (2004).

Several factors led to the selection of these Jesus films, from among others, for detailed comment. First, these films are most often cited in the literature, both film and religious literature, when the discussion centers around how Jesus has been treated on the screen. Secondly, these films are among those most frequently telecast on network and cable television, particularly during holiday seasons. Thirdly, these films were made by commercial studios for commercial use, not by religious organizations for evangelistic or educational purposes. John Heyman's *Jesus* (1979) constitutes an exception, although even this film was first shown in commercial theaters. Fourthly, and perhaps most importantly, all of these films are now available on VHS and most have become available on DVD. They can be easily obtained for purchase or rental, for home or classroom, through stores or web sites.

Finally, the third part of the guide, "The Cinematic Jesus in Retrospect and Prospect," represents an open-ended conclusion that includes generalizations about how Jesus has been portrayed on the screen over the first hundred or so years and considers how his story might be treated in the near future.

As a viewer's guide, this volume can be used in two related ways. On the one hand, the reader can approach the volume as he or she would any monograph by reading from the beginning through to the end. Since the films are reviewed in chronological order and placed within the framework of developments in the history of cinema and society, the reader will carry away an overview of the history of Jesus on the screen. On the other hand, the reader can treat the volume like a reference work and read the chapters on particular films as the occasion may dictate. Since every film receives similar treatment, the reader will develop an appreciation for a film—or films—in four areas: background information on the making of the film, including the names of the main contributors; how the film presents the Jesus story, with special attention given to the way material from the New Testament gospels has been used in the screenplay; how the film portrays Jesus and the relation of this portrayal to other characterizations of Jesus, such as those in the individual gospels and other writings; and, finally, the response to the film, by the general public and religious groups and by critics representing the religious and the secular press.

As a viewer's guide, this volume can also be used in association with screenings in group settings. Over the past thirty years, many of the films analyzed and mentioned herein have been used as teaching tools in film and in religion courses. Course syllabi, at the undergraduate and graduate levels, give evidence of the widespread use of Jesus films particularly in New Testament courses and increasingly in courses dedicated to the Jesus film genre. The Jesus film genre itself has become the subject for scholarly inquiry. In recent years, the program of the annual national meetings of the American Academy of Religion and the Society of Biblical Literature have featured the screening of a broad range of commercial films throughout their four-day gatherings as well as sessions devoted to presentations on particular films.

In order to enhance this volume's value as a viewer's guide, the book contains appendices and cameo essays on particular topics related to Jesus on film. The topics range from the question of gospel authorship to overviews of the geography and politics of first-century Roman Palestine. A bibliography and a filmography are also included.

The Cinematic Jesus
Promise and Problem

Jesus of Nazareth has been the dominant figure in western culture for most of the two thousand years since he lived and died in first-century Roman Palestine. Over the centuries, Jesus has also become a central figure in an emerging global culture. These were the underlying assumptions and the demonstrated conclusions of Jaroslav Pelikan's masterful 1985 book *Jesus Through the Centuries: His Place in the History of Culture*.[1]

Pelikan presents, roughly in chronological order, a series of eighteen images of Jesus that reflect the latter's place in the history of culture. These images include Jesus as "the Rabbi," "the Light of the Gentiles," "the King of Kings," "Christ Crucified," "the Universal Man," "the Prince of Peace," and "the Liberator." In support of his delineation of these images of Jesus, Pelikan calls upon a vast variety of cultural evidence—literary and visual.

From literature, Pelikan cites the writings of acknowledged theological greats: Athanasius, Augustine, and Aquinas; Bernard of Clairvaux and Francis of Assisi; Martin Luther, John Wesley, John Calvin, Friedrich Schleiermacher, and Karl Barth. Pelikan also utilizes comments from writers of a less traditional theological bent: Thomas Jefferson, Samuel Taylor Coleridge, and Ralph Waldo Emerson, among others. Furthermore, Pelikan invokes the teachings of such religious organizations and movements as the Benedictines, the Crusaders, and the Quakers. And he refers to the texts of papal bulls, hymns, poems, novels, and even to historical "lives" of Jesus.

From the visual arts, Pelikan displays and comments on works in different media by unknown and known artists: mosaics and frescoes; paintings and sculptures; wood carvings and manuscript illuminations; Giotto and Michelangelo; Dürer and Lucas Cranach the Younger; El Greco, William Blake, and Siegfried Reinhardt.

In establishing Jesus' place in culture over the centuries, Pelikan claims to rely on the artifacts of both "high culture" and what has become known as "popular culture." However, he omits the cultural evidence so characteristic of the twentieth and now the twenty-first century: *motion pictures, the movies,* or *cinema.* Pelikan makes not one reference to a film or to a filmmaker. However, it is precisely with

1

films and filmmakers that this volume concerns itself. We are interested in how the Jesus story has been adapted for the screen and focus our attention on the *cinematic* Jesus.

By common reckoning, commercial cinema was born on December 28, 1895, in Paris, France, in the basement of the Grand Café.[2] On that occasion, Auguste and Louis Lumière—using their Cinématographe—projected a series of ten films for a *paying* audience. Lasting only a minute or so each, these films showed scenes of everyday life—workers leaving the Lumière factory in Lyons where the brothers manufactured photographic equipment, a train arriving at a station with the passengers disembarking, the feeding of a baby, etc. The Lumière brothers had advanced, for the moment, beyond the American inventor Thomas A. Edison in their capability of projecting moving images on a screen for a viewing audience.

However, within four months of the projection of films by the Lumière brothers, Edison had acquired his own machine capable of projecting moving images and renamed it the Vitagraph. The first commercial showing of films using Edison's projector occurred on April 23, 1896, in New York City, at the Koster and Bial Music Hall, located at Broadway and 34th Street. As with his French rivals, many of Edison's brief early films showed scenes from everyday life.[3] Nonetheless, virtually from the beginning of the commercial use of moving pictures, filmmakers turned to the Jesus story as a source for subject matter and profit. All these pioneering films, of course, projected silent images. Talking pictures would not appear for another thirty years.

The Promise of Jesus in Film

That the Jesus story found expression through the medium of film is not surprising. As documented by Pelikan himself, Jesus and his story have been transmuted into a variety of visual forms over the centuries. However, significant differences between film and earlier artistic and cultural forms developed. These differences have made film an even more promising medium for telling the story of Jesus.

Firstly, film represents a medium with many dimensions that brings together virtually all the arts to create a moving picture. In cinema's earliest years, the traditional passion play—with its focus on the last week of Jesus' life—provided an immediate dramatic basis and model for a cinematic retelling of Jesus' life. The famed Oberammergau Passion Play first performed in Bavaria in 1634, and later every ten years, was well known throughout Europe and in this country.[4]

Before the turn of the century, several passion plays had been filmed on the European continent and in America. A brief film called

La Passion (1897), from France, has been identified by Richard H. Campbell and Michael R. Pitts as "the first film to chronicle the life of Jesus Christ and probably the first motion picture to be based on any portion of the Bible."[5] Like many early films, this cinematic passion play is no longer extant. The film has been described as consisting of twelve scenes with a screening time of five minutes. Other Jesus films soon followed.[6]

The so-called Horitz *Passion Play* (also 1897) earned its name from the fact that it had been filmed in Horitz, Bohemia (today the village of Horice in the Czech Republic). American theater producers Marc Klaw and Abraham Erlanger provided the financial support. The film captured scenes from the performance of a traditional passion play by the local villagers. The film was shown in Philadelphia beginning on November 22, 1897, first at the Academy of Music, later at the Horticultural Hall. At the outset of the next year, the film and its attendant program were taken to other northeastern cities—in January to Boston, in February to Baltimore, and in March to New York.

Even before the Horitz *Passion Play* reached New York City, Jesus had appeared there on the screen in the *Passion Play of Oberammergau* (1898). This cinematic presentation of the Jesus story, with twenty-three scenes and a twenty minute screening time, had received its first public showing in late January, 1898, at the Eden Musée, a well-known entertainment establishment in the city owned by Richard G. Hollaman. Like the Horitz *Passion Play*, the *Passion Play of Oberammergau* had no titles on the screen, thereby requiring a live narrator to provide commentary for the viewing audience. The moving images and narration were complemented by live music to lend solemnity to the occasion.

The favorable audience response to the initial presentations of the *Passion Play of Oberammergau* was duly noted in an article in the *New York Herald* (1 February 1898). The same article accused the exhibitors of the film of misleading the public:

> There was a large audience at the Eden Musee yesterday to witness what has been generally understood to be a cinématograph reproduction of scenes from the Oberammergau *Passion Play*. The spectators apparently were much interested in the pictures, and at the close generously applauded them. All the preliminary announcements of this exhibition have tended to convey the impression that this is a genuine reproduction of the celebrated *Passion Play* at Oberammergau. Of course the cinématograph has been invented since the last performance at Oberammergau. But a gentleman at the Eden Musee on last Friday, when a private exhibition of the scenes was given for the press, took the trouble to explain to a *Herald* reporter that the peasants who were accustomed to appear in the *Passion Play* at Oberammergau had been

induced to go through a special performance, at which the cinémato-gaph scenes had been taken. . . .

The truth is, however, that the cinématograph pictures at the Eden Musee were taken not at Oberammergau, but right here in New York on the roof of the Grand Central Palace early last December . . . . [7]

The investigative reporting of the *New York Herald* was accurate. The film shown at the Eden Musée had indeed been shot on a New York rooftop, not in a Bavarian village.

Hollaman had attended a viewing of the Horitz *Passion Play* in Philadelphia the preceding November, having failed to obtain the rights to that production for himself. He then decided to produce his own film for his New York entertainment house, the Eden Musée. Hollaman did so in collaboration with Albert G. Eaves, basing the film on the script of a theatrical passion play staged in this country years earlier.

The actual filming of the *Passion Play of Oberammergau* occurred over a six week period during the winter months of December and January, 1897 and 1898. Reminiscences about the making of the film point out the difficulties associated with its production. The cast, including animals, had to be transported to the rooftop of the Grand Central Palace by elevator. Actors wore heavy flannels under their bib-lical costumes. On occasion, snow had to be shoveled from the Garden of Gethsemane.[8] Viewers of this film today are also made of aware of the peculiar location of its making. The crosses of Jesus and the two thieves crucified with him cast shadows against the artificial backdrop that shields the New York skyline from the camera's view.[9]

In spite of the revelations by the *New York Herald* about the back-ground of the *Passion Play of Oberammergau*, the film proved itself to be a popular attraction for weeks and even received public praise from many church people, clergy and laity. The Eden Musée also sent out road companies to present two-hour passion play programs. Hollaman even made the film available for purchase.

As cinema matured, the production process came to involve collab-oration not only with the dramatic arts but also with the visual, the literary, and the musical arts. In the late 1920s, the silent movies gave way to the talkies as the voices of the characters themselves came to be heard. In the 1940s and 1950s, television joined the motion picture projector as a means of showing moving and talking images. In response, cinema developed the technology for even bigger images on still bigger screens. Along the way, color replaced black and white as the preferred film stock. Therefore, film increasingly developed an exceptional capacity for "bringing to life" Jesus and his story, just as so many other stories had come alive on the screen.

In addition to film's own capacity to "bring to life," there is a second reason why film holds such promise for telling the Jesus story. Film as an artistic and entertainment medium appeared over a hundred years *after* the commencement of—and has developed *alongside*—that scholarly and historical preoccupation with the Jesus story known as "the quest of the historical Jesus."

The so-called "quest" began in earnest, late in the eighteenth century, with the recognition that a distinction could be made between "the Christ of faith" and "the Jesus of history." The phrase "the Christ of faith" designated Jesus as confessed to be the Christ in the writings and traditions of the church—such as the New Testament, including the gospels of Matthew, Mark, Luke, and John. The phrase "the Jesus of history" designated Jesus as he walked and talked in first-century Palestine or, more accurately, Jesus as reconstructed to have lived in first-century Palestine based on the historical interpretation of all available evidence.

Although undertaken with a variety of motives, this ongoing "quest" has sought in its own way to bring to life Jesus and his story. The innumerable written "lives" and lesser sketches of "the historical Jesus" bear witness to this, with each claiming to present what Jesus was really like as a historical figure.

Over the past two centuries, this historical quest has expressed itself in three principal movements. The nineteenth-century quest, the "old" or "first" quest, was chronicled by Albert Schweitzer in his massive volume published in English as *The Quest of the Historical Jesus* (1906). Schweitzer concluded by sketching his own understanding of the historical Jesus. To him Jesus had been "a mistaken apocalyptist" (my phrase) who wrongly believed that the world as known would end in his own day. This "first" quest was drawing to a close just as cinema was beginning. As we have just seen, when filmmaking initially turned to Jesus, it turned to the church's tradition of the passion play—not to the conclusions of scholarly investigation.

My own *In Quest of Jesus* (rev. and enl. ed.; 1999) provides an overview of the historical quest that goes beyond Schweitzer's generation at the turn of the century through the late 1990s and encompasses both what has become known as a "new," or "second," quest and the beginnings of a "renewed" or "third" quest.[10] Among the varying historical reconstructions of Jesus discussed in my volume are Jesus as "the incarnation of God," "a zealot," "the suffering-servant messiah," "a magician," "the eschatological prophet," and "a sage."

By the close of the twentieth century, the discussion of Jesus as a historical figure had moved from academic circles into the public arena. This became evident when Jesus appeared on the covers of

Time, U. S. News & World Report, and *Newsweek* magazines the same week—Easter week, Passover week, the week of April 8, 1996. Among the profiles of the historical Jesus featured therein were those that described Jesus as "a Mediterranean Jewish peasant" and "a marginal Jew." Certainly a distinctive feature of the historical quest in recent decades has been the clear affirmation of Jesus' Jewishness—that he was a Jew.

Out of this quest—or quests—of the historical Jesus have come enlarged understandings of the gospels, which bear witness to Jesus, as well as renewed interest in Jesus himself as a flesh and blood human being. These literary perspectives and historical insights have become increasingly available to filmmakers as they moved away from the passion play model and began to create their own cinematic portrayals of Jesus. Audiences too, both professional film critics and the general public, have increasingly brought these literary perspectives and historical insights with them to their viewings of Jesus on the screen.

The Problem of Jesus in Film

In spite of its differences from other media, film has only occasionally realized its potential for telling the Jesus story because of what can be called "the problem of the cinematic Jesus." Actually, for the filmmaker and the viewer, the problem of the cinematic Jesus encompasses at least four dimensions: the *artistic,* the *literary,* the *historical,* and the *theological.* These four dimensions of the problem can be illustrated by seeing how film critics and commentators have recognized these dimensions in their reviews of Jesus-story films. Each of the films commented on here will be explored more fully later.

First, the problem of the cinematic Jesus has to do with the obvious recognition that Jesus-story films *are films.* This is the *artistic* dimension of the problem. Film possesses its own integrity as an art form and a storytelling medium. The film industry itself has come to recognize the artistic excellence of films by giving annual awards in different categories. In the United States, since 1927–1928, the Academy of Motion Picture Arts and Sciences has awarded Oscars. In Canada, there are Genies. Annual film festivals such as those at Toronto in Canada, Cannes in France, and Venice in Italy also bestow prizes.

Like all films, Jesus-story films should fulfill their artistic potential not just dramatically but visually as well. This point was made several decades ago by Gilbert Seldes—in *The New Republic* (4 May 1927)—when he judged Cecil B. DeMille's *The King of Kings* (1927) to be a cinematic failure. Contrary to the opinions of most reviewers, Seldes wrote:

Almost everything is treated graphically—is treated as painting-composition—and nothing as cinema, as moving pictures. All the great scenes seem to be reproductions of famous paintings; there is hardly an effect which could not have been achieved by the still camera.

Here Seldes has identified a problem not only for DeMille but for all makers of Jesus films. Long before there were moving pictures there were still pictures. The filmmaker must decide whether to duplicate these familiar images of Jesus or not. Because DeMille decided to duplicate rather than to create, Seldes even labeled his film "the anti-Christ." But Seldes made it quite clear that this represented an *artistic* and not a *theological* judgment. Professional reviewers for the press, secular and religious, routinely evaluate Jesus films in terms of their cinematic qualities: script, dialogue, lighting, cinematography, casting, acting, editing, music. That's the business of film critics.

Audiences also know whether they like or don't like what they have seen and experienced in Jesus-story films. People bring to their viewing preconceptions about how Jesus and scenes from his life look. Just by living in American or western society, we develop images of Jesus in our minds. Preconceptions about Jesus' visual appearance need not be derived from church attendance or membership. These preconceptions may represent remembrances of illustrations in family Bibles, come from familiarity with great works of art, or be derived from seeing billboards and watching television.

Secondly, the problem of the cinematic Jesus has to do with the written sources available for the fashioning of coherent screenplays—specifically those sources known from the New Testament by the names of Matthew, Mark, Luke, and John. This is the *literary* dimension of the problem. These four gospels are essentially confessions of faith in Jesus as the Christ. They contain only limited information about Jesus and his outer life. They report virtually nothing about his inner life and his motivation.

Moira Walsh, in her review of George Stevens' *The Greatest Story Ever Told* (1965) for the Catholic periodical *America* (27 February 1965), gave expression to the dilemmas presented to the screen writer by the gospels. She said:

> Any film-maker approaching the life of Christ—be he exegete or hack—is confronted with the same problem: the impossibility of piecing together a screen play using only the dialogue and specific information available in the New Testament. From this simple fact emerge all kinds of agonizing and insoluble dilemmas. Shall we write "additional dialogue" for Christ? What kind of small talk did He make, for example, at the marriage feast of Cana? Shall we provide motivation where none exists specifically, e.g. for Judas' betrayal? How shall we establish the

social, political, religious, etc., conditions of the world into which Christ came?

Although well stated by Walsh, the problem of literary sources extends beyond the meagerness of the information available in the four narrative gospels preserved in the New Testament. These four gospels themselves present two strikingly different characterizations of Jesus and his story: the portrayal of Jesus in the Gospels of Mark, Matthew, and Luke, on the one hand; and the portrayal of Jesus in the Gospel of John, on the other.

The Gospels of Matthew, Mark, and Luke have become known as the synoptic gospels because they present a common (syn-) view (optic) of Jesus and his ministry. In these gospels, Jesus centers his message around the phrase "the kingdom of God" (or "the kingdom of heaven," preferred by Matthew), delivers his message in striking parables, and maintains a certain secrecy about his work and identity. By contrast, in the Gospel of John, Jesus openly proclaims himself as one sent into the world by God, audaciously introduces sayings with the words "I am," and weaves these sayings into long, repetitive discourses. A challenge for any filmmaker will be how to bring together these two very different presentations, found in the gospels themselves, into a coherent characterization of Jesus and his story.

During the nineteenth century, or "first" quest of the historical Jesus, the issue of the literary relationship among the four gospels was addressed by the literary discipline of "source criticism." The dominant explanation for the similarity among Matthew, Mark, and Luke became, and remains, the "two-source" hypothesis. Accordingly, Mark constituted one source because it was the earliest gospel to be written (around 70 C.E.) and was subsequently copied by the authors of Matthew and Luke (in the 80s C.E.). The second source, no longer extant as a written document, is symbolized by the letter "Q" (for the German word *Quelle*, meaning "source") and represented the information preserved in Matthew and Luke but not in Mark (such as the Lord's Prayer). Because Mark and Q were understood to be the earliest sources, they were also considered in some scholarly circles to be the most accurate historically.

Correspondingly, in the nineteenth century, the Gospel of John came to be viewed as the last of the four to be written (before 100 C.E.) and was considered to be either literarily independent of the other three or intentionally quite different. The judgment today remains, in most scholarly quarters, that the teachings of Jesus in the Gospel of John result more from a creative process than from historical memory. Bluntly put, the lengthy discourses by Jesus in John represent statements put on Jesus' lips by his followers after his death, not sayings that he spoke during his lifetime. However, narrative details in John are often viewed by scholars as being more accurate historically than corresponding details in the synoptics. As presented in the Gospel of John, Jesus' ministry may have lasted as long as three years, may have rivaled the ministry of John the Baptist before the arrest of the Baptist, and may have included several visits from Galilee to Jerusalem before his final, fatal journey.

Thirdly, the problem of the cinematic Jesus has to do with the recognition that a distinction can be made between the stories about Jesus, as written in the gospels in the last third of the first century, and Jesus the historical figure who lived out his life in Roman-occupied Palestine during the first third of that century. This is the *historical* dimension of the problem characterized earlier as the relationship between the Christ of faith and the Jesus of history.

Whereas scholars in the nineteenth century approached the synoptic gospels with a certain confidence that they could recover what Jesus was really like, many scholars early in the twentieth century became less certain. This historical skepticism stemmed from the recognition that before the earliest written gospels there was a period of oral storytelling. The discipline of "form criticism" identified the individual units—or forms—of Jesus' words and deeds and studied how they had been shaped, or even fabricated, in the interests of the early church.

Film critic Dwight Macdonald learned the distinction between the Christ of faith and the Jesus of history the hard way, as attested by his reviews of William Wyler's *Ben-Hur* (1959) and Samuel Bronston's *King of Kings* (1961). Macdonald's evaluations of these films initially appeared in *Esquire* magazine (March 1960 and March 1962) and were later included in the published collection of his criticism.

About *Ben-Hur,* Macdonald wrote:

> Here is . . . a falsification of the Bible in which not the Jews but the Romans are responsible for Christ's martyrdom. According to Matthew, Mark, Luke, and John, it wasn't that way at all. *"Then said Pilate to the chief priests and the people, 'I find no fault in this man.' And they were the more fierce saying, 'He stirreth up the people . . . Crucify him, crucify him!'* But in this film, we see merely Pilate washing his hands and delivering Christ over to the brutal soldiery; ain't nobody here but just us Romans.

Macdonald's vociferous defense of the New Testament led him into an area confronted by every filmmaker who has adapted the Jesus story for the screen: the issue of anti-Semitism and the question of responsibility for the crucifixion of Jesus. Finally recognizing the difference between literary presentation and historical probability,

Macdonald later recanted his assessment of *Ben-Hur* (1959) in this review of Samuel Bronston's *King of Kings* (1961):

> When I reviewed *Ben-Hur* here two years ago and pointed out that the Gospels make the Jews chiefly responsible for the crucifixion and show Pilate as wanting to let Jesus go unpunished, this provoked a spate of angry letters. . . . When I made my gaffe two years ago, I took it for granted, as a WASP by upbringing, that the biblical account of the trial and crucifixion was correct. Since then, I've learned, by the chancy methods that journalists learn things, that a good case can be made out that the Gospel writers, for propagandistic reasons, played down the part of the Romans in the tragedy and played up that of the Jews. So I am willing to agree that the matter is obscure and that the hundred or so readers who wrote in objecting to my remarks may have been right about the historical fact. . . .

Jesus-story films regularly address the rather mundane issue of historical verisimilitude: how to make the settings, the characters, the clothing, the customs, etc., appear to be historically exact and accurate. Increasingly, filmmakers have had to deal with the issue of historicity: not "how did this look?" but "did this actually happen?"

As we have noted, scholars continue to use the available literary sources to reconstruct what they believe to be historically defensible profiles of what Jesus was like. In recent years, some scholars have even looked beyond the traditional four gospels for evidence about what Jesus said and did. The Gospel of Thomas, one of these other gospels, has been known only since 1945, when it was discovered in the sands of Egypt. This ancient document consists of 114 sayings of Jesus. Some of these sayings correspond to words found in the four gospels; others do not. Then there are still other gospels, among them the more familiar Infancy Gospels of Thomas and James and the less familiar Gospels of Peter and Mary (Magdalene).[11]

Fourthly, the problem of the cinematic Jesus has to do with the faith claims made about Jesus. This is the *theological* dimension of the problem.

Because of Jesus' place in culture at large as well as in church, most persons who see Jesus on the screen not only know what he looks like, and know his story, but they also have a personal stake in him and his story. Jesus' story is, in some sense, everyone's story. However, the Christian church or churches and their Christian constituents—in particular—view Jesus as belonging to them. Jesus is the Christ. He is *their* Jesus Christ.

A few years ago, over a closeup picture of Jesus as portrayed by Willem Dafoe in Martin Scorsese's movie *The Last Temptation of Christ* (1988), there was this bold headline in the *National Catholic Reporter* (29 June 1990): "What does a man who is also God look like?" In this

playful—but provocative—piece, Michael O. Garvey made this observation about those people who had voiced strong objections to him
about the Scorsese film:

> The main thing that seemed to bother these folks about the movie was
> what has been bothering people about the faith for some time now: the
> incarnation. And it's easy to imagine how a movie on the incarnation
> directed by the same guy who coached the protagonists of *Taxi Driver,*
> *Raging Bull,* and *The Color of Money,* might generate even more phone
> calls and letters to the editor than the book [by Nikos Kazantzakis] did.

In his attempt to understand the controversy swirling around the
Scorsese film, Garvey here points to the classic doctrine so central to
Roman Catholics and Protestants alike: the doctrine of the incarnation, the claim that God became human in the man Jesus. In support
of this basic teaching, the church at the Council of Nicea (325 C.E.) for-
malized the doctrine of the Trinity: God as one but three in one, Father,
Son, and Holy Spirit. Subsequently, the church at the Council of
Chalcedon (451 C.E.) articulated the doctrine of two natures: that Jesus
as the Son of God has two natures, divine and human, truly God and
truly man.

However, contrary to Garvey, *theological* objections to Jesus may
involve more, or less, than *just* the incarnation, with its related doc-
trines about the relationship between God and Jesus. Some Christians,
particularly evangelical or conservative Protestants, ascribe such
words as "inerrancy" and "infallibility" to those New Testament documents presupposed by all Jesus films. Any perceived departure by a
film from the written New Testament text can bring condemnation
and protest—particularly if that departure involves sexual temptation.

Other Christians, such as Protestants of traditional liberal leanings,
may be comfortable with the notion of Jesus as a fully human being—
even a man with domestic and sexual inclinations. Their understanding of Jesus may be in accord with the views reflected in such "social
gospel" hymns as "O Young and Fearless Prophet" and "O Master,
Let Me Walk with Thee" and in Charles M. Sheldon's popular 1897
novel *In His Steps.* Herein Jesus appears not as God to be worshipped
but as an example to be followed. These Christians could respond positively to a cinematic portrayal of Jesus in which his understanding of
himself and his mission develop over time. But even they may have
shared Harlan Jacobson's theological reservations about Scorsese's
Jesus.

Jacobson began his article on the Scorsese movie, in *Film Comment*
(September-October 1988), by identifying what he considered to be
the central question raised by that film's characterization of

Jesus: ". . . *not* was he man or God, but was he nuts?" Whatever the specifics of particular theological perspectives, the centrality of Jesus for Christian belief and practice represents still another dimension of the problem of the cinematic Jesus.

Therefore, for the viewer of a Jesus-story film, the problem of the cinematic Jesus can be expressed as a four-part question: To what extent is this film about Jesus not only *cinematically* interesting, but *literarily* sensitive to the gospel sources, *historically* probable, and *theologically* satisfying? Those filmmakers who have dared to bring Jesus to the screen have faced a difficult task indeed.

Two Trajectories of Jesus in Film

In spite of the complicated problem of the cinematic Jesus, a varied tradition of Jesus-story films has emerged—a tradition spanning the history of cinema.[12] The succession of Jesus films in this tradition has proceeded along two interrelated trajectories. Each of these trajectories represents an approach to the Jesus story that can be traced back into the history of the church and society long before there was cinema.

On the one hand, there have been those Jesus-story films that approached the Jesus story in encyclopedic fashion by drawing extensively on material from *all* four gospels. In our treatment of Jesus-story films, we use the word "harmony" to identify those films whose stories represent a straightforward blending of all four gospels into a single narrative without the mediation of another medium—such as a novel or a musical play.

Among the Jesus films taking this harmonizing approach and included herein for detailed comment are: Sidney Olcott's pioneering *From the Manger to the Cross* (1912); Cecil B. DeMille's popular classic *The King of Kings* (1927); Samuel Bronston's action-drama *King of Kings* (1961); George Stevens' meditative *The Greatest Story Ever Told* (1965); Franco Zeffirelli's ambitious made-for-television miniseries *Jesus of Nazareth* (1977); and Mel Gibson's more narrowly focused *The Passion of the Christ* (2004).

The films along this harmonizing trajectory become increasingly inclusive in terms of the amount of material incorporated from all four gospels, at least through *Jesus of Nazareth* (1977). Zeffirelli's film also projects the most coherent characterization of Jesus among its harmonizing predecessors by skillfully combining Jesus as presented in the synoptics with Jesus as presented in John.

The harmonizing approach to the four gospels was anticipated literarily in the earliest years of the church when Tatian, a Christian from Mesopotamia, combined the four gospels into one linear story about

Jesus. Known as the *Diatessaron* ("four-in-one"), this work was widely used as Scripture in the Syriac-speaking church of the Tigris-Euphrates region until the fourth and fifth centuries.

Over the centuries, literary harmonies of various kinds were similarly created by other prominent Christian thinkers, such as Augustine in the fifth century, John Calvin in the sixteenth century, and even by Thomas Jefferson in the nineteenth century. The harmonizing approach was also anticipated dramatically in the passion plays of Jesus' life, initially staged in Europe, that served as the basis for the earliest films about him. Thus by emphasizing the last hours of Jesus' life, Mel Gibson's *The Passion of the Christ* represents a return to cinema's origins more than a hundred years ago.

On the other hand, there have been Jesus-story films that represent an alternative approach. These films tell the Jesus story in more selective and imaginative ways. A number of the films analyzed herein represent this approach.

D. W. Griffith's *Intolerance* (1916) juxtaposes the Jesus story with three other stories from different time periods. Mervyn LeRoy's *Quo Vadis* (1951), Henry Koster's *The Robe* (1953), William Wyler's *Ben-Hur* (1959), and Dino De Laurentiis' *Barabbas* (1962) base their scripts on modern works of fiction that incorporate the Jesus story into another story from the ancient world of Rome.

In interesting departures from, and in contrast to all their cinematic predecessors mentioned here, Pier Paolo Pasolini's *The Gospel According to St. Matthew* (1964 in Italian, 1966 with English subtitles or dubbing) and John Heyman's *Jesus* (1979) rely on the texts of individual gospels for their screenplays; Pasolini on Matthew and Heyman on Luke. Whether knowingly or not, the makers of these films were taking approaches to the gospels that came into favor at mid-century in biblical scholarship and has flourished alongside the "second" and "third" quests for the historical Jesus. "Redaction criticism" became the name for the discipline that studies how each gospel writer had redacted—or edited—the received tradition about Jesus in order to identify the theological viewpoint of the individual writer. Redaction criticism was complemented by "narrative criticism," the discipline that evaluates the gospels as stories with such formal dimensions as plot, characters, and setting.

Other films have also approached the Jesus story, as narrated in the gospels, selectively and imaginatively. Norman Jewison's *Jesus Christ Superstar* (1973) and David Greene's *Godspell* (also 1973) represent cinematic versions of staged musical plays. *Monty Python's Life of Brian* (1979) drew on the Jesus story explicitly only at the outset and thereafter used the Jesus story as the subtext to its account about a lad named Brian. Martin Scorsese's *The Last Temptation of Christ* (1988), like other films already mentioned, draws on a novel, a work of fiction. Denys Arcand's *Jesus of Montreal* (1989 in.French, 1990 with English subtitles) presents an original screenplay that displays before its viewers a passion play within the film.

The films along the alternative trajectory, freed from the requirement of including material from all four gospels, exhibit increased sensitivity to the historical issues related to the projection of Jesus on the screen. In fact, two of the most recent films in this trajectory—*The Last Temptation of Christ* (1988) and *Jesus of Montreal* (1989, 1990)—include in their stories characters who explicitly raise the question of the relationship between the Christ of faith and the Jesus of history.

Therefore, the tradition of Jesus films has followed both harmonizing and alternative paths. The harmonizing path has led to greater dramatic coherence in the presentation of the Jesus character. The alternative path has led to increased sensitivity to Jesus as a historical figure. Consideration of the promise and the problem inherent in the adaptation of the Jesus story to film informs the discussion of individual films to which we now turn.

The Tradition of Jesus-story Films

For the filmmaker and the viewer, the problem of the cinematic Jesus encompasses four dimensions: the *artistic*, the *literary*, the *historical*, and the *theological*. The tradition of Jesus-story films follows two trajectories as evidenced by the films chosen for analysis in this book.

Harmonizing Trajectory	Alternative Trajectory
Sidney Olcott, *From the Manger to the Cross* (1912)	
	D. W. Griffith, *Intolerance* (1916)
Cecil B. DeMille, *The King of Kings* (1927)	
	Mervyn LeRoy, *Quo Vadis* (1951)
	Henry Koster, *The Robe* (1953)
	William Wyler, *Ben-Hur* (1959)
Samuel Bronston, *King of Kings* (1961)	
	Dino De Laurentiis, *Barabbas* (1962)
George Stevens, *The Greatest Story Ever Told* (1965)	
	Pier Paolo Pasolini, *The Gospel According to St. Matthew* (1964, 1966)
	Norman Jewison, *Jesus Christ Superstar* and David Greene, *Godspell* (both 1973)
Franco Zeffirelli, *Jesus of Nazareth* (1977)	
	Monty Python's *Life of Brian* (1979)
	John Heyman, *Jesus* (1979)
	Martin Scorsese, *The Last Temptation of Christ* (1988)
	Denys Arcand, *Jesus of Montreal* (1989, 1990)
Mel Gibson, *The Passion of the Christ* (2004)	

The Cinematic Jesus
Jesus-story Films

JESUS OF NAZARETH (over): Mary (Olivia Hussey) cradles her dead son Jesus (Robert Powell) beneath the cross. Source: Film Stills Archive, The Museum of Modern Art

The Cinematic Jesus
Jesus-story Films

The fourteen chapters that follow center around particular Jesus films. The chapters generally take up the films so featured in the chronological order in which they appeared. The chapters include comment on the broader social forces as well as the developments in cinema that informed the emerging tradition of Jesus-story films so that collectively these chapters constitute a history of Jesus in film.

For the benefit of the viewer, each chapter considers the featured film, or films, from four angles. First, by way of introduction, the chapter acknowledges the factors and credits related to the production of the film. Secondly, the chapter discusses the shape and content of the Jesus story in the film, with special attention given to the use of the gospels in the screenplay. Thirdly, the chapter considers how Jesus himself appears as a character in the film and selects a descriptive word or phrase to epitomize his portrayal. Fourthly, the chapter summarizes and evaluates the public and critical responses to the film. Although the artistic—or cinematic—qualities of the films are recognized, the emphasis throughout falls on their biblical, historical, and theological dimensions.

Also for the benefit of the viewer, the notes for each chapter identify the source of the particular film presupposed by the analysis, such as the specific videocassette version. In addition, the notes indicate whether the film is available on VHS and/or DVD. Since films display their credits on the screen, this volume does not reproduce in print the entire list of credits. However, the notes indicate where to locate basic data and information about each film in standard cinematic reference works and in works that catalog Jesus-story films. These include: *Magill's Survey of Cinema* (hereafter *MSOC*); *The American Film Institute Catalog of Motion Pictures (AFI Catalog)*; Richard H. Campbell and Michael R. Pitts, *The Bible on Film: A Checklist, 1897–1980*; and Roy Kinnard and Tim Davis, *Divine Images: A History of Jesus on the Screen*. The bibliography accompanying this volume contains detailed publishing information about these reference works.

The user of this guidebook should be aware of a convention followed in each chapter. In order to inform the viewer of the gospel—or gospels—from which a particular story about Jesus or a saying by him has been taken, terms such as the following are placed in parentheses:

19

Two Gospel Portrayals of Jesus

Within the New Testament itself are preserved two very different portrayals of Jesus. On the one hand, there is the synoptic portrayal reflected in the Gospels of Mark, Matthew, and Luke. On the other hand, there is the Johannine portrayal reflected in the Gospel of John. These differences appear both in the overall shape of Jesus' ministry and—more strikingly—in the characterization of Jesus himself.

Synoptic Portrayal	MINISTRY	Johannine Portrayal
Jesus receives baptism by John and testing by Satan.		Jesus receives the testimony of John.
Jesus begins his ministry after the arrest of John.		Jesus begins his public ministry before the arrest of John.
Jesus travels from Galilee to Jerusalem only once during his ministry.		Jesus travels from Galilee to Jerusalem several times during his ministry.
Jesus' ministry lasts as little as one year since only one Passover occurs.		Jesus' ministry lasts as long as three years since at least three Passovers occur.
Jesus cleanses the temple at the end of his ministry.		Jesus cleanses the temple at the outset of his ministry.
Jesus' last supper is a Passover meal, and he dies on Passover day.		Jesus' last supper is not a Passover meal, and he dies on the day before Passover.

Synoptic Portrayal	MESSAGE AND MEDIUM	Johannine Portrayal
Jesus' style and speech reflect "messianic secrecy."		Jesus' style and speech reflect "messianic openness."
Jesus proclaims and teaches "the kingdom of God" as he speaks in parables and aphorisms.		Jesus promises "life" or "eternal life" as he speaks in discourses containing "I am" sayings.
Jesus' miracles include healings and exorcisms, and are called "mighty works."		Jesus' miracles include healings, not exorcisms, and are called "signs."
Jesus addresses the issue of wealth and poverty.		Jesus does not address the issue of wealth and poverty.
Jesus repeats the "first" and "second" commandments of love.		Jesus gives a "new commandment" of love.

(Mark) — story or saying found only in Mark

(Matt) — story or saying found only in Matthew

(Luke) — story or saying found only in Luke

(Matt and Luke) — story or saying found in both Matthew and Luke, therefore, derived from that literary source often identified by the symbol "Q"

(synoptics) — story or saying found in Mark, Matthew, Luke, but not in John

(John) — story or saying found in John, but not in the synoptics

(all four) — story or saying found in Matthew, Mark, Luke, and John

Silent Jesus-story films, such as those analyzed in the initial three chapters, offer a rare benefit to viewers so accustomed to hearing narration rather than reading titles on the screen. The filmmaker frequently identifies on the screen for the viewer the gospel basis for the perceived action or the unheard dialogue—often giving chapter and verse, but not always with accuracy. Sometimes these gospel citations appear as intertitles between scenes, other times as subtitles beneath scenes. Therefore, for silent films a notation in parentheses, e.g. (Matt cited), means that the filmmaker has cited on the screen that particular gospel as the source for what the viewer sees.

FROM THE MANGER TO THE CROSS: Jesus (Robert Henderson-Bland) at
the home of Mary (Alice Hollister) and Martha (Helen Lindroth). Source: Film
Stills Archive, The Museum of Modern Art

CHAPTER ONE

1912 | Sidney Olcott
| From the Manger to the Cross

The opening years of the twentieth century saw Jesus on the screen in new films produced on both sides of the Atlantic.[1] The longer films, two reels in length with a screening time of twenty or so minutes, followed an extended passion play formula with scenes from throughout Jesus' life. Shorter films often focused on some aspect of Jesus' life—the star of Bethlehem and his birth, his raising of Lazarus from the dead, the parable of the prodigal son, his betrayal by Judas.[2]

However, no film from the early silent period was more important for the emerging tradition of Jesus-story films than *From the Manger to the Cross* (1912).[3] The film was produced by the Kalem Company, one of the leading American production companies of the era. The film was directed by Sidney Olcott. According to some sources, Olcott already had to his credit the first film version of *Ben-Hur* (1907), based on the 1880 novel of the same name by General Lew Wallace.[4]

Remarkably, *From the Manger to the Cross* was filmed on location in Egypt and Palestine.[5] Even in our day, the viewer who has been to that region will readily recognize familiar sites: the sphinx and the pyramids; Nazareth and the Sea of Galilee; the Via Dolorosa in Jerusalem; and the walled city of Jerusalem with its Muslim shrine, the Dome of the Rock, as seen from the east.

Although Kalem Company had distinguished itself as a production company that shot on location, the company did *not* send a team to the Middle East with the specific intention of making a cinematic life of Jesus. Company representatives had explored various filmmaking sites overseas, and the Middle East was selected as an area for making several one-reelers. These films were produced, but so was a multi-reel presentation of the Jesus story.

The author of the screenplay was a woman, the actress Gene Gauntier. She later claimed that it was while recovering from a sunstroke that she had the inspiration and the time to write the scenario that would become *From the Manger to the Cross,* subtitled simply *Jesus of Nazareth.* Gauntier also played the part of the Virgin Mary in the film and, during the shooting, married Jack Clark who played John the Beloved Disciple.

Visually, this Jesus movie was indebted to the work of the French artist James Joseph Jacques Tissot whose illustrated Bible was popular

23

at the turn of the century.[6] In fact, the Tissot Bible has been called a "sourcebook" for *From the Manger to the Cross*.[7]

THE FILM: A Silent Pageant

The film exhibits high production values for its time. The title frames include words ("The scene of this history is the Holy Land . . . ") that then dissolve into a map of the Holy Land. The map itself subsequently dissolves into other words ("With scenes filmed at Jerusalem, Bethlehem and other authentic locations in Palestine").

The title of the film accurately describes the framework within which the story of Jesus is told—from manger to cross, from birth to death. The story unfolds sequentially under a series of intertitles:

THE ANNUNCIATION—AND THE INFANCY OF CHRIST

THE FLIGHT INTO EGYPT

THE PERIOD OF YOUTH

AFTER YEARS OF PREPARATION: HERALDED BY JOHN THE BAPTIST

THE CALLING OF THE DISCIPLES

THE BEGINNING OF MIRACLES

SCENES IN THE MINISTRY

LAST DAYS IN THE LIFE OF JESUS

THE LAST SUPPER

THE CRUCIFIXION AND DEATH

Following each of these headings come subheadings consisting primarily of quotations from the gospels cited by chapter and verse. The scenes from the gospels are shown after the cited gospel texts. With only snippets of gospel text to explain what appears on the screen, the viewer must have prior familiarity with the Jesus story to fully appreciate many of the incidental moments on the screen that are not explained in writing—such as the brandishing of a sword by a disciple on the occasion of Jesus' arrest, or the washing of hands by Pilate after Jesus' trial.

Since *From the Manger to the Cross* draws on all four gospels for its script, the film represents the harmonizing trajectory of the Jesus film tradition. The film has the static character of a pageant with little dramatic movement. The translation used for the gospel texts is the King James Version thereby making the entire film something of an illustrated Authorized Version (AV), as the King James Version came to be called.

At the outset of the film, the annunciation to Mary is shown with amazing restraint, in comparison with other early Jesus films. A slightly earlier *Life of Christ* (1907) by the Pathé company, for example, dramatically shows the appearance of the angel Gabriel, wings and all, very much in the fashion of a church Christmas pageant.[8] But here, in the Kalem film—as directed by Sidney Olcott—it is the reaction of Mary that serves as the primary vehicle for suggesting that a heavenly communication has occurred (Luke cited); and no angel appears onscreen when Joseph receives the divine word not to put Mary away because of her pregnancy (Matt cited).

The segment on the youth of Jesus centers around the only story from the four gospels about his coming of age—the account of his dazzling the teachers in the Jerusalem temple with his wisdom at age twelve (Luke cited). The viewer today will see on the screen imaginative touches that stand up well in the entire history of Jesus cinema. Jesus stands beside his mother as she reads to him outside his father's carpentry shop in Nazareth. He rides a donkey en route to Jerusalem while his mother and father walk. Later, back in Nazareth, he emerges from the carpentry shop into the sunlight carrying a wooden beam; and the wooden beam casts a cross-like shadow on the ground.

The film introduces the ministry of Jesus with the preaching of John the Baptist (John cited) and his call of the four disciples beside the sea, Simon and Andrew, James and John (Matt cited). But the baptism of Jesus by John (synoptics) and the testing of Jesus by Satan (synoptics) are omitted, perhaps to avoid having to deal cinematically with the supernatural experience of Jesus at his baptism and his cosmic conflict with the devil in the wilderness.

However, the miracles of Jesus receive special emphasis with their own designated segment. Among the miracles depicted during this segment are the changing of water into wine (John cited) and a series of physical healings—a leper (Mark cited), a man stricken with palsy (Mark cited), and the widow of Nain's dead son (Luke cited). Accounts of Jesus' exorcisms, his casting out of demons, are not cited. This segment concludes with the spiritual healing of the sinful woman who anoints Jesus' feet in the house of a Pharisee (Luke cited).

Scenes from Jesus' ministry begin with a shot of his teaching from a boat next to the shore (Mark cited) followed by his walking on the water (Matt cited). Not even sizable waves require any special effort on Jesus' part to maintain his balance as he plows ahead. Subsequent scenes include: his dining with Mary and Martha (Luke cited), his teaching in the treasury of the temple (John cited), his raising of Lazarus from the dead (John cited), his healing of a blind man at Jericho (Matt cited), and his being anointed by a woman for burial (Matt cited).

In recent years, much has been written in scholarly and popular literature about the special relationship between Jesus and women, as depicted in the gospels.[9] The screenplay of this film highlights the role

of women throughout—from the manger to the cross. In recent literature on the relationship between Jesus and women, the Mary and
Martha story (Luke 10:38–42) has often been singled out for comment.
This story presents Jesus as something of a "feminist." He praises
Mary for learning at his feet instead of complimenting Martha who
has busied herself in the traditional woman's role of cook. Olcott
brings this brief episode to the screen in its entirety; and the sisters
Mary and Martha (from Luke) are identified in the film as the sisters
of Lazarus who also have the names Mary and Martha (John).

The screenplay also avoids casting women in the negative roles of
"seducer" and "harlot" by *not* filming gospel stories involving way-
ward women so popular in later Jesus movies: the dance of Salome
before Herod Antipas (Mark and Matt) and the threatened stoning of
the woman taken in adultery (John). No doubt the positive characterization of women throughout the film reflects the hand of the screenwriter herself, Gene Gauntier.

The last days in the life of Jesus open with his entry into the city,
shot from the Mount of Olives, as his followers descend with their
backs to the camera toward the walled city of Jerusalem waving palm
branches (Luke and Matt cited). In the temple, Jesus straightway
removes the rope serving as his belt, flails away, and scatters the people (Matt and Mark cited). As a result, the scribes and chief priests
seek his life and find assistance through the betrayal of Judas, one of
the twelve (Mark cited). During this segment, the camera captures
Jesus pensively seated on the Mount of Olives overlooking the city
across the valley.

The Last Supper that follows incorporates elements from the synoptics and John: Jesus' washing of the disciples' feet; his foretelling of
the betrayal of Judas; his words over the bread and wine; and the
flight of Judas (appropriately clad in black).

Jesus' words over the bread and wine are reported in some form in
all three synoptic gospels and in the writings of Paul (1 Cor 11:24–25).
These words serve as the basis for that sacrament known to Christians
variously as "the Eucharist," "the Lord's Supper," or simply as
"Communion" (with the latter presupposed in this film since Jesus'
words are introduced on the screen as "The First Communion"). By
contrast, the story of Jesus' washing the feet of the disciples appears
only in John 13:1–30; and foot-washing did not achieve status in the
church as a sacrament. Nonetheless, footwashing remains a ritualistic
act performed regularly in some churches and more occasionally in
informal worship settings. Thus it is remarkable that of all the Jesus
films analyzed in this volume, only this early film and the more recent
The Passion of the Christ (2004) bring Jesus' washing of the disciples'

feet to the screen. *The Gospel of John* (2003), of course, also includes the scene since it faithfully follows the text of the entire fourth gospel.

The crucifixion-and-death sequence also incorporates elements from the synoptics and John. As in the gospels, the capture of Jesus in Gethsemane is staged as occurring at night, with Judas leading the arresting party with a lantern. But for lighting purposes, the scene must be shot in the daylight in what became known as the day-for-night technique. An unidentified disciple resists with a sword; and Judas hangs himself, having failed in his attempt to return the blood-money (Matt cited).

No appearance of Jesus before Caiaphas and the Jewish authorities occurs. Taken to Pilate, then briefly turned over to Herod Antipas (Luke cited), Jesus is returned to Pilate. Pilate scourges him and presents him to the crowds with the familiar words: "Behold the man!" (John 19:5 cited). Cries of "crucify him" are followed by Pilate's washing of his hands. Soldiers drive Jesus to the cross with a chain around his neck, and they continue to whip him with motions reminiscent of his own actions in the temple in an earlier scene. He—and later Simon a Cyrenian—carries the "T" shaped cross (Mark cited).

At the place of crucifixion, a Roman soldier can be seen kneeling across Jesus' chest and pinning him down on the cross as he is nailed to it. He is crucified about the third hour, nine in the morning (Mark cited)—not at the sixth hour (as in John). Ropes and pulleys lift the cross upright. On the cross, Jesus utters two of the seven traditional last words: "Verily I say unto thee, Today shalt thou be with me in paradise" (Luke 23:43, but wrongly cited as Luke 23:49); and "I thirst" (John 19:28 cited). Darkness covers the land; and mention is made of an earthquake, but without dramatic visual display. When Jesus' head drops onto his chest, the film story concludes. But the final frame flashes John 3:16 before the eyes of the viewers: "For God so loved the world, that he gave his only begotten Son, that whosoever believeth in him should not perish, but have everlasting life."

As in its beginning, so in its ending, the film shows great restraint. The film concludes with the crucifixion. There is no attempt to bring to the screen the resurrection narratives, much less the ascension as narrated in Luke-Acts. By contrast, the Pathé *Life of Christ* (1907) mentioned earlier has Jesus as the Son ascend into heaven, while standing within a wreath-like cloud, and literally take his seat at the right hand of the enthroned Father. The Pathé film completes the Trinity by displaying a painted dove, representative of the Holy Spirit, above the seated Father and Son.

By concluding its Jesus story with the crucifixion, *From the Manger to the Cross* (1912) anticipates Jesus films later in the century that similarly end with Jesus' death: *Jesus Christ Superstar* (1973); *Godspell* (1973); and *The Last Temptation of Christ* (1988).

THE PORTRAYAL: Jesus as a Man of Good Deeds

Robert Henderson-Bland, an English actor, was summoned from his native land to Palestine to play the role of Jesus. Later in life, he wrote two books about his experiences: *From Manger to Cross* (1922) and *Actor-Soldier-Poet* (1939).[10] Henderson-Bland repeatedly emphasized how he had completely identified with his role as Jesus, or "Christus" (as he preferred to call him).

Henderson-Bland declared his determination "to bring out the force of [Jesus'] personality" and "to present Jesus as the *Lion of Judah* rather than as the Gentle Shepherd."[11] Although Henderson-Bland may have fulfilled his goal on the screen, the film remains a pageant about Jesus: a series of scenes with no dramatic development. Instead of Henderson-Bland's having transformed himself into Jesus, Jesus has been transformed into a bearded and robed actor who ably follows the script. Therefore, in Olcott's film, Jesus appears pre-eminently as an actor—a man of good deeds.

Nothing that Jesus does in this film should surprise the viewer. With the possible exception of the imaginative scenes of Jesus as a youth, every shot, scene, and sequence has a basis in the gospel texts. But clearly Jesus is represented by deeds and not words.

The synoptic theme of "the kingdom of God" appears on the screen in an occasional gospel text, but no mention is made about Jesus' teaching in parables. Not one parable is cited in the entire film. Neither is any one of the familiar sayings from the Sermon on the Mount cited—not a beatitude, not even the Lord's Prayer.

The Johannine phrase "I am" appears on one occasion when Jesus says, "Before Abraham was, I am" (John 8:58 cited). However, none of the metaphorical "I am" sayings from John are included. Jesus does *not* even comment on the raising of Lazarus with the usual "I am the resurrection and the life" (John 11:25). Consequently, Jesus' act of raising Lazarus from the dead does *not* explicitly constitute a sign pointing to his own identity as the one from God. This act becomes one more illustration of his miracle working—his "do-gooding" for the sake of Mary and Martha.

In fact, very little emphasis *in the film itself* falls upon Jesus' identity as the Christ, the Son of God. Those synoptic episodes and incidents which lift the veil of secrecy on Jesus' identity are *not* included in the film: not Jesus' baptism by John; not the confession by the disciple Peter at Caesarea Philippi; not Jesus' transfiguration on the mountain in Galilee; not Jesus' response to the high priest Caiaphas; and not even the declaration by the Roman centurion beneath the cross. Only John the Baptist, who does not baptize Jesus in the film, seems to affirm Jesus' special status when he identifies Jesus as "the lamb of God" (John 1:36 cited). Otherwise, Jesus is the Christ, the Son of God, because the viewers bring that understanding with them.

The physical setting of this Jesus story, as noted above, is quite literally the land of Palestine. But Jesus, as portrayed, is virtually without any social setting. He does call four disciples at the outset, but the disciples themselves play little role in his ministry. The sisters Mary and Martha have more individualized identity than any of the men. Also, Jesus' ministry is devoid of conflict until he goes to Jerusalem and cleanses the temple. That one act, and the collaboration of his disciple Judas, results in his eventual crucifixion by the Romans. There is no visual presentation of how or why that transfer from the Jewish authorities to the Roman authorities occurred. Such is the nature of a pageant. Such was the role required of Jesus.

THE RESPONSE: Protest and Acceptance

The earliest Jesus films screened commercially in the larger cities of this country evoked little public controversy. The producers and exhibitors of these films often sought and received the support of local church leaders, Catholic and Protestant.[12]

Hollaman's so-called *Passion Play of Oberammergau* (1898) even occasioned what may have been the initial discovery of the potential of film for spreading the Christian message. Colonel Henry Hadley, a noted Methodist evangelist of the day, saw the Hollaman film in New York City and adopted it for use in his preaching campaigns. He praised the film, and the medium itself, in these words:

> These pictures are going to be a great force. It is the age of pictures. See the billboards and the magazines and the newspapers; more and more pictures all the time. These moving pictures are going to be the best teachers and the best preachers in the history of the world. Mark my words, there are two things coming: prohibition and motion pictures. We must make the people think above the belt.[13]

However, from the beginning, the appearance of Jesus on the screen was not totally free of objection and opposition. Hadley himself was not allowed to show his moving pictures in Ocean Park, New Jersey, the home of a well-known religious colony. Instead, he set up a tent in nearby Asbury Park, and the next summer at Atlantic City. Then he took his show on the road, even into communities that had never seen motion pictures of any kind.

Nonetheless, what has become known in our day of television and cablevision as the "electronic church" has its origins in these turn-of-the-century occasions when film was used to communicate a Christian message. Contemporary televangelists, whether Jerry Falwell or Pat Robertson, can look to Henry Hadley and other early cinevangelists as their forebears.

Although the church generally may have initially perceived little threat from motion pictures, or motion pictures about Jesus, this tended to change as cinema increasingly became a form of mass entertainment and mass culture. By 1907, with the advent of theaters—the nickelodeons—dedicated to the commercial showing of films for a nickel, film as a medium came increasingly under attack as a corrupting influence on public morals—especially on the morals of the young. Although the subject matter of most films seemed to offend some group, it was the depiction of crime and sex that proved generally to be the most troublesome.

The "culture wars" of our day over the content of films, television programs, and song lyrics have their antecedents in the controversies surrounding cinema at the outset of the century. Michael Medved,[14] and other critics of Hollywood today, can trace their lineage back to the countless guardians of the public welfare of this earlier era.

Not surprisingly, in those days, churches themselves through representative bodies as well as individuals began joining the call for control and censorship at the local, state, and federal levels.[15] By 1910 such major cities as Chicago and New York had in place local censorship boards that required, and variously enforced, the prior approval of films to be publicly shown.

Therefore, by the time *From the Manger to the Cross* (1912) was released, the social environment and attitudes with regard to cinema had changed considerably. Not surprisingly, Henderson-Bland, who had played the part of Jesus in the film, could offer this retrospective assessment of the furor that had erupted surrounding the making and showing of the film:

> No film that was ever made called forth such a storm of protest as did the announcement of "From the Manger to the Cross." Criticism, like an avalanche literally poured down upon it from every quarter of the globe. The newspapers were full of it; the public talked of it; the clergy raved about the blasphemy of it. . . . [16]

Henderson-Bland even recalls how he had initially hesitated to accept the invitation to take on the role of "Christus." Nonetheless, several factors persuaded him to accept the challenge. In explaining these factors, Henderson-Bland reveals his own sensitivity to the varied dimensions of the problem of the cinematic Jesus: the literary, the theological, and even the historical. One factor was the stated intention of the filmmakers to make a picture "as true to the records of the Gospel as was humanly possible." Another factor was their intention for the picture to tell the story of Jesus "with such reverence, such sincerity, that it was hoped by this means to bring home to everyone of us, the immensity of the Sacrifice which that Life represented." Still another factor seems to have been his own familiarity with "many authors who have dealt with the historical Jesus."[17] This latter statement by Henderson-Bland indicates a growing public awareness of the biographies, or "lives," of Jesus written by scholars during the initial phase of the quest for the Jesus of history in the nineteenth and early twentieth centuries.

Uncertain of the responses of the church and church leaders to a cinematic Jesus, the makers of *From the Manger to the Cross* held initial screenings of the film before selected audiences, including clergy, in England and in the United States.

The film received its inaugural showing in London on October 3, 1912, at Queen's Hall. Among the church leaders present who later praised the film were the Rev. William Inge, the Dean of St. Paul's, and Francis Cardinal Bourne, the Catholic prelate of England.

The inaugural screening of the film in New York City occurred shortly thereafter on October 14, 1912, at Wanamaker's Auditorium. Reviewers for New York publications responded to the film with great appreciation.

The unnamed critic for *The New York Dramatic Mirror* (23 October 1912) evaluated the film primarily in terms of its cinematic qualities and commended it for its "general artistic excellence"—with the exception of the visual awkwardness of the walking on the water scene. However, W. Stephen Bush, in *The Moving Picture World* (26 October 1912), addressed more directly the theological aspects of the film. Bush praised the film as a "cinematographic gospel." He was enthralled by the scenes shot on location in Palestine where the original events allegedly occurred.

Bush also recognized that the scenes about the childhood of the Jesus were not derived from the four gospels. Nonetheless, he expressed great appreciation for these scenes and considered them to be quite effective. He observed that these scenes followed in the imaginative tradition of the apocryphal gospels, such as the Infancy Gospels of James and Thomas, that also tell stories about Jesus' early years not found in the four gospels.

These two New York critics differed only in the settings they deemed appropriate for future screenings of the movie. The former reviewer offered that the film should not be shown in entertainment establishments where it "would be both bad taste and artistically ineffective to sandwich the picture between a juggler's act and a Broadway song and dance." By contrast, Bush—with more than a little theological sensitivity himself—suggested that since Jesus had sought out the "plain people," so this film about Jesus should be taken into the picture houses to the masses.

The many uncertainties related to the projection of Jesus on screen during the opening decades of cinema find clear expression in an article written in response to the premier of Sidney Olcott's Jesus film. It appeared in *The Moving Picture World* (19 October 1912) bearing these headlines which accurately captured the substance of the article:

HANDLING THE KALEM RELEASE.
A FEW SUGGESTIONS AS TO THE METHOD OF ADVERTISING
"FROM THE MANGER TO THE CROSS."

Obviously written for exhibitors who might be considering the showing of the film, the article by Epes Winthrop Sargent offered many practical tips: how to involve ministers and churchworkers (offer an advance screening); how to obtain mailing lists (ask the minister); how to prepare written invitations (preferably in gothic type); how to use billboards (avoid sandwich boards); how to prepare the exhibition room (use a little incense); how to arrange for music (organ as the instrument of choice); etc. In this marketing article also appear those words that occur and recur throughout the literature at this early period of Jesus cinema: "reverent" and "reverence."

That Olcott's *From the Manger to the Cross* eventually found public acceptance is supported by the fact that it was periodically reissued. The 1938 release included a musical score and narration.[18] However, the filmmaker most responsible for enlarging the viewing public for films generally would not be Sidney Olcott, but D. W. Griffith. Griffith would also make his own contribution to the emerging tradition of Jesus-story films with his ambitious 1916 classic *Intolerance*.

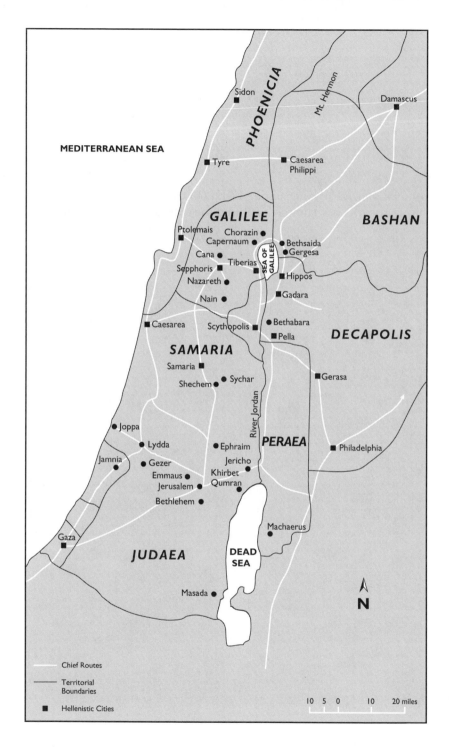

Map of Palestine in the Time of Jesus

INTOLERANCE: Jesus (Howard Gaye) bears the cross through the streets of Jerusalem. Source: Film Stills Archive, The Museum of Modern Art

CHAPTER TWO

1
9
1
6
D. W. Griffith

Intolerance

In a consideration of Jesus-story films, D. W. Griffith's ambitious *Intolerance* (1916) must be included—if for no other reason than his position and the place of this film in the history of cinema.[1] As much as any other single individual, Griffith transformed film from an entertainment medium into a medium of recognized social importance and artistic expression. However, as we shall see, Griffith's cinematic telling of the Jesus story within the broader context of this three-hour film occupies only twelve minutes of the viewer's time.

From 1908 through 1913, Griffith made nearly five hundred silent films while working for Biograph, one of the pioneering film companies, headquartered in New York City. Most of these films were one or two reels in length. He left Biograph, in part, because of his desire to make films of greater length. His relocation to southern California for the making of films was a contributing factor in the emergence of Hollywood as the film capital.

Griffith's first masterwork appeared in 1915. This was his stirring cinematic account of the Civil War and Reconstruction, *The Birth of a Nation*. Based on Thomas Dixon's popular 1905 novel *The Clansman*, the film tells its sweeping story through the experiences of two families, the Stonemans of the north, and the Camerons of the south. Then—as now—the film, with its glorification of the Ku Klux Klan, was condemned by many as racist. The recently founded National Association for the Advancement of Colored People (NAACP) opposed the showing of the film; and the film often precipitated civil unrest when screened, especially in the larger cities of the midwest and east. Consequently, the mayor of Chicago refused to issue a permit for the showing of the film in that city. Already, in 1907, Chicago had become the first major city to establish a local system of censorship whereby a film could be denied the permit required for public exhibition.

The Birth of a Nation was a dazzling production with daring camera work and editing that galvanized its audiences for two and one-half hours, some twelve reels in length. Audiences in America were beginning to discover the story-telling power of the movies.

The very next year, 1916, witnessed the release of Griffith's second masterwork *Intolerance*.[2] Filmed in Hollywood at the Fine Arts Studio

35

on Sunset Boulevard, the overall design and execution of this film even surpassed that of its cinematic predecessor. With *Intolerance,* Griffith underscored the theme of the film's title by telling not one but four stories from different time periods:

1. Modern story of a young man in the United States sentenced to die for a murder he did not commit
2. French story of the St. Bartholomew's Day massacre of Huguenots by Catholics in 1572
3. Judean story of the crucifixion of Jesus set, of course, in the first century C.E.
4. Babyl;onian story of the fall of the city of Babyon to Cyrus and the Persians in 539 B.C.E.

Griffith daringly tells these stories cinematically by using the technique of crosscutting—with the film shifting back and forth from one story to another. When publicly screened, the film had been edited to a mere fourteen reels, some three hours in length.

Griffith had begun planning for the project that would eventually become *Intolerance* even before the release of *The Birth of a Nation.* Therefore, *Intolerance* should not be considered, as it sometimes is, to be Griffith's public apology for the intolerant themes of its predecessor.

Nonetheless, *Intolerance* does represent Griffith's indictment of those social do-gooders (or "Uplifters," as he calls them in the film) whose claim to know what was best for society often expressed itself, in his eyes, as an intolerance toward others.

Before World War I, American society experienced a period of social activism that expressed itself in a myriad of so-called "progressive" causes and organizations. Women not only pursued the vote for themselves but played leading roles in the broader quest for human betterment, including limiting what could be exhibited on the screen.

Jane Addams, social worker and founder of Hull House in Chicago, sought varied reforms on behalf of the disadvantaged. When the nickelodeons were at the height of their popularity, she expressed concern for their influence on the youth even as she worked to provide recreational alternatives.[3]

The Woman's Christian Temperance Union (WCTU) had become a leader in the national movement to prohibit the manufacture and sale of alcoholic beverages. The WCTU also, in the name of protecting children from the addiction of movies, initiated a broad-based campaign of film censorship that included the call for federal governmental controls.[4]

In 1915, the Supreme Court of the United States, in decisions involving the Mutual Film Corporation, refused to extend First

Amendment protection to films thereby allowing for—and encouraging—the continued proliferation of censorship boards at the local, state, and potentially, the federal levels.

Understandably, Griffith himself became an outspoken advocate of artistic freedom and vigorously opposed those who would censor moving pictures, or limit their public exhibition, at whatever levels. In 1916, the very year *Intolerance* was released, Griffith published a forty-five page pamphlet entitled "The Rise and Fall of Free Speech in America."[5] This was also the year that two prominent Protestant denominations placed the issue of censorship on the agendas of their national meetings thereby signaling the church's concern to "clean up" the movies. Both the Methodist Episcopal Church, at its quadrennial General Conference, and the Protestant Episcopal Church at its triennial General Convention, received and adopted resolutions urging the United States Congress to pass legislation supportive of film censorship.[6]

THE FILM: The Judean Story as Thematic Footnotes

The title frame of *Intolerance* displays as its subtitle *Love's Struggle Throughout the Ages*. With introductory intertitles, Griffith explains to the viewers what to expect—four interwoven stories with a common theme. He uses the visual and written image of a young woman rocking a cradle to mark the transition from one story and time period to another. He develops this image from lines in a Walt Whitman poem in *Leaves of Grass*: " . . . endlessly rocks the cradle, Uniter of Here and Hereafter."

The didactic nature of *Intolerance* is evident throughout by the use of historical footnotes written on the screen for the viewing audience. These notes, for example, explain who Pharisees were, who Huguenots were, and how certain events in the Babylonian story were based on recent archaeological discoveries.

In the film, the Judean story is the least developed of the four stories. Among the many, many cuts from one story to the other, there are only *seven* relatively brief cuts to the Judean story. With a total screen time of no more than twelve minutes, such limited reference to the Judean story—the Jesus story—makes each cut to that story a thematic footnote.

All direct quotations from the gospels shown on the intertitles related to the Judean story follow the English of the King James Version—the so-called Authorized Version (AV). The sequences and scenes used in the telling of the Judean story draw on the following gospel material: the self-righteousness of the Pharisees (based on a parable in Luke 18); the changing of water into wine at Cana (John);

the woman taken in adultery (John); the association with children (synoptics); the way to the cross (four gospels) with the help of Simon of Cyrene (specifically synoptics); and the crucifixion itself (four gospels).

The *first* cut to the Judean story occurs after the opening sequence of the film that introduces the Modern story. Here the viewers meet the young woman and young man, the Dear One and the Boy, who have not yet met each other but whose lives will be disrupted by the actions of busy, moralizing do-gooders ("the vestal virgins of Uplift" as they are identified on the screen). These women would use civil law to make people good. The Judean story itself is then introduced by three intertitles, the last two of which appear imposed on two stone tablets of the Mosaic law with the beginning words of each of the ten commandments chiseled in Hebrew:

> Comes now out of the cradle of yesterday, the story of an ancient people whose lives, though far away from ours, run parallel in their hopes and perplexities.

> Ancient Jerusalem, the golden city whose people have given us many of our highest ideals, and from the carpenter's shop of Bethlehem [*sic*], sent us the Man of Men, the greatest enemy of intolerance.

> Near the Jaffa gate.

In the intertitle reproduced above, the reference to "Bethlehem" as the site of the carpenter's shop from which Jesus came surely represents a mistake since the gospels identify the Galilean village of Nazareth as the place of Jesus' upbringing.

The scenes that follow these intertitles show activity in the crowded streets of Jerusalem, the selling and buying of pigeons, and a young woman holding a baby—in a madonna-like pose—seated in a doorway. Then appears another intertitle:

> The house in Cana of Galilee.

After brief shots showing men seated along a deserted street, still another intertitle—with an explanatory footnote—reads:

> Certain hypocrites among the Pharisees.
> Pharisee—A learned Jewish party, the name possibly brought into disrepute by hypocrites among them.

The next sequence illustrates this hypocrisy with a focus on two men dressed in traditional fashion, heads covered, for prayer. One of them prays publicly and ostentatiously:

> "O Lord, I thank thee that I am better than other men." . . . "Amen."

Biblical scholars have sometimes claimed that the troublesome incident of Jesus' cursing the barren fig tree (reported in Mark 11 and Matt

21) originated as the parable of the barren fig tree (preserved in Luke 13). That is, the parable by Jesus was transformed into a narrative about Jesus by storytellers during the oral transmission of the gospel tradition. In this film, the depiction of the Pharisee hypocritically praying is clearly based on the parable of the Pharisee and the tax collector (preserved in Luke 18) wherein the Pharisee prays: "God, I thank thee, that I am not as other men . . . " Griffith the filmmaker has also transformed a parable into a narrative event.

After this three-minute introduction of the Judean story, the camera shifts to an introduction of the French story with an intertitle that labels Paris of 1572 as "a hotbed of intolerance, . . . " and then back to the Modern story where the moral "Uplifters" are designated as "modern Pharisees."

The *second* cut to the Judean story follows sequences of the Modern story in which the Dear One prays before a statue of the Madonna and child with the infant Jesus in her arms as the father of the Dear One dies. The consecutive intertitles read:

Out of the cradle endlessly rocking—
The Comforter, out of Nazareth.

Then:

There was a marriage in Cana of Galilee,
    John II.1.

Note—The ceremony according to Sayce, Hastings, Brown, and Tissot.

In the midst of a sequence showing the wedding ceremony, with closeups of the bride and groom, Jesus appears on the screen for the first time. Followed by his disciples, he walks through an arched doorway toward the camera. Suddenly two Pharisees pass by, take notice, and whisper to one another; and as Jesus stands facing the camera, he is identified by the intertitle "Scorned and rejected of men" (an allusion to Isa 53:3). Then a woman identified as "Mary, the mother" meets her son in a room containing large stone jars. As Jesus participates in the wedding festivities, the two Pharisees continue their hawkish observation of the celebration with the comment: "There is too much revelry and pleasure-seeking among the people." The embarrassment of the bride and groom at running out of wine is noted; and Jesus' changing of the water into wine is introduced with an intertitle based on the wording of John 2:11 followed by an interesting explanatory note:

The first miracle.

The turning of water into wine.

Note: *Wine was deemed a fit offering to God; the drinking of it a part of the Jewish religion.*

No other words appear during this Judean sequence. Jesus performs the miracle simply by stretching his hand over one of the stone jars, but with shadows in the shape of a cross superimposed on his white robe. That the water has become wine is validated by the response of those gathered—the approving look by his mother, the knowing glances of the groom and bride as they drink from a common cup, and the resumption of merrymaking by the wedding guests.

Consistent with his use of the Jesus story, Griffith has introduced into the brief gospel account of the changing of water into wine the two Pharisees with their censorious judgment about love of pleasure. The note on the use and meaning of wine within Judaism is certainly appropriate for an American viewing public at the height of the temperance movement. Only four years later, in 1920, Prohibition would begin with the implementation of the 18th Amendment to the United States Constitution that outlawed the manufacture, sale, and transportation of alcoholic beverages. Prohibition would last in this country until its repeal by the 21st Amendment in 1933.

After this four-minute sequence, the camera again cuts to the French story and then to the Modern story, both of which carry forward the love and marriage theme from the Judean story's depiction of the wedding at Cana.

The *third* cut to the Judean story also involves a shift away from the Modern story. The preceding sequence of events in the Modern story includes the notation that the moral "Uplifters" have become "the most influential power in the community." The intertitle that leads into the continuation of the Judean story lasting three minutes or less states simply:

Equally intolerant hypocrites of another age.

In what immediately follows, a Pharisee complains to his companion about Jesus' activity as "a man gluttonous and a winebibber, a friend of publicans and sinners" (with "St. Matthew XI.19" identified as the source for the words of accusation). The camera shows the Pharisees huddled together and Jesus' festive behavior. Then, these words introduce a well-known gospel incident: "the woman taken in adultery." The camera retells the story of accusation by the Pharisee, the intercession of Jesus, and his deliverance and dismissal of the woman with appropriate dialogue shown from "John VIII."

Then the film shifts back to the Modern story with an intertitle containing a question and a declaration:

Now how shall we find the Christly example followed in our story of today?

The Committee of Seventeen report they have cleaned up the city.

By prefacing the traditional story of the woman taken in adultery with the scenes showing the Pharisees in opposition to Jesus' eating and drinking, and by placing this Judean sequence within the framework of the Modern story, Griffith further underscores the equation now obvious to the viewer: Uplifters = hypocrites = Pharisees.

The *fourth* cut to the Judean story also occurs within the framework of the Modern story. The Boy and the Dear One have had a child. But the Uplifters accuse the Dear One of being an unfit mother and, using the law, take her baby away from her. Within this setting occurs a brief ten second cut away to the words "Suffer Little Children" (taken from the synoptic episode of Jesus' blessing of the children) and a shot of Jesus standing in the midst of a crowd of little ones with his hands resting on the heads of those nearest him.

This is the first sequence of the Judean story that does *not* depict Pharisees in opposition to Jesus. The juxtaposition of Jesus and his concern for children with the legal kidnapping of the baby by the Uplifters intimates that Jesus and the Uplifters are antithetical in their values and interests.

Again, the Modern story provides the context for the *fifth* cut to the Judean story. The Boy, falsely accused of murder, has just heard the verdict of "guilty" announced to the court. Then the intertitle:

Outside the Roman Judgment Hall, after the verdict of Pontius Pilate: "Let Him Be Crucified"

Here, words that appear on the lips of the crowds in the gospels are presented as though spoken by Pontius Pilate. Subsequently, from a distance, Jesus is shown struggling with the cross through crowded streets. He stumbles. Roman soldiers scourge him. Another man, from among the bystanders, takes up the cross. He joins Jesus. They make their way toward the place of crucifixion. No more than twenty seconds have elapsed. Then, back to the modern courtroom with the Boy standing before the judge and the Dear One nervously seated. The verdict: "To be hanged by the neck until dead, dead, dead!" Therefore, the Boy, like Jesus, heads toward his execution.

The events of the Babylonian and the French stories are also rapidly moving forward. Cyrus and the Persians are on the march against Babylon. The slaughter of the Huguenots has begun.

The *sixth* cut to the Judean story takes the French story as its point of departure. Suddenly, in the midst of the killing, the scene of the young woman and the rocking cradle appears. What follows, without any written comment, is a twenty second sequence showing Jesus continuing his way through the crowded streets toward his crucifixion. The camera cuts away to the Babylonian story, to "Babylon's last Bacchanal."

The *seventh* cut to the Judean story again takes place within the framework of the Modern story. As the Boy is being led to the gallows by two guards in the company of a priest, the camera shifts without notice to the crucifixion of Jesus. The entire scene is shot from a distance with Jesus already fixed to the cross on a hill—between two others—with masses of people gathered along the slopes of the hill. The figure of Jesus, in the upper left quadrant of the screen, is made to seem insignificant by the expanse of screen around him. The camera lingers for some seconds before cutting back to the Modern story as the Dear One speeds by automobile to the place of the Boy's execution. She brings the news that the real murderer has confessed to the crime. Unlike Jesus, therefore, the Boy does have his life spared. He and his beloved are melodramatically reunited beneath the gallows under the kindly gaze of the priest.

The film ends with scenes and comment from the contemporary world of the filmmaker's day that anticipate—in utopian fashion—the end of war and prison walls, the advent of "peace" and "flowery fields." Children play and people stand on the former sites of battle and imprisonment. A white cross-shaped light appears on the screen. The end.

THE PORTRAYAL: Jesus as Victim

In his presentation of the Judean—or Jesus—story, Griffith offers a very traditional portrayal of Jesus that should offend no one. Each of the *seven* sequences has its basis in a well-known gospel text or series of texts. Played by Howard Gaye, the Jesus figure looks and acts the part in ways intended to reinforce what the viewers might bring to the screen. However, this traditional portrayal grew out of considerable research and religious advice, as well as a bit of controversy.

The note on the intertitle introducing the water into wine episode, makes reference to "Sayce, Hastings, Brown and Tissot." Archibald Henry Sayce (d. 1933) was the author of several volumes on the empires of the Ancient Near East. James Hastings (d. 1922) was the editor of several reference works, including a dictionary on Jesus and the gospels. Francis Brown (d. 1916) was a scholar of Hebrew and other Semitic languages. Tissot was the French artist whose illustrations of the Bible had so influenced the makers of *From the Manger to the Cross* (1912).

Griffith used not only written authorities but also on-the-set religious advisors to assist him. Years later, Karl Brown, the assistant cameraman, remembered these advisors simply as Rabbi Myers and Father Dodd, an Episcopalian, not a Catholic priest. Brown wrote:

In a sense we had three directors on the picture. Griffith was there to make his wants known and to pass on the results. Rabbi Myers was there to direct the Jewish details of this Christian drama, while Father Dodd was there to keep this event in Jewish history in line with Christian beliefs. And so, between them, the filming proceeded quite smoothly, except for us in the camera department.[7]

The filming itself may have proceeded smoothly; but the presence of Rabbi Myers—Isadore Myers, the father of Carmel Myers, a young actress in the film[8]—did not ensure the absence of controversy. While production was still in process, representatives of the Jewish organization B'nai B'rith objected to Griffith's depiction of Jews actually crucifying Jesus.[9] Consequently, the film was drastically edited before its release. Griffith the opponent of censorship censored himself. Apparently, the eventual brevity of the Judean story (twelve minutes onscreen) was not his original design.

Therefore, viewers see *no* Jewish authorities mentioned or shown during the final *three* sequences related to the end of Jesus' life: no Caiaphas the high priest, only a passing reference to Pontius Pilate the Roman governor; no priests, only Roman soldiers leading the way to the cross; and no hypocritical Pharisees so prominent in the opening *three* episodes. Not even Judas and his betrayal are shown. How Jesus ended up on a Roman cross is not explained. The words spoken by the crowds in Jerusalem are shown on the screen as though spoken by Pilate: "Let him be crucified." Nonetheless, the overall impression of the film narrative is that the Pharisees who set in motion the events leading to Jesus' crucifixion bear the primary responsibility for his death.

Although the portrayal of Jesus in the abbreviated Judean story seems to be harmonious with the story of Jesus nurtured by the church for centuries, Griffith's retelling of the Jesus story—within the framework of *Intolerance*—has certainly given that story an alternative to the traditional Christian reading.

The film credits identify Howard Gaye as "Christ." However, nowhere on the screen is Jesus identified by such names of honor as "Christ" or "Son of God." Nowhere in the film is his death interpreted as having any saving significance for the sins of humankind. The resurrection is neither mentioned nor depicted. In the first Judean sequence, there is a reference to Jesus as "the Man of Men" and "the greatest enemy of intolerance." Thereafter, Jesus' opposition to intolerance expresses itself by his full participation in the wedding festivities at Cana, his resistance to those who would stone the adulterous woman, and his open association with children. Griffith has hypocritical Pharisees complain about Jesus and his activity. Griffith has even transformed Jesus' parable about the hypocritical Pharisee (Luke 18) into a narrative event making it an illustration of Pharisaic behavior instead of Jesus' critique of that behavior.

Therefore, Jesus the so-called "enemy of intolerance," even within the context of the traditional Judean story, becomes *a* victim of the intolerance he opposed. He appears as martyr, not savior. By using the Judean story primarily as a footnote to the Modern story, Griffith uses the story of Jesus—the best-known of all stories—to critique the behavior of the Uplifters in his own day. To Griffith, the attitudes and behavior of these "modern Pharisees" and "hypocrites" continued to victimize Jesus and what he represented—tolerance.

THE RESPONSE: A Failed Classic

Intolerance previewed at Riverside, California, on August 6, 1916, and opened in New York City at the Liberty Theatre on September 5, 1916, with the musical score played by the orchestra of the Metropolitan Opera House. Both the critical and the popular response to the film have been carefully documented.[10]

Critical response to *Intolerance* was somewhat mixed and concentrated primarily on its cinematic qualities. Only passing notice was given to its inclusion of the Judean story about Jesus. The review in *Variety* (8 September 1916), for example, was lavish with praise for D. W. Griffith and his film, referring to him as "the wizard director" and the production itself as "a film spectacle that goes a step beyond his contemporaries." However, the review included the observation that the intercutting from one story to another in the film "makes it so diffuse in the sequence of its incidents that the development is at times difficult to follow." This same review summarized the content of the Judean story as consisting of "Jerusalem at the birth of the Christian era, with one or two historical episodes in the life of Christ, and a shadow suggestion of the Crucifixion." This presentation of the Judean story received praise: "This vagueness was as effective in its artistry as any of the stupendous battle scenes also revealed."

Intolerance was widely shown throughout the country, and audiences attended in great numbers throughout the winter months of 1916–1917. Although war raged in Europe, Woodrow Wilson had been reelected President on the platform of having kept this country out of the conflict. But in April 1917, the United States entered the war to end all wars. The utopian vision of peace at the end of the film ceased to appeal to a public engaged in war. Therefore, Griffith halted the distribution of the film and announced plans to release two of the stories as individual films. In 1919, after the cessation of hostilities, the Modern story and the Babylonian story were released separately as *The Mother and the Law* and *The Fall of Babylon*.

Consequently, what would later become a film classic became in its own time a commercial failure. *The Birth of a Nation* recovered several times over its initial production cost of a hundred thousand dollars. The production cost for *Intolerance* approached or surpassed a million dollars—the highest of any film to that time. With this substantial initial outlay, and its subsequent withdrawal from movie houses, the film became a financial failure for Griffith.

The tradition of Jesus-story films was now clearly following two paths. D. W. Griffith's *Intolerance* (1916) represented an alternative approach to the Jesus story alongside the harmonizing treatment set forth by Sidney Olcott's *From the Manger to the Cross* (1912). The harmonizing trajectory of Jesus films continues with Cecil B. DeMille's *The King of Kings* (1927) to which we now turn.

However, the viewer of DeMille's silent movie will notice a striking difference between it and its silent predecessor *From the Manger to the Cross* (1912). This difference involves much more than advances in cinematic technology and technique. As we noted earlier, the Olcott film has the character of a pageant in which the scenes serve to illustrate broad themes and specific biblical texts that are displayed on intertitles. Dialogue in the films comes directly from the gospel texts themselves. In *The King of Kings*, DeMille too uses intertitles. But specific biblical texts are incorporated into a dramatic narrative in which much of the dialogue has been created by the screenwriter in the interests of the overall story.

THE KING OF KINGS: Jesus (H. B. Warner) with Mary his mother (Dorothy Cumming) and Peter his disciple (Ernest Torrence). Source: Film Stills Archive, The Museum of Modern Art

CHAPTER THREE

Cecil B. DeMille
1927 The King of Kings

The portrayal of Jesus on film received its most extravagant expression of the silent era from Cecil B. DeMille with his *The King of Kings* (1927).[1] This film became the most widely viewed Jesus film in the world over the next half century. In his 1959 autobiography, published after his death, DeMille claimed that more people had been told the story of Jesus through his film than any other medium except the Bible itself. He calculated that 800 million viewers had seen the film and even cited the use of the film by Catholic and Protestant missionaries in faraway jungles.[2]

Therefore, DeMille's film fulfilled both Jesus' command that his message be taken to the ends of the earth (Matt 28:16–20; Acts 1:8) as well as its own petition as they are displayed on the screen after the title frame. The viewer sees these words:

This is the story of JESUS of NAZARETH . . .

He Himself commanded that His message be carried to the ends of the earth. May this portrayal play a reverent part of that great command.

The continued popularity of *The King of Kings* stemmed in large measure from its reverence for the Jesus story, both off and on the screen. During the production of the film, DeMille sought the opinion of religious advisors. His advisors included the Rev. George Reid Andrews, Bruce Barton, and Father Daniel A. Lord, S.J.[3]

George Reid Andrews was the chairman of the Film and Drama Committee of the Federal Council of Churches. Founded in 1908, the Federal Council—the ecumenical organization representing primarily mainstream Protestant denominations committed to "the social gospel"—had increasingly concerned itself with cinema as a moral issue.

Bruce Barton was the author of a best-selling book about Jesus, *The Man Nobody Knows* (1924). Therein, he had presented the real Jesus as "the founder of modern business." Barton transformed this widely read book into a screenplay for a film that was much less successful than the book.[4]

Daniel A. Lord would become a leading advocate for morality in motion pictures. He was instrumental in the development of the

Production Code adopted by the movie industry in 1930 to regulate the content of films. He also played a key role in the creation of the Legion of Decency in 1934, the Roman Catholic agency given moral oversight for matters related to movies.

During the making of *The King of Kings,* DeMille not only utilized religious advisors but also encouraged worship on the set. The first day of shooting opened with a prayer service involving participants not only of the Protestant, Catholic, and Jewish faiths but of the Muslim and Buddhist traditions as well. Father Lord celebrated mass every morning outdoors when the company was on location on Catalina Island; and, at DeMille's behest, the entire cast paused for silent prayer after the shooting of the crucifixion scene in the Hollywood studio on Christmas eve, 1926. Years later, DeMille movingly recalled the latter experience as one of the high moments of his life.[5]

Furthermore, the actors and actresses in the cast had clauses in their contracts requiring exemplary conduct in their personal lives away from the set. H. B. Warner, chosen to play Jesus, rode from the dressing room to the set in a closed car and, while in costume, was spoken to only by DeMille himself. DeMille's protective shield around H. B. Warner's "Jesus" may have stemmed, in part, from collective memories of the time Howard Gaye had played "Jesus" for D. W. Griffith in *Intolerance* (1916). As Karl Brown, an assistant cameraman for Griffith, recalled many years later:

> During the long schedule of *Intolerance,* Howard made up every day and stood by during the filming of the Biblical story. He was in the habit of making up at home and riding to work all ready. Hollywood has not yet forgotten the sight of Jesus Christ riding down Sunset Boulevard at the wheel of a Model T Ford. [6]

Not only was reverence shown for the Jesus story during the production process but the completed film itself obviously caters to religious piety. *The King of Kings* reflects sensitivity to the kind of common piety characteristic of the United States during the first half of the twentieth century.

The musical score by Hugo Reisenfeld, now synchronized with the film, incorporates many traditional Christian hymns: "Fairest Lord Jesus," "Holy, Holy, Holy," and "Abide with Me," among others. The screen titles are, for the most part, quotations from the gospels identified by book, chapter, and verse. The camera work of Peverell Marley reflects the influence of many master painters of the Jesus story with tableaux of nearly three hundred paintings allegedly reproduced in the film.[7] More importantly, H. B. Warner looks and moves as many

Cecil B. DeMille (d. 1959), American film legend, on the set of *The King of Kings* (1927) surrounded by disciples. Source: Film Stills Archive, The Museum of Modern Art

imagined Jesus was supposed to look and move: with trimmed beard and white robe, with graceful movement and a benign smile.

DeMille's reverence for the Jesus story both on and off camera was consistent with his upbringing. His father, who died when DeMille was a boy, had been a candidate for ordination in the Episcopal Church and regularly read Bible stories to his children in the evenings. However, DeMille's reverence for the Jesus story was accompanied by the flamboyant filmmaking manner that, over his seventy-film career, made his name synonymous with showmanship and spectacle.

DeMille's silent *The King of Kings* (1927) had been preceded by his silent version of *The Ten Commandments* (1923) and was soon followed by his early talkie *The Sign of the Cross* (1932). These three were filmed in the grand, sweeping style and substance of the biblical epic.[8]

THE FILM: A Reverent Spectacle

The very opening scene of *The King of Kings* was intended by DeMille to jolt viewers out of their preconceptions of this familiar story, if not out of their seats.[9] He succeeds. The film opens with a banquet scene in Judea (with no biblical basis) showing Mary Magdalene's lavish and lascivious lifestyle. Surrounded by male admirers, she laments her desertion by her lover Judas (also with no biblical basis) who has joined "a band of beggars, led by a Carpenter from Nazareth."

The next scene, or sequence of scenes, occurs in a house where Jesus has gathered with his disciples and his mother and around which have congregated crowds of people (with explicit citation of Mark 2:1–2). Here on a Sabbath, Jesus as the "great physician" heals the lameness of a young lad named Mark (of later gospel fame) and subsequently a blind girl (through whose eyes the viewer initially sees Jesus' kindly face).

The worlds of Mary Magdalene and Jesus collide when she arrives with haste in her chariot outside his house. Instead of reclaiming Judas, she immediately falls under the spell of this "vagabond carpenter" who casts seven demons out of her—imaginatively filmed using the double-exposure technique, and interpreted as the seven deadly sins (lust, greed, pride, gluttony, indolence, envy, and anger, based on Luke 8:2 as cited).

With the introduction of Caiaphas as the high priest, the film links together familiar incidents and words taken from the four canonical gospels: the adulterous woman (John), the raising of Lazarus from the dead (John), the cleansing of the temple (four gospels), testing by Satan (Matt and Luke, but transposed to a temple setting), the Lord's Prayer (Matt and Luke, also transposed to a temple setting), the Last

Supper as a Passover meal with the breaking of bread and sharing of wine (synoptics), then the betrayal of Judas, the arrest in Gethsemane, a brief appearance before Caiaphas, the trial before Pontius Pilate, the crucifixion, and the resurrection (four gospels).

Jesus carries the entire cross to the place of execution (called "Calvary" following the King James Version of Luke 23:33) with the volunteered assistance of Simon of Cyrene (synoptics). Jesus is accompanied by the two thieves who carry only the cross-pieces for their impending crucifixions. On the cross, Jesus declares four of the so-called seven last words reported in the gospels: "Father, forgive them . . ." (Luke 23:34 cited); " . . . today shalt thou be with Me in paradise" (Luke 23:43 cited); "It is finished" (John 19:30 but not cited); and "Father, into Thy hands I commit My spirit" (Luke 23:46 cited). The lament from Psalm 22:1, "My God, My God, why hast Thou forsaken Me?" (Mark 15:34 and Matt 27:46) would not have been appropriate since the musical score plays the hymn "Nearer My God to Thee" as Jesus dies. The centurion beneath the cross, after rebuking his fellow soldier for piercing Jesus in the side (based on John), does exclaim, "Truly—this Man was the Son of God!" (Mark 15:39 cited).

The film, which opened with the attention-getting banquet scene and Mary Magdalene's departure to find Judas, reaches its visual climax with the crucifixion of Jesus. As Jesus hangs on the cross, darkness descends (Matt 27:45 cited) and an earthquake ensues (Matt 27:51 cited). Here is DeMille at his self-defining best—or worst. Wind howls, lightning flashes, and the earth splits. Judas hangs himself, and the tree with his dangling body falls into a yawning crevasse. Caiaphas loses his priestly headdress, and kneels—or cowers—before the rent veil of the temple (Matt 27:51a) set afire by a direct lightning strike. This Jesus film becomes something of a disaster movie.

The resurrection sequence includes the Roman soldiers guarding the tomb (from Matt but not cited), Jesus actually exiting the tomb (contrary to the canonical gospels) and appearing to Mary Magdalene in the garden (John cited), and his later appearance to the disciples, including Thomas, behind closed doors (John cited).

The final gospel text displayed on the screen as an intertitle—and cited by book, chapter, and verse—contains words similar to those with which the film was introduced:

> As My Father hath sent Me, even so I send you. Go ye, therefore, and teach all nations—and preach the gospel to every creature!
>
> —Mark 16:15

Thereafter, in a brief concluding sequence, Jesus is cinematically transformed (or ascends) from the limitations of his presence among his disciples to a more ethereal and universal presence with arms out-stretched over what appears to be a modern city. Jesus' image dis-solves leaving these words with which the gospel of Matthew concludes:

Lo

I am with you always

Throughout *The King of Kings,* the viewer should look for DeMille's effective use of animals, some having their basis in the gospel texts, others not: a monkey, a leopard, and zebras; sheep, cattle, and a lone lamb; doves, pigeons, and a vulture. Nonetheless, there is a glaring omission: *no* ass on which Jesus enters Jerusalem. Strictly speaking, in this film, there is *no* staged entry by Jesus.

THE PORTRAYAL: Jesus as Healer

The screenplay, credited to Jeanie Macpherson, obviously draws on all four of the canonical gospels, placing this Jesus-story film along the harmonizing trajectory. Nonetheless, the film represents a highly selective and imaginative retelling of the Jesus story as narrated in the four gospels.

The King of Kings omits any presentation of, or reference to, Jesus' birth and infancy as preserved in Matthew and Luke. Neither does the film mention any relationship between Jesus and John the Baptist, contrary to all four gospels. Instead, *The King of Kings* takes up the tra-ditional story of Jesus after he has begun to attract attention because of his healing activity. This is certainly appropriate within this narra-tive setting, for here Jesus appears preeminently as a mender of per-sons—as healer.

For many scholars involved in the nineteenth century quest of the historical Jesus, the miracles of Jesus presented a peculiar problem. Jesus' miracles, including his healings, were often considered to be contrary to "natural law" and, therefore, historically impossible. One of the first "lives" of Jesus published in the United States was Thomas Jefferson's *The Life and Morals of Jesus of Nazareth,* finally published in 1820. In this ambitious little work, Jefferson created his own story of Jesus by cutting and pasting all four gospels into a single narrative. Along the way, he also used the scissors of human reason to remove from his revised "life" of Jesus all the happenings considered by him to be "supernatural," thereby retaining primarily the teaching, or "morals," of Jesus.

Certainly the miracles of Jesus also present the filmmaker with the challenging question of how to treat them cinematically. Whether it be

DeMille's theology or his showmanship, he certainly does not shy away from displaying those miracles that can be broadly described as healings. In this respect, he anticipates those participants in the twentieth century quests for the historical Jesus who have argued that Jesus' healings are integral—even central—to his ministry.[10]

In *The King of Kings,* at the opening banquet scene, those being entertained by Mary Magdalene twice warn her of the difficulty in her wresting Judas away from Jesus. They claim that Jesus possesses "magical power" or "magic." One even claims to have seen Jesus *"heal the blind"* (italicized onscreen); and the other reports the claim that Jesus "hath *raised the dead."* At Jesus' trial before Pontius Pilate, Mary echoes these very words by shouting to the crowds who desire to have Jesus crucified: "His only crime has been to heal your sick, and raise your dead! Save him—ye may, yourselves, need mercy!"

Even with all the varied healing stories reported in the gospels and available to him, DeMille chose to invent two more healing episodes to which we have already referred—the healing of the lame Mark and the healing of the blind girl. The former scene enables DeMille to present Mark as an eyewitness to events throughout Jesus' ministry. The latter enables him to introduce Jesus to the viewing audience through her eyes as she gains her sight. In addition, and more tellingly, DeMille has Jesus repair a broken doll upon the request of one of the little ones he suffers to come unto him (a scene shot in DeMille's own garden).[11] In the film, Jesus' mending of the doll becomes the symbol for Jesus as the mender of persons—Jesus as healer.

Therefore, in *The King of Kings,* actions do speak louder than words. Jesus' teaching is minimal. Sayings about the "kingdom" appear only sparingly on Jesus' lips, and then as a kingdom not of this world (John 18:36 cited). Jesus uses not one parable (from the synoptics), although there are occasional words about his identity as the one from God (from John). Jesus declares: "I am come a light into the world . . . " (paraphrase of John 8:12); "I am the resurrection, and the life . . . " (John 11:25 cited); and "I am the way, the truth, and the life" (John 14:6 cited). Consequently, Jesus is called a blasphemer for having made himself equal to God (also based on John).

The film recognizes Palestine in the first century to be occupied territory—a land occupied by the Romans. Even before the title frame, over the signature of Cecil B. DeMille himself, appear these explanatory words:

> The events portrayed by this picture occurred in Palestine nineteen centuries ago, when the Jews were under the complete subjection of Rome—even their own High Priest being appointed by the Roman procurator.

However, the villains in the film are neither the Romans nor the Jews collectively, but Judas and Caiaphas. Judas, identified on intertitles as "the Ambitious," had joined the band of disciples with the expectation that Jesus would become king and he would receive glory and reward. Caiaphas, the appointed high priest, "cared more for revenue than religion" and viewed the temple itself as "a corrupt and

---

Cecil B. DeMille and Who Wrote the Gospels?

In Cecil B. DeMille's *The King of Kings* (1927), a young boy named Mark appears as an important figure associated with Jesus throughout the film. This lad represents the Mark considered by early Christian writers to have written the gospel of the same name.

In his history of the church, Eusebius (d. 340) cites a passage from Papias, the Bishop of Hierapolis, who wrote toward the middle of the second century (ca. 130). Papias claimed that the Gospel of Mark had been written after the death of Peter by the John Mark who had accompanied both Peter (1 Pet 5:13) and Paul (Acts 12:12, 25; 13:5; 15:36–41; Phlm 24; Col 4:10; 2 Tim 4:11).

However, the headings over the four gospels—"According to Matthew," "According to Mark," "According to Luke," "According to John"—were added to the gospels no earlier than the second century when these diverse writings were collected together and the need arose to distinguish among them. All four gospels are anonymous documents. Not one of the four authors identifies himself by personal name in his gospel.

The Gospel According to Matthew became associated with the disciple of Jesus named Matthew (Mark 3:18; Matt 10:3; Luke 6:16). The gospel that bears his name also identifies Matthew as a tax collector (Matt 10:3) and claims that Matthew the tax collector and the tax collector named Levi are the same person (compare Matt 9:9 with Mark 2:13–14 and Luke 5:27).

The Gospel According to Luke became associated with the companion of Paul referred to as a "physician" in the letters of Paul (Col 4:14; Phlm 24; 2 Tim 4:11).

The Gospel According to John became associated with the enigmatic figure known in this gospel as "the beloved disciple"

profitable market-place" to be used for his own economic gain. And so, Judas betrayed Jesus to Caiaphas "after hope of an earthly kingdom was gone" for thirty pieces of silver; and Caiaphas urged Pilate to crucify Jesus because he perceived Jesus to be "a menace to his profits from the Temple." That Jesus was a menace was dramatized by his disruptive action in the temple, on which occasion he was hailed as

---

(John 13:23; 18:15–16; 19:26–27; 20:2, 8; 21:7, 20). But the gospel itself omits any reference to John by personal name. Nonetheless, the "beloved disciple" was eventually identified as John the son of Zebedee, although other ancient traditions attributed the authorship of the Fourth Gospel to an elder named John or to a "heretic" named Cerinthus.

A few modern scholars continue to defend the so-called "apostolic authorship" of the four gospels by Matthew, Mark, Luke, and John respectively. In *Jesus Christ Superstar* (1973), the "apostles"—at the last supper—sing a poignant refrain anticipating their retirement when they would write the gospels. Most scholars would question or deny such authorship of all—or some—of the four canonical gospels.

Certainly, contrary to DeMille, Mark the boy does not appear in the Gospel of Mark as a youngster healed of a crippling ailment by Jesus who thereafter follows him about. Nonetheless, scholars who detect the presence of the young Mark in the gospel have sometimes identified him as the nameless "naked" lad who barely escaped apprehension by the authorities when Jesus was arrested in Gethsemane (Mark 14:51–52).

The argument supporting the identification of the "naked boy" as Mark goes something like this: The Book of Acts (12:12) refers to the house of Mary, the mother of John also named Mark, as a place in Jerusalem hospitable to the early church. If the followers of Jesus, such as Peter, gathered there after the crucifixion and resurrection, perhaps that was the house where they had celebrated the Last Supper before Jesus' death (Mark 14:12–26). After the Passover meal, Jesus and his followers departed for the Garden of Gethsemane at the foot of the Mount of Olives. Curious Mark—wearing only his bedclothes—followed the celebrants to Gethsemane. There in the commotion of the moment, the party apprehending Jesus tried unsuccessfully to take Mark into custody. He fled naked, leaving his bedclothes behind.

"King" (with "Hosannas" taken from the entry into Jerusalem passages from the gospels and the refrains of the "Hallelujah Chorus").

In the end, Caiaphas nobly takes all responsibility for the death of Jesus. To Pilate he says: "If thou . . . wouldst wash thy hands of this Man's death, let it be upon me—and me alone!" Later during the fearsome crucifixion scene, he prays: "Lord God Jehovah, visit not Thy wrath on Thy people Israel—I alone am guilty."

THE RESPONSE: Much Praise

In our day, we have become accustomed to scandals of sex and murder involving persons prominent in the entertainment field. Such scandals in the early 1920s reinvigorated the call for the federal regulation and censorship of the movies.

To counter the threat of governmental control, film industry leaders turned to self-regulation. In 1921, they formed the Motion Picture Producers and Distributors of America (MPPDA), and selected Will Hays to lead the organization. An elder in the Presbyterian Church from Indiana and a prominent Republican politician, Hays had served as Postmaster General in the administration of President Warren G. Harding.[12]

Hays created a Public Relations Committee made up of representatives from leading civic, benevolent, and church organizations. The latter included the Federal Council of Churches (FCC), whose George Reid Andrews later served as an advisor for Cecil B. DeMille, and the National Catholic Welfare Conference (NCWC), initially established during World War I—under a different name—to give the Catholic church a nation-wide voice on social issues, including films.

Hays' strategy was to assure the public through the committee that the public good was being served. Over the next decade, he secured agreements from the members of the MPPDA that motion picture studios would submit materials being considered for adaptation to readers for advice and, later, this was extended to the review of scripts themselves. In 1927, the year of *The King of Kings*, Hays distributed to the studios the so-called list of "Don'ts and Be Careful's," eleven subjects to be avoided in films and thirty-five subjects about which to be careful in the manner of presentation.

The "Don'ts" that involved religion and religious subjects and that had a bearing on Jesus-story films included: "Pointed profanity—by either title or lip—this includes the words 'God,' 'Lord,' Jesus, Christ (unless used reverently in connection with proper religious ceremonies) . . ."; "Any licentious or suggestive nudity . . ."; "Ridicule of the clergy"; and "Willful offense to any nation, race, or creed." Among the "Be Carefuls" were: "Brutality and possible gruesomeness"; "Actual hangings or electrocutions as legal punishment for crime";

"Sympathy for criminals"; and "Attitude toward public characters and institutions."[13] Historically, of course, the Roman practice of crucifixion involved both nudity (to shame the criminal on the cross) and gruesome brutality (to use the criminal as a public example).

These efforts under the leadership of Will Hays did hold at bay the push for Congress to adopt legislation regulating the movies. But he had difficulty enforcing the established procedures and guidelines with the movie makers. Incidents along the way, often involving specific films, failed to produce general trust between the industry and the public. The possibility of governmental intrusion remained.

However, by the late 1920s, at least the mainline Protestant and the Catholic churches had come to recognize the potential in movies for the good; and that good included the portrayal of Jesus on the screen. Gilbert Simons begins his article on "Christ in the Movies," in *World's Work* (May 1928), with this paragraph:

> Christ in the movies? Sacrilege! Ten years ago that would have been the reaction, but it is not today because, in a decade, the moving picture as an art has grown vastly in prestige, and because the Protestant churches, especially in the large cities, have become accustomed to modern methods of attracting members.

In support of his claim, Simons cites a series of non-commercial, non-sectarian films about incidents from the life of Jesus made for use in church services by the Religious Motion Picture Foundation—a private foundation established by philanthropist William E. Harmon. Simons also supports his claim by noting the reception and success of the recently released commercial film *The King of Kings*.

DeMille's production, costing more than two million dollars, premiered at the Gaiety Theatre in New York City, on April 19, 1927. The film also opened the newly built Grauman's Chinese Theatre in Hollywood, on May 18, a month after the New York premiere.[14]

The critics and the public responded favorably to the film. Mordaunt Hall, writing for *The New York Times* (20 April 1927) described the premiere in these terms:

> So reverential is the spirit of Cecil B. DeMille's ambitious pictorial transcription of the life of Jesus of Nazareth, the Man, that during the initial screening at the Gaiety theatre last Monday evening, hardly a whispered word was uttered among the audience. This production is entitled *The King of Kings*, and it is, in fact, the most impressive of all motion pictures.

Most other film critics for the New York press were just as positive in their evaluations of the film.[15] Reviewers representing publications with varying readerships similarly considered *The King of Kings* to be a superb film with high cinematic values—including the performance of H. B. Warner as Jesus. Although complimentary, these writers differed in their varied assessments of the degrees of faithfulness of the film to the biblical texts.

The reviewer in the entertainment weekly *Variety* (20 April 1927) clearly recognized the challenge faced by any screen writer who must transform the gospel texts into a dramatically interesting presentation. Accordingly, screen writer Jeanie Macpherson had to exercise "screen license" at the expense of "Biblical accuracy" in order to produce "a splendidly sketched scenario and continuity." As a result, ". . . the story runs logically, building up finely to its impressive, gripping finale."

The commentator for the religious publication *The Outlook* (18 May 1927) discovered the film to contain—paradoxically—elements of too much license and too much literalness. The opening sequences centering around Mary Magdalene and Judas, with no basis in the gospels, were said to result from "the Hollywood complex"; but the concluding presentation of the resurrection, perhaps Jesus' actually exiting the tomb, was said to have descended to "the standards of Easter cards" by leaving nothing to the imagination.

Frederick James Smith, in the popular magazine *Photoplay* (June 1927), apparently with less knowledge of the gospels than his fellow reviewers, claimed: "DeMille has followed the New Testament literally and with fidelity. He has taken no liberties." Nonetheless, like his fellow reviewers, Smith here reflects a concern for what we have called the *literary* dimension of the problem of the cinematic Jesus— the relationship between the written gospels and a screenplay.

All things considered, *The King of Kings* was well received upon its release. However, DeMille's own recollection of the initial public response to the film included opposition by "tiny but militant atheist societies" and by "certain Jewish groups."[16] DeMille's rejoinder to the former, at least in part, came in the form of his next film *The Godless Girl* (1929)—a story about a high school atheist club and the eventual redemption of the young woman of the title. His answer to the Jewish groups resulted in his making alterations to *The King of Kings* as originally released. A brief news article in *The New York Times* (6 January 1928) signaled these changes under the headline:

'KING OF KINGS' FILM WILL BE REVISED
DeMille to Change Scenes and Titles
as Jews Asked and Add a Foreword

The specific changes are not detailed in the newspaper article; but the Jewish organizations requesting the changes included the B'nai B'rith that had also objected to D. W. Griffith's intended portrayal of the Jews in the Jesus story in *Intolerance*. Neither does DeMille identify the specific scene and title changes in his autobiography. But the film still in circulation in videocassette format gives evidence of his attempt to guard against the often heard anti-Semitic charge that the Jews collectively bear the responsibility and guilt for the death of Jesus.

First, there is the foreword to the film, placed before the title frame itself and bearing DeMille's own signature, which declares that the Jews were under Roman control with even their high priest appointed by the Roman procurator.

Secondly, there is the repeated cry of Caiaphas the high priest that he alone is responsible and guilty for the death of Jesus. The words themselves are an obvious refutation of the gospel text where the gathered crowds cry out before Pilate: "His blood be on us and on our children" (Matt 27:25).

Thirdly, there is no trial scene before Caiaphas and the Sanhedrin—only an intertitle and a passing shot indicating that Jesus upon his arrest was taken to Caiaphas before his transferal to Pilate. In spite of these efforts, the film retains something of an anti-Semitic tone by associating Caiaphas with the love of money.

The silent Jesus in DeMille's *The King of Kings* walked across the screen only a few months before Al Jolson would play the part of the Jewish cantor's son in *The Jazz Singer* (1927). Because of its use of sound, this film began to change forever what audiences expected of motion pictures. By the late 1920s, radio had joined the phonograph as a sound machine. The screen could no longer remain silent. The talkies arrived and soon rendered silent films into artifacts of a bygone era. The year 1929 has been called "the first year of talkie supremacy" in the history of American cinema.[17] Although not dubbed later, *The King of Kings* was released in 1931 with a synchronized musical soundtrack.

When Jesus spoke for the first time on the commercial screen it was probably in French, not English. The Julien Duvivier film *Ecce Homo* appeared in 1935 with Robert Le Vigan in the title role. Two years later, 1937, the film was dubbed in English and shown in the United States as *Golgotha*.[18] As the title suggests, this Jesus film focused on the events of passion week much in the tradition of the passion play. Years later, in his reflections on the making of his own *Jesus of Nazareth* (1977), Franco Zeffirelli remembered this Duvivier film as the "most beautiful" of all the Jesus films he had seen.[19]

Nonetheless, in the United States, it was DeMille's *The King of Kings* (1927)—not Duvivier's *Golgotha* (1935, 1937)—that remained without a serious harmonizing rival for more than thirty years. When that rival film finally did appear, it tried to pass itself off under the same name as the DeMille epic, and eventually did so, but without the definite article. That film was Samuel Bronston's *King of Kings* (1961).

BEN-HUR: Judah Ben-Hur (Charlton Heston) offers Jesus (Claude Heater) a drink of water. Source: Cinema Collectors

CHAPTER FOUR

William Wyler
Ben-Hur (and others)

1
9
5
9

After World War II, with the emerging rivalry of television and advances in its own technology, cinema turned in earnest to the Bible as a thematic basis for displaying itself in grandiose and overpowering ways.[1] Cecil B. DeMille both advanced and expanded his reputation as the impresario of the lavish biblical spectacle with his *Samson and Delilah* (1949) and the dramatic remake of his own 1923 version of *The Ten Commandments* (1956).

DeMille did not undertake a remake of his silent *The King of Kings* (1927). Neither did anyone else in Hollywood extend the harmonizing trajectory of Jesus films until the appearance of Samuel Bronston's Jesus film of similar title, *King of Kings* (1961).[2] Several factors account for this thirty-four year gap between the release of commercial films that approached the Jesus story in a harmonizing way.

Perhaps the overriding factor was DeMille's own continued presence and prominence in Hollywood through the 1930s, 1940s, and 1950s—the first three decades of the sound era. DeMille died in 1959. Two years later, in 1961, Samuel Bronston's harmonizing epic production of the Jesus-story appeared.

Another factor, along the way, involved developments related to the film industry that discouraged filmmakers from bringing the Jesus-story to the screen. In the 1920s, the film industry had experienced ongoing public controversy over the issues of regulation and censorship. Finally, in the early 1930s, there emerged a system whereby the industry regulated itself under vigilant watch of, and in co-operation with, an external pressure group.

In 1930, the Motion Picture Producers and Distributors of America (MPPDA) adopted a Production Code. The Production Code consisted of standards, in twelve categories, to which all films were expected to conform. Among the standards were guidelines against "blasphemy" and guidelines protective of "religion." Thus: "Reference to Deity, God, Lord, Jesus, Christ shall not be irreverent"; and "no film or episode shall throw ridicule on any religious faith."[3] Will Hays, the head of the MPPDA, enthusiastically supported the Code; but the Code actually originated with Martin Quigley, a Catholic layperson who published the trade paper *Motion Picture Herald,* and Father Daniel A. Lord, S.J., the priest who had served as a religious advisor on the set of *The King of Kings* (1927). Joseph Breen, another Catholic, became the head of the Production Code Administration (PCA)—the office responsible for enforcing the Code. The PCA certified films with a seal of approval that was required for the showing of films in most theaters.

In 1934, the Catholic bishops in this country established the Legion of Decency. The Legion was formed to make sure that the film industry did enforce the Production Code and to give moral guidance about films to its own Catholic constituency. The organization even instituted a rating system for films: A-I, morally unobjectionable; A-II, morally unobjectionable for adults; B, morally objectionable in part; and C, condemned. For the next thirty years, the Production Code Administration and the Legion of Decency controlled, formally and informally, what viewers would see on the screens of American motion picture theaters, including cinematic portrayals of Jesus. Catholics were even asked, through their churches, to subscribe to a pledge in support of the principles and judgments of the Legion and to be in solidarity with those who openly opposed the exhibition of immoral films.[4]

Still another factor to account for the long period between harmonizing presentations of the Jesus story was the rediscovery by American filmmakers, in particular, of how to use the Jesus story for box office appeal without focusing the camera directly upon the person of Jesus throughout. The 1950s and 1960s witnessed the continuation and full-flowering of a particular alternative approach to Jesus on film: telling the Jesus story in association with, but in subordination to, another story or other stories.

Whereas D. W. Griffith's *Intolerance* (1916) had subordinated the Jesus story to stories from other historical periods by crosscutting from one to the other, these later Jesus films told the story of persons who also lived under the aegis of the Roman Empire, but whose lives had been touched directly by Jesus himself. More often than not, Jesus appears in these films as "the undefined Christ."[5] That is, the presence of Jesus is more suggested than displayed frontally and up close. While he is the subject, he is not the focus of the films. The viewer sees Jesus from a distance, simply views his hand or feet, or hears his voice.

Among the Jesus films taking this alternative approach were Mervyn LeRoy's *Quo Vadis* (1951), Henry Koster's *The Robe* (1953), Dino De Laurentiis' *Barabbas* (1962) and, of course, William Wyler's *Ben-Hur* (1959).[6] All of these films were based on works of literary fiction that centered around the struggle between emerging Christianity and the Roman Empire. Two of these films had cinematic predecessors of the same name.[7]

These four films belong cinematically to what has been identified as a sub-genre of the biblical epic—the Roman/Christian epic.[8] Invariably the Roman/Christian epic features protagonists wrestling with, and acting out, the decision to follow Jesus as the Christ, not to obey Caesar and the demands of Rome. Of these four epics, *Barabbas* received an A-II rating from the Legion of Decency, the other three an A-I rating. *Barabbas* continues to offer the most interesting challenge to the thoughtful viewer.

THE FILMS: Roman/Christian Epics

Quo Vadis (1951), *The Robe* (1953), and *Barabbas* (1962)—in varying ways—center their stories in the city of Rome sometime after the crucifixion of Jesus, although principal characters have been eyewitnesses to the event.

Quo Vadis (1951), produced by Sam Zimbalist for Metro-Goldwyn-Mayer and directed by Mervyn LeRoy, had at least two cinematic predecessors by that name from the silent movie era (1913, 1923). The silent versions were Italian productions; and the 1951 movie was also filmed in Italy. All versions represent adaptations of the 1895 novel of the same name by Nobel Prize winning author Henryk Sienkiewicz.

This story of conflict between the eagle of Rome and the cross of Christianity, set in Rome during the reign of Nero (54–68 c.e.), involves the triumph of romantic love between the military hero Marcus Vinicius and a female hostage of the state named Lygia, with Robert Taylor and Deborah Kerr in the leading roles. Against all odds, Marcus and Lygia survive the persecution of Nero; and, after Nero's death, they become free to begin their married life together.

The films and the novel derive their name from words allegedly spoken by Peter as he flees the burned city of Rome. In this film, confronted by a light in the shape of the cross, Peter asks, "Quo vadis, Domine?" ("Whither goest thou, Lord?"). Jesus—unseen, but heard—declares: "If thou desert my people, I shall go to Rome to be crucified a second time." Therefore, Peter returns to Rome and suffers crucifixion himself—upside down, in accordance with church tradition. The genial face of the disciple Peter in *Quo Vadis* will reappear as the face of the wise man Balthasar in *Ben-Hur*, since the same actor plays both parts—Finlay Currie.

The principal visual appearances of Jesus in *Quo Vadis* occur midway through the film at a gathering of believers outside Rome. Peter boldly preaches by recalling the shape of Jesus' ministry—including Jesus' call of the disciples, his teaching and his miracles, and specific events leading to his crucifixion and resurrection (synoptics and John).

Occasionally, the camera shot of Peter dissolves into a flashback of Jesus to illustrate Peter's words.

The Robe (1953) did not have the film history of *Quo Vadis;* but the film made history by using the widescreen technique known as CinemaScope for the first time. Produced by Frank Ross for 20th Century-Fox and directed by Henry Koster, the film was based on the 1942 novel, *The Robe,* by popular, best-selling author Lloyd C. Douglas. The robe, in the title, refers to the garment worn by Jesus to the place of execution and for which the soldiers cast lots beneath the cross.

Here is another story about the conflict between the entrenched power of Rome and the emerging power of Christianity. Only, now, the story begins in the eighteenth year of the reign of Tiberius (14–37 C.E.) and ends during the rule of his successor Caligula (37–41 C.E.). This story also centers around a love relationship—between the Roman Tribune Marcellus Gallio and Diana, a longtime acquaintance who has come under the guardianship of Tiberius. Posted to Judea out of spite, Marcellus leaves for that distant land with his Greek slave Demetrius. Richard Burton plays Marcellus, with Jean Simmons as Diana and Victor Mature as Demetrius.

It is in conjunction with Marcellus' brief tour of duty in Judea that Jesus appears visually in the film. As Marcellus and Demetrius approach Jerusalem, the camera shows Jesus—from a distance—entering the city on an ass (four gospels) with the crowds waving palm branches (only John). Within the week, Marcellus receives the order from Pontius Pilate to command the execution squad responsible for carrying out the sentence of crucifixion for this man. Again, the camera shows Jesus—on his way to his death, but with his face hidden by the bulky cross (four gospels). Still again the camera films Jesus—affixed to the cross, but from a distance, or from foot level, or from the rear. From Jesus on the cross, spoken by Cameron Mitchell, comes his one line in the movie: "Father, forgive them. . . . " (Luke).

Beneath the cross, Marcellus wins the robe and suddenly feels bewitched and crazed by it. By contrast, Demetrius his slave—also under the spell of this "carpenter from Galilee"—deserts Marcellus with the parting accusation that Marcellus had crucified the one called "messiah" and "Son of God."

Marcellus' long journey back to sanity and forward to faith returns him to Italy through the intervention of Diana, then to Cana in Galilee, and—finally—back to Rome. At the end, Marcellus stands trial before Caligula in Rome where he receives the sentence of death for treason. His beloved Diana joins him; and they march to their executions as believers with his having announced that Jesus' kingdom is not of this world (John 18:36).[9]

Early in the next decade, *Barabbas* (1962) became still another film with a Roman/Christian theme that projected Jesus on the screen in an indirect way. The film was a Dino De Laurentiis production, filmed in Italy, with Richard Fleischer as director and released through Columbia Pictures.

Based on the 1951 novel by the Nobel Prize winning Swedish author Pär Lagerkvist, the story revolves around the character named Barabbas who, in the gospels, was set free by Pontius Pilate instead of Jesus. Anthony Quinn plays the title role. The story carries Barabbas from Jerusalem—where he witnesses events related to the crucifixion—through a long sentence of forced labor in the sulfur mines of Sicily for having resumed his rebellious ways against Rome, to his final years in Rome where he has earned his freedom as a gladiator. Along the way, Barabbas becomes a Christian, of a sort. Having misunderstood the statement that God would burn away the old world to make way for the new, he actually participates in the burning of Rome, thinking that he is doing the Christian thing.

Jesus, played by Roy Mangano, appears on screen at the very beginning of the film. In fact, the viewer sees Jesus even before seeing Barabbas. However, closeups of Jesus' face and words spoken by him are avoided. The film opens with Jesus on trial before Pontius Pilate for "sedition" and "blasphemy"—but the camera shows Jesus standing to one side in the shadows. After the film credits, Jesus experiences the humiliation of scourging and mocking by the soldiers—but the camera avoids showing his face. When Barabbas exits his darkened hole of captivity, he briefly sees Jesus—standing in the blinding light of day with a red robe and a crown of thorns. Later, as Barabbas celebrates his own release, he looks out of his window and sees Jesus struggling with his cross—but at a distance. Barabbas also visits the site of crucifixion as Jesus hangs on the cross and later has his body removed—but again the camera moves around the periphery of the Jesus figure.

The crucifixion sequence in *Barabbas* has a distinction that sets it apart from all other Jesus films. There is neither storm nor earthquake nor tearing of the temple veil. There is just an eerie darkness as the dimmed sun hangs in the sky at midday over the cross of Jesus (synoptics). The crowds stand around in stunned silence. As reported by Dino De Laurentiis, the camera here has captured an actual solar eclipse visible in the Italian village of Roccastrada, a hundred or so miles north of Rome, on February 15, 1962.[10]

As in similar films, there is in *Barabbas* a love connection—here between the title character and a woman named Rachel who had been attracted to Jesus as a man come from God. Barabbas and Rachel visit the empty tomb on the third day after Jesus' death. She believes in Jesus as the resurrected Christ. He scoffs and considers Jesus' body to have been stolen. Rachel pays for her convictions by being stoned to death in Jerusalem.

In the film *Barabbas,* as in similar films, the disciple Peter has a significant role. He enters into theological discourse with Barabbas twice, shortly after the crucifixion and then years later after the burning of Rome. Throughout the film, Barabbas—haunted by the memory of the one who died in his place—mirrors the modern agony of struggle between non-belief and belief. More than once, Barabbas cries: "Why can't God make himself plain?" By contrast, Peter becomes a defender of God. As though addressing modern humans, Peter puts forth the argument that the wrestling about the God-question in the human soul in itself represents knowledge of God. Finally, Barabbas does die as a Christian—whether or not a true believer—on a cross amidst a forest of crosses. His dying words are directed to God: "I give myself up into your keeping . . . It is Barabbas."

The claim, in this film, by Barabbas that Jesus' body was stolen—not resurrected—has its basis in the gospels themselves (see Matt 28:11–15). This so-called "stolen body theory" of the resurrection was accepted as historical by Hermann Samuel Reimarus, the eighteenth-century German scholar often credited with initiating the quest for the historical Jesus. Reimarus argued that historically Jesus was a "political messiah" whose intention was to establish a political kingdom in Jerusalem but who failed to achieve his goal, as his crucifixion attests. Subsequently, Jesus' disciples stole his body and made up the notion of Jesus as a "spiritual messiah" who went to Jerusalem to die for the sins of humankind, who was raised from the dead by God, and who would come again for final judgment. According to Reimarus, therefore, Christianity originated as a conscious fraud perpetrated by Jesus' followers.[11]

Quo Vadis, The Robe, and *Barabbas* dramatized the conflict between Rome and emerging Christianity. *Ben-Hur,* however, reflects more directly the Roman challenge to Judaism and Judaism's resistance. The film pits Judah Ben-Hur, the ever loyal Jew, against Messala, the patriotic Roman, in a friendship turned to enmity that culminates in the famous chariot race.

Ben-Hur (1959) was produced for Metro-Goldwyn-Mayer by Sam Zimbalist, the same studio and producer who had brought to the screen *Quo Vadis* (1951). Here, too, Miklos Rosza provided the sweeping music. William Wyler was chosen as director. Wyler had already received two Academy Awards and, more recently, had dealt with the moral issue of pacifism in the westerns *Friendly Persuasion* (1956) and *The Big Country* (1958).[12] The debate over pacifism also surfaces in *Ben-*

Hur, but in more subtle ways. That veteran of big picture shows, Charlton Heston, was cast as Judah Ben-Hur.

Filmed in Rome at Cinecittà Studios, *Ben-Hur* had an advertised cost of some fifteen million dollars. The running time of the film was nearly four hours. Upon its release, viewers were immediately greeted on the screen by something they had never seen. The trademark MGM lion, which customarily growls, was silent. The request to silence the lion for this picture was made by Wyler so that the opening of the film would not be disturbed by the roar.[13]

Ben-Hur—like *Quo Vadis*—had dramatic predecessors. There had been two earlier silent films (1907, 1925) and a staged predecessor (1899). The 1925 film, directed by Fred Niblo, represents a film classic in its own right. At a cost of four million dollars, it had been the most expensive movie made in its day. William Wyler himself, as a young man, had been involved in the making of Niblo's version. All these productions for screen and stage were adaptations of the novel *Ben-Hur* (1880) by General Lew Wallace, who had received his military rank in the Union army during the Civil War.[14]

The Wyler film—like the Wallace novel—has an appropriate subtitle: *A Tale of the Christ.* This tale of Ben-Hur is set in its entirety within the framework of the life of Jesus. Even before the title frames and credits, the viewers are introduced to a Christmas pageant as Mary and Joseph make their way to Bethlehem for the census and are greeted there, after the birth of their child, by shepherds (Luke) and wise men (Matt).

Immediately after the credits and the display of the date "ANNO DOMINI XXVI," Roman soldiers march through Nazareth as Joseph, in his carpenter's shop, engages in a brief conversation with a fellow villager about his son's apparent neglect of his carpentry work. Joseph gives assurance that his son is "about his Father's business" (Luke). A brief shot shows Jesus in the distance walking in the hills above the village.

That Jesus has begun his public ministry receives notice when Messala and his fellow soldiers arrive in Jerusalem. Messala's predecessor talks about Jesus. He calls Jesus a "carpenter's son" who does "magical tricks" and teaches that "God is near—in every man."

Other references to Jesus occur in the film; and Jesus himself can be seen in the distance as crowds gather for the Sermon on the Mount (Matt). But there are *two direct encounters* between Judah Ben-Hur and Jesus (with Claude Heater as Jesus). Both encounters are shot obliquely with the face of Jesus not seen.

The *first encounter* occurs after Judah and Messala have become enemies. Judah's mother and sister have been imprisoned; and he has been sentenced to hard labor as a galley slave. As Judah and other prisoners are led through Nazareth, the chain-gang stops for water. Not allowed by his guard to drink, Judah collapses, crying, "God, help me!" Suddenly a hand with a gourd offers him water as Judah gazes transfixed into the stranger's face. The viewer sees only the man's hand and later his back and his head with long wavy hair.

The *second encounter* between Judah and Jesus occurs toward the end of the film in conjunction with the trial and crucifixion of Jesus. Judah has returned to Judea. He has defeated and killed Messala in the chariot race. He has even been reunited with Esther, a love interest of many years, and his mother and sister, both of whom he discovered to be lepers living in a leper colony. As Jesus makes his way to the place of crucifixion carrying a "T" shaped cross, he stumbles before Judah and the three women in his care. Judah cries out, "I know that man." He rushes to fill a gourd with water and extends a drink to Jesus. Again the viewer only sees Jesus' prostrate form from the rear. The lengthy sequence from Jesus' trial before Pilate through the crucifixion itself is shot from a distance or with angles that avoid showing Jesus' face. Neither does one hear his voice, although Judah later reports that he heard him say: "Father forgive . . ." (Luke).

At the end, Judah—through Esther—finds reconciliation with his mother and sister who have had their leprosy miraculously washed away during the dark moments of Jesus' crucifixion. The very last scene of the film shows a shepherd and his sheep moving across the screen beneath three empty crosses on the hill in the distance.

THE PORTRAYALS: Jesus as Crucified Redeemer

Roman/Christian epics—as alternative approaches to the Jesus story that subordinate his story to another—must be by their very nature very selective in what they present about Jesus and his activity. Each of the four Roman/Christian films considered here centers around one moment of his life—the final moment, his death. These films also highlight Jesus' teaching on forgiveness and love. Therefore, Jesus appears in these films *as* a non-violent, crucified redeemer—although the films interpret the meaning of redemption with different nuances.

In *Quo Vadis*, the opening voice-over narration declares: "Thirty years before this day, a miracle occurred on a Roman cross in Judea, a man died to make men free, to spread the gospel of love and redemption. . . . " Although emphasized in the narration, the crucifixion itself is not shown on film. But Peter, in his sermon to the believers in Rome, recalls how Jesus had been crucified on Calvary. He mentions Jesus' words from the cross, "Father forgive . . ." (Luke) and concludes by citing Jesus' sayings from the Sermon on the Mount about turning the other cheek, loving one's neighbor, and doing to others as you would have them do to you (Matt). Over against Marcus' glorification of war and his sanctioning of slavery before he became a Christian, Christian believers in the film express opposition to war and slavery, in the name of Jesus.

Quo Vadis, like most Roman/Christian films, represents a tale of martyrdom. After the burning of Rome, Christians are mauled by lions and are themselves burned alive on crosses in the arena. Therefore, the redemption brought by Jesus' death clearly involves deliverance from death and life everlasting. Before his own martyrdom, Peter enters the arena and, with words borrowed from Jesus, declares to the believers awaiting death that they will soon be with him in paradise.

When finally married, Marcus and Lygia become united as husband and wife in this life *and the next,* although they escape death in the film. The closing scene shows them leaving Rome. As they pass the spot where Jesus had earlier directed Peter to return to Rome, these words are heard (voice-over): "I am the way, the truth, and the life" (John).

The Robe and *Barabbas* are also tales of martyrdom. Marcellus and Barabbas, the central characters who witness Jesus' crucifixion, have difficulty accepting their respective roles in that drama. Marcellus feels responsible for Jesus' death as the commander of the execution detail. Barabbas struggles with the issue of why he was allowed to live and Jesus to die. But when the end comes, each goes to a state-imposed death bearing the label "Christian"—the one by order of Caligula, the other at the instigation of Nero. In *The Robe,* Marcellus is joined in his martyrdom by his beloved Diana. In *Barabbas,* the title character experiences the loss of Rachel who is martyred by stoning in Jerusalem shortly after the crucifixion itself. He too eventually dies by crucifixion alongside dozens of others.

How Marcellus and Barabbas understand their respective martyrdoms—and, therefore, their redemption—differs. Marcellus understands redemption in terms of forgiveness and eternal life. This expresses itself most obviously in the film's closing scene. Before the emperor Caligula, Marcellus declares that he enters a kingdom not of this world. He and Diana then march toward their deaths with the camera angle suggesting that they are ascending into the heavens. For Barabbas, however, redemption may be of a different kind. Although characters in the film express confidence in the resurrection of Jesus and life everlasting, Barabbas continues to express a certain agnosticism about life—and about God. His last words have an ambiguity suggesting that he delivers himself over not to God but to the darkness, or to God who is the darkness. Death itself may be his redemption from the burden of life.

Also, Marcellus and Barabbas only gradually learn that being

Christian involves non-violent love. Marcellus sees and hears this among the Galilean Christians of Cana, including Peter. Barabbas first hears this from Rachel, but sees it in the action of his fellow gladiator Sahak. In the arena, Sahak refuses to kill a fallen opponent—in spite of the wishes of the crowds—because of "the law of love."

Unlike the other films that focus on Christian/Roman relations in the empire, *Ben-Hur* is *not* a tale of martyrdom. Jesus still appears as a non-violent crucified redeemer. In fact, redemption for Judah Ben-Hur involves his transformation from one who vengefully wields the sword to one committed to the way of love. This transformation occurs near the end of the film. After he returns from the crucifixion of Jesus, Judah reports to Esther how he heard Jesus on the cross say: "Father, forgive . . . " (Luke) With that, he says, he felt the sword being taken out of his hand. Jesus' words about loving your enemies, as relayed to him by Esther earlier, had finally struck home.

This presentation of redemption as transformation from warmaking to peacemaking occurs in the film alongside the view of redemption as victory over death. Esther herself gives voice to this outlook when she urges Judah to take his leprous mother and sister to see Jesus in Jerusalem so that " . . . they will know that life is everlasting and death nothing to fear if you have faith."

However, in the film, it is Balthasar—one of the three wise men—who functions as the principal theological commentator on the events that have transpired. Balthasar was present in Bethlehem shortly after the birth of Jesus. He also attended the Sermon on the Mount, and on that occasion expressed confidence that Jesus was indeed the "Son of God." He joins Judah at the crucifixion as they both look on. To Judah he summarizes the meaning of what they are seeing: "He has taken the world of our sins onto himself. . . . To this end he said he was born in that stable when I first saw him. . . . For this cause he came into the world. . . . "

The film itself places this "tale of the Christ" into still a broader context of meaning. Michelangelo's painting of "The Creation of Adam" from the Sistine Chapel serves as the background to the opening credits and the concluding shot.[15] God stretches forth his right hand toward the left hand of the seated Adam, index fingers nearly touching. This "touch of new life" is duplicated visually in the film in the two dramatic scenes where Jesus offers a cup of water to Judah in Nazareth and later when Judah reciprocates by offering a cup of water to the fallen Jesus in Jerusalem. These themes of touching and water extend themselves during the crucifixion sequence. The rain mixes with blood, runs down the hillside, and gathers in a pool that reflects the image of Jesus hanging on the cross. Suddenly, the women in a nearby cave—where they had sought refuge—discover that their leprosy has been washed away. After the storm, Judas returns home and reports to Esther the transformation that has occurred in his life through the death of Jesus. Then his mother and sister approach with their new-found wholeness. Judah touches their faces. The untouchables have become touchable. God has touched the world through Jesus. Herein lies redemption.

THE RESPONSES: Box Office Successes

The 1950s was the decade of the Biblical epic. Cecil B. DeMille's *Samson and Delilah* (1949) became the top box office attraction for 1951 by generating nine million dollars. His *The Ten Commandments* (1956) brought in thirty-four million dollars.[16]

The reviews of *Quo Vadis* and *The Robe* in *Variety* (14 November 1951 and 23 September 1953), the show business trade publication, saw big bucks in these spectacles when they premiered in New York City on November 8, 1951, and September 16, 1953. The former was identified as a box office "blockbuster"; and it was predicted that the latter "will get its money back by the bucket full." These prognostications came true. *Quo Vadis* brought in more than eleven million dollars, the second highest box office total for 1952, against a production cost of some six million dollars. *The Robe* produced seventeen million dollars in the last few months of 1953 alone, against a production cost of only four million dollars, on the way to becoming one of the top box office draws of the decade. Both *Quo Vadis* and *The Robe* also received Academy Award nominations as Best Picture. For his performance in *The Robe*, Richard Burton received a Best Actor nomination; and the film received Oscars in the categories of Art Direction, Set Decoration, and Costume Design.

Reviewers of these films in the religious and the secular press evaluated them as cinematic spectacles rather than focusing specifically on their treatments of Jesus. But the reviews by critic Bosley Crowther for *The New York Times* (9 November 1951 and 27 September 1953) reflected often-expressed opinions. The way the camera in *Quo Vadis* showed tableaux of Jesus during the sermon of Peter—on the shore, at the last supper, after the resurrection—was considered to be a tasteless distraction. The presentation of the crucifixion sequence in *The Robe* received praise for its reverential dignity.

Ben-Hur became the greatest success among the alternative Jesus films that subordinated the Jesus story to a tale with a Roman/Christian theme. In fact, by most objective criteria, William Wyler's *Ben-Hur* (1959) represents one of the most successful films in the history of cinema. The biggest box-office draw of the decade 1951–1960, the film garnered eleven Academy Awards, including the awards for Best Picture, Best Director, and Best Actor. Not until *Titanic* (1997) and *The Lord of the Rings: The Return of the King* (2003) did other movies garner that many Oscars.

The film also received positive critical response, although not without dissenting opinions.

Variety (18 November 1959) greeted *Ben-Hur*'s premiere in New York City on November 16, 1959, with praise for the way the movie had distinguished itself from all its grand predecessors, biblical and non-biblical. This film reflected "a genuine concern for human beings" who were "not just pawns reciting flowery dialogue to fill gaps between the action and spectacle scenes." The phrase which would often recur in assessments of the film was "intimate spectacle." Wyler was able to make the audiences care about those whose lives appeared on the screen.

For all its intimacy, *Ben-Hur* remained a spectacle. As such, the anonymous reviewer for *Time* magazine (30 November 1959) called the film "the biggest and the best of Hollywood's superspectacles." But the reviewer for rival publication *Newsweek* (30 November 1959) was not impressed and dismissed it with the claim that "this three hour and 32-minute production becomes . . . merely a stultifying series of predictable 'big' scenes."

No publication had been, or would prove itself to be, more critical of the biblical epics of the 1950s and the glossy Jesus epics of the 1960s than the liberal Protestant weekly *The Christian Century*. An editorial critical of biblical epics (28 October 1959) that appeared *before* the release of *Ben-Hur* even elicited public rejoinders by director William Wyler and star Charlton Heston.[17] But Martin E. Marty, writing for the same periodical *after* viewing *Ben-Hur* (13 January 1960), acknowledged appreciatively that the film belonged in a category all by itself. Specifically, Marty says:

> Religiosity is not conspicuous: the script devotes at least as much attention to the object of faith as to its human subjects. The authentic Christian note is not evaded. The personal element, paradoxically, does again and again win over sight sensations and sound shocks.

Marty concludes by citing the two personal encounters in the film between Jesus and Judah Ben-Hur: "When it is all over, we ask: What was it really about? It was about someone who gave a parched man a cup of cold water. He in turn later gave one to a suffering man. That is what it always was supposed to have been all about."

Critics for the Roman Catholic periodicals *America* and *Commonweal*, however, saved their greatest praise for the Dino De Laurentiis production of *Barabbas*. The film played in Italy and Great Britain before coming to the United States in the fall of 1962. In their reviews, neither Moira Walsh for *America* (6 October 1962) nor Philip T. Hartung for *Commonweal* (9 November 1962) commented specifically on the handling of the opening Jesus sequences. Both concentrated on the broader story and title character and talked in similar terms. She: "I think *Barabbas* is that *rara avis:* an excellently made biblical spectacle that is genuinely religious." He: "It is an elaborate religious spectacle that is genuinely religious." She: "It is a story of degradation and human perversity, of grace frequently proffered and just as frequently rejected, but it is also, in every frame, the story of the Hound of Heaven who prevails at the last moment." He: "Although the script . . . has made changes in expanding the original story, it has caught well its main theme—that of a man fleeing from the Hound of Heaven."

These positive assessments of *Ben-Hur* and *Barabbas* by representatives of leading Protestant and Catholic periodicals suggest that the *theological* questions raised in the 1950s and 1960s about these alternative Jesus-story films differ significantly from the questions asked of Jesus films earlier in the century. Then the theological question often expressed itself in terms of their "reverence" for Jesus and his story. Both *From the Manger to the Cross* (1912) and *The King of Kings* (1927) received high marks for exhibiting such reverence. Now, especially with *Ben-Hur* (1959) and *Barabbas* (1962), the question had become not so much one of *reverence* for Jesus and his story but one of *meaning:* What's it all about?

Another question that came to the fore in the earliest years of Jesus films, both the harmonizing and the alternative traditions, was the question of anti-Semitism. D. W. Griffith, with *Intolerance* (1916), and Cecil B. DeMille, with *The King of Kings* (1927), had made editorial changes in their films in response to criticism by leaders of Jewish organizations.

If there be anti-Semitic tendencies in these Roman/Christian spectacles of the 1950s and 1960s, these tendencies express themselves not so much through the depiction of Jews but by their absence. This absence has been spoken of as "the disappearing Jew."[18] In the films whose stories play themselves out in the city of Rome—*Quo Vadis, The Robe,* and *Barabbas*—there is no indication of a Jewish presence in Rome and no clue that the movement called "Christian" still struggles with its identity both within and over against emerging Judaism. In those films where Jesus actually stands trial for his life in Jerusalem, the viewer first meets him standing before Pilate. Each of these films— *The Robe, Ben-Hur,* and *Barabbas*—shows Pilate's washing of his hands. In the gospels, this act (only in Matt 27:24) represents one of the narra-

tive details by which responsibility for the crucifixion is shifted from
the Romans to the Jews. But in these alternative Jesus films, the Jewish
authorities and Caiaphas the high priest have no stated role in the
events unfolding.

The omission in these films of the gospel-based scene of Jesus' trial
before Caiaphas the high priest (especially Mark and Matthew), found
historical support among those scholars who claimed that Jesus'
appearance before Caiaphas was "made up" by the church in order to

Flavius Josephus
Does Hollywood

Some Jesus-story films concentrate on events reported only in
the gospels. Other films draw on non-gospel sources for thematic
material. The writings of the Jewish historian Flavius Josephus
(ca. 37–100 C.E.) represent invaluable sources for understanding
the history of Roman Palestine.

Flavius Josephus was born into a priestly family in Jerusalem
with the given name of Joseph—Joseph ben Matthias. Having
explored other sectarian options, he eventually associated himself with the Pharisees. At the outset of the first Jewish war
against Rome (66–70 C.E.), Joseph served as the military commander of the Jewish army in Galilee. During the war, he sur-
rendered to the Romans.

As a prisoner-of-war, Joseph found favor first with the Roman
general Vespasian and then with Vespasian's son Titus.
Vespasian returned to Rome to become emperor (69–79 C.E.), and
Titus assumed the command of the Roman legions. Joseph then
served as advisor to Titus during the siege of Jerusalem which
ended in the fall of the city and the destruction of the temple.
Titus himself eventually succeeded his father as emperor (79–81
C.E.)

After the war, Joseph took up residence in Rome under the
patronage of the Flavian emperors, including Vespasian and
Titus. Joseph honored his benefactors by taking the Roman name
Flavius Josephus, man of letters. In the closing decades of the
first century, he produced two major historical works.

The Jewish War, in seven books, begins with the threat of
Antiochus IV Epiphanes whose actions precipitated the
Maccabean revolt (167–164 B.C.E.) but concentrates its narrative

shift responsibility for Jesus' death from the Romans to the Jewish authorities.[19] More recently, the historicity of Jesus' trial before Pontius Pilate also has been called into question.[20]

But the Jewish authorities reappear on the screen along with the face of Jesus himself in those two ambitious harmonizing Jesus films of the 1960s: Samuel Bronston's *King of Kings* (1961) and George Stevens' *The Greatest Story Ever Told* (1965).

around the events related to the war between Jews and Romans (66–70 C.E.). The Jewish Antiquities, in twenty books, traces the history of the Jews from creation down into Josephus' own life-time, thereby retelling much of the story told in his earlier work on the war. Therefore, Josephus writes from Rome as an apologist explaining his people to a wider Graeco-Roman audience.

In Denys Arcand's *Jesus of Montreal* (1989, 1990), the narrator of the passion play mentions Flavius Josephus alongside other ancient Roman historians—Tacitus, Suetonius, and Pliny. But well before Josephus appeared in Montreal, he had done Hollywood, thanks to the two harmonizing Jesus films of the big-screen 1960s: Samuel Bronston's *King of Kings* and George Stevens' *The Greatest Story Ever Told*.

King of Kings (1961) opens, in epic fashion, with a sequence based on Josephus' accounts of the Roman conquest of Jerusalem in 63 B.C.E. (War 1.141–154; Ant. 14.64–76). Josephus had told how the Romans took the city in the third month of a siege, how Roman soldiers slaughtered priests in the temple, and how Pompey profaned the temple by entering the holy of holies.

The Greatest Story Ever Told (1965) also incorporates dramatic material from Josephus' writings into its story by showing an incident that happened in Jerusalem when Herod the Great died (4 B.C.E.). A Jewish mob tore down an eagle that had been placed over the gate to the temple by Herod, the Roman-appointed "King of the Jews" (War 1.648–655; Ant. 17.149–168).

Josephus' influence on Hollywood extends beyond these three cinematic moments. Several films include the gospel-based dance of Herodias' daughter before Herod Antipas and her subsequent request for John the Baptist's head on a platter (in Mark and Matt). The gospels nowhere report the name of the dancing daughter. From Josephus comes her fabled name, Salome, although Josephus does not report her dance (Ant. 18.137).

KING OF KINGS: Jesus (Jeffrey Hunter) and the Sermon on the Mount.
Source: Cinema Collectors

CHAPTER FIVE

1961 | Samuel Bronston
King of Kings

Not long after Cecil B. DeMille's death in 1959, producer Samuel Bronston announced his intention to bring to the big screen the Jesus story in the harmonizing tradition of DeMille and his *The King of Kings* (1927). The American public again would be directly confronted by the face of Jesus.

Bronston even declared his intention to call his film *The King of Kings* and so registered the title with the Motion Picture Association of America's Title Bureau.[1] This created legal problems between Bronston and the Cinema Corporation of America that controlled DeMille's Jesus film of the same name. However, since neither the Cinema Corporation nor DeMille had protected the title by properly registering it with the MPAA, Bronston's production eventually did appear as *King of Kings* (1961), with the definite article missing.[2]

The Bronston film occasionally pays tribute to the earlier DeMille movie. For example, the former duplicates a closeup shot of the end of the cross as Jesus drags it up steps while making his way to Golgotha. But it is difficult to understand how anyone who has seen both films could ever call *King of Kings* (1961) a remake of *The King of Kings* (1927), as has sometimes been done.[3]

Bronston assembled an impressive production crew.[4] For director, he chose Nicholas Ray, whose credits included *Rebel Without a Cause* (1955), a cult classic after actor James Dean's premature death. In fact, Bronston's Jesus film is sometimes referred to as Nicholas Ray's *King of Kings*.[5] However, *King of Kings* was edited without Ray's having the final cut.[6] Philip Yordan wrote the screenplay. Miklos Rosza, who had scored *Quo Vadis* (1951) and *Ben-Hur* (1959), composed the music; and Orson Welles, who had made film history with his stunning *Citizen Kane* (1941) at age twenty-five, served as the omniscient narrator.

Spain became the site of production because Bronston had built enormous studios in Madrid. The surrounding countryside served as surrogate for Galilee and Judea. It was in Spain also that Bronston made his monumental *El Cid* (also 1961) about the eleventh-century Spanish hero who collaborated with local Moors to drive invading Moors from Spain. The final words of this film could have been adapted for the ending of his Jesus film: "Thus the Cid rode out of the gates of history into legend."

King of Kings, with a final production cost at around eight million dollars, was distributed by Metro-Goldwyn-Mayer. In conjunction with its release, a thirty-two page souvenir book was prepared—an item that would occasion no small amount of comment of its own. This book includes a reference to a visit by Bronston to Pope John XXIII to elicit papal approval for the project.[7]

THE FILM: An Action-Drama

The issue of how to begin his Jesus story had been important to DeMille. He opened with an intimate setting, with the camera centering on Mary Magdalene as a beautiful courtesan at a banquet with her male admirers.

Bronston's three hour film "experience" begins, in operatic fashion, with a musical overture and includes an intermission between two acts. The Jesus story itself has been placed within the framework of world history—ancient and modern.

The film begins visually with panoramic shots showing Roman legionnaires marching across the barren countryside toward Jerusalem with the city in the background.

The film begins verbally when the narrator—with a God-like voice and perspective—speaks the appropriately biblical sounding words, "And it is written. . . ." The tramping soldiers represent the command under Pompey, who brought the city and the land under Roman jurisdiction in 63 B.C.E.

The ancient texts referred to by the narrator, and the events displayed on the screen, find their basis not in Scripture but in the writings of the Jewish historian Flavius Josephus. His two monumental histories *The Jewish War* and the *Antiquities of the Jews,* written in the first century C.E., represent the most important narrative sources for understanding what happened in Palestine during the Roman occupation.

However, the viewer who listens with care during the opening sequences will recognize allusions to important world events that had occurred between the release of DeMille's *The King of Kings* in 1927 and Bronston's *King of Kings* in 1961: the holocaust of the Jews by the Germans during World War II; and the conflict between the Jews and the Arabs after the 1948 establishment of the state of Israel. The narrator intones: "Jews went to the slaughter . . ." as villages are torched and bodies tossed on burning piles of wood. The narrator later describes Herod the Great, named "King of the Jews" by Rome, as "an Arab of the Bedouin tribe" and thus, by implication, not a Jew himself but an enemy of the Jews.

With this grand opening, the Bronston film in its own way achieves the objective sought by DeMille—to jar the viewers out of their preconceptions about Jesus and the Jesus story. Bronston has also subtly drawn a correlation between the world of antiquity and the modern world and led the viewers to identify not with the Roman oppressors but with the oppressed Jews.

At last, the face of Herod the Great dissolves into an image of a man and his wife making their way by donkey across the barren countryside. The narration had already mentioned the Jewish hope for a messiah to deliver them from Roman tyranny. Now the narration makes the transition to the familiar gospel story of the birth of Jesus: "And it came to pass in those days that a decree went out from Caesar Augustus . . . " (Luke).

With these words, the Bronston epic—unlike the DeMille film—takes up the life of Jesus with episodes from his birth and infancy (Luke and Matt). The initial dialogue in the film comes from Joseph in Bethlehem, who asks a man in a doorway, "Are you the innkeeper?"

Before the formal intermission, the film brings to the screen several of the best-known episodes from Jesus' ministry prior to his fatal visit to Jerusalem: Jesus' baptism by John, perhaps not by immersion but pouring (synoptics) and his threefold testing in the wilderness by Satan, with the latter heard but not seen (Matt and Luke); the gathering of the first three "apostles" (John); the woman taken in adultery (John); events related to the execution of the Baptist, including the dance of Salome (Mark and Matt); and an extended Sermon on the Mount, shown as a dialogue sermon as Jesus walks among his hearers responding to their questions (Matt). As Jesus' ministry unfolds, he expands the number of his disciples to twelve (especially synoptics); and a roll-call occurs as the disciples walk past the camera singly and in small groups.

After the intermission, the film concentrates on events related to the final days of Jesus' life: the entry into Jerusalem (four gospels); an insurrection led by Barabbas (based on Luke 23:19); the Last Supper with words over the bread and wine (synoptics); the betrayal by Judas (four gospels); the trial before Pontius Pilate (four gospels) with an appearance before Herod Antipas (only Luke); the way to the cross with the assistance of Simon of Cyrene (synoptics); and the crucifixion itself (four gospels).

On the cross, Jesus utters six of the seven last words. To God: "Forgive them, Father . . ." (Luke 23:34). To a thief on an adjacent cross: "You will be with me this day in paradise" (Luke 23:34). To his mother beneath the cross: "Woman, behold your son" (John 19:26). To God: "My God, my God . . ." (Mark 15:34 and Matt 27:46). To whomever: "It is finished" (John 19:30). And finally, to God: "Father into your hands I commend my soul" (Luke 23:46). When Jesus dies, the centurion beneath the cross mutters: "It is truly the Christ" (based on synoptics).

The crucifixion scene shows a number of crosses on a rocky hill, with most crosses empty, except for the three on which Jesus and the two thieves hang. An imaginative overhead shot enables the viewer to see, from on high, the raising of the cross of Jesus.

All four gospels, with slight variation of wording, agree that the charge affixed to the cross read: "King of the Jews." John 19:20 even notes that the charge was written in three languages: Hebrew, Latin, and Greek. DeMille, in *The King of Kings* (1927), followed the gospel of John by spelling out the charge in all three languages.

By contrast, in the Bronston film, the sign over Jesus' head reads in bold letters INRI. Here the staging (or presentation) follows the common iconographic tradition by using the letters INRI to represent the charge on the cross—an abbreviation for the Latin, IESUS NAZARENUS REX IUDAEORUM, "Jesus of Nazareth, King of the Jews."

This film's faithfulness to the iconographic tradition at the crucifixion represents a surprise. Earlier the staging of the Last Supper had departed from the artistic tradition. Jesus and his disciples were arranged along a "Y"-shaped table instead of sitting on the far side, facing the viewer, in the compositional manner of Leonardo da Vinci.

The resurrection sequence includes the discovery of the empty tomb by Mary Magdalene, the appearance of the risen Jesus to her, and later an appearance to the disciples on the shore of the Sea of Galilee (all from John). The film concludes there on the beach with an inventive shot of the risen Jesus' shadow intersecting with a line of fishing nets to form a cross-like image on the sand. As with DeMille, so here the final spoken words are: "I am with you always even to the end of the world" (Matt).

Although *King of Kings* incorporates many familiar stories and sayings from all four gospels into its Jesus story, these actions and words are placed in the service of a broader plot that involves expanded roles for four supporting characters in the gospels: the Roman centurion, present at the cross, identified herein by the name Lucius; Barabbas the Jewish prisoner, released by Pilate, who bears the full name of *Jesus* Barabbas; Judas the disciple, who betrays Jesus to the authorities; and Mary, the mother of Jesus.

The gospel basis for Lucius lies in the unnamed Roman military commander beneath the cross who, depending on the particular gospel and translation, confesses Jesus to be "the Son of God" (Mark and Matt) or "innocent" (Luke). Later church tradition identifies this centurion by the name Longus. The Gospel of Peter, fragments of which were discovered in Egypt in the nineteenth century, identifies the centurion in charge of the squad guarding the tomb by the name of Petronius (Pet 8:4). In *King of Kings*, he receives the name Lucius.

Jesus (Jeffrey Hunter) with the Roman centurion named Lucius (Ron Randell). Source: Larry Edmunds Book Shop

The viewer should keep an eye on Lucius, played by Ron Randell.[8] His presence runs throughout the entire film, since his tour of duty in Palestine extends from the birth of Jesus in Bethlehem through the crucifixion of Jesus outside Jerusalem. First assigned by Caesar to serve Herod the Great, Lucius later serves Pontius Pilate. He commands the soldiers who massacre the infants in Bethlehem. He visits the house of Jesus in Nazareth for census purposes when Jesus has become a young lad. Assigned to spy on Jesus and his movement in Galilee, Lucius periodically reports his findings to Pontius Pilate—often in the presence of Pilate's frequent companions Herod Antipas and Caiaphas, sometimes in such intriguing settings as a barber shop and a spa. At the trial of Jesus, Lucius becomes Jesus' court appointed attorney and later has the unwelcome task of visiting Barabbas in his cell and setting Barabbas free. Lucius' associations with Jesus lead him to move from the explicit espousal of atheism to his eventual confession of Jesus as "the Christ."

The biblical basis for Barabbas is the character by that name—a prisoner—who, in keeping with the alleged Passover custom, was freed by Pilate, whereas Jesus was executed. All four gospels include the character with the name of Barabbas—*bar abbas,* a Jewish surname meaning "son of the Father." He even became the star of his own film entitled *Barabbas* (1962). That this gospel character had "Jesus" as a given name is mentioned in several ancient manuscripts of the gospels in Greek and in other languages. However, most English translations of the gospels omit this reading as a secondary addition to the no longer extant original manuscript. But in *King of Kings,* Barabbas bears his full name: Jesus Barabbas.

Identified in one gospel as an insurrectionist and murderer (Luke 23:19), Barabbas in this film becomes the leader of ten thousand Jewish rebels, or zealots, who seek freedom from Rome by means of the sword. They scour the hills for the Roman enemy, even attacking the column of Roman legionnaires escorting Pilate and his wife. Barabbas and his men have a weapons factory in Jerusalem, which they use as a base for an uprising to coincide with Jesus' peaceful entry into Jerusalem at Passover time.

Judas, a follower of Barabbas in the film, becomes attracted to Jesus as a prophet of peace and joins his band of disciples. But Judas maintains an ongoing debate with Barabbas about the relative merits of non-violence versus violence. Eventually disillusioned by the failure of Jesus' way of peace as a means of bringing freedom, Judas betrays Jesus in an attempt to force him to use his miraculous powers to defeat the occupying Romans.

Still another character from the gospels also has an interestingly developed role in the film: Mary the mother of Jesus. Mary attends the baptism of her son Jesus by John. Throughout her son Jesus' ministry, she maintains a home in Nazareth, fully aware of her son's identity and mission, although there are only the slightest allusions to the virginal conception and birth. She receives visitors—notably John the Baptist and Mary Magdalene—who want to chat about her remarkable boy. Earlier, Mary Magdalene had been identified as the woman taken in adultery. So it is to Mary Magdalene that Mary the mother of Jesus speaks the parable of the lost sheep. When Jesus himself returns for a farewell visit with his mother before his final departure to Jerusalem, his mother seems to have become conscious of his fate even before he does. Beneath the cross, his mother is entrusted by Jesus to the care of John, his "beloved disciple."

Although the role of Mary Magdalene has not been greatly expanded, the film exhibits the tendency—so obvious in the medieval tradition of the church—to make Mary Magdalene into a "penitent sinner" in contrast to the "virgin" Mary.[9] All four canonical gospels portray Mary Magdalene as a faithful follower of Jesus. In Luke (8:1–3), she becomes a follower after having seven demons exorcised. In John (20:1, 11–18), she—first among the followers—discovers the empty tomb and experiences an appearance of the resurrected Jesus. However, Luke (7:35–50) does *not* identify her as the sinful woman who anoints Jesus' feet *nor* does John (8:1–11) identify her as the woman taken in adultery. More positively, the Gospel of Mary (Magdalene)—probably second century—portrays her as having received privileged teachings from Jesus, to the dismay of Andrew and Peter.[10]

THE PORTRAYAL: Jesus as the Messiah of Peace

In *King of Kings*, Jesus was played by the thirty-three year old Jeffrey Hunter. He had appeared in the western *The Searchers* (1956) and in the political drama *The Last Hurrah* (1958). Whereas the *King of Kings'* souvenir book claimed that many candidates were considered for the role, Hunter's widow later asserted that he was the only one who would take the part. Her comment indicates how wary actors were of the Jesus role. She also said that Hunter himself had been deeply affected by his experience.[11]

The film acknowledges in various ways that Jesus, as played by Jeffrey Hunter, was a miracle worker. The narrator declares Jesus' day to be "a time of miracles." The camera shows the healings of a crippled boy and a blind man. A written report of Jesus' activities, read to Pilate by the ubiquitous Lucius, refers to his having fed a crowd of five thousand with five loaves and two fishes, having walked on the water, and having stilled a storm. References are also made to Jesus' having cast out demons and having raised the dead. However, the film omits the cinematically popular raising of Lazarus from the dead.

The film affirms that Jesus was a teacher. The narrator also declares Jesus' day to be "a time of teaching." In fact, the Sermon on the Mount (Matt 5–7) serves as the centerpiece for this dimension of Jesus' ministry and, in many ways, for the film itself. Many of Jesus' teachings on the mountainside are gathered together from elsewhere in the gospels themselves. As a teacher, Jesus makes occasional references to "the kingdom of God" and occasionally delivers a parable. He can also speak about himself in words that begin, "I am . . ." and be said to call himself "Son of God."

Nonetheless, Jesus' message finds its center neither in the kingdom (as in the synoptics) nor in himself (as in John). As might be expected, Lucius the Centurion gives the definitive summary of what Jesus and his message are all about. After the Sermon on the Mount, Lucius dutifully reports to Pilate what Jesus taught: ". . . peace, love, and the brotherhood of man."

Indeed, the words "peace" and "love" are the words most often associated with Jesus throughout the film. Early in Jesus' ministry, the narrator had distinguished the options available to Judas: Was he to run with Barabbas as "the messiah of war" or to follow Jesus as "the new messiah of peace"? After the Sermon on the Mount, when Jesus withdraws to teach the twelve, the narrator explains that Jesus taught them "peace and love. . . ." And Barabbas complains to Judas that Jesus speaks "only of peace." Both the "great commandment" and the "new commandment" find their way into the script. Jesus declares the "great commandment" in response to a question during the Sermon on the Mount: "Love the Lord your God . . . and love your neighbor . . ." (synoptics). He gives the "new commandment" to his disciples at the Last Supper: "Love one another . . ." (John).

Therefore, an emphasis on peace and love emerges in the midst of the traditional story of Jesus. All the traditional titles are associated with Jesus: "Son of God," "Christ," "Son of man," and even "King of Kings." But no designation fits him better than "the new messiah of peace" declared from on high by the narrator—God?—himself.

In sharp contrast to Barabbas the revolutionary, Jesus appears as a pacifist advocating peace and love. Here is further support for the claim that this film universalizes "the Christ story in a way that upgrades humanism over divinity."[12] Or, from a different angle, the film upgrades humanism over human violence. The film completely omits many confrontational scenes from the gospels: *no* preaching in the synagogue at Nazareth; *no* cleansing of the temple in Jerusalem; and *no* armed struggle between Jesus' disciples and the arresting party in Gethsemane.

The harmonizing *King of Kings* (1961) shares an obvious strength with its immediate alternative predecessors—such as *Ben-Hur* (1959). Like those Roman/Christian epics, *King of Kings* recognizes that Roman rule provided the oppressive political framework for the life and death of Jesus, and that Roman rule thereby engendered a potentially violent response among the Jewish populace. These films also share a weakness. They present Jesus as so non-violent and non-threatening that they leave viewers wondering how such a nice guy ended up on a Roman cross.

THE RESPONSE: A Film Without Honor

Bronston's *King of Kings* was the first commercially produced film in this country to tell the Jesus story in the harmonizing tradition, with the camera focused throughout on the Jesus character, since the adoption of the Production Code by the film industry in 1930 and the creation of the Legion of Decency by the Catholic Church in 1934. Bronston's experience with the Legion dramatizes why filmmakers had been reluctant to bring the Jesus story to the screen except in the alternative approach taken by such films as *Quo Vadis* (1951), *The Robe* (1953), *Ben-Hur* (1959), and subsequently, *Barabbas* (1962).

The Legion of Decency refused to classify *King of Kings* according to any of its "morally unobjectionable" categories. Instead, the film received a "special classification" with this explanation:

> While acknowledging the inspirational intent of this motion picture, the poetic license taken in the development of the life of Christ renders the film theologically, historically, and scripturally inaccurate.[13]

The position taken by the Legion of Decency immediately complicated the marketing of the film to the American public. Nonetheless, Bronston's *King of Kings* opened around the country in October, 1961.

Ironically, this film—with its introductory allusions to recent world events and its projection of Jesus as "a messiah of peace"—was released during a period in the "Cold War" when it seemed most likely that the world would destroy itself. This was the period between the United States-backed invasion of Cuba known as "the Bay of Pigs," in April of 1961, and the "Cuban missile crisis," in October of 1962, when President John F. Kennedy and the United States confronted Nikita Khrushchev and the Soviet Union over the placement of missiles with nuclear warheads in that island nation.

Although there is no demonstrable evidence that the international situation in the early 1960s influenced the public's acceptance, or non-acceptance, of this Jesus film, perhaps this should not be discounted. The failure of D. W. Griffith's *Intolerance* (1916) at the box office has often been attributed to the incongruity between his plea for tolerance in the face of a world gone berserk over World War I. Certainly the Jesus portrayed in *King of Kings* appears as out of place in the post-World War II world of power politics as he had in that earlier era.

The critical response to *King of Kings* by the secular and the religious press was devastating. In fact, seldom has a film of such magnitude been met with such scorn. In spite of the accolades bestowed on *Ben-Hur* (1959), critics during the 1950s had obviously developed not only immunity from, but hostility toward, Hollywood extravaganzas with biblical subject matter. *King of Kings* bore the brunt of this hostility and ultimately became a box office failure, grossing less than its eight million dollar cost.

Many representatives of the secular press simply saw the film as another example of "bad cinema." Brendan Gill, in *The New Yorker* (21 October 1961), dubbed the film "a bore" and described it as "a sort of Macy's Thanksgiving Day parade for simple-minded grownups, in which outsize rubber dolls labeled Herod, Salome, Herodias, Mary Magdalene, and John the Baptist go jogging past our astonished eyes." The unidentified reviewer for *Time* magazine (27 October 1961) found merit in the "precisely organized and competently prosed" script by Philip Yordan, but the review concluded that the most telling criticism lay in the indelicate subtitle by which the film had become known in film circles, "I Was a Teenage Jesus." The similarly unidentified critic for *Newsweek* magazine (30 October 1961) praised director Nicholas Ray for handling "the huge screen and the cast of thousands better than his predecessors," but the reviewer still dismissed the finished product as "a long, slow, static movie. . . . "

The reviewers for leading Protestant and Roman Catholic periodicals were no less dismissive. Tom F. Driver of *The Christian Century* (11 November 1961) imagined a conversation between a press agent and a critic. In response to the question of how he would characterize the film, the critic answered, "As the King James Version of 'Gone With the Wind.'" The imaginary critic continues with observations about this auburn-haired and blue-eyed Jesus as a "true American" and a "good boy" because he visits his "Irish mother" before the crucifixion. In a footnote, Driver even offers to send his *King of Kings* souvenir book, with plates suitable for framing, to anyone who would pay the postage.

Moira Walsh of the Jesuit weekly *America* (21 October 1961) writes more extensively and in a less playful vein. Her concluding indictment of the film lies in its possible reinforcement of "secular humanism" or the "American Way of Life" under the guise of the central Christian story. The film, she says, "equates the Christian moral code with such terms as decency, brotherhood, the Golden Rule." That is, the film beckons its viewers not to take up a cross but rather, "Take up your credit card and follow me." She obviously sees in the film not just bad cinema but bad theology.

One dimension of the film that continued to engender lively substantive discussion, particularly in the Catholic press, was the way it had handled the role of "the Jews" in the death of Jesus. Walsh, while acknowledging herself to be a film critic and not a biblical scholar, observed that most Jesus films like *King of Kings* share the tendency of "rearranging facts to absolve the Jews of all blame for Christ's death."[14]

The DeMille *The King of Kings* (1927) had underscored the culpability of one Jew, the high priest Caiaphas, for Jesus' death by placing on his lips the words: ". . . I alone am guilty." The Bronston *King of Kings* (1961), in what sounds like a play on these lines, has Pontius Pilate, the Governor of Judea, say: "I, and I alone, have the authority to sentence you to crucifixion. . . . " The trial scene before Pilate takes place without the presence of Jewish crowds and even without Barabbas. Jesus dies, apparently having been found guilty of the specific charge of sedition.

The discussion among Catholics about *King of Kings* and its treatment of the responsibility for the death of Jesus occurred before the 1965 Vatican Council II pronouncement about the Jews as God's people: *Nostra Aetate* ("Our Times"). This document rejected the notion that Jews collectively bear the responsibility for the death of Jesus and that God has thereby rejected the Jews.

The year 1965 was also the year for the release of a Jesus film even more ambitious than its epic harmonizing predecessors. This cinematic presentation of the Jesus story originated with the man who had received an Oscar for directing *A Place in the Sun* (1951). He had also brought to the public such engaging stories of the American west as *Shane* (1953) and *Giant* (1956), receiving another Oscar for the latter film. George Stevens soon turned his attention to an even greater story—in fact, *The Greatest Story Ever Told* (1965).

THE GREATEST STORY EVER TOLD: Jesus (Max von Sydow) at the last supper. Source: Larry Edmunds Book Shop

CHAPTER SIX

1965 | George Stevens
The Greatest Story Ever Told

George Stevens initiated plans for his own cinematic presentation of the Jesus story even before the premiere of Samuel Bronston's *King of Kings* in October of 1961. Stevens had already visited Israel to locate sites for what was projected to be a ten million dollar extravaganza. He had also already discarded the notion of shooting in that troubled land because of changes wrought in the topography since the first century by war and erosion.[1] Instead, Stevens chose sites in the American west, especially the Glen Canyon area of southern Utah. The Colorado River became the Jordan. The desert became the setting for a built-for-the-occasion Jerusalem with its holy temple.

In the movement from an idea to the screen, as is often the case, there was squabbling relative to backing and funding for Stevens' project. Originally, Stevens had the support of 20th Century-Fox. But when Metro-Goldwyn-Mayer agreed to distribute Bronston's *King of Kings*, the leadership of 20th Century-Fox charged MGM with "unfair competition" and asked the Motion Picture Association of America to intervene. The MPAA (formerly the MPPDA) rejected the claim. As a result, 20th Century-Fox both withdrew from the organization and dropped its support of the project itself.[2]

In the long run, United Artists became the distributor of the film that eventually cost nearly twenty million dollars. George Stevens both produced and directed *The Greatest Story Ever Told*.[3] The film title, but little else, comes from the popular 1949 book about Jesus by Fulton Oursler. Stevens also wrote the screenplay in association with James Lee Barrett, who later collaborated on the script for the three hour made-for-television presentation *The Day Christ Died* (1980), based on the 1957 book by Jim Bishop.[4] The music was composed and arranged by Alfred Newman.

The credits also recognize that the film was produced in "creative association" with the poet Carl Sandburg. Film critic Dwight Macdonald, perhaps failing to establish exactly what this meant, spoke of Sandburg as something of a "cinematic Holy Ghost."[5] However, Carl Sandburg—then in his eighties—did move to Hollywood in mid-July 1960, and over the next year and a half met with George Stevens and his staff to help clarify their vision of the film.[6]

89

Max von Sydow, the Swedish actor, was cast in the role of Jesus with top billing. At the time, he was known to a limited American audience, having appeared primarily in the films of his fellow countryman, Ingmar Bergman.

On the screen, Max von Sydow was surrounded by faces all too familiar to an American audience. In Bronston's *King of Kings* (1961), Jesus had competed cinematically with the characters of Lucius, Barabbas, Judas, and Mary; but in Stevens' *Greatest Story*, Jesus competed with the likenesses of Hollywood's brightest stars.

Among the familiar faces around Jesus appear the easily recognizable features of Pat Boone, Jamie Farr, Jose Ferrer, Charlton Heston, Van Heflin, Martin Landau, Angela Lansbury, David McCallum, Roddy McDowall, Dorothy McGuire, Sal Mineo, Donald Pleasance, Sidney Poitier, Telly Savalas, John Wayne, Shelley Winters, and Ed Wynn—to list only a few of those whose names appear, in alphabetical order, in the on-screen credits. The casting-according-to-type included John Wayne as the Roman centurion and Pat Boone as the angel in the tomb. In a kind of cinematic rehabilitation, Joseph Schildkraut, who had played the traitor Judas in DeMille's *The King of Kings* (1927), appears here as the more sympathetic character of Nicodemus.

In *The Greatest Story Ever Told*, Jesus was forced to compete for the viewer's attention not only with well-known Hollywood actors but also with an American landscape readily recognizable to moviegoers from countless "western" films. Twentieth-century Palestine may not be first-century Palestine, but neither is Utah. Panoramic shots of towering mountains with snow-capped peaks show ant-like figures moving slowly across vast spaces punctuated by buttes so characteristic of the American southwest. Filmed in this natural setting, the Mount of Temptation becomes the Moun*tain* of Temptation as Jesus struggles up the steep, sharp cliffs. The following sequence features a closeup of a full moon that fills the screen and, in its own way, detracts from Jesus. The Sermon on the Mount also becomes the Sermon on the Moun*tain*. When Jesus addresses his disciples and the crowds, he stands precariously with his back to a precipice of several thousand feet.

By all outward appearances, Stevens intended to equal—and even to surpass—Samuel Bronston in the grandeur and the scope of his own cinematic presentation of the Jesus story. Seemingly, Stevens meant his film to be *the greatest version* of *the* greatest story. Like its immediate predecessor, the Stevens film was designed to be shown in two acts with a formal intermission, but with a longer screening time. The lengths of varying versions of the film have been identified as ranging downward from as much as 260 minutes.[7] The Stevens film also appears more inclusive of specific stories and sayings from the four gospels. Like Bronston, Stevens circulated a promotional book thirty-two pages in length.

However, whereas Bronston's *King of Kings* displayed the characteristics of an action-drama with big fight scenes, Stevens approached *The Greatest Story* with an avowed concern for ideas. While on location in Utah in December of 1962, Stevens expressed his own cinematic vision in these words: "We are doing simply the story of Jesus, with no interruptions for theatrical embroideries. Our contacts are with ideas rather than spectacle." He continued by explaining the ideas with which his film was concerned: "Our theme—compassion and man's humanity to man—is desirable to men of all faiths."[8] Later, in February of 1965, as the film was preparing to open in New York City, Stevens reiterated his understanding of the film's theme in similar words: "The basic theme of the story is one which, unfortunately, has not always been associated with it in the past. It relates to the universality of men and how they must learn to live together."[9]

Ironically, Stevens' statements about the basic theme of *The Greatest Story ever Told* seem, in some ways, more appropriate for Bronston's *King of Kings*. Bronston's film also focuses rather sharply on love, peace, and brotherhood, but in the midst of armed conflict. Stevens' film spreads before the viewer both more and less, more thought on a wider range of issues, less frantic action.

THE FILM: A Meditation

The Greatest Story Ever Told opens in a church with the camera angled upward into the dome around which are seen frescoes depicting scenes from the life of Jesus. As the camera moves downward from the interior of the dome, the voice of a narrator intones the lines which introduce the story of Jesus according to the gospel of John: "In the beginning was the word, and the word was with God, and the word was God. . . . " The camera continues moving downward past a fresco of Jesus bearing the cross and then a medallion with the Greek words ΕΓΩ ΕΙΜΙ, translated by the narrator as "I am He." Then comes into view, painted on the wall, the face of Jesus, in a white robe and with arms outstretched. The image of Jesus has a traditional look, but it does not represent any known painting. This Jesus is none other than Max von Sydow; or, one might more aptly say, Max von Sydow is this Jesus.

The narrator continues with words from the prologue to the gospel of John, with references to "life" and "light"; and the image of Jesus in the church dissolves into a starry night in which one star appears brighter than all others. This star dissolves into a flame burning from a small oil lamp carried by a woman in a stable. As a baby cries, and as the hand of that baby comes into view, the narrator concludes this prologue to the film by verbalizing the title words: "The Greatest Story Ever Told."

The film concludes by returning the viewer to the church with which it opened. After the discovery of the empty tomb, Jesus appears to the disciples, and others, as they are seated and/or standing on a cloud-shrouded mountain. With a close-up of Jesus, the camera follows Jesus ascending skyward. The image of Jesus dissolves into clouds, and he speaks those words with which cinematic stories of Jesus so often end: "Lo, I am with you always, even to the end of the world" (Matt).

Then the camera, back in the church, moves downward from the interior of the dome of the church, past the fresco of Jesus bearing the cross, past the medallion with the words ΕΓΩ ΕΙΜΙ, to the face of Jesus—Max von Sydow—painted on the wall.

Stevens also uses another visual framing device for his retelling the greatest of all stories. The transitions to and from the earthly life of Jesus are marked by four heralds blowing their trumpets atop the walls of Jerusalem. They appear announcing the birth of Jesus. They also appear announcing his resurrection from the dead.

It is within these frameworks, and in two acts, that Stevens retells the Jesus story, based on a script that includes the most familiar episodes from the four gospels. Among the episodes presented *before* intermission are: the infancy stories (Matt and Luke); the baptism by John followed by the testing in the desert by the devil (synoptics); the declaration of the great commandment of loving God and loving neighbor (synoptics); the woman caught in adultery (John); the execution of John the Baptist (Mark and Matt); the Sermon on the Mount (Matt); the confession of Peter and Jesus' response (Matt); Jesus' rejection at Nazareth (synoptics); and the raising of Lazarus from the dead (John).

The episodes presented *after* intermission are those that occur during passion week. They include: the entry into Jerusalem (four gospels); the cleansing of the temple (four gospels); the betrayal of Judas (four gospels); the Last Supper (four gospels); the trial before Caiaphas and the Sanhedrin (especially Mark); an initial hearing before Pontius Pilate and an appearance before Herod Antipas (Luke); the trial and sentence of death before Pontius Pilate (four gospels); the way to the cross with the assistance of Simon of Cyrene (synoptics); and the crucifixion outside the city walls (four gospels). The comprehensive treatment of the Jesus story in the film is suggested by the inclusion of all *seven* of the traditional last words of Jesus.

Stevens' film about Jesus incorporates the familiar episodes from the gospels, but his presentation certainly contains the unexpected as well, both in terms of interpretation and staging.

Satan—or the devil—plays a relatively minor role in the four gospels. Satan's greatest prominence occurs in the earliest written account of the testing in the wilderness (Mark) that has been expanded into a threefold temptation of Jesus in other gospels with additional information from the "Q"-source (Matt and Luke). He dares Jesus to change the stones into bread, to throw himself off the pinnacle of the temple, and to worship the devil instead of God. Also, in two gospels, Satan enters into Judas leading Judas to betray his master (Luke and John).

DeMille, in his *The King of Kings* (1927), has the devil make a brief personal appearance to Jesus during the last days in Jerusalem. There, in the temple, the devil tempts Jesus to worship him by showing him the kingdoms of the world. In Bronston's *King of Kings* (1961), the devil makes no personal appearance but becomes a disembodied voice leading Jesus through the prescribed threefold temptation—immediately after his baptism and before the inauguration of his public ministry.

However, in Stevens' *Greatest Story*, the devil has been transformed into a major character, one whom the credits identify as "the dark hermit." This character, played by Donald Pleasance, becomes a sinister presence throughout the film. The viewer can expect to see and hear him at crucial moments in the story: on the mountain top for the testing in the wilderness; in the crowd at Capernaum when Mary Magdalene as the adulterous woman escapes stoning; before Judas in Jerusalem as Judas leaves the Last Supper heading for Caiaphas' house; to Peter in the courtyard eliciting a denial while Jesus stands trial before the Sanhedrin; and among the people during the interrogation of Jesus by Herod Antipas and Pontius Pilate. Remarkably, as Jesus makes the transition from Herod back to Pilate, the camera shows a close-up of the dark hermit with a voice-over of John 3:16 as though these words are running through his mind ("For God so loved the world that he gave his only Son, so that everyone who believes in him may not perish but may have eternal life"). Nonetheless, shortly thereafter, the dark hermit will lead the crowds in screaming: "Crucify him!"

Lazarus appears as a narrative character only in the gospel of John where, as the brother of Mary and Martha, he dies only to be resuscitated from the dead by Jesus. Since in John the cleansing of the temple occurs at the outset of the gospel, it is the incident involving Lazarus—not the action in the temple—that becomes in that gospel the precipitating factor leading to the final plot against Jesus.

Although DeMille included both the raising of Lazarus and the cleansing of the temple in his film, the Bronston *King of Kings* omitted both gospel incidents. *Greatest Story* includes these two gospel stories; and they become the basis for expansions within the cinematic narrative.

The resuscitation of Lazarus from the dead, with his being called forth from his mountainside tomb, serves as the finale for the film's first act as those who have witnessed the event rush toward the city walls of Jerusalem acclaiming what Jesus has done. The music breaks into the "Hallelujah Chorus," leaving the viewer to wonder what musical underscoring will be left for the resurrection of Jesus himself.

This Lazarus, and his sisters Mary and Martha, have already been introduced to the viewer at an earlier moment. As Jesus and his first disciples head from the Jordan River back to Galilee, they are invited into the home of Lazarus and his sisters. In this film, Lazarus has become a man of some learning and wealth—in fact, a composite character. He incorporates into himself features of the man who asked about the greatest commandment and traits of the rich young man who could not divest himself of his worldly possessions (both of synoptic fame).

The action of Jesus in the temple, with the crowds—including Judas—watching passively, serves as a springboard for two scenes that run counter to the claims of the gospels and defy historical possibility from the viewpoint of life-of-Jesus research. Jesus returns to the temple after nightfall and preaches from the steps of the high altar—a scene that has Jesus verbalize words about faith, hope, and love (taken from Paul, I Cor 13). When Judas, in remorse, finally dies, he does so not by hanging himself (as in Matt) nor by a clumsy fall (as in Acts). Instead, Judas returns to the temple courtyard deserted by the priests and crowds who have presumably followed Jesus toward the place of execution. Then, at the very moment a nail fixes Jesus' hand to the cross, Judas casts himself into the flames of the altar of sacrifice—as a burnt offering, a holocaust.

THE PORTRAYAL: Jesus as Incarnate Word

Throughout the film, Jesus appears unmistakably as the fulfillment of the Davidic messianic hope of Israel. Several persons apply scriptural texts to him.

Herod the Great no longer appears as the dissipated Arab of Bronston's *King of Kings*. Here Herod identifies himself as an Idumean from the territory south of Judea, who knows the scriptures even better than the Judean priests. In the presence of the three wise men, his advisors, and his son Antipas, Herod—called a pious man by his son—recalls the words of the prophet Micah: "From you Bethlehem shall he come forth who is to be ruler in all Israel . . . " (Mic 5:21). This same text appears on the lips of John the Baptist after the baptism of Jesus and, much later, on the lips of Herod's son Antipas when Jesus appears before him in Jerusalem. Herod also justifies his command to massacre the infants at Bethlehem by quoting other words from the prophets: "A voice was heard in Bethlehem weeping and mourning . . . " (Jer 31:15). And Joseph, having fled from Bethlehem to Egypt with wife and child, stands under a palm tree reading from a scroll words from the prophet Isaiah: "For unto us a child is born . . . " (Isa 9:6).

Even more striking than the citation of these traditional messianic texts by those around Jesus is the use in the film of texts that refer to God—notably from the Psalms—to refer to Jesus. After the baptism of Jesus, John stands waist deep in the River Jordan crying out: "Lift up your heads, O gates . . . that the King of glory may come in" (Ps 24:8–9). By implication, Jesus is that "King of glory." After Jesus' nighttime oration in the temple, as he departs, one of his followers leads the gathered crowd responsively in the 23rd Psalm ("The LORD is my shepherd . . .") with the implication that Jesus is that "LORD" and "shepherd." As guards move in to disperse the crowd, those present can be heard repeating the words initially verbalized by John: "Lift up your heads, O gates . . . that the King of glory may come in."

In the film, Jesus just as clearly understands himself to be the fulfillment of the hope for a messiah. This is implied at his baptism by John and his testing by the devil and is later made explicit. He accepts Peter's confession that he is "the messiah," "the Christ." Upon his return to Nazareth, he responds to a question about his messiahship with the claim that he fulfills scripture, "The Spirit of the LORD is upon me . . ." (Isa 61:1–2). Before the Sanhedrin, when asked by Caiaphas about his identity as the Christ, the Son of God, Jesus answers with an unequivocating, "I am" (as in Mark). It is precisely Jesus' perceived and self-claimed fulfillment of the messianic hope that leads to his difficulties with the authorities.

Unlike the easy-going relationship among Pontius Pilate, Herod Antipas, and Caiaphas in *King of Kings,* their relationship here appears less friendly and more pragmatic. The film draws upon the writings of Josephus, the Jewish historian, for a sequence that shows unrest in Jerusalem upon the death of Herod the Great. Although the film leaves unclear the exact nature of the succession after Herod's death, there remains the unmistakable affirmation that his son Antipas and the ruling high priest owe their positions to the Romans.

Pilate, Antipas, and Caiaphas are shown to be united in their opposition to John the Baptist, although the responsibility for executing him falls upon Herod Antipas. They also become increasingly one in their opposition to Jesus as they individually receive reports of his activities in Galilee—particularly his healings—but also other reported miracles, such as his feeding the multitudes, walking on water, and changing water into wine. Caiaphas dispatches representatives in response to a report that Jesus practices "sorcery." Antipas hears about Jesus' healings, but becomes apprehensive about him only when he perceives Jesus to be a "Galilean rebel" who seeks his kingdom. Further reports come to Antipas and to Pilate that Jesus has been hailed as "king" in Galilee. After Jesus' entry into Jerusalem, Caiaphas too recognizes that the people call him "king" and "messiah" and subsequently orders his arrest.

The film repeatedly emphasizes the Roman interest in maintaining law and order. Early on, the return of Joseph and Mary from Egypt to Nazareth takes them along a road lined with crucified rebels. Pilate himself displays an ongoing concern about the threat of unrest posed by John and—later—Jesus. Therefore, it is not very convincing in the film when Pilate at the very end, in a manner consistent with the gospels, tries to weasel out of turning Jesus over for crucifixion. Although Caiaphas as high priest and Judas as betrayer are involved in the events that eventuate in Jesus' execution, the film ultimately places the responsibility for his death on that shady character identified as the "dark hermit." That is, the devil made 'em do it!

This film portrays Jesus as the messiah in fulfillment of the promises in the Scriptures. The film does emphasize his miracle-working activity as that which both attracted a crowd and threatened the authorities. But Jesus appears as much more than a traditional messianic figure who works miracles. He appears as the incarnate Word—the incarnation of God.

More than any other Jesus film, *The Greatest Story Ever Told* moves under the influence of the gospel of John. Not only does the film begin with words about the "Word" from the prologue of John, but the camera moves into the world, and then—after the resurrection—out of the world. Throughout the film, Jesus repeatedly refers to the *world* as that which, in some sense, stands over against God and into which he has come with "light" and "life" and "love" (prominent themes in John). In his programmatic nighttime address on the altar steps in the temple, Jesus declares: "I have come to bring salvation *to the world*." As he stands holding aloft a torch, Statue-of-Liberty-like, he continues: "I have come as a light *into the world*." In Gethsemane, as he prays, he says: "For this cause I have come into *this world*." Before Pilate, he understandably declares that his kingdom is "not of *this world*." Along the way, he articulates familiar "I am" sayings: "I am the bread of life," "I am the resurrection and the life," "I am the way, the truth, and the life." At the last supper, he sets forth his new commandment that his followers "love one another" as he has loved them.

Within this conceptual framework of coming into and taking leave of the world, Jesus becomes not only *in the world* and *not of the world*, but also *in Judaism* but *not of Judaism*. This film is not about a Jew who was Christ but about Christ who happened to appear in first-century Palestine as a Jew.

George Stevens, as an official photographer with the U. S. 6th Army in World War II, was present during the liberation of the Dachau concentration camp in the spring of 1945; and photographs of him and his work hang in the U. S. Holocaust Memorial Museum in Washington, D.C. Stevens had also directed, for the screen, *The Diary of Anne Frank* (1959). Both personally and professionally, Stevens was sensitive to the issue of anti-Semitism. Within *Greatest Story* itself, he uses Nicodemus and Joseph of Arimathea as members of the Sanhedrin who are sympathetic to Jesus in opposition to Caiaphas the high priest. Stevens also uses the "dark hermit" as the cheerleader for those in the crowd who scream for the crucifixion of Jesus. Nonetheless, in spite of all this, there appears in *Greatest Story* the implication that Christianity was in the process of superseding Judaism—at least superseding the Judaism centered in the sacrificial cult of the Jerusalem temple.

In a manner consistent with the synoptics, Jesus enters Jerusalem and immediately proceeds to "cleanse" the temple. To a moneychanger he declares, just before overturning his table, words from Jeremiah the prophet: "'My house shall be called a house of prayer,' says the LORD, 'but you have made it a den of thieves.'" But this initial scene of Jesus in the temple has been expanded to include comment not only on commercial activity in the temple but also on the religious rite of sacrifice itself. As Jesus sets free the caged birds and tethered animals, he further says: "It is written in the scriptures, 'I desire mercy, not sacrifice . . . rather knowledge of God than burnt offerings. . . . '" These words from Hosea 6:6 echo words spoken by John the Baptist in the wilderness at the outset of the film. Although Jesus accuses these moneychangers and sacrifice sellers of having defiled the temple, he himself proceeds to defile it as a non-priest who proceeds to the altar of sacrifice. Later that night, he delivers an oration about salvation from the steps of the altar. That Jesus has replaced the temple as the avenue to God seems quite clear. When he dies on the cross, all temple activity has ceased and the courtyard stands empty—except for Judas who sacrifices himself on that altar, the efficacy of which has been replaced by the sacrifice of the one he betrayed.

Within the conceptual framework of coming into and taking leave of the world, Jesus' teachings also find their proper setting. There is in the film not only an *other*-worldliness but an *anti*-worldliness. This is a Jesus far removed from the merrymaking Jesus of D. W. Griffith's

Intolerance. This Jesus can cry, at least in a controlled way, as a tear makes its way down his cheek when Lazarus dies; this Jesus does not laugh. His face has a northern gothic look, appropriate for a Swede, dour and pained.

The *anti*worldliness in the film, and Jesus' teachings, has to do with the repeated counsel against a comfortable life made possible by the "stuff" of this world. The so-called "dark hermit" serves as a spokesman for the life of ease. Lazarus and his sisters live it.

Jesus first encounters the "dark hermit" in the wilderness after scaling the heights of a mountain. The latter speaks invitingly from his shallow rock shelter: "Long hard climb, wasn't it? Come on in, if you like. Some think the whole of life should be hard like that. An easy life is a sinful life. That's what they think." But the hermit immediately counters this view: "Not so. Life should be as easy as a man can make it. It can be easy, friend, if a man knows the way to power and glory in *this world*." Then before the three traditional temptations, at night in the limited light of the moon, the hermit tempts Jesus with food—worldly stuff. Jesus declines, saying simply: "I'm fasting."

Jesus' fasting does not last forever. His initial association with Lazarus and his sisters takes place in their comfortable home when he and his disciples are invited in, as pilgrims, for food and rest. As all sit around leisurely talking, Jesus replies to a question about the greatest commandment by citing Deuteronomy 6:4f and Leviticus 19:18: ". . . love the Lord thy God . . . and love thy neighbor as thyself. . . ."

Then the conversation between Jesus and Lazarus takes a more serious turn when Lazarus asks to go with him; and Jesus says, "You are wealthy." When asked if wealth were a "crime," Jesus denies such. But Jesus suggests that wealth may become "a burden" because "it is easier for a camel to go through the eye of a needle than for a rich man to enter the kingdom of heaven." Jesus further denies that wealth and goodness are mutually exclusive. But he affirms that a man "cannot serve both God and money"; and he praises a widow who gave two pennies—all that she had. When Jesus asks Lazarus if he would divest himself of all he owns to follow him, Lazarus looks wistfully at his sisters and says, "Who could do such a thing?" Judas first, and then Jesus, with the other disciples, arise and leave.

Even Judas must have learned something from the discussion between Jesus and Lazarus. Judas' eventual betrayal of Jesus to Caiaphas brings with it both the declaration that he still loves Jesus and the request that Jesus not be harmed. Furthermore, Judas does not seek money and disavows any interest in monetary gain for his duplicitous act.

The film—as expressed most directly in the exchanges between

Jesus and the hermit, as well as between Jesus and Lazarus—does reflect a critique of the materialism and consumerism in post-Depression and post-World War II America. This film of the early 1960s does not call for the kind of transvaluation of life-styles that came with the counter-culture of the late 1960s.[10] Jesus has accommodated himself, at least in an equivocating way, to the possibility that money and goodness can co-exist. Even though Lazarus does not give away his riches and follow Jesus, Jesus does not forget him; and, later, Jesus returns to raise Lazarus from the dead. However, there is irony in finding even the slightest critique of wealth in *The Greatest Story Ever Told*, since the film—all twenty million dollars' worth—has such a lushness about it, even in a desert. Austerity never looked so good.

THE RESPONSE: Another Film Without Honor

The Greatest Story Ever Told opened in New York City on February 15, 1965, nearly two years after the completion of the actual shooting of the film.[11] Although the Legion of Decency had given *King of Kings* a "special classification," this Jesus film received an A-I classification, morally unobjectionable for all ages. However, the system by which the film industry had regulated itself for three decades would soon come to an end.

Later in 1965, the Legion of Decency became the National Catholic Office for Motion Pictures (NCOMP). This change reflected the reforms occurring worldwide in the Catholic Church as a result of the Second Vatican Council—Vatican II, as it became popularly known. This change also signaled that the Catholic Church in the United States was continuing to adjust to the far-ranging developments in the film industry.

In 1952, a United States Supreme Court decision involving Roberto Rossellini's Italian-made film *The Miracle*, extended First Amendment, freedom of speech protection to motion pictures. Intellectually challenging, artistically interesting, and sexually frank European films increasingly entered the United States without the limitations required by the Production Code.[12] In 1957, Eric Johnston the head of MPAA and the successor to Will Hays, announced revisions in the Code that allowed for the treatment of more varied adult subject matter on the screen.

That same year, 1957, the Legion of Decency redefined and expanded its range of classifications beyond A-I to include: A-II, morally unobjectionable for adolescents and adults; and A-III, morally unobjectionable for adults. Still another category was added in 1963: A-IV, adults, with reservations. In 1968, three years after the Catholic bishops transformed the Legion of Decency into the NCOMP, the

MPAA replaced the Production Code with a ratings system that also labeled films according to age level suitability, but without moral judgment: G, general audiences; M, mature audiences; R, persons under sixteen restricted unless accompanied by a parent or guardian (later raised to under seventeen); and X, no one under seventeen admitted.[13]

When *The Greatest Story* opened, its smart look elicited much comment. No less than five, supposedly independent, movie reviewers suggested that the film had the appearance of a series of Hallmark greeting cards.[14] Whether or not these specific comments were intended as compliments, and they were not, Stevens' film—like Bronston's four years earlier—received little honor in its own day. Ultimately, this twenty million dollar production also became a loser at the box office. Hollywood would not risk this much money on a Jesus film again.

The critics pounced, especially those representing secular publications. Brendan Gill, still writing for *The New Yorker* (20 February 1965), reduced his overall evaluation of this film to one word: "A disaster." The anonymous reviewers for *Newsweek* (22 February 1965) and *Time* (26 February 1965), Hollis Alpert in *Saturday Review* (27 February 1965) and Robert Hatch in *The Nation* (1 March 1965) were not much kinder. Among the negative judgments: the slow pace, the distraction of familiar actors as gospel characters, the shifts in dialogue from traditional King James prose to folksy Americanisms, and the biblically unfounded depictions of Lazarus as the rich young man and the devil as the dark hermit.

Although Bosley Crowther—in *The New York Times* (16 February 1965) expressed similar reservations about the film, he concludes his review with the acknowledgment that, overall, "the quality of [Stevens'] reverence should captivate the piously devout." The introduction of the word "reverence" by Crowther into his review recalls the single most important criterion for evaluating Jesus films earlier in the century.

Representatives of the religious press tended to respond to the film with slightly more favor—especially those writing reviews for Catholic publications. The most surprising assessment of the film came from Moira Walsh, the film critic for *America* (27 February 1965). Years earlier she had harshly dismissed Bronston's *King of Kings* for trivializing the Christian message. She acknowledged that she expected the worst, on the eve of viewing Stevens' production. But her experience contradicted her expectation:

> I don't know how Mr. Stevens did it, but for the most part he communicated with this spectator in the way he evidently intended. In other

words he confronted me with wonder and awe and mystery and with some fresh awareness and insight into the greatest story ever told.

Perhaps the framing of the Jesus story, beginning and ending in church, was one of the ways Stevens did it.

Philip T. Hartung, in *Commonweal* (12 March 1965) ranked the film midway between "a masterpiece" and "a disaster." Nonetheless, he praised the film as "a reverently [that word, again] told Life of Christ" that represented "by far the best" effort to bring the story of Jesus to the screen. He also observed that "the vexing Jewish situation is extremely well handled." Edward H. Peters, in *The Catholic World* (April 1965), similarly claimed that "the Christ we meet is in general the one which Christianity has presented to the world." With regard to the miracles, he expressed the view that "the handling of this vexing theme is thoughtful and reverent."

However, Fred Myers, in a lengthy critique in *The Christian Century* (21 April 1965), expressed that Protestant publication's usual disdain for biblical epics. Nearly alone among reviewers, Myers picked up on the emphasis in the film on detachment from the world. He observed "that this film's insistence on the otherworldliness of Jesus undercuts . . . a widely shared contemporary understanding of the gospel. . . . " Just as the Catholic reviewers had found in the film a reverence for Jesus congenial to their *theological* points of view, so Myers' objection to *The Greatest Story* was centered in a *theological* perspective that saw the depiction of Jesus as irrelevant to the contemporary Protestant understanding of him.

The understanding of the gospel to which Myers refers is, no doubt, that of the "social gospel"—the application of the Christian message of love to the complicated social realities of modern life. This Christian concern for the social order expressed itself in social creeds adopted by Protestant denominations beginning with the declaration on "The Church and Social Problems," adopted by the Methodist Episcopal Church in 1908. This concern received literary expression in the writings of theologian Walter Rauschenbusch, including his influential 1917 volume *A Theology for the Social Gospel*. In fact, the publication for which Myers wrote—*The Christian Century*—had adopted its name at the turn of the century, before two world wars, when many believed optimistically that the twentieth century would be the Christian century through the Christianizing of the social order. This publication became the leading nondenominational periodical for social Christianity.

The Greatest Story Ever Told premiered at the height of the civil rights struggle—one month before the march from Selma to Montgomery, Alabama, in the spring of 1965. This was also the period of growing opposition to American involvement in Vietnam. Little wonder that the otherworldly Jesus in *The Greatest Story* seemed out of sync for many persons involved in the struggles for social justice at home and abroad. Perhaps the ascetic detachment of Jesus in *The Greatest Story* was more congenial to traditional Catholic understandings with various holy orders committed to lives of chastity, poverty, and obedience.

In spite of such harsh criticism of the film, there often appeared in secular as well as religious reviews great appreciation for the *persona* of the Jesus character as projected by Max von Sydow. One wonders whether or not this kinder treatment of Max von Sydow as Jesus, in contrast to the evaluation of Jeffrey Hunter just four years earlier, did not stem from von Sydow's prior reputation and association with Ingmar Bergman.

Even before the screening of the Stevens harmony, a radically alternative approach to the Jesus story had been seen in Europe. Pier Paolo Pasolini's *Il Vangelo Secondo Matteo* had been released in Italy, in 1964. It would soon immigrate to America as *The Gospel According to St. Matthew* (1966).

The Seven Last Words of Jesus

On Good Friday, from 12 noon until 3 o'clock in the afternoon, many churches have traditionally remembered the crucifixion of Jesus with a worship service centered around the so-called Seven Last Words of Jesus—the seven sayings reportedly spoken by him from the cross. No one gospel contains all seven sayings; and a study of these sayings discloses that they often represent or recall, texts from Hebrew Scripture, the Old Testament. Mark reports one saying; and Matthew carries over the same saying. Luke reports three sayings different from the one in Mark and Matthew. John records still three more.

These seven words (my translation) in a traditional liturgical order are as follows:

Luke 23:34	"Father, forgive them; for they do not know what they're doing."
Luke 23:43	"Truly I say to you, today you'll be with me in paradise."
John 19:26–27	"Woman, look, your son! . . . Look, your mother!"
Mark 15:34	"My God, my God, why have you abandoned
	Matt 27:46 me?" (from Ps 22:1)
John 19:28	"I'm thirsty." (compare Ps 69:21)
John 19:30	"It's completed."
Luke 23:46	"Father, into your hands I entrust my spirit." (compare Ps 31:15)

Among the Jesus-story films reviewed thus far, only George Stevens' *The Greatest Story Ever Told* (1965) portrays Jesus as saying all seven words from the cross. Bronston's *King of Kings* (1961) and Zeffirelli's *Jesus of Nazareth* (1977) include six of the seven, omitting the word about thirst. Mel Gibson's *The Passion of the Christ* (2004) also incorporates all seven words into his cinematic story of Jesus' last hours.

THE GOSPEL ACCORDING TO ST. MATTHEW: Judas (Otello Sestill) betrays Jesus (Enrique Irazoqui) with a kiss. Source: Jerry Ohlinger's Movie Material Store

CHAPTER SEVEN

Pier Paolo Pasolini
The Gospel According to St. Matthew

1
9
6
6

Pier Paolo Pasolini seems an unlikely person to bring the Jesus story to the screen: a prolific poet, novelist, screenwriter, and filmmaker, he was also an avowed Marxist and atheist.

His first two films, like much of his work, explored the sordid underside of Italian life. *Accatone* ("Beggar," 1961) focused on the life of a pimp; *Mamma Roma* (1962), on the life of a prostitute. Pasolini was even prosecuted for having insulted the Roman Catholic Church for the segment he contributed to the film *RoGoPaG* (also 1962).[1] The capital letters in the title represent the names of the filmmakers each of whom contributed one of the four stories—Roberto Rossellini, Jean-Luc Godard, Pier Paolo Pasolini, and Ugo Gregoretti. His segment told the story of the filming of a passion play and sharply contrasted the solemnity of the subject matter with the ribald lives of the actors playing the parts. Throughout his career, Pasolini's artistic work and his personal life created great controversy. He was eventually murdered in 1975 by a young man who belonged to the underclass so vividly depicted in his writings and movies.

Pasolini's *The Gospel According to St. Matthew* made its debut in the United States in February 1966 and was distributed first with English subtitles and later dubbed in English.[2] The "St." in the title was added for its English distribution, against Pasolini's wishes. The film received an A-I classification from the National Catholic Office for Motion Pictures (NCOMP).

Produced by Alfredo Bini for L'Arco Film/Lux Compagnie Cinématographique de France, the Italian original had appeared simply as *Il Vangelo Secondo Matteo*, in 1964. Pasolini himself receives credit as director and author of the screenplay. The running time of the film has been listed downward from as long as 142 minutes.[3] The film bears a dedication to Pope John XXIII who had died in 1963 during Vatican Council II—that reforming council of the Roman Catholic Church that he had convened.

TO THE DEAR, FAMILIAR
MEMORY OF
POPE JOHN XXIII

This dedication seems quite appropriate, since Pope John XXIII himself had inspired the making of the film, at least in a roundabout way, according to a frequently repeated story.[4] Pasolini was in the central Italian town of Assisi. A visit to the area by the Pope caused such a traffic jam that Pasolini was forced to remain in his hotel. Casting about for reading material, he found a copy of the New Testament in his room and began reading. He was struck by the drama of the Jesus story in the gospel of Matthew. Then and there, he decided to bring that version of the Jesus story to the screen. When it did appear, *The Gospel According to St. Matthew* stood over against its predecessors both in terms of its basic approach and in terms of its cinematic style. The film has rightly been called "in a class by itself."[5]

First, the approach of the Pasolini film was distinctive within the cinematic succession of Jesus films. Films in the harmonizing tradition of Jesus films had re-presented the story of Jesus by combining the Jesus story from all four gospels. This approach expressed itself from Olcott's *From the Manger to the Cross* (1912) through DeMille's *The King of Kings* (1927) and, even more inclusively, in Bronston's *King of Kings* (1961) and Stevens' *The Greatest Story Ever Told* (1965). An alternative tradition of Jesus films had also emerged in which the Jesus story was subordinated to another story, whether a modern story as in *Intolerance* (1916) or an ancient story as in such Roman/Christian epics as *Ben-Hur* (1959).

Pasolini also takes an alternative approach to the Jesus story, but charts new territory by pursuing another option. He bases his cinematic portrayal of Jesus not on the four gospels, but on the story of Jesus as narrated in a single gospel. Whether knowingly or not, Pasolini takes an approach favored by biblical scholarship in his day. The 1960s was the period of a growing emphasis on the theology of the individual gospel writer. "Redaction criticism," as the discipline came to be called, studied how a gospel was organized, what was included and excluded, as a means of determining the theology peculiar to the author of that gospel.[6]

Secondly, the cinematic style of the Pasolini film was certainly distinctive in comparison with the most recent Jesus films of his day that had used color and the big screen.[7] The Pasolini film was shot in black and white stock in a style often described as neo-realistic, a style suggestive of the documentary film. This gives the film the look of earlier black-and-white Jesus films of the silent era.

The filming took place in the barren wasteland of southern Italy, with every location chosen by Pasolini himself. He used the stark countryside, contemporary villages, and ancient ruins. Members of the local populace were chosen as supporting players in the film. In fact, instead of casting well-known actors, Pasolini generally employed amateurs, including some of his own intellectual friends.

His mother—Susanna Pasolini—played the role of the aged Mary, the mother of Jesus. Enrique Irazoqui, a Spanish student, was cast as Jesus.

Pasolini's selections of style, location, and actors enabled him to retell the story of Jesus in accordance with what he referred to as "analogy."[8] By "analogy," he meant "the transposition from the ancient world to the modern world without having to reconstruct it archaeologically or philologically."[9] Contrary to what might be expected from a Marxist, his intention was not to debunk the familiar story of Jesus. Instead, he sought to "re-mythicize" that story. Looking back at what he had done, Pasolini concluded: "I, a non-believer, was telling the story through the eyes of a believer."[10] Or, as he stated it slightly differently: "My film is the life of Christ plus two thousand years of story-telling about the life of Christ."[11] The artistic tradition of those several centuries asserts its influence at a number of points. For example, the attire of the Jewish leaders, most notably their waste-basket-shaped headgear, owes a special indebtedness to the Italian artist Piero della Francesca (d. 1492). Also, at different points in the movie, the viewer hears music from a variety of eras: the mournful sounds of Odetta's rendering of the African-American spiritual "Sometimes I Feel Like a Motherless Child" (in English), the rhythms of the Congolese "Missa Luba" (a Catholic mass scored for African voices and drums), and the moving refrains of Johann Sebastian Bach's "St. Matthew Passion" (a more obvious choice).

THE FILM: An Adaptation of the Gospel of Matthew

The gospel of Matthew provides the narrative and teaching material for *The Gospel According to St. Matthew.* Like the gospel, the film moves from the conception and birth of Jesus to his crucifixion and resurrection. The film moves forward by linking together stories about and sayings by Jesus from that gospel. The film avoids the imaginative subplots and created conversations that mark so many of the Jesus films that preceded it. Virtually all incidents and dialogue in the film have their basis in the gospel text. An omniscient narrator is not used; and the technique of voice-over is reserved for words from the gospel itself—such as Old Testament quotations in the infancy narratives and the divine voice at the baptism.

However, *The Gospel According to St. Matthew* in no way represents just a visual illustration of the written gospel. The screenplay represents a creative adaptation of the gospel text. Pasolini has selected certain actions and teachings and thereby omitted others. He has rearranged the exact sequence of the material chosen. He has emphasized some dimensions of the gospel story while minimizing others. Throughout, Pasolini brings the gospel to the screen through a strik-

ing and varied use of the camera—long-shots and close-ups, sometimes connected with zoom shots and at other times joined by quick
cuts and fades. The viewer will better understand Pasolini's adaptation of the written gospel for the screen by examining how the literary
shape of the gospel has been modified for the film, and by noting the
resultant shape of Jesus' ministry in the film.

The gospel of Matthew begins with a carefully structured genealogy of Jesus and stories about events related to the conception, birth,
and infancy of Jesus (chapters 1–2). But Pasolini omits the genealogy
and begins his film with the stories. Specifically, the film opens with
an initially silent confrontation between Mary and Joseph. The first
words heard are those of the angel, in the form of a young girl, when
she says: "Joseph, son of David, be not afraid to take thy wife Mary
unto thyself . . . " (1:20). The film thereafter closely follows the infancy
narratives—visit of the wise men to Herod and the holy family, the
flight of the family to Egypt, the massacre of the infants, the subsequent death of Herod, and the return and settlement in Nazareth.

The gospel of Matthew includes a large amount of Jesus' teaching,
much of which has been arranged into five collections or speeches.
Each of these discourses centers around a specific theme:

Chapters 5–7	Discourse on the higher righteousness (Sermon on the Mount)
Chapter 10	Discourse on discipleship
Chapter 13	Discourse on the secrets of the kingdom of heaven
Chapter 18	Discourse on the church
Chapters 24–25	Discourse on the close of the age

Pasolini has incorporated these discourses into his film *as discourses*
very unevenly, or not at all. The initial discourse on the higher right-
eousness, the Sermon on the Mount (chapters 5–7), does find its way
into the film as a distinct entity. The sayings Pasolini selected from the
gospel for the film include such familiar teachings as the beatitudes,
the Golden Rule, and the Lord's Prayer. In the film, the sermon represents a *tour de force*. The sermon is shot as a series of a dozen or more
close-ups of Jesus' face with a cut to a different pose between each of
the spoken segments of the sermon. For example, the viewer sees
Jesus with his head uncovered when he declares the beatitudes but,
immediately thereafter, with his head covered for his pronouncement
of the Golden Rule. Throughout the sermon, therefore, Jesus appears
as "a talking head."

The discourse on discipleship, with its list of the twelve disciples
(chapter 10), also finds its way into the film. But it has been relocated
so that the sayings from it, and the introduction of all twelve disciples, follows the call of the first disciples beside the sea and precedes
the Sermon on the Mount.

Only a few sayings from the discourse on the church (chapter 18) are included in the film. Pasolini does not include any sayings material, much of which consisted of parables, from the discourse on the mysteries of the kingdom (chapter 13) nor from the discourse on the close of the age (chapters 24–25). In a later interview, Pasolini seemingly acknowledged this omission when he said that he had shot footage of, but removed from the film, what he called "all Christ's eschatological sermons."[12] By removing these "sermons," with their talk about the future, Pasolini makes Jesus' message more this-worldly.

The gospel of Matthew draws to a close with stories related to Jesus' passion, crucifixion, and resurrection (chapters 26–28). Pasolini incorporates most of the specific episodes in his film—including the betrayal of Judas, the last supper, the arrest in Gethsemane, the trial before Caiaphas, the denial of Peter, the hanging of Judas, the trial before Pilate, and the crucifixion followed by burial. When the women go to the tomb, they are confronted by an angel in the form of the same young girl who had earlier appeared to Joseph. She says to them: " . . . Go and tell his disciples that he is risen. He is going to Galilee before you. . . . " The resurrected Jesus does appear and, as in the gospel so in the film, declares his "great commission" that they go forth baptizing and teaching. Therefore, *The Gospel According to St. Matthew* becomes still another Jesus film that ends with Jesus' promise: ". . . I shall be with you always even until the consummation of the world."

Although Pasolini has not carried over into the film the five great discourses so literarily characteristic of the gospel of Matthew, he has retained the underlying shape of Jesus' ministry. Pasolini's cinematic adaptation of the gospel presents the public ministry of Jesus as falling into two periods, with substantial screen time devoted to each: an early period in Galilee and the later period in Jerusalem, with Peter's confession and Jesus' three "passion predictions" as transitional markers from the former to the latter.

The *Galilean period* of Jesus' ministry opens with his baptism by John, his testing by the devil, his return to Galilee, and his call beside the sea of Peter, Andrew, James and John (chapters 3–4). His introduction of, and charge to, the twelve (chapter 10) and the healing of a leper (chapter 8) give way to the Sermon on the Mount (chapters 5–7). Controversies over plucking grain and healing lead to the resolve by the religious leaders that he be put to death and to his application of Isaiah 42:1–4 to himself (chapter 12). The miracles of his feeding the multitudes and walking on the water (chapter 14) are followed by extensive teaching on a variety of subjects (chapters 11–12). Subsequently, Jesus rejects his mother (chapter 12), receives rejection by his townspeople (chapter 13), challenges a young rich man (chapter 19), and exalts younger children (also chapter 19). The execution of

John the Baptist, with a sedate dance by Salome (chapter 14), and brief comment by Jesus on the demands of discipleship (chapter 8) serve as appropriate preparation for Jesus' questioning of his disciples and the close of the Galilean phase of his ministry (chapter 16).

On a wind-swept mountain (identified as near Caesarea Philippi in the gospel), Jesus asks: "Who do men say the Son of man is?" And: "Who do you say that I am?" Peter replies: "Thou art the Christ, the Son of the living God." Then Jesus blesses Peter and confirms him as the rock on which the church would be built: "Blessed are you Simon born of Jonah. . . . " Pasolini later divulged that he removed these words of the so-called investiture of Peter after the initial editing; but because the Catholic Church has seen in them a basis for the authority of Peter and his papal successors, Pasolini returned them to the script as a gesture of goodwill toward his Catholic friends.[13] Jesus then gives, in close proximity to one another, the three "passion predictions" that he must go to Jerusalem, be put to death, and be raised on the third day (16:11, 17:22–23, 20:18–19). Jesus utters the last of these pronouncements after he and his disciples have seen Jerusalem for the first time—a drab city, without walls, clinging to a hillside.

The *Jerusalem period* of Jesus' ministry begins with his entry into the city riding on an ass, his cleansing of the temple, and his cursing of the fig tree (chapter 21). There follows extensive teaching by Jesus during his stay in the city (chapters 21–22). He enters into debate with authorities—and others—over such issues as his and John's authority, the lawfulness of paying taxes to Caesar, and the great commandment. Along the way he confronts the religious leaders with the parable of the two sons and its application that tax collectors and harlots enter the kingdom before the religious leaders. He also confronts them with the parable of the wicked vinedressers; and they draw the conclusion that the owner will destroy the vinedressers and give the vineyard to others. Jesus scathingly indicts the scribes and Pharisees with his series of "woes" (chapter 23). Little wonder that the Jewish authorities, led by Caiaphas, resolve that they must bring him within their power and put him to death (specifically 26:3–5). Events then unfold that enable them to accomplish their objective (chapters 26–28).

THE PORTRAYAL: Jesus as Prophet and Sage

In *The Gospel According to St. Matthew,* Jesus comes in fulfillment of the messianic promises made to Israel by God in the scriptures. He goes from Galilee to Jerusalem with the stated intention of being put to death in accordance with the will of God.

However, Jesus—as played by Enrique Irazoqui—comes across as a hurried and harried teacher with unusual, even miraculous, powers. Above all, Jesus appears as a social critic whose words and deeds often run afoul of those whom he encounters. He is a man at odds with his social environment—especially the religious authorities. Although Pasolini has not incorporated all the great discourses from the gospel into his film, he has included most of those sayings and stories which show Jesus engaged in conflict with authorities, in Galilee and in Jerusalem. Furthermore, by omitting entirely the futuristic eschatological material from two of the discourses (chapter 13 and chapters 24–25), Pasolini makes Jesus even more into a man of the moment, uttering words of condemnation, not a man speculating about the end of the world.

Therefore, Jesus appears in Pasolini's film, above all else as prophet and sage. Jesus appears as prophet to those viewers who see and hear what is presented on the screen. He appears as sage to those viewers who also comprehend the subtleties of how Pasolini uses what appears on the screen. Both the prophet and the sage, within Israel, and later Judaism, engaged in social criticism—the prophet through an open declaration of God's judgment, the sage through a more subversive critique of human behavior.

Within life-of-Jesus research, scholars have used both of these categories, prophet and sage, as the basis for interpreting what Jesus was like as a historical figure. American scholars, in particular, have often described Jesus as some kind of prophet who declared God's word of doom and hope to his contemporaries. Among these scholars are: Shirley Jackson Case, *Jesus: A New Biography* (1927); Morton Enslin, *The Prophet from Nazareth* (1961); E. P. Sanders, *Jesus and Judaism* (1985); Richard A. Horsley, *Jesus and the Spiral of Violence* (1987); R. David Kaylor, *Jesus the Prophet: His Vision of the Kingdom on Earth* (1994); Dale C. Allison, *Jesus of Nazareth: Millenarian Prophet* (1998); Paula Fredriksen, *Jesus of Nazareth: King of the Jews* (1999); and Bart Ehrman, *Jesus: Apocalyptic Prophet of the New Millenium* (1999).

During the "third quest," the most recent period of Jesus research, there has also appeared an emphasis upon Jesus as a sage—a Jewish cynic who intended to undercut the social pretensions and hierarchical ideologies of his contemporaries. Those setting forth this interpretation include: John Dominic Crossan, *The Historical Jesus: The Life of a Jewish Mediterranean Peasant* (1991); Burton L. Mack, *The Lost Gospel: The Book of Q and Christian Origins* (1994); Robert W. Funk, *Honest to Jesus* (1996); and Stephen J. Patterson, *The God of Jesus: The Historical Jesus and the Search for Meaning* (1998).

In Pasolini's cinematic retelling of the Jesus story, the dimension of social criticism in the ministry of Jesus can be seen most clearly at two moments in that story—both of which have their foundation in the gospel text. These moments involve the preaching of John the Baptist and the lengthy series of "woes" by Jesus against the scribes and Pharisees.

In many Jesus films, John the Baptist serves the sole purpose of announcing the coming of the messiah in the person of Jesus. But this film carefully reproduces all of John's words prior to his baptism of Jesus (chapter 3). These words include the condemnation of the religious leaders: "O generation of vipers. . . . " As John speaks these words, these leaders with their unmistakable headdresses make their way along the riverbank watching John's baptizing activity. The viewer sees them even before seeing Jesus. The polemic against the authorities in the message of John will be carried forward by John's successor; and Jesus does carry it forward.

In most Jesus films, the long diatribe by Jesus against the religious leaders for their hypocritical behavior is minimized or omitted altogether. But this film includes virtually all the discourse material from the gospel: "Woe upon you scribes and Pharisees, you hypocrites . . . " (chapter 23). Pasolini has Jesus deliver these condemnations word-for-word and in the gospel sequence; but in order to keep the interest of the viewer, he has Jesus deliver these words to the crowds at three different locations in Jerusalem. Each change of location leads to greater involvement of soldiers in controlling the masses. Although the intention to put Jesus to death had already been announced by religious leaders in Galilee, Caiaphas now responds to Jesus' verbal attack in Jerusalem with the declaration: "We must bring him within our power, but cunningly, of course, and put him to death. . . . " (based on 26:3–5).

No Jesus film more exclusively places the responsibility for Jesus' death on the Jewish religious authorities than *The Gospel According to St. Matthew*. Their responsibility also suggests itself by the way the film presents the appearances of Jesus before Caiaphas and then before Pilate. Both scenes are shot in open courtyards in the style of *cinema verité*—as though the viewer is standing with the crowd at a distance and looking on.

The appearance of Jesus before Caiaphas and the whole council closely follows the gospel account. Witnesses testify that Jesus had spoken about the destruction of the temple. Then Caiaphas pointedly says: " . . . tell us whether thou art the Christ, the Son of the living God." Jesus replies: "Thou hast said it." Then he continues: "Moreover, I tell you this, hereafter you shall see the Son of man sitting at the right hand of the power and coming upon the clouds of heaven." Cries of "Blasphemy!" ring out. The next morning, when the council reconvenes, Caiaphas says simply: "He shall be put to death."

The appearance of Jesus before Pilate has been greatly abbreviated from the gospel account. Pilate does *not* ask Jesus, "Art thou the King of the Jews?" Pilate simply announces: "Today is the paschal feast . . .

I shall release a prisoner . . . Barabbas or Jesus, whom they call the Christ?" The crowds cry out for the release of Barabbas and the crucifixion of Jesus. Pilate disavows any responsibility for the fate of this "just man" and motions that he be taken away.

In Pasolini's film, Jesus dies at the instigation of the Jewish authorities on the *religious* charge of blasphemy with the support of the crowds. There is no intimation whatsoever that Jesus posed a *political* threat. Ironically, Pasolini the Marxist has completely de-politicized the crucifixion.

Furthermore, there is a striking suggestion in the film that the responsibility for Jesus' death extends beyond just the Jewish religious leaders, perhaps to all the people, even all humanity. As Jesus hangs on the cross, the screen suddenly goes dark; and a voice repeats the words from Isaiah 6:9–10 that appear at a much earlier point in the gospel itself (chapter 13):

Hearing you will hear, but not understand
 and seeing you will see but not perceive
for the heart of this people has been hardened
 and with their ears they have been hard of hearing . . .

When light returns to the screen, and Jesus reappears, he utters his cry of dereliction: "My God, my God, why hast thou forsaken me?" Although there is the suggestion of an earthquake, there is no tearing of the curtain in the temple; and there is no confession of divine sonship by the Roman soldiers beneath the cross. Although Pasolini acknowledges this transferral of the Isaiah text to the crucifixion scene as one of his few liberties, he does not comment on the intended meaning.[14]

In spite of Pasolini's assignment of responsibility for the death of Jesus to the religious authorities, he does—in his own way—downplay the tendencies in the gospel text that have supported anti-Semitism. In the hearing before Pilate, Pasolini does *not* have the Roman governor wash his hands *nor* does he have the Jewish crowds ask that Jesus' blood be on themselves and on their children (as in 27:24–25).

Perhaps Pasolini's explanation of "analogy" as foundational for his bringing the Jesus story to the screen discloses what lies implicitly in his presentation. As Pasolini himself said, he was not trying to reconstruct the past but rather to find some equivalence between that past and his own present. This led him away from Palestine to southern Italy as the site for filming. The logic of analogy draws an equivalence not between the Jewish leaders in first-century Palestine and twentieth-century Judaism, but between the religious establishment of ancient Palestine and the religious establishment of contemporary

Italy—that is to say, the present-day church, specifically the Roman Catholic Church.

Therefore, the re-mythicized story of Jesus as portrayed in *The Gospel According to St. Matthew* confronts the Roman Catholic Church even as Jesus challenged the religious leaders of his day. The de-politicized Jesus of the film is by no means a-political, but rather a subversive character who undercuts ecclesiastical authority in the modern world. Within the framework of the film, Jesus looks and sounds like a prophet. In the interaction between that Jesus and the modern viewer, Jesus comes across as a sage. However, if *The Gospel According to St. Matthew* represented a critique of the church, surprisingly little notice of this critique came from the institutional church—or churches.

THE RESPONSE: A Film with Great Honor in Its Own Day

Pasolini's *The Gospel According to St. Matthew* was an entry in the Venice Film Festival in the summer of 1964. The filmmaker and his work were confronted by Catholic and neo-fascist pickets and hecklers.[15] The film itself received a Special Jury Prize. In a review of the film with the dateline of Venice, September 4, that appeared in *Variety* (9 September 1964), the reviewer suggested that the commercial success of the film would require some kind of church endorsement. Endorsement was forthcoming in the form of the many honors conferred upon it by the church—by the churches in Europe and in the United States, Catholic and Protestant.

In the fall of 1964, the film received a special screening in conjunction with Vatican Council II then in progress in Rome; and later the International Catholic Film Office bestowed on the film its Grand Prize as the best film of the year. The National Council of Churches in this country, the successor to the Federal Council of Churches, granted a special award to the film. The film was recognized "for its retelling in imaginative cinematic terms one version of the New Testament story, thus revealing Christ's life and passion as a realistic and human experience for contemporary audiences."[16]

First shown commercially in New York City on February 17, 1966, at the Fine Arts theater as a benefit for the Msgr. William R. Kelly School, Pasolini's film had its strongest appeal in the United States in church settings, and on college campuses, where it was projected in sixteen millimeter format. Not only the churches but critics for the religious press also responded with enthusiasm to Pasolini's cinematic portrayal of the Jesus story.

Both Philip T. Hartung and Moira Walsh, critics for Catholic periodicals, gave Pasolini high marks. Although neither saw in the film a critique of the institutional church, both did see the film as presenting a *theological* challenge for Christians. Writing for *America* (26 February 1966), Walsh concluded:

> It is ironic that it is a Marxist who most nearly succeeds in capturing on the screen (or projecting off it) the salutary but embarrassing reminder that if Christians only learned to live up to the teachings of their master they could make the world a wonderful place.

Writing for *Commonweal* (6 March 1966), Philip T. Hartung made a similar observation:

> And if Pasolini has anything to say in the way of propaganda, he is saying, "This is the founder of Christianity." And he might ask if Christians live according to his teaching. "The Gospel" could be considered a dialogue between its Marxist makers and its Christian and non-Christian viewers.

Reviewers for the liberal Protestant weekly *The Christian Century* also bestowed praise on the film. In the March 16, 1966, issue, Robert J. Nelson referred to the film as "a miracle" and personalized his response: "And before Pasolini we must now confess how little was our faith in filmmaking." Nelson also thought that the category "prophet" was an appropriate way of describing the film's presentation of Jesus and further said:

> Instead of standing still on the hillside, preaching with rich modulation of voice and benign visage, Jesus speaks right into the camera at close range, piercing the minds of the audience. Some of the uncompromising injunctions exposed my complacency and selfishness in a way that actually made me shiver.

Two years earlier, Martin E. Marty had commented on the film for the December 23, 1964 *The Christian Century*. Having seen the special viewing in Rome in conjunction with Vatican Council II, Marty expressed concern that the film might give "a distorted picture of Jesus as a hasty and harrying haranguer." Nonetheless, he extended overall praise to the characterization of Jesus in the film: "Everything then turns on Jesus, well played by Enrique Irazoqui, a black-eyed 'Jesus' who shares with Pasolini the responsibility for removing so many images of the pale, frail Jesus we have come to know. . . . "

Certainly much of the applause received by Pasolini's alternative adaptation of the Jesus story stemmed from its immediate comparison with those pretty and pretentious harmonizing epics that were its contemporaries: Bronston's *King of Kings* (1961) and Stevens' *The Greatest Story Ever Told* (1965). Even today, Pasolini's *The Gospel*

According to St. Matthew (1966) will probably elicit greater appreciation from viewers if seen in association with these high gloss presentations of the Jesus story.

Representatives of the secular press were less charitable in their
assessments of Pasolini's accomplishments. Film critic Pauline Kael,
at her caustic best, wrote: "Pasolini's 'The Gospel According to St.
Matthew' was so static that I could hardly wait for that loathsome
young man to get crucified. Why do filmmakers think that's a good
story anyway?"[17] As clearly attested by Kael's remarks, reviewers no
longer felt constrained to judge Jesus films on the basis of reverence
for the story, nor to be reverent themselves. Increasingly, Jesus films
were expected to meet the same *cinematic* standards as other films.
The difficulties inherent in making a Jesus film *as a film* were openly
recognized.

The anonymous reviews in *Newsweek* (28 February 1966) and *Time*
(18 February 1966) differed over Pasolini's achievement, or lack
thereof, in the film's characterization of Jesus. *Newsweek* favorably
described Enrique Irazoqui's portrayal of Jesus as

> strong, tough, and stern, a matchless orator, not above spellbinding, a
> dangerous, demanding leader who asks for total filial devotion, who
> smiles only at innocent infants and almost laughs only when a giggling
> gaggle of barefoot children tug at his robes and beg a little blessing.

By contrast, *Time* (18 February 1966) spoke of Pasolini's failure "to
match his vivid re-creation of time and place with an equally fresh
portrait of Jesus." Other critics too echoed the latter sentiment that a
different characterization does not necessarily mean a *better* one.[18]

Robert Hatch in *The Nation* (7 March 1966) and Bosley Crowther in
The New York Times (18 February 1966) were divided in their assessments of how well the film brought the teachings and miracles of Jesus
to the screen—the *literary* dimension of the problem of the cinematic
Jesus. Hatch considered the film to be a failure in this regard, but considered this failure to be inevitable:

> These flaws, though blatant in the present film, are generic to all New
> Testament pictures. The Bible is metaphor, allegory, poetry: it is not a
> movie script. It requires distance, imagery, tableau, if it is to be made
> visually persuasive and moving.

By contrast, Crowther spoke with approval of the way the film handled both the teachings and miracles. About Jesus' teachings, he said:
"His words are the straight words of the gospel . . . " About Jesus' miracles, he continued: "Likewise, the cryptic performances of the miracles . . . are pictorially done so that they seem the simple, straight,
quick-change recordings of inexplicable phenomena."

Stanley Kauffmann, in *The New Republic* (26 March 1966), recognized dramatic weaknesses in the movie. Nonetheless, he called it "the best film about Jesus in film history."

The film that would rival Pasolini's *The Gospel According to St. Matthew* as the best Jesus-story film ever—in the judgment of many—was still more than ten years in the future. That film too would be the work of an Italian artist. But before Franco Zeffirelli's *Jesus of Nazareth* (1977) came to the screen, there appeared the singing Jesus of *Jesus Christ Superstar* and *Godspell* (both 1973).

JESUS CHRIST SUPERSTAR: Jesus (Ted Neeley) and the triumphal entry into Jerusalem. Source: Cinema Collectors

CHAPTER EIGHT

1973 | Norman Jewison / David Greene
Jesus Christ Superstar / Godspell

Norman Jewison's *Jesus Christ Superstar* and David Greene's *Godspell* (both 1973) actualized another alternative for bringing Jesus and his story to the screen.[1] Both films presented a singing Jesus supported by a choral cast; and each film was based on a previously staged musical of the same name: The Tim Rice/Andrew Lloyd Webber rock opera; and the John-Michael Tebelak/Stephen Schwartz musical.

Although the films did not appear until 1973, they—like their staged predecessors—grew out of and reflected the youth culture that came into prominence during the preceding decade. The 1960s saw the ascendancy of rock music and that movement, or movements, of young people variously identified as student activists or social dropouts, campus radicals or flower children, yippies or hippies. Racial segregation and then the war in Vietnam gave these representatives of the so-called counter-culture foils against which they rebelled or from which they withdrew. Berkeley, Haight-Ashbury, and Woodstock became geographical markers along the way. Other musicals from that era that celebrated this generation, and eventually found themselves on the screen, included *Tommy* (1975) and *Hair* (1979).

However, the youth movement was not without a more traditional religious component. So-called "freaks" for Jesus were "turned off" drugs by the Spirit—or, were "turned on" by the Spirit instead of drugs. Tim Rice and Andrew Lloyd Webber, the youthful English composers of *Jesus Christ Superstar*, and John-Michael Tebelak, the young American originator of *Godspell*, may not have been directly related to this Jesus movement, but they were certainly sensitive to their contemporaries and the cultural forces that shaped them.

Jesus Christ Superstar began as a single song by that name. It was later released as a two disc record album, and eventually found its way on tour in this country with road companies performing the rock opera in concert format.[2] In the fall of 1971, the rock opera was elaborately produced for the stage at the Mark Hellinger theater in New York City under the direction of Tom O'Horgan, who had earlier directed the stage musical *Hair*. The New York production of *Jesus Christ Superstar* was given cover story treatment by *Time* magazine (25

October 1971) with the cover itself displaying the 21 year old star Jeff Fenholt—later a television evangelist—dressed in what was reported to be a $20,000 robe. As the old story was told with new glitz inside the theater, police patrolled outside as pickets marched with signs in protest.

Years later—in 1987—after establishing himself as the composer of such Broadway hits as *Evita* and *Cats*, but before the success of *Phantom of the Opera* and *Sunset Boulevard*, Andrew Lloyd Webber recalled the basic question underlying *Jesus Christ Superstar*. The question: "Did Judas Iscariot have God on his side? . . . how much was the whole thing in the end an accident or what was necessary given the politics of the day?"[3]

Filmmaker Norman Jewison became interested in bringing *Jesus Christ Superstar* to the screen while in what was then Yugoslavia filming another Jewish story—the musical *Fiddler on the Roof* (1971). Jewison eventually involved himself in the making of *Jesus Christ Superstar* on several levels. He co-produced the film with Robert Stigwood for Universal Studios; he wrote the screenplay in association with Melvyn Bragg; and he also directed it.

The film was shot in the summer and fall of 1972, in Israel, on a three and a half million dollar budget.[4] Although ancient sites were used as settings, the intersection between the ancient past and the present world became evident throughout the film in sometimes startling ways: an army tank here and a screaming fighter plane there, occasional modern dress and contemporary scaffolding, and a temple sign in Arabic and English reading "Money Changer." Ted Neeley and Carl Anderson were cast as Jesus and Judas respectively, with Yvonne Elliman as Mary Magdalene. The men had played the same roles in the Los Angeles stage production; she, the same role in the New York stage production.

By comparison with the rock opera *Superstar*, the musical *Godspell* (Old English for "gospel") developed out of John-Michael Tebelak's master's thesis at Carnegie Tech, now Carnegie Mellon University, in Pittsburgh. Tebelak later recalled how the original play resulted from a church experience while working on his thesis:

> I went to the Easter Vigil service at the Anglican Cathedral in Pittsburgh. It was snowing, and I was aware of the proper setting for a tremendous religious experience. But the people in the church seemed bored, and the clergymen seemed to be hurrying to get it over with. I left with the feeling that, rather than rolling the rock away from the tomb, they were piling it on. I went home, took out my manuscript and worked it to completion in a non-stop frenzy.[5]

After an off-Broadway run at Café La Mama in New York City, *Godspell* reopened with a musical score and lyrics by Stephen

Schwartz at the Cherry Lane Theater in May, 1971. There was considerably less fanfare than would accompany the Broadway opening of *Superstar* a few months later. Tebelak assessed the musical in these words: "The Church has become so dour and pessimistic, it has to reclaim its joy and hope. I see 'Godspell' as a celebration of life."[6]

One way that the celebration of *Godspell* continued beyond the initial run in New York was its adaptation for the screen. Whereas the film *Superstar* transported Jesus back to Palestine, *Godspell* the movie kept him in New York. The city itself became the set for the film. The role of the clown-attired Jesus figure was given to Victor Garber who, twenty years later, would play the devil in the Broadway revival of the musical *Damn Yankees*. The camera moves with Garber and the troupe of nine other actors around town from one familiar site to another—from the Brooklyn Bridge to Central Park, from Lincoln Center to the now lamented World Trade Center, from Times Square to the Cherry Lane Theater.

Godspell was produced by Edgar Lansbury and released through Columbia Pictures.[7] Direction was by David Greene who also wrote the screenplay with John-Michael Tebelak. Tebelak himself stayed in New York throughout the shooting of the film which began with a prayer service in front of the Empire Diner on 10th Avenue at 22nd Street, in August, 1972.[8]

THE FILMS: Rock Opera and Musical

As films and stage plays, *Jesus Christ Superstar* and *Godspell* find their textual basis in the four gospels. However, their Jesus stories are limited in scope and highly imaginative in presentation. Both films tell the Jesus story as a play within a play.

The movie *Jesus Christ Superstar* opens with a company of actors riding in an old bus, with a large cross atop, out into the Israeli desert where the staging of the Jesus story occurs. The story itself has the scope of a passion play since it focuses on the last week of Jesus' life. Although all four gospels are utilized for the narrative and the lyrics, the gospel of John provides much of the dramatic structure.

Among the recognizable events drawn from the gospels are these: the conspiracy under the leadership of Caiaphas (John); Jesus' anointing by Mary at Bethany (John), identified here as Mary Magdalene; Jesus' entry into Jerusalem (four gospels) and his cleansing of the temple (at the end of his ministry as in the synoptic placement, not in the beginning as in John); the betrayal of Judas (four gospels); the Last Supper (synoptic version); agony and arrest in Gethsemane (synoptics); Jesus' appearance before Caiaphas and Annas (John); the denial of Peter (four gospels); Jesus' appearance before Pilate (four gospels); Jesus' appearance before Herod Antipas (Luke); the suicide of Judas by hanging (Matt); Jesus' reappearance and trial before Pilate (especially John); the way to the cross *without* the assistance of Simon of Cyrene (John); and the crucifixion (four gospels).

The sequence of events in the Jesus story concludes with his crucifixion. With arms lashed and hands nailed to the cross, Jesus verbalizes three of the seven last words: "God forgive them . . . " (Luke); "My God, my God . . . " (Mark and Matt); and "Father, into your hands . . . " (Luke). From the artistic tradition, the sign posted over the head of the crucified Jesus reads: INRI. Jesus dies on the cross. There is no tomb—full or empty—and there are no resurrection appearances.

The movie *Jesus Christ Superstar* ends with the actors boarding the same bus that transported them into the desert. As they board, they look over their shoulders at the place where the play was performed. Now the viewer recognizes the actors according to their roles—Pilate, Herod Antipas, Caiaphas, Mary Magdalene, and even Judas. However, Ted Neeley who played Jesus is missing. After the bus departs, the final scene shows a solitary cross on a hilltop as the sun sets. (Or is it rising?) In a shot reminiscent of the ending of *Ben-Hur* (1959), the camera captures a shepherd with his flock moving in the shadows from left to right.

Godspell the movie begins with a John the Baptist figure, played by David Haskell, walking across Brooklyn Bridge into Manhattan. He pulls a brightly colored cart and blows a traditional *shofar*, or ram's horn. He sings the opening musical number, the appropriate "Prepare Ye the Way of the Lord." Then he proceeds to summon eight young people away from their daily tasks. They include a taxi driver, a parking lot attendant, a dancer, a waitress, a model, a delivery man, a student, and a career woman. The small band also reflects ethnic and gender inclusiveness—black and white, female and male. Those in this diverse group become disciples of Jesus and later act out his story with him at various sites around the city.

Within this framing, *Godspell* takes up the Jesus story not with the last week of Jesus' life—as did *Superstar*—but at the outset of his public ministry. Its screenplay draws on the synoptic gospels, not on the gospel of John. In fact, the film and its staged predecessor were billed as musicals based specifically on the synoptic gospel of Matthew.

Certainly the few recognizable events from the gospels that have been adapted for the stage and screen are found in Matthew. These include: the baptism of Jesus by John (Matt 3); the debate between Jesus and the authorities over such issues as the authority of John, the payment of taxes to Caesar, and the greatest commandment (Matt 21–22); the Last Supper with the disciples (Matt 26); the withdrawal to Gethsemane for prayer (also Matt 26), which provides the setting for the threefold testing by the devil (Matt 4); and, finally, the execution (Matt 27)—not by crucifixion, but by electrocution.

Although these events appear in one, or both, of the other synoptic gospels of Mark and Luke, their adaptation in *Godspell* often makes it evident that the play and film presuppose the version in Matthew. For example, the presentation of the baptism includes the conversation between John and Jesus peculiar to that gospel; and the words over the bread and wine at the last supper reflect the phrasing in Matthew. Also, incidental sayings of Jesus scattered throughout the screenplay are drawn from Matthew—especially from the Sermon on the Mount (Matt 5–7).

However, the claim that *Godspell* was based on Matthew is somewhat misleading. What really sets this cinematic portrayal apart from *all* other Jesus films is its abundant use, and creative presentation, of Jesus' parables. These parables are derived not only from Matthew, but from Luke and Mark as well. They include: the Pharisee and the tax collector (Luke 18); the unforgiving servant (Matt 18); the good Samaritan (Luke 15); the rich man and Lazarus (Luke 16); the sower (synoptics); and the prodigal son (Luke 10). The nine—not twelve— disciples who make up Jesus' traveling company act out the parables using song, word, and mime.

The greatest deviation of the *Godspell* screenplay from the gospel of Matthew lies in the overall scope and structure of its Jesus story. Whereas Matthew has an infancy narrative (chapters 1–2) and five great collections of Jesus' teachings (chapters 5–7, 10, 13, 18, 24–25), *Godspell* moves from the baptism of Jesus to his crucifixion and falls into two clearly delineated parts. In terms of dramatic development, *Godspell* more closely resembles Mark, as did Pasolini's *The Gospel According to St. Matthew* (1966) itself.

Part one opens, as we have noted, with the proclamation of John the Baptist, John's call of the disciples, and John's playful baptism of them and him in a fountain. The newly constituted band then withdraws into a junkyard. The mood becomes one of unrestrained joy as Jesus and his followers draw closer together, inviting the viewers themselves to feel kinship with them. All the teachings from the Sermon on the Mount spoken and all parables enacted in the film are incorporated into this initial segment as the group moves about the miraculously deserted city. The songs celebrate the love and mercy of God who calls upon those who love God to love one another: "Save the People"; "Day by Day"; "Turn Back, O Man; "Bless the Lord"; "All for the Best"; "All Good Gifts"; and "Light of the World."

The transition between parts one and two occurs not at Caesarea Philippi, as in Mark, but on a pier on the New York waterfront. A robot monster suddenly appears stylistically representing, by implication, the threat of the Jewish authorities. The robot mouths words from the so-called "conflict" stories (Mark 11–12). This encounter with the robot interrupts the idyllic romp of Jesus and his company. The song "Alas for You" (based on Jesus' words of condemnation of the Jewish leaders in Matt 23) ensues with stanzas that begin:

> Alas, alas for you, lawyers and Pharisees,
> Hypocrites that you be.

Part two opens with the return of Jesus and his followers to the junkyard. The mood suddenly becomes one of poignant sadness as Jesus prepares his followers—and the viewers—for his leave-taking. The latter is accomplished when Judas departs from the last supper and returns with the police, perhaps suggestive of Roman authority, but indicated here by flashing blue light and wailing siren. Among the songs in this closing sequence are "By My Side," "Beautiful City," and "On the Willows" (the latter recalling Psalm 137). Jesus dies by electrocution on a chain link fence as he sings, "O God, I'm bleeding . . . dying . . . dead." As day breaks, the faithful including Judas—bear Jesus' cruciform body into the city singing "Long Live God" (not Jesus) and, wearing their everyday guises, disappear into the crowds that suddenly appear on Park Avenue.

Like its musical counterpart *Superstar*, *Godspell* ends the Jesus story with his death. Whatever resurrection occurs does so in the transformed lives of the participants in the drama. Both productions imply an existentialist understanding of the resurrection consistent with the proposal of theologian and biblical scholar Rudolf Bultmann that generated much discussion in this country in the 1950s and 1960s—although first proposed by him in a 1941 essay, "The New Testament and Mythology."[9] Therein, Bultmann understood resurrection to be *not* an occurrence that happened to the dead Jesus, but a happening in the lives of people of all generations as faith rises in them in response to the church's proclamation about Jesus.

THE PORTRAYALS: Jesus as Superstar and Jesus as Hippie

In spite of much in common, as we have just seen, *Jesus Christ Superstar* and *Godspell* differ in their adaptations of the Jesus story. They also differ in their characterizations of Jesus himself.

In *Jesus Christ Superstar*, Jesus may be the title figure, but the roles of Judas and Mary Magdalene have been greatly expanded. Indeed, the film projects not only the passion of Jesus but also the passions of Judas and Mary.

The play within the play opens with a sequence dominated by Judas. The opening number sung by Judas, "Heaven on Their Minds," articulates a clearly delineated point of view. Judas is alarmed. Things have gotten out of hand. Jesus, the carpenter's son from Nazareth, began his public career as a man known for his teaching and for doing good. But increasingly Jesus has become mythologized as more than a man—as "the new messiah," or even, in some sense, as "God." Worse still, according to Judas, Jesus has begun to believe the things said about him by others. Consequently, the growing commotion will likely call down upon Jesus and his followers the retribution of the Romans. Viewers see on the screen only events from the last week of Jesus' ministry. But at the outset they are given a retrospective glance at that ministry through the eyes and voice of Judas.

Whereas Judas warns—and even accuses—Jesus, Mary Magdalene comforts him. She soothingly sings "I Don't Know How to Love Him," the most popular single from the rock opera, to Jesus as he sleeps. Later, Judas, just before his suicide, echoes the words first sung

GODSPELL: John the Baptist (David Haskell) baptizes Jesus (Victor Garber).
Source: Cinema Collectors

by Mary. Although neither Mary nor Judas may know exactly how to love him, both do love him. They also agree that "he's a man, he's just a man."

The expanded roles of Judas and Mary, and their assessments of him, do not detract from, but enhance, the characterization of Jesus himself. Jesus appears as a man with a mission unto death caught in the squeeze between the varying expectations of his contemporaries and the demand of God.

Jesus also appears caught between the masses and the Jewish authorities, notably Caiaphas the high priest. The crowds, dazzled by Jesus' mighty works (referred to repeatedly in the lyrics of various songs), believe that they have found in him the fulfillment of their messianic hopes. The crowds, on the occasion of Jesus' entry into Jerusalem, become the first participants in the unfolding drama to bestow upon Jesus the name above every name in a mass communication and mass entertainment society: "Superstar!"

By contrast, Caiaphas shares Judas' apprehension about possible Roman reprisals and decided that "for the sake of the nation this Jesus must die" (based on John 11:50; also 18:14). To avoid these reprisals Caiaphas and Judas link up to effect what the latter calls "the sad solution."

It is Caiaphas, dressed in black attire like the other Jewish leaders, who is singled out as the person most responsible for the fatal conspiracy again Jesus. After Jesus' arrest in Gethsemane, he appears before Caiaphas and faces the charge of having called himself "the Son of God" (especially John 19:7). But because the Jewish leaders are limited in their authority to impose capital punishment (John 18:31), they take Jesus to Pontius Pilate.

Before the Roman governor, Jesus experiences interrogation about the claim of his being "King of the Jews"; but Jesus asserts that his kingdom is not of this world (John 18:36). As a Galilean, Jesus soon finds himself before Herod Antipas. In the film's funniest—and tackiest—scene, Herod in his own song acknowledges reports that Jesus has even called himself "God." Finally, Pilate must resolve the case. Although he finds no reason for a death sentence, and washes his hands of the matter, Pilate gives in to the request of Caiaphas and the cries of the crowds. Thus Pilate consigns Jesus to death by crucifixion as "an innocent puppet."

As Pilate's words suggest, Jesus goes to his death as a puppet—as God's puppet, in obedience to God's demand. In spite of the film's occasional artistic excesses, the scene of Jesus in Gethsemane is profoundly moving and far removed from the plastic poses and perfunctory lines in other Jesus films. Jesus cries out to God: "Why should I die?" Although admitting that he does not understand why, Jesus finally does accept that he must die. Die he does. This portrayal of Jesus as a man with limited understanding may confound some traditional biblical and theological viewpoints, but it—ironically—heightens the degree of Jesus' faithfulness. Jesus remains faithful to his divine call in spite of his lack of understanding.

Just as Jesus in Gethsemane before his death interrogates God, so Judas after his own death interrogates Jesus—from on high, accompanied by a Motown-like chorus signing the title song, "Superstar." Herein Judas asks Jesus: "Why'd you choose such a backward time and such a strange land?" The chorus asks Jesus: "Who are you? What have you sacrificed?" And Judas again asks: "Did you mean to die like this?" But then Judas concludes by apologetically saying: "Don't get me wrong—I only want to know."

Neither Jesus nor Judas receives answers to their ultimate questions. However, there is a more mundane, forward-reaching knowledge among many of the participants in the story. They know that they will be remembered by later generations. Judas knows that he will be "damned for all time." Pilate foresees that millions will heap on him "the blame." The apostles collectively admit that they aspired to apostleship so that they could retire and write the gospels "so they'll still talk about us when we've died."

In the film, as in the stage play, Jesus appears as just a man. But, like so many rock musicians in our day, without fully understanding why or how, this scruffy-looking man named Jesus suddenly finds himself to be a "superstar."

By contrast, the Jesus character in *Godspell* appears in a Superman shirt, striped trousers, and the makeup of a clown—with marks beneath his eyes and a red heart on his forehead. Unlike other cinematic Jesuses, he has no beard, but his curly hair stands like a halo around his head.

This cinematic portrayal of Jesus as a clown was not without precedent. At the New York World's Fair in the early 1960s, at the Protestant-Orthodox Pavilion, sponsored by the Protestant Council of New York, Rolf Forsberg's brief twenty-two minute film *Parable* (1964) was projected. This film shows a white-faced, white-cloaked clown moving through the "great circus of life" as "a man who dared to be different," according to the spoken prologue. The film itself did not have dialogue and was more an allegory than a parable.

Parable stirred up controversy in the New York City area, as reported in the national press.[10] Two members of the pavilion's steering committee resigned claiming that the portrayal of Jesus as a clown was sacrilegious. Some local clergy were offended by what were alleged to be the Buddhist leanings of Rolf Forsberg, the film's writer and producer. Others noted that the film ended with a death but no resurrection. Even Robert Moses, the director of the World's Fair itself, asked that the film be withdrawn; but the leaders of the Protestant Council resisted. The film became a popular attraction throughout the duration of the fair and circulated widely in church circles for years thereafter. The popularity of *Parable* probably helped prepare the public for an appearance of Jesus as a clown in *Godspell*.

In many ways, the characterization of Jesus in *Godspell* in terms of substance, not make-up, resembles Jesus as presented in the synoptic gospels. Like Jesus in the synoptics, Jesus in the film generally avoids self-referential statements about himself as Christ, Son of man, Son of God. Like Jesus in the synoptics, Jesus in the film uses the parable as his most characteristic form of teaching. The film, therefore, draws heavily on that portion of the synoptic teaching tradition that shows Jesus as proclaimer and inaugurator of "the kingdom of God," or "the kingdom of heaven" (to use the phrasing preferred in Matthew). Consequently, as expressed in word and action, God—not Jesus himself—constitutes the theological center of *Godspell*.

However, the playful manner in which the parables are dramatized by Jesus the clown, and his followers, tends to undercut both their promise and their threat. This contributes to the overall portrayal of Jesus in *Godspell* as a loving dropout from the society that eventually kills him. In the language of its own day, the musical portrays Jesus as "hippie."[11]

Not only have Jesus and his followers been separated from ancient Palestinian society in this film, they have separated themselves from New York society as well. The streets stand empty during their travels about town. The junkyard becomes their haven. Therefore, *Godspell* leaves unanswered the question of why this Jesus came to be put to death. Pharisees are condemned by name in the film; and the viewer is left with the impression—perhaps consistent with the gospel of Matthew and D. W. Griffith's *Intolerance* (1916)—that Pharisees represent the principal opponents to Jesus. Although Judas acts out his obligatory role as betrayer, neither Caiaphas nor Pilate has a part in the story. Jesus seemingly dies simply because that is the way the story ends.

The creators of *Jesus Christ Superstar* and *Godspell* have succeeded in making Jesus into a figure of their own time—the 1960s. Nonetheless, the characterizations of Jesus in these two productions diverge from one another. *Jesus Christ Superstar* portrays Jesus as a man, but a man elevated by his public performance to fame and superstardom. On the other hand, *Godspell* portrays Jesus as a playful clown who does not perform before public audiences, but drops out of society for the amusement of himself and his friends.

The divergent cinematic characterizations of Jesus cohere with their earlier stage personae, as accurately epitomized by a religion commentator who saw both stage productions. Elliott Wright spoke about Jesus in *Superstar* as a "woe-woe Jesus" and Jesus in *Godspell* as a "ho-ho Jesus."[12]

THE RESPONSE: Entertainment Blockbusters

The film *Jesus Christ Superstar* returned more than twelve million dollars in rentals, the film *Godspell* less than one million.[13] In spite of this difference in receipts, both *Jesus Christ Superstar* and *Godspell*—in their varied cultural incarnations as films, plays, albums, solo records—represent enormous commercial success for the many layered entertainment industry.

Godspell continues to be performed as a musical play around the country by churches, schools, and community theater groups. Jewison's cinematic adaptation of *Superstar* became a regular offering on music cablevision. Over the years, the Andrew Lloyd Webber-Tim Rice rock opera has continued to be taken on the road by traveling companies and, on occasion, experienced revivals in London and in New York. The production directed by Gale Edwards, that opened in London in 1996 and ran briefly in New York four years later, was filmed, made available in a videocassette format, and telecast on PBS. By contrast with its cinematic predecessor, this version has the intimate feel of a stage play and a more contemporary urban look. Glenn Carter appears in the role of *Jesus Christ Superstar* (2000).[14]

If both *Godspell* and *Jesus Christ Superstar*—with their differing portrayals of Jesus—have found such continued commercial success, that success may stem more from "how" the Jesus story is told instead of "what" the story is about. In the 1960s, the issue of the relationship between medium and message, in the dawning age of mass communication, was creatively and influentially addressed by Marshall MacLuhan in his book *Understanding Media*. In fact, his theory of communication became popularly identified with the slogan, "the medium is the message."

Much of the critical response to the films *Jesus Christ Superstar* and *Godspell*, when they first appeared, involved the issue of the relationship between the medium of film and the message of Jesus. Although the categories of "medium" and "message" were not used in the early years of Jesus on the screen, there was then some controversy about whether the film represented an appropriate medium for portraying the Jesus story. However, by the 1970s, the concern was not whether Jesus ought to be shown on film, nor whether the Jesus story had been told reverently on film, but the extent to which these two films had made Jesus over into images of the youth generation.

Several critics found *Godspell* to be an engaging film experience, but a film with little relationship to the Jesus of the gospels. Vincent

Canby, reviewer for *The New York Times* (20 March 1973), said that the movie was "less a celebration of the life and teachings of Jesus than . . . a celebration of theater, music, youthful high spirits, New York City locations, and the zoom lens." Similarly, Penelope Gilliatt, in *The New Yorker* (7 April 1973), wrote that the cinematic version of the off-Broadway musical was "a version of the Gospels to be read as show-biz literature by the Woodstock generation." And Stanley Kauffmann, in *The New Republic* (12 May 1973) repeated this sentiment by declaring: "In anything remotely resembling something that could begin to be called a religious sense, 'Godspell' is a zero; it's Age-of-Aquarius Love fed through a quasi-gospel funnel, with a few light-hearted supernatural touches."

This assessment of *Godspell* as a statement about the 1960s generation, not about the Christian gospel, did not confine itself to the secular press. In the Jesuit periodical *America* (14 and 21 April 1973) Richard A. Blake and Moira Walsh expressed similar reservations.

Blake rather harshly said:

> for some believers, the exuberant joy of a youth-cult Christ and his swinging disciples may even provide a quasi-religious experience. But quasi-religious expressions call for hard second looks. A second and coldly exegetical look at 'Godspell' reveals that what is proclaimed in this musical gospel is not Christ, but a nostalgic escape into a lost childhood, when, according to most adults, the grass was always green and every day was Saturday.

Moira Walsh who had so strongly dismissed the Jesus epics of the early 1960s, agreed with much of Blake's contention about *Godspell* when she said: ". . . I don't think this is the Christian message in relevant contemporary form. It may even, as some critics have suggested, stroke the self-congratulatory reflexes of the drop-out flower children." But she concluded on a more positive chord with a comment about how one leaves the theater: "You even come away temporarily loving your neighbors in the theater, and maybe that is not such a bad beginning of a Christian message."

Nonetheless, there were those who found in *Godspell* a fitting blend between the medium and the message. Arthur Knight, writing for *Saturday Review* (28 April 1973) said that the film ". . . with no religious trappings whatsoever provides a religious experience of extraordinary intensity." Cheryl Forbes, in the conservative Protestant publication *Christianity Today* (10 April 1973) understandably called attention to a few "biblical inaccuracies" in the film—such as the depiction of Jesus' kissing Judas instead of Judas' kissing Jesus at the moment of arrest. But, surprisingly, Forbes thanked Columbia Pictures for bringing this "infectious musical" to the screen and praised its portrayal of the "free frolicking joy of following Christ."

Godspell the movie opened around the country in March, 1973. When *Jesus Christ Superstar* arrived in theaters later that summer, the dominant issue eliciting comment was not that of medium versus message, but an issue present throughout the entire history of Jesus films: anti-Semitism.[15] *Godspell* in its very stylized presentation had been virtually apolitical. It had no characters identifiable as either Caiaphas or Pilate. But *Superstar* portrayed Caiaphas and his fellow black-clad priests as the chief perpetrators of the plot against Jesus. By contrast, it showed Pilate as the unwilling participant in the events leading to the death of Jesus.

James M. Wall reviewed *Superstar* for the liberal Protestant weekly *The Christian Century* (27 June 1973) and, to his own surprise, had kind comments about the film. Admitting a long-standing aversion to movies based on the Bible, Wall claimed that this movie "accomplishes something I have never seen in a biblical film: it portrays Jesus in a first century setting with twentieth century sensitivity." Summarily: "It is superb cinema, stimulating theology, and in no way anti-Semitic."

Wall's review elicited a response from Rabbi Marc Tanenbaum that also appeared in *The Christian Century* (5 September 1973). Central to Tanenbaum's statement was the claim that passion plays—like *Jesus Christ Superstar*—are

> by their very genre anti-Jewish, and quite frankly, ought to be abandoned voluntarily until some morally sensitive creative artist finds it possible to write one that allows the professed Christian message of love for fellow man and reconciliation to prevail as a dominant motif, rather than hatred and vilification.

In a column for *Christianity Today* (12 October 1973), Cheryl Forbes—who had spoken well of *Godspell*—gives a very different evaluation of *Superstar.* She says that the film "though a theological disaster, has become an ecumenical triumph." In her review, she cites the articles by Wall and Tanenbaum, the former disapprovingly and the latter seemingly with appreciation. Forbes characterizes the film as a theological disaster because, among other reasons, "Jesus, played by Ted Neeley, looks and acts incompetent, insecure, and petulant." She calls the film an ecumenical triumph because of the diverse religious groups that had condemned the film: "Protestants, Catholics, Jews for Jesus, and Jews for Judaism. . . . "

However, Moira Walsh the long-time film critic for *America* (1 September 1973)—who had expressed misgivings about *Godspell*—found *Superstar* more to her liking. She acknowledged that Jewish concerns about the film might be justified, but she also recognized that blacks might be offended by the casting of the black actor Carl Anderson in the role of Judas and that fundamentalists might be scandalized by the unorthodox approach to Jesus and his message. She also expressed appreciation for the way Norman Jewison had captured for the screen "the essence of the original work." She describes that essence as "the attempt by two young agnostics, Tim Rice and Andrew Lloyd Webber, to express their bemused admiration for the life and teachings of Jesus in terms that are comprehensible to them."

The critical assessments of *Godspell* and *Jesus Christ Superstar* were sharply divided. Reviewers were seldom indifferent. Perhaps the division of opinion is well illustrated in the contrary evaluations in two widely circulated weekly news magazines. The reviews in *Time* introduce *Godspell* with the headline "Godawful" (9 April 1973), but claim that *Superstar* "has reverence, taste, good vibes, and it really rocks out" (30 July 1973). In a reversal of assessment, the reviews in *Newsweek* state that *Godspell* "has a few strong points" (9 April 1973), but say that *Superstar* represents "one of the true fiascoes of modern cinema" (9 July 1973).

With *Jesus Christ Superstar* and *Godspell*, the alternative trajectory of Jesus-story films had clearly expressed itself in a new way. Both films had transmuted the Jesus-story from staged musicals into celluloid. Both films had also projected onto the screen images of Jesus not seen before. These film images of Jesus were possible because there was a new cinematic freedom abroad in the land, both in subject matter and in the treatment of subject matter.

In 1966, Jack Valenti, a special assistant to President Lyndon B. Johnson, accepted the invitation to become the head of the Motion Picture Association of America (MPAA). Two years later, the MPAA finally replaced the Production Code, by which the film industry had regulated itself since 1930, with a rating system based upon age levels. The Production Code Administration (PCA) was replaced by the Classification and Rating Administration (CARA). The ratings system that was adopted continues in slightly revised form into our own day. Today the classifications are:

G   general audience;
PG   parental guidance suggested;
PG-13   parents cautioned to give special guidance for attendance
           by children under 13;
R   restricted with anyone under 17 required to be accompa
           nied by parent or adult guardian;
NC-17   no one 17 and under admitted (replaced X rating in
           1990).[16]

Both *Jesus Christ Superstar* and *Godspell* appeared in 1973 with G-ratings. In the same year, another G-rated film that told the Jesus story using song was released. This was *The Gospel Road* (1973)—produced by Johnny and June Carter Cash, directed by Robert Elfstrom, and shot on location in Israel. The film represents an unusual mixture of ways of telling the Jesus story. Johnny Cash, also the narrator, points out local sites in the manner of a travel guide and sings songs written for the occasion like the country singer he is. Elfstrom plays the part of Jesus in those segments that recreate the ministry of Jesus. June Carter Cash plays Mary Magdalene.[17]

However, the new freedom of expression in film led to the making of other Jesus films in the 1970s considered by many to be utterly outrageous, even by the more relaxed standards of that era, such as Robert Downey's *Greaser's Palace* (1972), not rated. The intended humor in *Greaser's Palace*, with a cast of little-known actors, often degenerates to a tasteless level. In the film, the Jesus character, in a zoot suit, parachutes into the "old west." There he repeatedly confronts gunslingers at Greaser's Palace, a saloon, and eventually dies by crucifixion, but not before dazzling bystanders with some rather remarkable feats. In one of the more memorable and less disgusting moments, a man—having been healed of his lameness—drags himself up the steps of the saloon shouting, "I can crawl! I can crawl!"[18]

The 1970s also saw the brief appearance on American screens of *The Passover Plot* (1976). The film was based on the controversial, but widely read, 1966 book of the same name by Hugh J. Schonfield. Schonfield was a scholar whose writings represented "revisionist" interpretations of the origins of Christianity. The "plot" of the title involved Jesus' convoluted plan to fake his death on the cross—a plan that failed because of the Roman centurion's spear thrust in his side. Because of its dependence on Schonfield's book, *The Passover Plot* represents a film that at least implicitly claimed to be based on the conclusions of historical research, however improbable Schonfield's own historical reconstruction of Jesus' ministry may have been.[19]

The announced intention of Jens Jørgen Thorsen, a Danish filmmaker, to make a pornographic film about Jesus did not materialize—at least not in the 1970s. The film had such working titles as *The Many Faces of Jesus* and *The Love Affairs of Jesus Christ*. But as Thorsen cast about Europe in the mid-1970s, unsuccessfully seeking a site hospitable to his project, he left controversy in his wake—from his native Denmark, through Sweden, France, Italy, and finally to the United Kingdom.[20]

However, the decade of the 1970s that witnessed such a proliferation of alternative ways to bring Jesus to the screen also became the decade during which the Jesus harmony reasserted itself in what many still consider to be the finest Jesus-story film ever made. That film was Franco Zeffirelli's *Jesus of Nazareth* (1977).

Vatican Council II
on the Jews

Vatican Council II issued the declaration *Nostra Aetate* ("Our
Times") on October 28, 1965. The statement addressed the issue
of the relationship of the Roman Catholic Church to all non-
Christian religions, including the relationship of the Church to
Judaism. The statement's affirmation of the common heritage
between Christians and Jews and its condemnation of anti-
Semitism greatly influenced Franco Zeffirelli and led to his
determination to underscore the Jewishness of Jesus in his film:

> Sounding the depths of the mystery which is the Church,
> this sacred Council remembers the spiritual ties which link
> the people of the New Covenant to the stock of Abraham.
> The Church of Christ acknowledges that in God's plan of
> salvation the beginning of her faith and election is to be found
> in the patriarchs, Moses and the prophets . . .
> Likewise, the Church keeps ever before her mind the words
> of the apostle Paul about his kinsmen: 'they are Israelites, and
> to them belong the sonship, the glory, the covenants, the giv-
> ing of the law, the worship, and the promises; to them belong
> the patriarchs, and of their race according to the flesh, is the
> Christ' (Rom. 9:4–5), the son of the virgin Mary. She is mind-
> ful, moreover, that the apostles, the pillars on which the
> Church stands, are of Jewish descent, as are many of those
> early disciples who proclaimed the Gospel of Christ to the

world. . . . Since Christians and Jews have such a common spiritual heritage, this sacred Council wishes to encourage and further mutual understanding and appreciation. This can be obtained, especially, by way of biblical and theological enquiry and through friendly discussions.

Even though the Jewish authorities and those who followed their lead pressed for the death of Jesus (cf. John 19:6), neither all Jews indiscriminately at that time, nor Jews today, can be charged with crimes committed during his passion. It is true that the Church is the new people of God, yet the Jews should not be spoken of as rejected or accursed as if this followed from holy Scripture. Consequently, all must take care, lest in catechizing or in preaching the Word of God, they teach anything which is not in accord with the truth of the gospel message or the spirit of Christ.

Indeed, the Church reproves every form of persecution against whomsoever it may be directed. Remembering, then, her common heritage with the Jews and moved not by any political consideration, but solely by the religious motivation of Christian charity, she deplores all hatreds, persecutions, displays of anti-Semitism leveled at any time or from any source against the Jews. . . .

(Text reprinted from Flannery, *Vatican Council II*, 740–41)

JESUS OF NAZARETH: The Crucifixion of Jesus (Robert Powell). Source:
Jerry Ohlinger's Movie Material Store

CHAPTER NINE

Franco Zeffirelli
Jesus of Nazareth

1
9
7
7

Franco Zeffirelli, a few days before Christmas, 1973, made one of the most important decisions of his professional life. He agreed to direct for television the film about the life of Jesus that would become *Jesus of Nazareth.*[1]

The initiative for the production had originated with RAI, the Italian state television organization; and the production became a joint venture between RAI and ATV, the British commercial television network. Lew Grade of ATV assumed overall responsibility for the project with Vicenzo Labella as producer. The Italian Zeffirelli had been invited to direct the movie, although Zeffirelli himself claims that Swedish filmmaker Ingmar Bergman had been favored by executives within the Italian network.[2] Several factors prompted Zeffirelli, after some six months of indecision, to accept the assignment.

One factor was the status of his own career. He had been active in the theater and opera, in television and cinema. His previous films had been the highly acclaimed *Romeo and Juliet* (1968), an adaptation of the Shakespeare tragedy, and the just released *Brother Sun, Sister Moon* (1973), the story of the young Francis of Assisi. But suddenly other projects on which he was working collapsed, and he had time for Jesus after all.

Another factor in Zeffirelli's acceptance of the offer was the additional length of time that television would give him to develop the story of Jesus. The made-for-big-screen Jesus films of the 1950s and 1960s had running times of around four hours. But this made-for-small-screen movie could be designed for six or more hours of viewing in a miniseries format.

A third factor in Zeffirelli's decision to make the film was the opportunity it gave him to fulfill his longstanding dream of portraying Jesus, the Christ of Christianity, as a Jew who was no enemy to his people, past or present. Zeffirelli recalls having been deeply affected by the 1965 Vatican Council II statement, *Nostra Aetate* ("Our Times"). Late in 1973, he went to the Vatican library and read again this statement on Judaism. Then he, as a self-described "lazy Catholic,"[3] accepted the invitation to bring the Jesus story to the screen with a sense of "moral responsibility."[4] He later described that responsibility in these words: "The point I wanted to make was that Christ was a

137

Jew, a prophet who grew out of the cultural, social, and historical background of the Israel of his time. . . . "[5]

From the outset, Zeffirelli intended to base *Jesus of Nazareth* (1977) on all four gospels. Although conversant about the issues of biblical scholarship with regard to the gospels and the historical Jesus, Zeffirelli expressed particular appreciation for the narration and the trustworthiness of the gospel of John. In fact, contrary to most modern scholars, he considered John to be an eyewitness account by the so-called "beloved disciple."

Therefore, Zeffirelli's film would carry forward that harmonizing trajectory of Jesus films extending from the earliest made-for-the-camera passion plays through Olcott's *From the Manger to the Cross* (1912) and DeMille's *The King of Kings* (1927) to Bronston's *King of Kings* (1961) and Stevens' *The Greatest Story Ever Told* (1965).

Zeffirelli's decision to direct the film, of course, required him to make many other decisions. These decisions involved location, cast, script, and music.[6]

Like George Stevens, his immediate predecessor in the harmonizing tradition of Jesus films, Zeffirelli visited the state of Israel, the land of Palestine, to consider locations for the filming—Bethlehem, Nazareth, Jerusalem. Like Stevens, he also concluded that he must look elsewhere. He found ancient Palestine not in Utah but in Morocco and Tunisia. Among the extras in the cast, in the synagogue scenes, were members of the ancient Jewish community that still lived on the Isle of Djerba off the coast of Tunisia.

Also like Stevens, Zeffirelli selected many well-known movie stars for significant roles: Laurence Olivier as Nicodemus, James Mason as Joseph of Arimathea, Anne Bancroft as Mary Magdalene, Peter Ustinov as Herod, Rod Steiger as Pontius Pilate, Anthony Quinn as Caiaphas, Ernest Borgnine as the Roman centurion, and Michael York as John the Baptist. Zeffirelli chose Olivia Hussey, the Juliet of his earlier film, to play Mary the mother. For the title role of Jesus of Nazareth, he considered American actors who were then at the beginning of distinguished careers—Dustin Hoffman and Al Pacino. Eventually he named an English actor to play Jesus—Robert Powell.

The first version of the script was written by Anthony Burgess, the English novelist. The final version was the work of Suso Cecchi d'Amico and Zeffirelli himself. Maurice Jarre, who had written the soaring musical scores for *Lawrence of Arabia* (1962) and *Doctor Zhivago* (1965), was chosen to compose the music. The musical score is not only an underlying support for the finished film, but enlivens the action as the participants break forth into joyous singing and dancing.

The actual filming took place from late 1975 until May, 1976, first in Morocco and then in Tunisia. Shooting the film in Muslim lands brought its own special misunderstandings because of the honor repeatedly accorded both Mary the mother of Jesus and Jesus himself in *The Koran (Qur'an)*.

The Koran affirms Mary to be the virgin mother of the prophet Jesus (especially surah 19). Because of Mary's special status, and Islam's traditional modesty with regard to women, there were Muslim men on the set who refused even to look at the actress playing Mary. Accordingly, on one occasion when Olivia Hussey arrived for work in jeans and a t-shirt, an elder of the small Moroccan village approached Zeffirelli and asked that she dress more modestly.[7]

Or again, *The Koran* suggests that Jesus may not have actually been killed or crucified (surah 4). In his role as Jesus, Robert Powell insisted on carrying a heavy wooden beam, not a fake one, for the sequence of events related to the crucifixion. His sufferings, as much actual as acted, became obvious as he made his way to the place of execution and then was fixed to the cross. The Tunisian extras suddenly reacted with a muttering that gave way to despair. The extras came to believe that the blood-covered Powell had been beaten and nailed. Calm was restored only with the assistance of the Tunisian members of the crew who assured those present that Powell only appeared to have been crucified. Finally, Powell himself gave an out-of-character command for everyone to get on with it.[8]

THE FILM: The Jesus Story as a Jewish Story

Jesus of Nazareth underscores throughout the spiritual vitality of first-century Judaism. The viewer should watch for the participation of the people in a broad range of religious ceremonies, in Galilee and Jerusalem, in synagogues and the temple.

The film begins by placing the story of Jesus within the context of Jewish messianic expectation. After a brief exterior shot of a small village, later disclosed to be Nazareth, the camera moves into the interior of a crowded synagogue. The rabbi holds, with both hands, an open scroll and comments on the text before him with words that begin: "In the hour when the king messiah comes. . . . "

The following sequences present many familiar moments related to the *infancy* of Jesus: the annunciation to Mary and her visit to her kinswoman Elizabeth (Luke) and the reluctance of Joseph to wed his betrothed (Matt); the announced Roman census and visit of the shepherds (Luke) and the visit of the wise men (Matt); the presentation in the temple (Luke) and the flight to Egypt to escape the clutches of Herod the Great (Matt).

These familiar stories are used by Zeffirelli to establish the Jewish heritage of the child born to Mary and adopted by Joseph. Anna, the mother of Mary, known from the apocryphal Infancy Gospel of James, plays a prominent role. There are many touching scenes: the betrothal and later the wedding of Joseph and Mary; the circumcision and *bar mitzvah* of Jesus; and the latter's precocious performance in the temple at age twelve. In these stories appears the first of many recitations in the film of that traditional Jewish credo, the *Shema*: "Hear, O Israel, the LORD Thy God, the LORD is One" (Deut 6:4f).

The film itself does not identify Caesarea Philippi as the place of the confession of Simon called Peter. But this identification of Jesus as messiah serves as something of a turning point in the lengthy presentation of Jesus' activity as an adult. Before that pivotal scene, Jesus has centered his teaching and healing in *Galilee*. Shortly after that scene, *Jerusalem* becomes the site of his teaching and healing.

A partial catalog of the stories related to Jesus' ministry in *Galilee* disclose the inclusive, harmonizing character of the script: Jesus' encounter with John the Baptist and the Baptist's disciples (John); his baptism by John, but *no* testing in the wilderness (synoptics); his rejection in the synagogue at Nazareth (Luke); his exorcism of the boy with an unclean spirit in the synagogue at Capernaum (synoptics); his miracle of the catch of fish in the presence of Simon, not yet known as Peter (Luke); his dining with Matthew, or Levi (synoptics), as the setting for the parable of the prodigal son (Luke); his healing of the paralytic lowered through the roof (synoptics); the raising or healing of Jairus' daughter (synoptics); the execution of John the Baptist, with the dance of Salome (Mark and Matt); Jesus' feeding of the crowds with five loaves and two fish (all four gospels); his dining in the house of Simon the Pharisee and being anointed by a sinner (Luke), identified here as Mary Magdalene; his sending forth of the disciples two by two (synoptics); and—then—the confession of Simon that Jesus is the messiah, the Son of God (synoptics) and Jesus' responding blessing of Simon as Peter, the Rock (Matt).

Two of the best-known, and often-filmed, gospel episodes serve as the transition between Galilee and Jerusalem. They are presented without the grandeur and drama often associated with them in the cinematic tradition: the Sermon on the Mount, consisting only of beatitudes and the Lord's Prayer (Matt); and the raising of Lazarus from the dead at Bethany (John).

In addition to showing the well-known events from Jesus' last week in *Jerusalem*, the film has relocated to these days many events that occur in other settings in the gospels. Another partial catalog further underscores the comprehensive nature of the script: the entry into Jerusalem (all four); the cleansing of the temple (all four); the woman taken in adultery (John); the healing of the Roman centurion's servant (synoptics); the healing of a blind man (John); the visit of Nicodemus (but by day, not by night as in John); the Last Supper (all four); the arrest in Gethsemane (all four); the trial before Caiaphas (especially Mark); the denial of Peter (all four) and suicide by hanging of Judas (Matt); the trial before Pilate and release of Barabbas (all four); the way to the cross, *without* Simon of Cyrene (John); crucifixion with six of the seven words from the cross (all four); and—beyond death—the empty tomb and resurrection appearances (all four). The film ends with a paraphrase of the words of promise uttered by the resurrected Jesus to his disciples from the gospel of Matthew: "I am with you everyday until the end of time."

Such listings of episodes, however, misrepresent the texture of the narrative. Stories from the gospels are not strung together side by side but woven into a fine tapestry. This is accomplished by imaginative story-telling through the expansion of characters known from the gospel accounts and through the creation of other characters and sub-plots—not unlike that seen in Bronston's *King of Kings*, but with greater dramatic subtlety and artistic sensitivity.

In Capernaum, the impetuous fisherman named Simon—later Peter—who harbors resentment against Romans for their heavy taxa-tion and Matthew the tax collector are at odds with each other until they find common ground as followers of Jesus. Simon—the one called "the zealot," not Peter—and Judas Iscariot leave the zealot movement and become disciples of Jesus. Barabbas surfaces as the leader of that band of zealots and suffers arrest in Jerusalem because of an attempted uprising and his killing of a Roman legionnaire.

Nicodemus and Joseph of Arimathea represent members of the Sanhedrin sympathetic to Jesus. Then there is Zerah—a recognized leader of the Sanhedrin, without textual basis in the gospels, who serves as principal adversary of Jesus on his arrival in Jerusalem at Passover time. Zerah is a betrayer. He betrays Judas, the traditional betrayer, by leading Judas to believe that arrangements have been made for Jesus to explain himself to the Sanhedrin, not for Jesus to be tried by that body. In many ways in the film, Caiaphas and Pilate play greatly reduced roles. They have little regard for, and communication with, one another. Unlike their counterparts in the Bronston film, Caiaphas and Pilate respond to—rather than initiate—the events swirling around them. At the center of these events stands Jesus of Nazareth.

THE PORTRAYAL: Jesus as Suffering-Servant Messiah

Zeffirelli has wonderfully achieved his stated objective in his charac-terization of the title character: Jesus does appear as a Jew who emerged out of the Israel of his time. More particularly, the messianic expectation of Israel—as articulated in the film's opening scene in the synagogue at Nazareth—finds its fulfillment in Jesus of Nazareth.

Following this opening scene, there are numerous affirmations that the divinely conceived son of Mary is the expected messiah. Affirmations come from Elizabeth his aunt, the aged Simeon, the three wise men, the shepherds, Herod the Great, and the messianic forerunner, John the Baptist, who must decrease even as Jesus increases.

The film does not divulge how Jesus himself became aware of his messiahship, although as a youth he exercises the devotional practices of his Jewish heritage. Nonetheless, after his baptism by John—through whose eyes the viewer sees the adult Jesus for the first time—Jesus returns to the synagogue at Nazareth fully conscious of his messianic identity. There, he reads from the scroll of Isaiah and applies the text to himself: "The Spirit of the Lord is upon me . . . " (Isa 61); and "Today the scriptures are fulfilled. . . . " (Luke). Here Jesus is denounced as a blasphemer by those present. Already, at this early point, the charge has been made that will echo throughout his ministry and ultimately lead to his death.

Jesus' messianic self-understanding is confirmed by his own disciples in the confession of Simon called Peter: " . . . you are the messiah, the Son of the living God." As in the synoptic gospels, so in the film this occasion serves as the turning point in Jesus' public ministry because only now does he begin to talk with them about his impending death in Jerusalem: "The Son of man must be rejected by the elders and chief priests of the temple. . . . "

Also, only after this scene from the synoptics does Jesus openly declare his identity as the one from God through those "I am" sayings so characteristic of the gospel of John. On the way to Jerusalem, at the raising of Lazarus, Jesus declares: "I am the resurrection and the life." In Jerusalem, having restored sight to a blind man, he says: "I am the light of the world." At the Last Supper with his disciples, he ends his discourse with the statement: "I am the way, the truth, and the life." During these final days, Jesus also declares: "I and my Father are one." This openness by Jesus continues throughout his trials before the authorities. When asked by Caiaphas if he is the messiah, the Son of God, he forthrightly affirms: "I am. . . . " When asked by Pilate if he is a king, he likewise affirms: "I am. . . . " The blasphemer before his own people has become a traitor in the eyes of Rome, and dies accordingly—on a cross, the traditional Roman means of executing traitors.

The central issue throughout the film, both for the ancient participants portrayed and the modern viewer, is the identity of Jesus himself. Jesus performs an abundance of easily recognizable miracles—although he does not curse and wither the fig tree, as he does in Pasolini's *The Gospel According to St. Matthew* (1966). Jesus also declares many familiar teachings, including many parables—although he does not proclaim the parable of the vineyard, as he does in the Pasolini film. Perhaps this particular incident and this specific parable have been omitted from the Zeffirelli script because they have often been interpreted within Christianity as statements about God's rejection of Israel.

What really matters in *Jesus of Nazareth* is neither what Jesus did nor what he said but who he claimed to be—who he was and is! His claims about himself result in his death. As Jesus hangs on the distinctive lattice-like cross, Nicodemus gazes upon him and offers the viewers the definitive interpretation of Jesus' identity as the messiah. Nicodemus recites the "suffering-servant" passage from Isaiah 53 that concludes with those familiar words: ". . . he was wounded for our transgressions, he was abused for our iniquities."

Nicodemus' identification of Jesus as suffering-servant messiah, who vicariously suffered and died on behalf of others, was anticipated in the film by Jesus himself. Earlier Jesus had said to the crowds seated around him in the temple: ". . . the Son of man came not to be served, but to serve, and to give his life as a ransom for many" (Mark 10:45). Jesus had also said to Barabbas during those final days: "I have come to take on my shoulders the sins of the world. . . ."

Zeffirelli's decision to give the role of theological commentator to a Jew, Nicodemus, explains why in the film the Roman centurion beneath the cross does *not* utter those familiar words from the gospels: "Truly, this man is the Son of God" (Mark 15:39).

The emphasis upon Jesus' having intentionally defined his messiahship as a messiahship in fulfillment of such servant passages as Isaiah 53 finds its counterpart in scholarly tradition—particularly in British scholarship in the years just prior to the Zeffirelli film. The very title of T. W. Manson's 1953 monograph signals this understanding of Jesus: *The Servant-Messiah.* Other contemporaries of Manson, also representatives of the "second" quest of the historical Jesus, shared his focus on Jesus as suffering-servant: A. M. Hunter, *The Work and Words of Jesus* (1950); Vincent Taylor, *The Life and Ministry of Jesus* (1955); C. H. Dodd, *The Founder of Christianity* (1970).[9] More recent British participants in the "third quest" also emphasize Jesus' intentionality about his death on the cross. However, they are less confident that Jesus went to his death in conscious fulfillment of Isaiah 53: J. D. G. Dunn[10] and N. T. Wright.[11]

In Zeffirelli's *Jesus of Nazareth,* there is nothing apocalyptic, coming again at the end of history, about the cinematic portrayal of Jesus as suffering-servant messiah. The phrases "kingdom of God" and "kingdom of heaven" appear interchangeably on Jesus' lips, as in the synoptic gospels. Jesus, at an early point of his ministry in Galilee, responds to the question of "when" the kingdom will arrive by saying emphatically that "the kingdom of heaven is here, now" (recalling Luke 17:20–21).

There is also nothing political about this present "kingdom" as proclaimed by Jesus. Throughout his ministry, Jesus—as John the Baptist before him—calls upon his hearers to have a change of heart and takes his stand against political action as advocated by the zealots. Twice, in Jerusalem, Jesus says to Barabbas: "love your enemies." And Judas, still wrestling with the issue of the outwardness versus the inwardness of the kingdom, explains to Zerah the differences between his own view and that of Jesus: "I always believed action, political action, could solve everything . . . thought it was enough to think clearly; act clearly. . . .He says the heart is more important. . . . " Therefore, understandably, before Pilate, Jesus qualifies his claim to kingship with the statement that his kingdom is *not* of this world (John 18:36).

THE RESPONSE: From Protest to International Acclaim

Jesus of Nazareth received its first telecasting in the United States on the NBC network in two three-hour presentations in prime time, on Palm Sunday and Easter Sunday, April 3 and April 10, 1977. The film was also shown during the same Easter season in Great Britain and Italy, as well as in other countries. Even before its television premiere, Zeffirelli's film had received praise from Pope Paul VI. In an unprecedented statement in his Palm Sunday address to the world, the Pope had said: "Tonight you are going to see an example of the fine use which can be made of the new means of communication that God is offering man. . . . " Perhaps this commendation rested, in part, on the recognition that the film included the so-called investiture of Peter— the words of Jesus used over the centuries to support the authority of the Pope as the successor to Peter (Matt 16:17–19). No doubt this commendation helped swell the size of the viewing audience, especially in Italy. Reportedly, 80% to 83% of the populace in that country watched the program.[12]

The size of the viewing audience in the United States was no less impressive. The film achieved a 50 share of the market for its debut on Palm Sunday and Easter Sunday, thereby attracting an estimated audience of 90 million viewers.[13] The overall quality of the film was recognized the next year by an Emmy nomination as the Outstanding Special, Drama or Comedy, for 1977–1978.

However, in the United States, the television premiere of the film had been preceded by public controversy. The announcement that NBC had purchased the fifteen million dollar film for future showing appeared in newspapers as early as August 1, 1974, three years before it aired.[14] General Motors Corporation had already committed itself to full sponsorship; and the film, when aired, was not to be interrupted for commercials.

Later statements made by Zeffirelli in anticipation of the film aroused the interest and the ire of religious leaders in the United States who represented conservative, or fundamentalistic, Protestantism. Zeffirelli had emphasized in an interview how Jesus would be portrayed as "an ordinary man—gentle, fragile, simple." Bob Jones III, president of Bob Jones University in Greenville, South Carolina, immediately attacked the film on the assumption that it would in some way compromise Jesus' divinity. He called for a letter-writing protest campaign that reportedly produced some 18,000 angry letters to General Motors. Although the automotive giant had already invested several million dollars as sponsor of the telecast, the threat of potential customers taking their money elsewhere led to the cancellation of the sponsorship. In turn, General Motors opened itself to frequent ridicule in the American press.[15] The television sponsorship was eventually assumed by Procter and Gamble.

The release of *Jesus of Nazareth* brought with it compliments from representatives of Christian, Jewish, and Muslim religious organizations who had served in an advisory capacity.[16] They included: Monsignor Pietro Rossano of the Pontifical Commission for the Relations with Non-Christian Religions and the Commission for the Study of the Bible; Father Agnellus Andrew, O.F.M., National Catholic Radio and Television Centre, England; Rabbi Marc H. Tanenbaum, American Jewish Committee; Rabbi Albert Friedlander, the Leo Baeck Rabbinical College, London; Augusto Segre, the European Jewish Cultural Committee; and Mohammed Ben Bouroue, the Koranic School in Meknes, Morocco. One of these advisors, Rabbi Marc H. Tanenbaum, frequently commended the film in this country for its avoidance of anti-Semitism and its corresponding sympathetic depiction of first-century Judaism.

Reviewers and representatives of many evangelical Protestant publications spoke well of the film. One of these publications was *Christianity Today*, a weekly periodical founded in 1956 as an alternative to the more liberal Protestant weekly *The Christian Century*. An editorial in *Christianity Today* (15 April 1977) approvingly observed that "Zeffirelli's film follows the gospel accounts almost to the letter." The editorial cited the evangelist Billy Graham and Bill Bright, the head of the Campus Crusade for Christ evangelistic organization, as religious leaders supportive of the film and, correspondingly, criticized Bob Jones III for his sight-unseen attack. Cheryl Forbes, also in *Christianity Today* (20 May 1977), praised the film and identified the ingredient that set it apart from other like films: "its naturalness, its simplicity." These authors expressed appreciation for the inclusion and handling of the resurrection in *Jesus of Nazareth*. No doubt these comments were elicited by the fact that the two most successful recent Jesus films, *Jesus Christ Superstar* and *Godspell* (both 1973), had ended with a dead Jesus.

However, reviewers in the more liberal Protestant and in the Catholic religious press were less enthusiastic for Zeffirelli's accomplishment. The thoughtful review by Charles P. Henderson, Jr., in *The Christian Century* (20 April 1977), recalled what we have identified as the several dimensions of the problem of the cinematic Jesus. Henderson recognized the *artistic* strengths of the film, but found the film lacking *literarily, historically,* and *theologically*. Basic to the film's literary and historical weaknesses was the way it accepted literally the gospel of John, and ignored "the long-established distinction between the Jesus of history and the Christ of faith. No attempt whatsoever is made to separate the affirmations of the early church from the events which make up a biography of Jesus." Furthermore, and this was the film's theological weakness, the Jesus that appears in the film avoids social engagement with the world around him:

> Caught between the imperial power of Rome and the ruthless terror of the zealots, Jesus and his small band of disciples operate from an enclave of spirituality. . . . This film follows the conventional and popular notion that salvation involves an act of separation from the world and its politics.

These differing responses to *Jesus of Nazareth* by Protestant commentators mirror the ongoing debate within Protestant circles about the authority of scripture and the nature of the "gospel." Those representing evangelical Christianity, operating out of a framework of biblical inerrancy and emphasizing personal salvation, generally liked the film as a Christian statement. The writer representing liberal Christianity, assuming that the gospels cannot be accepted at face value and stressing the social implications of the Christian message, found the film wanting as a theological statement.

Richard A. Blake, in the Catholic periodical *America* (9 April 1977), unintentionally staked out a middle position between those of Forbes and Henderson. Blake recognized that the script deviated from the gospel accounts in several ways and at a number of points, but these deviations did not bother him. On the other hand, he found the production "unbearably slow and tedious," or as he puts it, "not as strong as 'The Gospel According to St. Matthew' and not as painful as 'The Robe.'" Also recognizing that the film affirms the humanity and the divinity of Jesus, he saw in the film "a respectable presentation of the New Testament. . . . "

Writing for *Time* and *Newsweek* magazines, respectively (both 4 April 1977), Richard N. Ostling and Harry F. Waters favorably compared the film with its cinematic predecessors. Ostling noted the way the film had placed Jesus within the social and religious context of first-century Judaism; and Waters saw in the film a theological balance between Jesus' humanity and divinity.

In spite of the many words written about *Jesus of Nazareth* by critics representing the religious and the secular press, the critics did not identify precisely *how* Zeffirelli created such a coherent characterization of Jesus out of the diversity of the four gospels. This is *how* Zeffirelli harmonized Jesus the "open messiah" of John with Jesus the "secret messiah" of the synoptics: he places the "I am" sayings from John on Jesus' lips only after the confession of Peter. Therefore, in Galilee, Jesus maintains a certain reticence about his identity; but, in Jerusalem, he fully reveals who he is.

With this skillful harmonizing of the four gospels, Zeffirelli had given the harmonizing trajectory of Jesus films possibly its finest expression. *Jesus of Nazareth* became a television regular, especially during the Christian seasons of Christmas and Easter. However, *Jesus of Nazareth* was not the last film about Jesus to appear during the decade of the 1970s. Two very different films, to be analyzed in the next two chapters, extended the alternative trajectory: *Monty Python's Life of Brian* (1979) and a film called simply *Jesus* (also 1979).

LIFE OF BRIAN: Brian (Graham Chapman) acclaimed as messiah. Source:
Jerry Ohlinger's Movie Material Store

CHAPTER TEN

1979 | Monty Python's Life of Brian

In the 1970s, the United Kingdom and North America witnessed the growing prominence of a provocatively wacky comedy troupe known as Monty Python.[1] With a keen sense of life's absurdity, the group dared to cross conventional social boundaries and to poke fun at most things others hold dear.

The group of six had been brought together in 1969 to develop a new comedy show for the BBC. Later that year, on October 5, the first series of *Monty Python's Flying Circus* began airing. Subsequent series would also be aired, ending with the final show of the fourth series on December 5, 1974. By then, the programs were also being telecast on CBC in Canada and PBS in the United States.

Of the six members comprising Monty Python, five were British. Graham Chapman, John Cleese, and Eric Idle first knew each other as students at Cambridge University. Similarly, Terry Jones and Michael Palin met at Oxford. Terry Gilliam, the lone American, graduated from Occidental College, California, before wending his way from Los Angeles to New York and then to London. Gilliam became the graphic artist and animator for the group.

The creative output of Monty Python, collectively and individually, was enormous—not only television shows, but also records and books, stage performances and feature films.[2] Their film *Monty Python and the Holy Grail* appeared in 1975. The Holy Grail, of course, refers to the cup used by Christ at the Last Supper and allegedly brought to England by Joseph of Arimathea. As repeatedly recounted by members of the troupe, the occasion that gave impetus for their doing a movie about the Jesus story happened during their promotional tour for *Holy Grail*. Someone asked what their next film would be, and Eric Idle immediately gave a Pythonesque rejoinder, "Jesus Christ: Lust for Glory." This initiated discussions among members of the group who were attracted, according to Idle, by "the freshness of the subject—nobody had made a biblical comedy film."[3]

The initial formal writing session for the prospective Jesus film was held in December of 1976. A first draft was completed by the summer of 1977. Subsequently, in January of 1978, the troupe spent two weeks on the Caribbean island of Barbados to finish rewriting the screenplay.

149

Along the way, the Pythons had decided that the film itself, although set in the time of Jesus, would focus not on Jesus but on a contemporary of Jesus with the improbable name of Brian. Thus the title became *Monty Python's Life of Brian*.

The group also made other decisions among themselves. Terry Jones would serve as director of the film, with Terry Gilliam as production designer. Graham Chapman, who had played King Arthur in *Holy Grail* would play the title role of Brian. But none of them would play Jesus, whose minimal screen time rivaled that of Jesus in the Roman/Christian epics of the 1950s. Instead, the part of Jesus went to English actor Ken Colley. All Pythons, in characteristic fashion, would play multiple parts.

John Goldstone, the producer of *Holy Grail*, agreed to produce *Life of Brian*. He secured financial backing of £2 million for the project from a British company, EMI, with the understanding that changes would not be made in the script and Python would retain the final cut. But Lord Bernard Delfont, the chairman of EMI. vetoed the promised support after he had read the script. Perhaps he had personal as well as corporate reasons for withdrawing from the agreement. His involvement with this Python film could have put him in an embarrassing position in comparison to his brother, Lew Grade. It was Grade who had so recently been instrumental in the production of Franco Zeffirelli's highly successful and widely acclaimed made-for-television movie *Jesus of Nazareth*.

The Python troupe, through Eric Idle, eventually found a willing financial backer for *Life of Brian* in ex-Beatle George Harrison. Harrison formed Handmade Films, with Denis O'Brien; and they became executive producers of the movie. Ironically, even without the backing of Lew Grade's brother, the Python movie was filmed in the fall of 1978 in a locale that had served Zeffirelli so well—Tunisia. Sites and sets that had been used for the Zeffirelli film were utilized in the making of this film. During the shoot, George Harrison even made a brief visit to Tunisia so that the attentive viewer will discover not only Harrison's name in the credits but also his face on the screen in a cameo appearance.

As had Zeffirelli's production crew, so had the crew of *Life of Brian* experienced memorable moments with extras from the local populace, most of whom were Muslim and knew little or no English. Terry Jones, who directed the film, recalled two such moments that involved large crowds and thus many extras: the scene beneath Brian's bedroom window and the scene in the courtyard before Pontius Pilate. [4]

The scene beneath Brian's window required those gathered below to shout back to Brian in unison, in English. Jones thought the scene would need to be dubbed into English later. But a dozen or so English-speaking tourists were recruited and placed up front. In cheerleader fashion, Jones shouted out a line of words, which the crowd repeated, and the routine continued. With the English-speakers to the fore in the crowd, dubbing became unnecessary.

The scene before Pilate required the masses to respond to the verbally challenged governor by falling to the ground with gales of laughter. Jones brought in a Tunisian comedian to elicit laughter from the extras. When this failed, Jones had his assistant tell the crowd in their own language simply to do what the director himself was about to do. Then Jones fell down on his back, kicked his legs in the air, and laughed hysterically. The crowd promptly responded in kind. But, of course, the cameras were not rolling; and the subsequent takes were not as funny as the initial fall. Nonetheless, the scene was eventually printed as filmed.

THE FILM: A Biblical Comedy

Monty Python's Life of Brian is, to use Eric Idle's phrase, a biblical comedy; and the film has rightly been associated with the comedic categories of satire and parody.[5] The title serves public notice that the film reflects the style and substance of the Python troupe. The title also declares that the film centers around a character named Brian.

However, Jesus himself appears as a character on the screen. Jesus' gospel-based story, familiar to viewers, provides the narrative framework for the Brian story. Both Jesus' and Brian's stories begin with a lowly birth in a stable. Both stories move toward a crucifixion at the behest of Pontius Pilate, the Roman governor over Judea. Thus, although Jesus is not the main character, this movie belongs to the tradition of Jesus-story films in which an actor plays Jesus in a first-century setting. The relationship between the Jesus story and the Brian story in this original screenplay and the film's genre as a comedy place it along the alternative trajectory of Jesus-story films.

Moments in Brian's life continuously recall occasions and motifs associated with Jesus in the gospel accounts. Thus, Brian comes to represent a Christ-figure who anachronistically lives during Jesus' own lifetime.[6] As Terry Jones and his confederates have repeatedly claimed, the film—with its Brian character— is used to ridicule *not* Jesus but the ways Christians have often responded over the centuries to Jesus as their Christ. But one can understand how Monty Python humor might not appeal to everyone and how this film could offend believers, both Jewish and Christian.

Life of Brian has the look of biblical epics, including such Jesus-story films as *Ben-Hur* (1959), *King of Kings* (1961), *Barabbas* (1962), *The Greatest Story Ever Told* (1965), and *Jesus of Nazareth* (1977). Although the counter-cultural musicals of the early 1970s had placed their cinematic Jesus stories within a twentieth- century setting—modern Israel for *Jesus Christ Superstar* and New York City for *Godspell*—this Python movie maintains its ancient appearance from beginning to end. The one deviation, as though the troupe could contain themselves no longer, occurs midway through the film with a *Star Wars* moment when a spaceship suddenly rescues Brian.

Life of Brian also captures, in its own playful way, the political dynamics of first-century Judea under Roman occupation. To establish historical context for their Jesus stories, both *King of Kings* (1961) and *The Greatest Story Ever Told* (1965) turned to the writings of the ancient Jewish historian Flavius Josephus. Details in *Life of Brian* also find support in Josephus' writings, especially *The Jewish War*.[7] The factionalism among Jewish liberationist groups depicted in the film rings true given the infighting among the Jews prior to the Roman destruction of Jerusalem in 70 C.E. The Roman use of crucifixion as a routine means of maintaining order and the Jewish use of suicide as a response to oppression also presuppose documented occasions in the history of first-century Judea.

However, in spite of setting Brian's life in the time and place of Jesus' life, the moviemakers carefully and immediately signal to viewers that Brian is *not* Jesus. The first two sketches, which frame the animated presentation of credits, make this distinction obvious.

The film begins with a star-filled but moonless sky when suddenly a bright star appears moving across the heavens. Dawn breaks. Three silhouetted camels and their riders appear and follow the star. They move down a narrow village lane and stop outside a stable. Inside, a lone women, a.k.a. Terry Jones, sits dozing as the three men enter and startle her. "Who are you?" she asks, only to learn that they are wisemen bearing gifts of gold, frankincense, and myrrh for "the Son of God," "Messiah," "King of the Jews." In response to the mother's disclosure of her child's name, the men kneel beside the manger and declare: "We worship you, Oh Brian, who are Lord over us all. Praise unto you Brian and to the Lord our Father. Amen." Having left their gifts and departed, the wisemen suddenly reenter the stable, reclaim their gifts, and depart. Wrong stable. Wrong mother. Wrong child. The wisemen are then seen moving up an adjacent street toward another stable—this time a traditional crèche with a man standing and a woman seated, both with halo-like glows about their heads, next to a manger. Brian is *not* Jesus.

As the animated presentation of the credits flash on the screen, the viewer hears the lyrics and the music of the title song. The humorous lyrics celebrate the humanity of Brian as he grows from babe to teenager to manhood. The flamboyant music is reminiscent of the typical theme of a James Bond movie. This Brian is *not* Jesus.

When the narrative resumes, the camera shows a blue sky and then pans down to reveal crowds moving across a rocky countryside, some walking alone, others leading donkeys or camels. To establish place and time, three captions appear successively:

Judea A.D. 33

Saturday Afternoon

About Tea Time

As the crowds begin to make their way up a slope, the camera cuts to a figure dressed in an off-white cloak, wearing long hair, and standing on the knob. He is speaking:

> How blest are the sorrowful, for they shall find consolation. How blest are those of gentle spirit. They shall have the earth for their possession. How blest are those who hunger and thirst to see right prevail. They shall be satisfied. . . .

The camera pulls back and shows large crowds gathered around the speaker. His voice becomes fainter and fainter. The viewer is suddenly located amidst a small group of hearers on the outer fringe straining to hear the words. Abruptly, a voice nearby shouts, "Speak up!" Another rebukes the shouter: "Quiet, Mum!" Here stand Mandy—Brian's mother, played by Terry Jones—and her adult son. This Brian is *not* Jesus.

In *Life of Brian*, only these introductory episodes of infancy (based primarily on Matthew) and the Sermon on the Mount (adapted from Matthew) directly involve Jesus as a character. The viewer sees Jesus only in the second episode. Besides Jesus, the only other named character in the gospel-based Jesus story who appears in Monty Python's Brian story is Pontius Pilate. The viewer may detect allusions to events from the gospel passion narratives involving Simon of Cyrene and Barabbas, but there will be neither references nor allusions to the high priest Caiaphas. Whether intended or not, this decision not to have a Caiaphas character avoids the possibility that the film might be viewed as anti-Semitic. Herein Pilate and the Romans bear exclusive responsibility for all crucifixions.

This Sermon on the Mount sequence serves not only to reinforce the distinction for the viewer between Jesus and Brian, but also encapsulates the perspective of the entire film. Humor lies not in the Jesus story *per se* but in how Jesus' followers have appropriated, or misappropriated, that story. A man in the crowd, near Mandy and Brian, mishears one of Jesus' beatitudes as, "Blessed are the cheesemakers." A woman asks, "What's so special about the cheesemakers?" Her husband explains, "Well, really, it's not meant to be taken literally. It refers to any manufacturer of dairy products." Herein lie the perennial hermeneutical problems of hearing and remembering, understanding and interpreting that have divided believers and churches over the centuries.

This Sermon on the Mount sequence also introduces other characters who become prominent throughout the film. As Brian and his mother prepare to leave, a small group passes by them. These four are members of the Peoples' Front of Judea (PFJ), one of the competing revolutionary factions. They include: Reg, their leader; Francis and Stan; and Judith, later Brian's love interest. Commenting on what they heard Jesus say, Francis declares, "Well blessed is just about everyone with a vested interest in the status quo, as far as I can tell, Reg." And Reg replies, "What Jesus blatantly fails to appreciate is that it is the meek who are the problem."

The story of Brian involves Brian's association with this rather loony bunch of revolutionaries, his repeated encounters with Roman authority, and eventually his crucifixion following his second appearance before Pontius Pilate. After the episode involving Jesus' sermon, the film continues with sketches characteristic of Monty Python, but which for this film have been placed within a broader narrative structure. These sketches can be identified in ways that highlight Brian's role:[8]

Brian and Mandy attend the stoning of Matthias on a charge of blasphemy, and the presiding official gets stoned instead.

Brian hears the complaint of an ex-leper cured by Jesus that he has no income, and he learns from Mandy that his own father was a Roman soldier.

Brian sells snacks as a vendor at a matinee in the "Colosseum, Jerusalem," and he meets four members of the PFJ.

Brian paints "Romans go home" graffiti on city walls to establish credility, and he receives a lesson in Latin grammar from a Roman centurion.

Brian attends a conspiratorial meeting of the PFJ, and he hears a discussion about the non-benefits or benefits of Roman rule.

Brian participates in a raid on the palace of Pontius Pilate, and he finds himself imprisoned with Ben, an admirer of all things Roman.

Brian receives a hearing before Pontius Pilate but escapes, and he is rescued serendipitously by a spaceship.

Brian becomes a fugitive from the Romans, and at the marketplace he
receives a lesson on how to haggle.

Brian remains a fugitive from the Romans, and he pretends to be a holy
man and attracts a following.

Brian remains a fugitive from the Romans, and in the wilderness he is
acclaimed messiah by his followers.

Brian remains a fugitive from the Romans, and the next morning crowds
gather beneath his window.

Brian is finally recaptured and again taken before Pontius Pilate, and
Pilate gives his traditional Passover address to the crowds.

LIFE OF BRIAN: Brian (Graham Chapman) on trial before Pontius Pilate.
Source: Jerry Ohlinger's Movie Material Store.

Brian is crucified among an alleged 140 prisoners, and the surviving
members of the PFJ wish him well.

With the extended crucifixion sketch, the film reaches its conclusion. The victims have been fixed to the cross, but tied, not nailed.
There is neither blood nor death. They are quite chatty and become
rather cheery.

Several skits are incorporated into the final sketch. Reg leads a
party of PFJ members out to the site and reads a proclamation salut-
ing Brian on the occasion of his "martyrdom." Then Brian's PFJ bud-
dies sing to him, "For he's a jolly good fellow . . . ." A Roman
centurion, who has received an order from Pontius Pilate to have
Brian released, rushes up asking, "Which one is Brian of Nazareth?"
Several of the condemned immediately identify themselves as
"Brian." One is set free, but not Brian himself. Judith appears. She tells
Brian how proud she is of him and promises never to forget him. Then
Brian's shrewish mother Mandy approaches, complains about how
disappointed she is in her son, and sarcastically tells him to go on and
be crucified. As she turns and scurries away, Brian pleadingly call out,
"Mum, mum. . . ."

Then a fellow victim on a nearby cross, played by Eric Idle, says,
"Cheer up, Brian . . . ." He proceeds to lead those on the crosses in
singing a song written by Eric Idle himself, "Always Look on the
Bright Side of Life."

The lyrics give expression to the philosophy underlying not only
this film but Monty Python's entire body of work. There is the absurdity of life and the finality of death; nonetheless, those who live must
not forget to embrace the joys of life while yet alive. Through the lyrics
sound thematic echoes of the biblical book of Ecclesiastes, which similarly counsels its readers to recognize that all is vanity, or lacking in
lasting meaning, but to find provisional meaning in the food, the drink
and the toil during one's life under the sun.

As the crucified chorus sings, the camera pulls back. The crosses
recede into the distance and appear silhouetted above the barren landscape. The camera pans upward and leaves the viewer with white
clouds in a blue sky.

THE PORTRAYAL: Jesus as Christian Icon

In *Monty Python's Life of Brian*, the two gospel-based episodes that
involve Jesus—the birth in a stable and a sermon on a mount—portray him visually in ways that recall traditional Christian iconogra-
phy. Both images look like pictures cut from an illustrated Bible or

removed from the wall of a religious classroom. Both images also have antecedents in such stylistically divergent films as *The Gospel According to Matthew* (1964, 1966) and *The Greatest Story Ever Told* (1965). Thus the portrayal of Jesus in the Python film can best be described as that of a Christian icon.

Moreover, what little we glean from this movie about Jesus corresponds to traditional Christian doctrine. After Jesus' sermon, Reg, the leader of PFJ dismisses Jesus' teaching as supportive of the status quo. This Jesus is a pacific figure, not a political revolutionary. Later when Brian encounters an ex-leper, the one healed explicitly acknowledges that Jesus had cured him through a miraculous act. This Jesus is not only teacher but miracle worker.

Jesus the Christian icon serves as a foil for Brian and his story. After the first few sketches, all visual sightings of Jesus and all references to him stop. Jesus decreases even as Brian increases. But the Jesus story continues as the subtext of the Brian story. Jesus' traditionally understood messianic career underlies Brian's own non-messianic career, which results in his becoming acclaimed as messiah.

Although the opening infancy episode contains the explicit recognition by the three wisemen that the one they seek is "Son of God," Messiah," and "King of the Jews," the circumstances of Brian's own origin emerges when Mandy as mother has a parental chat with her son about his maculate conception. Mandy informs Brian that his father was a Roman centurion. Nonetheless, Brian instantly repudiates the notion that he is Roman and embraces his Jewishness. Underlying this claim of illegitimacy is the ancient polemical tradition that a Roman legionnaire by the name of *Ben-Panthera* fathered Jesus—a tradition also used in the film *Jesus of Montreal* (1989, 1990).

Brian's professed hatred of the Romans leads him to associate himself with the PFJ and to act subversively against Roman rule. And therein, and unwittingly, he launches his strange career that leads to a Roman cross.

Brian participates in a raid against the palace of Pontius Pilate and finds himself hauled before the governor for the first time. Pilate addresses Brian as a Jew, but Brian now calls himself a Roman. Brian escapes from the distracted governor, flees from the palace, and the chase commences. As the result of a pratfall, or two, Brian eventually finds himself standing among holy men on speakers' corner—holy men identified in Python literature as "prophets." Compelled to disguise himself from the attendant Roman soldiers and to prove himself before small groups of hearers, Brian must act like a prophet himself.

Before Brian opens his mouth, three speakers articulate garbled messages using snippets that vaguely recall apocalyptic "doom" passages from the Bible, such as Revelation 17 and Mark 13: "the whore of Babylon;" "rumours of things going astray;" and "a friend shall lose his friend's hammer." However, Brian declares directly and with great clarity:

> Don't pass judgment on other people or else you might get judged yourself.

These words express sentiment articulated by Jesus in the gospels (especially Matt 7:1-2; also Luke 6:37-38). The viewer has returned to the Sermon on the Mount with which the film opened. Whereas gospel-based words of Jesus appeared on the lips of Jesus there, here they are spoken by Brian without attribution to Jesus.

Brian continues speaking words of Jesus familiar to the viewer because of their basis in the gospel text. Brian mentions "birds . . . " and "lilies . . ." (Matt 6:25-33, also Luke 12: 22-31). But listeners interrupt. Brian then mentions "a man and two servants" and some "talents" (Matt 25:14-30; compare Luke 19:12-27). Listeners continue to interrogate and heckle him. Roman soldiers move toward Brian. Suddenly Brian becomes as confused and garbled as the prophets who spoke before him.

By now Brian has attracted a following. He runs. They pursue. They become convinced that he is withholding "the secret of eternal life." They call him, "Master." He says repeatedly, "Leave me alone." Soon his increasingly frantic followers beg for a sign. They become divided into factions, each claiming a special relic: Shoe-ites, his shoe; Sandalites, his sandal; and Gourdenes, his gourd. Brian the revolutionary has, in the eyes of his followers, become a prophet—even more than a prophet.

Brian is pursued into the desert, a traditional place of withdrawal and miracles. There Brian's unintended confrontation with a hermit named Simon leads to shouts among his followers that miracles have occurred. Then it happens. They acclaim Brian to be messiah. Brian emphatically responds: "I am not the messiah." But his denial is taken as clear evidence that Brian is indeed "the messiah—the chosen one." When Simon the hermit himself agrees with Brian and disagrees with Brian's followers, those followers turn on Simon with cries of "heretic," "persecute," "kill." Brian has indeed become their messiah—an accidental messiah.

The next morning a huge throng has gathered in the street beneath the shuttered window of Brian's house desiring to see "the messiah." Disturbed by all the commotion outside, Mandy creates a commotion of her own inside when she discovers that Brian has had Judith as an overnight guest. Finally Brian appears at the open window in a fashion reminiscent of the Pope preparing to bestow a blessing on the masses in St. Peter's Square. But instead of a blessing, Brian shares with those gathered this bit of wisdom: "Look . . . you've got it all wrong. You don't need to follow me. You don't need to follow anybody. You've got to think for yourselves. You're all individuals."

These words complement Brian's earlier saying about not judging others. And they serve as Brian's and Monty Python's central counsel on how to conduct oneself given the fundamental absurdity of life and the finality of death.

The nineteenth-century quest of the historical Jesus considered the issue of Jesus' "messianic consciousness" to be of central concern. Clearly Brian has no sense of being a messianic figure and becomes messiah in the consciousness of his followers because of a comedy of errors. However, for a moment—before the gathering at speakers' corner— Brian articulates words of Jesus that he does not attribute to Jesus. Did Brian remember them from the Sermon on the Mount? Regardless, the Monty Python troupe, by placing these words of Jesus on Brian's lips and by placing the garbled apocalyptic statements on the lips of the other holy men, has aligned Brian not with the prophets of doom and gloom but with sages who offer advice about life here and now.

THE RESPONSE: Opposition but Success

Warner Brothers-Orion Pictures obtained the distribution rights to *Life of Brian* in the United States, and the film was released with an "R" rating. The world premiere was held in New York City, at Cinema One, on August 17, 1979. The film's opening in the United Kingdom occurred three months later, in London, at the Plaza Cinema, on November 8. The film had earlier received an "AA" certificate from the British Board of Film Censors (BBFC), restricting the film to those over 14, but requiring no cuts. However, objections were raised against *Life of Brian* in both countries.[9]

The premier in New York immediately elicited negative responses from leaders and representatives of Jewish, Catholic, and Protestant groups.

Rabbi Benjamin Hecht, speaking on behalf of three orthodox organizations, dismissed *Life of Brian* as "blasphemy" and "a crime against religion." The Rabbinical Alliance of America, the Union of Orthodox Rabbis of the United States of America and Canada, and the Near Eastern Sephardic Communities of America claimed to represent a thousand rabbis and a half million Jews. Other Jews too might have considered offensive the pervasive use in the film's dialogue of epithets that have historically been used to slander Jews.

The National Catholic Office for Motion Pictures, successor to the Legion of Decency, bestowed a "C" (condemned) rating on *Life of Brian*. The Archdiocese of New York strongly supported this judgment with censorious statements. One spokesman for the Archdiocese declared, "The picture holds the person of Christ up to comic ridicule and is, for Christians, an act of blasphemy." Another said, "This is the most blasphemous film I have ever seen and it pretends to be nothing else." Catholics also might have viewed the obvious contrasting parallel between the non-virgin Mandy and the virgin Mary to be ridiculing the mother of Christ.

The Reverend Roger Fulton, Pastor of the Neighborhood Church in Greenwich Village, participated in a demonstration outside the Warner Communications building at Rockefeller Center. On this occasion, he delivered a lengthy address, which contained words describing *Life of Brian* as "vulgar, anti-Christian, and anti-Semitic." The diverse gathering of protestors then marched to Cinema One, on Third Avenue. No doubt the charge of vulgarity stemmed not only from the language used throughout the film but also from the frontal nudity of Brian and Judith, however brief.

On August 27, a month before this public demonstration against the film and ten days after its premier, Warner Brothers defensively released an explanatory statement:

> The public has been enthusiastic, having flocked to every theater now playing the picture. It is entertainment and, to many, *Monty Python's Life of Brian* is an enjoyable movie experience. It was never our intention to offend anyone's beliefs, and we certainly regret having done so. The film is satire, it is a spoof, and it should be viewed in that context.[10]

One object of the film's spoofing that received little notice in the reviews of the time was the emerging feminist movement. Near the beginning of the movie, the character named Stan introduces the issue of gender equity within the circle of the PFJ by correcting his revolutionary comrades whenever they use inappropriately male nouns and pronouns. He eventually expresses the desire to be called not Stan but Loretta. However, by the end of the film, Stan (or Loretta) has not only raised the consciousness of his (or her) colleagues but also has altered their use of exclusive language. The members of the PFJ refer to each other not as "brother," not as "sister," but as "sibling." They also honor Stan's request by addressing him as Loretta.

Many reviews of *Life of Brian* in the secular press acknowledged the potential offensiveness of the film to believers and referred to the publicly expressed objections to the film. They then expressed varying degrees of appreciation for its humor.

In his review for *The New York Times* (17 August 1979), Vincent Canby wrote favorably about the movie's "bad taste," "delirious offensiveness," and the "not-so-reverent account of the life, times, and apotheosis of one Brian of Nazareth . . . . " In a follow-up column, he refused to label *Life of Brian* as "blasphemous" and unequivocally denied that the film "manifests a contempt of God" (30 September 1979). Writing for *The New Republic* (22 September 1979), Stanley Kauffmann said that just as Monty Python had "reamed the stupidities and cruelties of the Middle Ages" so the comic band had used similar inventiveness "to ream the stupidities and delusions of religiosity." He added: "They will not destroy true, unpompous faith. (How could they, anyway, even if they wanted to?)"

David Ansen for *Newsweek* (3 September 1979) and Richard Schickel for *Time* (17 Sept 1979) also wrote brief reviews for their respective weekly magazines. Both make passing comparisons between traditional biblical epics and *Life of Brian*, although Ansen observes that the crucifixion scene in the Python film "owes as much to Busby Berkeley as to the Bible" and Schickel describes the comic troupe as "funny lads" who "detest all formal systems of belief, all institutions . . . . " Lawrence O'Toole, in the Canadian weekly *Macleans* (10 September 1979), concludes his review by agreeing with those who found the film insulting, but "for reasons of banality rather than blasphemy."

Variety (22 August 1979), the entertainment weekly, anticipated a complaint about *Life of Brian* sometimes made in other American periodicals: "the frequent impenetrability of the English accents." However, as might be expected, the complaint in the religious media went well beyond accents.

The Catholic publication *America* (15 September 1979), within the context of a commentary titled "Parody and Pluralism," declared the film to be "a deliberate, self-conscious mockery of the Judeo-Christian tradition." The Protestant periodical *Christianity Today* (16 November 1979) assessed the film with greater theological subtlety and depth. Harvie M. Conn, the author of the critique, acknowledged the film to be humorous, but—in his own intriguing way—allowed the charge of "blasphemy" to stand.

Monty Python's Life of Brian continued to be attacked as blasphemy in many communities across the United States. Pressure was brought to bear on theater owners and managers not to screen the film, and individuals were urged not to attend. Among the oppositional groups were the California-based Interfaith Committee Against Blasphemy and the Mississippi-based National Federation for Decency.

Organized opposition to the film certainly had its local successes. But overall, this Python movie enjoyed a successful and profitable run.

In the United States, there is First Amendment freedom of speech protection for movies and *no* establishment of religion; but in the United Kingdom, there is *no* First Amendment freedom of speech protection for movies and an established church. Whatever the legal, religious, and social differences between the two nations, the opening of *Life of Brian* in London in early November also produced opposition.

Although the BBFC issued certificates for films to be screened, there were more than three hundred district councils that had the power to change the conditions granted by the BBFC for the showing of a particular film in local cinema houses.

The Festival of Lights, an organization concerned with public morality, lobbied against *Life of Brian*. On the day after the London premier, the Archbishop of York, Dr. Stuart Blanch, referred to the film and called for vigilance on the part of local councils: ". . . in their own areas the local viewing committee is alerted to the need to see the film before it is publicly shown and, having done so, to take responsible decisions as to whether and on what conditions it should be shown."[11]

A few district councils, such as those in Cornwall in the southwest and West Yorkshire in the midlands, banned the film—although the residents of West Yorkshire had only to drive a short distance to the city of York, the see of the Archbishop, to take in the film. Others councils changed the BBFC certification of "AA" to a more limiting "X," with the result that the distributors of the film refused to screen it with the revised designation.

Several Anglican Bishops forthrightly opposed *Life of Brian*, none more so than Mervyn Stockwood, the Bishop of Southwark. Bishop Stockwood was a participant in one of the most memorable moments in the public discourse about the film.[12] On the evening of November 9, there was a televised debate, moderated by Tim Rice, the lyricist of *Jesus Christ Superstar*. On the one side, Stockwood appeared with Malcolm Muggeridge, the well-known author and defender of the faith. On the other side, they were opposed by two Pythons, John Cleese and Michael Palin. The debate soon degenerated into acrimony as Cleese and Palin fended off charges of Monty Python's having belittled such cherished Christian claims and moments as the incarnation, the Sermon on the Mount, and the crucifixion. But again, in spite of public discord over *Life of Brian*, the film enjoyed a successful and profitable run in the United Kingdom as it had in the United States.

Twenty-five years later, as Mel Gibson's *The Passion of the Christ* continued to draw crowds into American theaters, *Monty Python's Life of Brian* also found its way back into theaters. Through Moira

Macdonald, the movie critic of *The Seattle Times* (12 May 2004), Terry Jones thanked Mel Gibson on behalf of the Python troupe for providing them with the opportunity to re-release their film. Anthony Lane, in his review in *The New Yorker* (3 May 2004), as though pronouncing absolution after all these years declared, *"Life of Brian* contains not a shred of blasphemy."

The other Jesus-story film that opened in the United States shortly after *Life of Brian*, also in 1979, was a movie never considered blasphemous. That film bore the simple title *Jesus*. Posters announcing the film's theatrical release promised, "You'll believe in miracles," and showed a close-up of empty sandals in the sand.

JESUS: Jesus (Brian Deacon) performs the miracle of the loaves and fishes.
Source: The JESUS Film Project, Campus Crusade for Christ

CHAPTER ELEVEN

John Heyman
Jesus

Cecil B. DeMille casts his shadow over the tradition of Jesus-story films. He became the impresario of the biblical epic; and his silent *The King of Kings* (1927) set the standard by which his successors in the era of sound often judged themselves.

In 1950, or thereabouts, Bill Bright—the founder of Campus Crusade for Christ evangelistic organization—felt led by God to make a film on the life of Jesus. Without the money to produce the film, Bright says that he approached Cecil B. DeMille about the possibility of DeMille's involving himself in such a project. Nothing happened then, but thirty years later something did. What happened has been chronicled in a volume with an introduction by Bill Bright but written by Paul Eshleman, a longtime leader with Campus Crusade for Christ.[1]

John Heyman, born in Germany, had come of age in Great Britain after his family sought refuge there from Nazism. In the 1960s, he produced a series of British films, including *Boom!* (1968), an adaptation of the Tennessee Williams play *The Milk Train Doesn't Stop Here Anymore*. In the 1970s, he continued his work in the United States and contributed to the production of such films as *Chinatown* (1974), *Saturday Night Fever* (1977), and *Grease* (1978).

During this period, Heyman became interested in the Bible and eventually committed himself to filming the entire work—beginning with Genesis 1:1. His production company became known as the Genesis Project. He even completed work on a major portion of the Book of Genesis, but needed financial backing to proceed. Therefore, Heyman turned for assistance to Bill Bright—in 1976—thinking that support might be found in religious circles.

Bright had a long-standing interest in making a film about Jesus. Heyman had a production company that could make it. Together, through a series of circumstances, they secured an agreement from Bunker and Caroline Hunt, of Texas oil and silver fame, to underwrite the film to the amount of three million dollars in support of the larger goal of world evangelism.

Decisions had to be made; and those decisions led away from the harmonizing epic approach of DeMille. The script would be based on the story-line from only one gospel. Every word spoken by Jesus would be taken from that gospel: Luke.

The resulting film was named, quite simply, *Jesus*.[2] The final cost of production approximated six million dollars. As the headline in the evangelical weekly periodical *Christianity Today* (5 October 1979) declared: "Luke Belatedly Gets His Film Credits."[3]

By bringing to the screen the Jesus story based on a single gospel, the film called *Jesus* (1979) followed the path taken in the alternative tradition of Jesus filmmaking pioneered by Pier Paolo Pasolini and his *The Gospel According to St. Matthew* (1964, 1966). However, in spite of similar approaches to the Jesus story, no two films could be more different in terms of their stated purposes, their cinematic qualities, and their eventual audiences.

Where Pasolini the Marxist and atheist sought to provoke, Heyman, and those Christians working with him, would seek to persuade. The film was designed for use by the outreach ministry of Campus Crusade for Christ, and so it bears that evangelistic stamp.

The filmmakers' styles contrasted as sharply as had their purposes. The Pasolini film was shot in black and white, in the style of neo- realism, in southern Italy, without any attempt to reconstruct the Palestine of the first century. The Heyman film was filmed in color, in the land of Israel itself, with every effort made to replicate historical exactitude in terms of dress, customs, architecture. Israelis were cast in most of the parts, but the title role was given to a non-Jew, an English gentile actor—Brian Deacon.

The two films appealed to different audiences. The Pasolini film became a favorite among those Christians and non-Christians with an intellectual and artistic bent, particularly in Europe and North America. The Heyman film would be shown around the world particularly to the unchurched and those not "born again."

Another key decision, beyond that of basing the script on one gospel, was to circulate a preliminary script among several hundred religious leaders and biblical scholars for comment. The script was written by Barnet Fishbein. Among those asked for advice included the Roman Catholic prelate Archbishop Fulton J. Sheen and Rabbi Marc Tanenbaum of the American Jewish Committee. The latter expressed his ongoing concern that the film not portray "the Jews" as "Christ-killers." The screenwriter obliged by his handling of the script at a number of points.

Jesus was directed by Peter Sykes and John Kirsh. They experienced awkward moments in the actual shooting of the film. The filming of the baptism of Jesus constituted just such a moment.

Two details in the brief report of the baptism in Luke are peculiar to this gospel. Luke 3:21–22 omits any explicit statement that Jesus was actually baptized by John; and these verses contain the interesting notation that when the Holy Spirit descended on Jesus like a dove it did so in "bodily form." Faithful to the letter of the text, the completed film shows Jesus dunking himself under the water and a dove alighting on his shoulder. When the scene was shot, Jesus—alias Brian Deacon—had to stand in the waist-deep water for two hours while men elevated on ladders tossed doves toward him. Even with birdseed on his shoulders, the doves kept landing on his head or facing away from the camera. Although success finally came, Deacon contracted a case of pneumonia because of his prolonged soaking.[4]

THE FILM: More than Just the Gospel of Luke

The gospel of Luke provides the narrative and teaching material for the film called *Jesus*. Like the gospel, the film moves from the conception and birth of Jesus to his crucifixion, resurrection, and ascension. Nearly all episodes and dialogue in the movie have their basis in the gospel text. A narrator, Alexander Scourby, reads the gospel text or, at other times, makes explanatory comments. By contrast to other Jesus films, the music—when present—is non-obtrusive and often unnoticed.

On the screen, at the outset, *Jesus* claims not only to be literarily faithful to the gospel of Luke but to be historically accurate by identifying itself as a "documentary." Nonetheless, some stories and teachings in the gospel have been included, others excluded. Of those included, some have been rearranged in sequence, others reduced in scope.

In spite of a certain pageant-like quality, *Jesus* also reflects a creative use of the medium of film. The raising from the dead of the widow of Nain's son (chapter 7) appears as a flashback, related to John the Baptist by a visitor through the bars of his prison cell. The parable of the Good Samaritan (chapter 10) appears as imagined by a young girl, while she listens to Jesus' narration of the parable. Many of Jesus' teachings are prompted by objects at hand: a sack of seed brings on the interpretation of the parable of the sower (chapter 8); a lamp on the wall, the saying about putting a lamp on a stand (chapter 8); a passing camel, the saying about a camel going through the eye of a needle (chapter 18).

We can see how the literary shape of the gospel has been modified for the screen by noting the resultant shape of Jesus' life, according to the movie. The broad outline of the Jesus story in the gospel appears as follows:

Preface (1:1–4)
I.   John and Jesus (1:5–2:52)
II. Ministry of Jesus
         in Galilee (3:1–9:50)
         from Galilee through Samaria to Jerusalem (9:51–19:27)
         in Jerusalem (19:28–23:56)
III. Resurrection and Ascension of Jesus (24:1–53)

The gospel of Luke begins with a formal preface that sets forth the author's purpose (1:1–4). The gospel then tells stories about the births of John and Jesus followed by the account of Jesus' visit to the temple in Jerusalem at age twelve (chapters 1:5–2:52).

The opening sequences of the film *Jesus*, based on these two chapters, are labeled on the screen as "prologue." The film script omits the material related to the birth of John, but faithfully presents the events related to the birth and childhood of Jesus.

The gospel of Luke, in its presentation of the ministry of Jesus, has two distinctive features that distinguish it from the gospels of Mark and Matthew. Both features in Luke underscore Jesus' concern for non-Jews.

First, after Jesus' baptism and testing, he immediately returns to his hometown of Nazareth (chapter 4). There, in the synagogue, he reads from the scroll of Isaiah: "The Spirit of the Lord is upon me. . . . " He announces that the text has that day been fulfilled. As long as Jesus presents himself as the Jewish messiah, he receives applause from his hearers. But when he claims that his ministry—like the ministries of the prophets Elijah and Elisha—will involve outreach to gentiles, his hearers turn nasty and try to kill him.

Secondly, Jesus' public ministry involves an extended journey through territory inhabited by non-Jews. The journey takes him from Galilee in the north, through Samaria in the central hill country, to Jerusalem in the south (chapters 9–19). That Jesus makes his way through Samaria is suggested by references to Samaria and Samaritans in this section of the gospel. Jesus begins his journey by sending followers into a village of the Samaritans (chapter 9). Later, Jesus declares his parable of the Good Samaritan (chapter 10) and praises a Samaritan, who happens to be the only one of ten healed lepers to return and thank him (chapter 17).

The gospel of Luke also has a distinctive ending. Only this gospel reports the resurrection and additionally describes an ascension into heaven (chapter 24)—an event repeated at the outset of the book of Acts, the second volume of the two-volume work Luke-Acts.

In the film *Jesus*, the title frames mark the transition from the presentation of Jesus' early years from infancy to the presentation of his ministry: "The public life of . . . JESUS." Faithful to the gospel, the film moves Jesus from his preaching and rejection at Nazareth (although references to Elijah and Elisha have been deleted from his homily) to his ascension outside Jerusalem (shot not from the viewpoint of observers on the ground but from the perspective of Jesus, with the earth receding beneath him, as though he were in a space rocket).

The film obscures the possibility that Jesus' journey went specifically through the territory of Samaria. Neither the entry of the disciples into the Samaritan village nor the story of the thankful Samaritan leper is included in the film. However, Heyman's *Jesus*—like the gospel on which it depends—does present the public life of Jesus as falling roughly into three periods during which he spends considerable time on the road between the northern and the southern territories: an *early* period in Galilee, a *transitional* period from Galilee to Jerusalem, and the *later* period in Jerusalem.

The *early* period of Jesus' public ministry begins with his baptism, testing, and rejection at Nazareth (chapters 3–4). Then he moves to Capernaum where he calls Simon, James, and John to be disciples through effecting a miraculous catch of fish (chapter 5). There, from the boat next to the shore, he delivers the parable of the Pharisee and tax collector (chapter 18). Next he resuscitates from the dead—or heals?—Jairus' daughter (chapter 8). Having called Matthew Levi the tax collector as a disciple (chapter 5), he withdraws into the hills where he introduces the full complement of twelve—including Judas the "traitor" (chapter 6). The so-called Sermon on the Plain follows as he walks among the people personalizing his bits of wisdom (chapter 6). Thereafter, he dines in the home of a Pharisee where a sinful woman enters and anoints his feet (chapter 7). That woman—Mary Magdalene, of course—joins his band along with Joanna and Susanna (chapter 8). Subsequently, Jesus receives visitors from John the Baptist (chapter 7) and delivers the parable of the sower (chapter 8). This initial period of his activity draws toward a close as he performs such feats as the stilling of the storm, the exorcism of the naked Gadarene demonic, and the feeding of the crowds with five loaves and two fish (chapters 8–9).

The *transitional* period of Jesus' public life opens with his questioning the disciples and the confession of Peter: "You are God's messiah" (chapter 9). Jesus commands secrecy and gives his first "passion prediction": "The Son of man must suffer. . . . " Thereafter, talk turns to suffering and death—of Jesus and those who would be his followers. Withdrawing to a mountain with Peter, James, and John, he is transfigured before them, appearing in the presence of Moses and Elijah (chapter 9). As Jesus and his band move toward his destiny of suffering, he finds time to exorcise an epileptic boy (chapter 9) and to teach the Lord's Prayer in a hybrid version that combines lines from the prayer in Matthew and Luke (chapter 11). He shares the parable of the mustard seed with his followers and then creates controversy in a synagogue on the sabbath by healing a woman of an eighteen year infirmity (chapter 13). Walking beside the moving wagon of a rich man, Jesus talks with him about wealth (chapter 18) and sets forth another "passion prediction." Then he tells the parable of the Good Samaritan (chapter 10), blesses little children (chapter 18), and heals a blind man (chapter 18). This transitional period of Jesus' activity draws to a conclusion in the house of Zacchaeus the tax collector (chapter 19). At table, Jesus announces to the disciples that " . . . You are going to Jerusalem," And he continues with his third "passion prediction."

The *final* period of Jesus' public life embraces most of those familiar events in Jerusalem related to his death. He approaches the city astride a small colt as his followers wave branches and speaks about the city's coming destruction. Once in the city, Jesus proceeds to cleanse the temple (chapter 19). His public teaching and public debate include praise of a widow for her offering, an answer to the question about his authority, a parable about the killing of the vineyard owner's son, and an answer to the question about payment of taxes to Caesar (chapters 20–21). With the approach of the feast of Passover, he sends Peter and John to prepare for the meal—the Last Supper. With his small band seated in a semicircle, Jesus offers words over the cup, the bread, and (again) the cup, plus the extended teaching at the meal characteristic of this gospel (chapter 22). His arrest in Gethsemane and detention in the house of the high priest involve both the betrayal of Judas and the denial of Peter (chapter 22).

The next morning sees Jesus taken before the council, before Pilate, before Herod Antipas, back to Pilate (chapter 23). On the way to the cross, Jesus carries the cross-piece until Simon of Cyrene is pressed into service. Later at the place of execution, Jesus and two others are affixed to crosses with their arms bound by ropes and nails driven through their wrists. On the cross, Jesus speaks *all* three sayings preserved in the gospel itself: "Forgive them, Father. . . . " And: " . . . today you will be in paradise. . . . " Finally: "Into thy hands. . . . " Then Jesus dies, with the moment of death captured in a striking overhead shot as his head falls forward to his chest. The voice of the Roman centurion can be heard: "Glory be to God, certainly this was a righteous man" (chapter 23).

The gospel of Luke has provided the screenplay for *Jesus* the movie. But there is much more to the film than the screenplay based on Luke. Consistent with its evangelistic purpose and use, the film narrative has been placed in a broader theological framework. In this regard, the film *Jesus* has kinship with George Stevens' *The Greatest Story Ever*

Told. Both frameworks interpret the significance of Jesus for the viewer.

THE PORTRAYAL: Jesus as the Unique Person

In the film *Jesus*—as released in 1979—before the story begins, the viewer sees and hears words from John 3:16–17 scrolling upward over the screen. Then the viewer sees and hears these words:

> Today Jesus Christ has
> more than 1,000,000,000 followers.
> Four Gospels record
> the humble beginnings of the Christian Faith,
> and while other Gospels tell of some other events,
> or even of the same events
> somewhat differently. . . .
>
> this is His story taken
> entirely from the Gospel of Luke.

As the story ends, the viewer hears the concluding words of Jesus from the gospel of Matthew with which so many Jesus films end: " . . . Lo, I am with you always, even to the end of the world. Amen." There follows a seven minute commentary on the film that represents a cinematic counterpart to the traditional altar call in many Protestant churches: as the viewer sees still pictures from the film, the unseen narrator invites the viewers to pray with him and to accept the living Jesus as Lord over their lives. He cites scriptural verses from the synoptic gospels, the gospel of John, the letters of Paul, and the Book of Revelation. He also provides a summary theological, or christological, interpretation of Jesus: "He is the most unique person who has ever lived. His birth was unique. . . . His life was unique. . . . His message was unique. . . . His death on the cross was unique. . . . His resurrection was unique. . . . "

Jesus the film does offer a balanced presentation of Jesus the person as portrayed in the gospel of Luke—and, more generally, in the synoptic gospels. Jesus preaches "the kingdom of God," often using parables. He speaks about himself as "the Son of man," both in terms of suffering, death, resurrection, and in terms of coming again for final judgment. Jesus' ministry and message have a universal appeal as he associates with all social types, including Pharisees, tax collectors, and women. He also performs miracles. His mighty works include physical healings, exorcisms, and control over nature. Jesus goes to Jerusalem to die and establishes a new covenant through his death on the cross. Jesus is resurrected from the dead.

Jesus the film avoids the implication that *all* Jews—past or present—bear the responsibility for Jesus' crucifixion. This avoidance expresses itself in at least four ways.

The first way has to do with the film's adaptation of the "passion predictions" (9:22; 17:25; 18:31–33). The initial "prediction" by Jesus given in conjunction with Peter's confession has been edited in the film to exclude any reference to the Jewish leaders—the elders, priests, and scribes. The second "prediction" that refers to neither Jewish leaders nor to gentiles has been simply retained in the film. The third "prediction" that refers to the gentiles and omits any reference to the Jewish authorities has been included in the film word-for-word and relocated so that Jesus speaks the words in the house of Zacchaeus just prior to his final departure for Jerusalem.

The second way the film avoids the implication that all Jews bear responsibility for the crucifixion involves the creation of a scene that has no basis in the gospel text. After Jesus' entry into Jerusalem and his actions in the temple, Pontius Pilate, Caiaphas, and Annas are seated at a table. The dialogue goes something like this:

Pilate:	I understand that many have already hailed him as king.
Caiaphas:	A king *(he chuckles)* . . . a king of beggars, whores, and thieves. We've seen his like before. They come. They make their claims. They go. They are forgotten.
Annas:	Don't be blind. His following is growing by the day. The people admire him. . . .
Pilate:	. . . and think he is a king *(he rises)*. Let me give you a warning. If this man should threaten the peace further, I shall look to you.
Caiaphas:	Perhaps he's right. It's time we confronted the Galilean.

A third way the film avoids the implication that all Jews bear responsibility for the crucifixion involves commentary by the narrator that has no basis in the gospel text. As the scene shifts away from the meeting among Caiaphas, Pilate, and Annas, Jesus reenters the temple. The voice of the narrator declares: "And as the hypocritical section of the scribes and Pharisees came increasingly under his attack, so his following among the Jews grew . . . and so did the opposition of those he condemned."

Later, after the council of elders has conspired to put Jesus to death, and as they deliver him over to Roman authority, the narrator again says: "And they took him before Pontius Pilate, the most vicious of all Roman procurators, alone responsible for the crucifixion of thousands."

Still a fourth way the film avoids the implication that all Jews are responsible for the crucifixion of Jesus is by its characterization of

Caiaphas, Annas, and Pilate near the end. Caiaphas and Annas involve themselves directly in all the events of Jesus' last hours. They are present in Gethsemane at Jesus' arrest; and they accompany Jesus as he makes the rounds from Pilate, to Herod, and back to Pilate. They even suggest to Pilate that he release Barabbas and do away with Jesus. Pilate releases Barabbas but does not verbally sentence Jesus. In an intriguing camera shot from the courtyard below, where Jesus stands, Pilate tosses toward Jesus and the soldiers a small scroll, presumably containing in writing the order of execution—a scroll filmed in slow motion as it falls toward the viewer.

Therefore, by contrast to the gospel of Luke, the film gives Pontius Pilate a more active role in the final conspiracy against Jesus and describes him as one fully capable of passing the sentence of crucifixion. The film also places oversight for the conspiracy against Jesus squarely upon Caiaphas and Annas. According to the film, Jesus' death cannot be construed as an indictment of an entire people.

THE RESPONSE: 196 Million Decisions for Christ

Jesus, G-rated, opened on October 19, 1979, in 250 theaters. Initially released in the western and southern regions of the United States, the film appeared in theaters in the northern and eastern regions the following spring, 1980.

The film had originated as a collaboration between Campus Crusade for Christ, a cinematically inclined religious organization, and the Genesis Project, a religiously oriented film organization. An agreement with Warner Brothers enabled the film to be booked into commercial theaters. Inspirational Film Distributors was formed to oversee the marketing of the film and the advance sale of tickets through local committees representing various religious and church organizations. Over four million people had seen the film by the end of its year-long showing in commercial movie houses.[5]

Already, by the spring of 1980, the film was being dubbed in other languages, and its worldwide distribution by Campus Crusade for Christ soon began. A decade after the initial release of the film, the weekly religious periodical *Christianity Today* (20 October, 1989) introduced an article with the headline: "Ten Year Run for 'Jesus'." Reported statistics were impressive: dubbed into 130 languages, shown in 155 countries, viewed by more than 325 million people.

Toward the end of his life in 1959, Cecil B. DeMille could claim that more persons had been introduced to Jesus through *The King of Kings* than any medium other than the Bible itself. In his autobiography, he used the figure of 800 million people.[6] Thanks to television, Zeffirelli's *Jesus of Nazareth*, first telecast in America and Europe during the Easter season in 1977 and many times since, soon surpassed DeMille's film in size of viewing audience. As early as 1984, in his personal account of the film, Zeffirelli suggested that his film had probably been seen by more than a billion people.[7]

Through its aggressive use by Campus Crusade for Christ, Heyman's *Jesus* now claims to be not just the most widely viewed Jesus film but the most widely viewed film in history. Two weeks before the public release of Mel Gibson's *The Passion of the Christ*, a feature article by Franklin Foer appeared in *The New York Times* (8 February 2004) under the headline "*The Passion's* Precedent: Has a 1979 Bible Film Become the Most-Watched Movie Ever?"

A statistical profile of The JESUS Film Project, obtained from its Web site (dated April 1, 2004) indicates that 5,760,925,245 people in 228 countries have seen *Jesus* the movie.[8] Of that number, more than 196 million claim to have accepted Jesus as Christ as a result of viewing the film. Whatever its ranking in Jesus film history relative to the total number of viewers or decisions for Christ, there can be no doubt that *Jesus* has become available in more languages than any film of any kind—857 languages, and counting.

Given the non-commercial genesis of the film, the critical response in the national press at the time of its premier was somewhat limited. The entertainment weekly *Variety* (24 October 1979) reviewed the film based on a pre-release Hollywood screening. *Time* magazine (5 November 1979) featured the film in its religion section, offering many details about how the movie came to be. Reviews in religious publications appeared in the Protestant *Christianity Today* (21 December 1979) by Thomas Trumbull Howard and in the Catholic *America* (10 May 1980) by John W. Donahue.

All of these publications evaluated the film *Jesus* within the context of other recent cinematic portrayals of Jesus. On the one hand, the film was generally considered different from, or superior to, the stark black-and-white treatment of Pasolini's *The Gospel According to St. Matthew* (1994, 1966), the glossy color approach of Bronston's *King of Kings* (1961) and Stevens' *The Greatest Story Ever Told* (1965). On the other hand, Heyman's *Jesus* was said to fall short of the religious and emotional power of Zeffirelli's *Jesus of Nazareth* (1977).

However, Thomas Trumbull Howard, in *Christianity Today,* while still expressing reservations about putting any Jesus on the screen, concludes: "The film deserves a great deal of praise, and has done, we venture to guess, as good a job as anyone has ever done with the attempt."

Although *Jesus* (1979) had initially been shown in commercial theaters, the film itself was not a commercial enterprise. As the 1970s gave way to the 1980s, two Jesus films appeared that were commercial ventures: *The Day Christ Died* (1980) and *In Search of Historic Jesus* (1980).

A 20th Century-Fox film produced for CBS-TV, *The Day Christ Died* (1980), was telecast on May 26, 1980. Based on a historical novel of the same name by Jim Bishop, the film focused on the last days of Jesus' life giving it the scope of a traditional passion play.[9]

A Sunn Classics production, *In Search of Historic Jesus* (1980), G-rated, represented a pseudo-documentary in a succession of films that tantalized audiences with the promise of answers to questions related to such topics as Noah's ark and life beyond death. The company would rent theaters, saturate the local market with advertising, and screen the film for a limited time, with the income from ticket sales going to the company itself.[10]

The importance of these two films lies in their expressing a growing recognition, both by filmmakers as well as the general public, of the difference between the presentation of Jesus in the four gospels and what Jesus was like historically.

Interestingly enough, the next major contribution to the ongoing tradition of Jesus-story films was based on a work of fiction and disclaimed any pretension of being based on the gospels themselves, much less historical research. That film, of course, was Martin Scorsese's *The Last Temptation of Christ* (1988). The film would generate much public controversy.

The Politics
of Roman Palestine

Herod the Great. Archelaus. Herod Antipas. Philip. Pontius
Pilate. Caiaphas. Annas. These are the politically prominent figures of Roman Palestine who are mentioned in the gospels and,
therefore, appear on the screen in the long procession of Jesus-
story films.

In 40 B.C.E., the Roman Senate appointed Herod to be "King of
the Jews" over a geographical area that approximated that of
King David centuries earlier. Although a Jew in religious matters,
Herod was a native of Idumea (ancient Edom)—the territory
south of Judea that had traditionally been an enemy of Israel. Not
until 37 B.C.E. when local resistance was quelled did Herod
assume full control over his vassal kingdom. What followed was
a reign marked by political astuteness, court intrigue, and an
ostentatious building program. The latter included the transformation of the Jerusalem temple into one of the great sanctuaries
of the ancient world.

The gospels present Jesus as having been born during the latter years of Herod's reign (Matt 2:1; Luke 1:5). Those cinematic
epics that include an account of Jesus' infancy, especially the massacre of the children at Bethlehem (Matt 2:16), highlight the role
of Herod the Great in interesting ways.

The death of Herod the Great was accompanied by complicated political maneuvering among those sons who had survived
their father's murderous wrath. Consequently, the Romans
divided Herod's kingdom among three of his sons and denied all
three the title of "king." They were named either tetrarch, rulers
of a fourth part of the province, or ethnarch, ruler of a people.

Philip became Tetrarch of areas north and east of the Sea of
Galilee (4 B.C.E.–34 C.E.). In the gospels, his name is preserved in
the name of his capital city, Caesarea Philippi (Mark 8:27; and
Matt 16:13). Personally, he plays no role in the story of Jesus in
the gospels or on screen.

Herod Antipas became Tetrarch over Galilee (4 B.C.E.–39 C.E.).
There Jesus came of age and began his public ministry. John conducted his baptizing ministry in the Jordan River Valley, including Perea. This is the Herod responsible for beheading John
(Mark 6:14–29; Matt 14:1–12; Luke 9:7–9) and for interrogating

Jesus in Jerusalem (Luke 23:6–17; also Luke 13:31–33). Therefore, those films—and there are many—that portray either, or both, of these episodes include a characterization of Herod Antipas.

Archelaus became Ethnarch over Samaria and Judea (4 B.C.E.–6 C.E.). In the gospels, he is mentioned only in passing (Matt 2:22). His rule was short-lived, although lasting some nine years until he was deposed. *The Greatest Story Ever Told* (1965) does more with the political transition after the death of Herod the Great than any other film, but it deletes Archelaus from its story of the succession. In Archelaus' place, the Romans appointed a series of prefects, or procurators, who governed directly for Rome (6–66 C.E.) until the outbreak of war between the Jews and Rome (66–70 C.E.).

After Archelaus was deposed, the most famous of the Roman governors who ruled Judea and neighboring territories was, of course, Pontius Pilate (26–36 C.E.). Because of his association with Jesus, Pilate plays a prominent role in the trial of Jesus in all four gospels—and in most Jesus films.

Therefore, political jurisdiction in Palestine during the ministry of Jesus (ca. 30 C.E.) was divided three ways: Philip governed over the Northeast Territory; Herod Antipas over Galilee and Perea; and Pontius Pilate over Samaria and Judea.

Under this Roman umbrella, and answerable to the Roman prefect, was the most powerful representative of historic Israel— the high priest. The holder of this office presided over the temple in Jerusalem and, usually, over the Sanhedrin, the chief judicial body of the Jews. The best known high priest under Roman rule was Joseph Caiaphas (18–36 C.E.), son-in-law to Annas, a predecessor as high priest (6–15 C.E.)

All four gospels present the high priest as involving himself in the final proceedings against Jesus, albeit in various ways. Two gospels present these proceedings as a trial (Mark 14:53–64, 15:1, and Matt 26:57–68, 27:1–2). The other two present the proceedings against Jesus as either an inquiry (Luke 22:54–23:1) or as a conversation (John 18:12–14, 19–24). Several films omit any depiction of an appearance between Jesus and the high priest.

The gospel of Luke represents the gospel most intentional about correlating its narrative with the political arrangements of Jesus' day (especially 1:5, 2:1–2, 3:1–3). Understandably, the film based on this gospel—the film named *Jesus* (1979)—offers viewers characterizations of Herod Antipas, Pontius Pilate, Caiaphas, and Annas.

THE LAST TEMPTATION OF CHRIST: Jesus (Willem Dafoe) holds the cup of wine at the Last Supper. Source: Larry Edmunds Book Shop

CHAPTER TWELVE

Martin Scorsese
The Last Temptation of Christ

In the early 1970s, a young American filmmaker by the name of Martin Scorsese unknowingly took his first step toward making his own contribution to the ever-lengthening tradition of Jesus-story films. A friend, actress Barbara Hershey, gave him to read a copy of the Nikos Kazantzakis novel *The Last Temptation of Christ*, first published in Greek in 1955, and in English translation in 1960.

Kazantzakis himself was best known to the American public through the 1964 Hollywood adaptation of his 1946 novel *Zorba the Greek*. Born and finally buried on Crete, Kazantzakis' entire life was something of a pilgrimage from Christ to Christ—from the Christ to whom he had been introduced through the Greek Orthodox culture and Roman Catholic schooling of his youth to the Christ about whom he wrote during his later years. Geographically, the author's pilgrimage carried him from Greece to France, from Germany and Austria to the Soviet Union. Intellectually and spiritually, his pilgrimage took him from the philosophers Henri Bergson and Friedrich Nietzsche to the religion founders Moses and the Buddha, from the Christian Saint Francis to the Marxist theorist Lenin.

Kazantzakis' novel *The Last Temptation of Christ*, written toward the end of his life, represented an admittedly fictional account of the life of Jesus but also an autobiographical statement. Kazantzakis was using the Jesus story to continue working through his own lifelong *struggle between the flesh and the spirit*—a struggle he considered to be the universal human struggle. Accordingly, the "last temptation" experienced by Jesus on the cross was the temptation with which he had been confronted throughout his life. He had been tempted to embrace the domestic—or fleshly—pleasures of wife and home, of sex and children, and thereby to abandon his spiritual call to sacrifice himself on the cross. Although Jesus has an extended vision of the good life while hanging on the cross, he dies with the glorious knowledge that he had been faithful unto death—*flesh* had been transcended by *spirit*.

By his own admission, Scorsese did not finish reading the novel *The Last Temptation of Christ* for six years.[1] By then he had distinguished himself as the director of such films as *Mean Streets* (1973), *Alice Doesn't Live Here Anymore* (1974), and *Taxi Driver* (1976). He would soon receive acclaim for *Raging Bull* (1980), the story of prizefighter Jake LaMotta.

179

Having completed the Kazantzakis book, Scorsese—an Italian from New York City who had at one time considered becoming a Roman Catholic priest—immediately committed himself to transforming the literary work into film. Twelve more years passed before Kazantzakis' novel became Scorsese's film *The Last Temptation of Christ* (1988).[2]

With a commitment to make the film, Scorsese asked Paul Schrader—a collaborator from other productions—to write the screenplay. Paramount Pictures agreed to provide backing. The project received a budget of some twelve million dollars. Both Morocco and Israel were scouted for possible locations, but Israel was selected. Casting proceeded, and—reportedly—Aidan Quinn received the title role.

With shooting scheduled to begin, protest began. As had been the case a decade earlier prior to the telecast of Zeffirelli's *Jesus of Nazareth*, protest expressed itself in the form of a letter-writing campaign. The campaign was initiated by The National Federation for Decency, under the leadership of the Rev. Donald Wildmon, based in Tupelo, Mississippi. Just as General Motors had responded to the objections to Zeffirelli's film by dropping its television sponsorship, so Paramount gave in to the pressure and dropped its support of Scorsese's project.[3] Early in 1984, therefore, Scorsese found himself looking for another backer.

Finally in 1987, Universal Pictures agreed to provide support for the project, but with changes in the cast, with shooting in Morocco instead of Israel, and with a budget reduced to six million dollars. Scorsese later looked back with humor on the impact of a reduced budget. Instead of twelve stunt men, he could afford only five during the cleansing of the temple sequences in Jerusalem. The same five play the Roman soldiers who surround the temple, the locals who riot when Jesus starts throwing things, the Levites who come down the stairs, and the five men who go up the stairs against the Levites—that is, against themselves.[4]

A general release date for the film was set for September, 1988. As the date neared, public pressure against the film began to build anew. In an age of cable television and televangelism, the film became the object of scorn and the basis of threats in many fundamentalist circles. Central to the charge of blasphemy against the production was its expected portrayal of Jesus as one who resisted messiahship and engaged in various sex acts.

Universal Pictures had taken measures to anticipate and to counter negative publicity. The studio hired a consultant who had experience promoting films to the evangelical Christian market. After several months, in June 1988, Tim Penland the consultant resigned.[5] He expressed an ongoing concern that the script was blasphemous and claimed that Universal had failed to keep its promise to provide a pre-view screening for such Christian leaders as Bill Bright, the leader of Campus Crusade for Christ and the force behind the film *Jesus* (1979). A representative of Universal denied Penland's charges, claiming that Penland had resigned over an old version of the script and that the screening had been postponed, not cancelled, because production was running behind schedule.

The studio proceeded to open the film in selected cities in August so that the movie-going public could judge the film for themselves. The cities chosen for initial screenings included New York, Washington, Chicago, Minneapolis, Seattle, San Francisco, and Los Angeles. Along the way not-so-funny things happened, as reported in the press. The furor was featured in a *Time* cover story and a spread in *Newsweek* (both dated 15 August 1988).

Jerry Falwell, the founder of the by-then-disbanded Moral Majority, called for boycotts of all theaters showing the film and all products of MCA, Universal's parent company. Bill Bright reportedly offered to raise ten million dollars to reimburse Universal if the studio would render unto him for destruction all copies of the Scorsese film. Furthermore, the issue of anti-Semitism that had bedeviled the entire history of the cinematic Jesus surfaced in new ways. As the Chairman of MCA, Lew Wasserman—himself a Jew—was accused by Christians of fomenting anti-Jewish hatred by allowing the distribution of the film. Demonstrators appeared near his home; and an airplane flew overhead with a banner:

WASSERMAN FANS JEW HATRED W/TEMPTATION

When released amidst controversy in theaters, *Last Temptation* bore credits that identified Harry Ufland as executive producer and Barbara de Fina as producer, Paul Schrader as scriptwriter and Scorsese as director. The exotic musical score was written by Peter Gabriel, the popular songwriter and performer. Willem Dafoe, who had recently faced the Viet Cong in the Academy Award winning *Platoon* (1986), now confronted the Romans in the featured role of Jesus. The supporting cast included Harvey Keitel as Judas and Barbara Hershey as Mary Magdalene. The latter two actors were veterans of earlier Scorsese films; and Hershey, as we have noted, was the person who introduced Scorsese to the Kazantzakis novel many years earlier.[6]

THE FILM: An Acknowledged Work of Fiction

The Jesus-story films of the 1950s, epitomized by *Ben-Hur* (1959), were based on works of literary fiction. These so-called Roman/Christian epics represented the alternative—not harmonizing—trajectory of

Jesus films. Their Jesus stories were adapted from modern works of fiction; and they subordinated the story of Jesus to other stories set in the Graeco-Roman world.

The Last Temptation of Christ, with a screening time of nearly three hours, also projects the grandeur and sweep characteristic of a cinematic epic.[7] The Scorsese film takes its place in the alternative trajectory of Jesus films because it too is mediated by a novel. Only now the Jesus story is not subordinated to another story as it had been in *Ben Hur*. As in the Kazantzakis novel, so in the film, the Jesus story stands front and center; and its characterization of Jesus at many points challenges traditional ecclesiastical understandings of what he was all about.

The movie *The Last Temptation* immediately establishes its relationship to the novel. Even before the title frame these words scroll upward across the screen:

The dual substance of Christ—
the yearning so human,
so superhuman,
of man to attain God . . .
has always been a deep
inscrutable mystery to me.
My principle [sic] anguish and source
of all my joys and sorrows
from my youth onward
has been the incessant,
merciless battle between the spirit and the flesh ,. . .
and my soul is the arena where these two armies
have clashed and met.
       —Nikos Kazantzakis from the book "The Last Temptation of Christ"

These words are followed by a disclaimer that was—no doubt— added by Scorsese, before the release of the film, in response to the charges that the movie was a blasphemous distortion of the biblical story:

This film is not based on the Gospels but upon the fictional exploration of the eternal spiritual conflict.

These latter words, of course, disclaim too much. As with the Kazantzakis novel, the film is based in some sense on the story of Jesus as narrated in the four gospels. In order for the viewer to understand the relationship between the film and the biblical narrative, it may be helpful to consider *the underlying structure of the film as falling into three parts*. Parts one and three represent the highly imaginative framework within which Scorsese—following Kazantzakis—has placed the more recognizable gospel-based story of Jesus.

Part one of the film begins with Jesus' laboring in his carpentry shop. Jesus appears as a cross-maker for the Romans. His friend Judas, a participant in the zealot movement, chastises him for being a Roman collaborator. Subsequent scenes include: Jesus' participation in the crucifixion of a fellow Jew; his visit to his childhood friend Mary Magdalene at her place of prostitution, where he waits his turn, for conversation and not for sex; his withdrawal to a desert monastery in search of spiritual guidance; and his reconciliation with Judas, who joins him instead of assassinating him.

Part two of the film includes stories drawn from the gospels, but with a dramatic rearrangement of sequence and sometimes surrealistic staging. Jesus rescues the woman taken in adultery (John) identified as Mary Magdalene the prostitute. He delivers a modest Sermon on the Mount (Matt). He calls disciples (four gospels). All this occurs before his baptism by John (synoptics) and his three-fold testing in the wilderness by Satan (Matt and Luke). Thereafter, Jesus visits the house of Mary and Martha (Luke), who are presented as sisters of Lazarus (John). Subsequent episodes include exorcisms and healings (four gospels), attendance at a wedding where he changes water into wine (John), rejection at his hometown of Nazareth (synoptics), and the raising of Lazarus from the dead (John).

When Jesus arrives at Jerusalem, he cleanses the temple (four gospels). Having withdrawn from the city, he enters riding side- saddle on an ass and cleanses the temple a second time. He commemorates the Last Supper with his disciples, including the women, and prepares them for his death with words over the bread and wine (synoptics). Having cajoled Judas into betraying him, Jesus is arrested in Gethsemane and denied by Peter (four gospels). Jesus appears briefly, and even somewhat casually, with Pontius Pilate who finally gives him over for scourging, mockery, and crucifixion by Roman soldiers (four gospels). Jesus makes his way to Golgotha—a place of three thousand skulls, according to Pilate—bearing only the crosspiece, alone and without assistance (John). Therefore, neither Caiaphas, nor Barabbas, nor Simon of Cyrene appears as Jesus takes his final and fatal walk. On the cross, Jesus utters three of the seven last words: "Father, forgive . . . " (Luke); "Father, why have you forsaken me?" (Mark and Matt); and "It is accomplished" (John).

Part three of the film, the controversial vision sequence, takes place between the second and third of Jesus' last words from the cross. Here Jesus experiences his "last temptation" to forsake his call unto death for a domestic life with wife and child. Jesus imagines that he has been rescued from the cross by the intervention of God through his guardian angel; and he considers what his life could have been like. In his mind, he marries Mary Magdalene. She dies. Then he marries Mary the sister of Lazarus, and enjoys life with Mary, her sister Martha, and their children. Along the way, Jesus confronts Saul—now Paul—who proclaims Jesus to be the resurrected messiah; and, as Jerusalem burns, Jesus has deathbed conversations with his surviving disciples, including Peter and Judas. But at the end, Jesus' guardian angel is disclosed to have been Satan, and his imagining to have been just imagining. He awakens to the harsh reality of the cross and dies—faithful to the end, with a smile on his lips and a crown of thorns on his head.

The Last Temptation of Christ ends with the death of Jesus on the cross. The Scorsese film takes its place alongside those Jesus films that conclude with his crucifixion and death, not his resurrection—at least not resurrection in the sense of the dead Jesus' having been resurrected to new life by God. Among the films concluding with the cross are the silent Jesus harmony From the Manger to the Cross (1912) and the alternative musicals Jesus Christ Superstar and Godspell (both 1973).

However, The Last Temptation goes beyond these films by explicitly raising for the viewer the possibility that belief in the resurrection of Jesus had been fabricated. The claim that belief in the resurrection of Jesus represented a conscious fraud is as old as the quest of the historical Jesus. In the eighteenth century, H. S. Reimarus claimed that the disciples not only stole Jesus' body from the tomb but concocted the notion that he had been resurrected by God.[8] In The Last Temptation, the hint of fraud arises through the surprising and provocative role in this Jesus story of Saul—the one also called Paul.

Saul makes his initial appearances during the narration of the ministry of Jesus. He appears as a zealot who maintains contact with Judas and assassinates a recovering Lazarus in order to destroy the evidence of Jesus' life-giving power. Saul, now Paul the apostle, later appears during the imagined vision sequence while Jesus hangs on the cross. Having been spared the crucifixion, Jesus stops to hear Paul as the latter preaches his "gospel" of crucifixion and resurrection. Jesus calls Paul's message a lie and denies that he had been the messiah, crucified and resurrected. To this Paul responds: "I created the truth out of what people needed and what they believed. If I have to crucify you to save them, then I'll crucify you. If I have to resurrect you, then I'll do that too. . . . "

Although this exchange between Paul and Jesus may be negated in the mind of the viewer by the realization that it occurs only in the imagination of the dying Jesus, the question of the relationship between the Christ of faith as preached by the church and the Jesus of history has been raised more explicitly here than in any other Jesus story film to this time.

The Last Temptation of Christ also represents another film in which the roles of Mary Magdalene and Judas have been greatly expanded and sharpened. Mary, of course, embodies that temptation of the domestic and carnal life, which Jesus resists. By contrast, Judas represents the zealot option of those willing to bear arms for God's sake against Rome. It is in the ongoing interaction between them and Jesus that the person and mission of Jesus receives clarification and definition.

THE PORTRAYAL: Jesus as Reluctant Messiah

Near the beginning of the film, when Judas challenges Jesus to forsake his collaboration with the Romans as a cross-maker, Jesus declares that the messiah will not come through force. After Jesus has withdrawn into the desert seeking direction from the community of monks, Judas confronts Jesus, having been commissioned by his fellow zealots to assassinate him. Instead, Judas joins Jesus—but with a vow to kill Jesus if he deviates from the path of revolution.

Much later, after the initial cleansing of the temple, Jesus secretly shares with Judas—whom Jesus calls his "strongest friend"—the reason for their visit to Jerusalem. Jesus informs the incredulous Judas, who still thinks in terms of armed revolt, that he has come to die as a sacrificial lamb in fulfillment of scripture and that he must die on the cross willingly. Still later, after the entry into the city on the ass and another disturbance in the temple where he refuses to signal rebellion against Rome, Jesus reminds Judas of his vow to kill him if he deviates from the path of revolution. Therefore, Judas betrays Jesus in response to Jesus' own urging that he, Judas, simply keep his word as his friend.

During one of the last conversations between Judas and Jesus, Judas offers a succinct and helpful summary of the *three stages* of Jesus' ministry as portrayed in the film. Judas says to Jesus: " . . . first it's love . . . then the axe . . . now you have to die." The love-stage had begun in the desert among the monks. The axe-stage began after Jesus' baptism by John and his succession of John. The death-stage begins after his arrival in Jerusalem and a night-vision in which the prophet Isaiah appeared and pointed him to the "suffering-servant" passage in Isaiah 53:

> He has borne our faults;
>> he was wounded for our transgressions;
>>> yet he opened not his mouth.
> Despised and rejected by all,
>> he went forward without resisting,
>>> like a lamb led to the slaughter.

Throughout the three stages of Jesus' ministry, his message shuttles back and forth somewhat confusedly on at least *three levels* of discourse and meaning.

On *one level*, Jesus' speech resembles that of the synoptic gospels, although he prefers the expression "the world of God" rather than "the kingdom of God." His ministry opens with the Sermon on the Mount in which he proclaims blessings, woes, and the only parable from the gospels cited in the film: the parable of the sower. Jesus interprets the parable allegorically with the sower representing Jesus himself and the seed representing love. Much of Jesus' synoptic-like talk suggests a kind of realized eschatology, God as present, without his using "kingdom" language. On one occasion, for example, Jesus declares: "God is here . . . I am here." But Jesus does sound, however briefly, a futuristic note when he affirms: "After the cross, I will return to judge the quick and the dead." These words recall not a saying of Jesus from the gospels but the familiar Apostles' Creed.

So, on a *second level*, Jesus' speech recalls the theological categories of the later church which no doubt Kazantzakis and Scorsese learned through their Greek Orthodox and Roman Catholic heritages respectively. Conversations between Jesus and others often revolve around the ideas of body and soul, heaven and hell. When Jesus tells Mary Magdalene that God will save her soul, she responds by urging Jesus to save her body. After the death of the head of the monastery, it is said that his soul has gone to heaven and the body has finished its work.

The dualism between flesh and spirit announced on the screen, at the outset of the film, in the words of Kazantzakis, obviously finds its way into the fabric of the film itself. It is also this traditional dualism that probably accounts for the blatant sexism that jars the viewer of a film made in the 1980s. The temptation of the domestic life with a woman represents Satan's way. The rejection of such temptation becomes God's way. Indeed, Satan as serpent speaks with a throaty woman's voice; and, Satan, deceptively, in the form of the young girl as guardian angel—in the fantasy sequence—consoles Jesus upon the death of Mary Magdalene: "There's only one woman in the world; one woman, with many faces. This one falls; the next one rises." On at least one occasion, Jesus refers to Satan as Lucifer—a name for the devil from ecclesiastical Latin meaning "Light-bringer."

But Jesus' speech also operates on a *third level*. On this level, his words reflect the philosophical perspective adopted by Kazantzakis, especially under the influence of Henri Bergson. Jesus' comments are sometimes avowedly pantheistic. For example, he can tell Judas that when he gazes into the eye of an ant he sees the face of God.

Although Jesus must share screen time with Judas, and less so with Mary Magdalene, *The Last Temptation* remains very much the story of Jesus. More specifically, Kazantzakis' *The Last Temptation* becomes very much Scorsese's story of Jesus. Scorsese dares to do what no other filmmaker has done with Jesus, at least not with such sustained intensity. He dares to get into the mind of Jesus so that the viewer not only hears Jesus speak, not only hears Jesus speak about what he has been thinking, but actually hears Jesus think! Scorsese uses the cinematic technique of voice-over to open up the interior life of Jesus even as he had, in an earlier film, opened up the interior lives of such characters as Travis Bickel in *Taxi Driver.* Therefore, through its exploration of Jesus' inner self, *The Last Temptation* portrays Jesus as a reluctant messiah—ultimately, a reluctant suffering-servant messiah.

Scorsese introduces Jesus to the viewer with an overhead shot—another of his signature techniques—showing Jesus lying on the ground, and then with a closeup of his face. The voice-over: "The feeling begins, very tender, very loving . . . and the pain starts . . . claws slip beneath the skin, and tear their way up . . . just before they reach my eyes they dig in and I remember. . . . " The scene shifts to the carpentry shop. The camera shows Jesus as he fashions a wooden cross. And the voice-over continues: "First I fasted for three months . . . I whipped myself before I went to sleep. Then the pain came back, then the voices . . . They called me by name . . . JESUS." Throughout the film, Jesus' inner struggle becomes known to the viewer. The questioning. The equivocation. The anxiety. The fear. But also, finally, understanding and conviction! At first uncertain whether Satan or God was speaking to him, Jesus finally comes to the realization that God speaks—and requires him to die. Yet even on the cross, the domestic life still beckons him.

Nonetheless, unlike the Jesus of *Superstar,* this Jesus does eventually understand *why* he must die. Interestingly, in spite of vast differences between the films, both Zeffirelli's *Jesus of Nazareth* and Scorsese's *The Last Temptation* interpret Jesus' messiahship in terms of the servant passage in Isaiah 53.

The Last Temptation of Christ moves directly, and swiftly, from Jesus' arrest in Gethsemane to Jesus' trial before the Roman governor, Pontius Pilate—omitting any depiction of his appearance before the Jewish authorities. The charges against Jesus are assumed to be political as Pilate, in a low-key manner, refers to Jesus as "King of the Jews," or "another Jewish politician." Pilate pronounces Jesus to be more dangerous than the zealots while Jesus here—as in most Jesus films—suggests that his kingdom is not of this world. But Jesus continues by referring to the great image in Daniel 2 and identifies himself as the stone that smashed the image—that is, smashed Rome. After a severe whipping by Roman soldiers, Jesus is put on public display. But no crowds cry out for his blood. No Barabbas has a part. The film appears to avoid some of the gospel-based anti-Semitic tendencies in other Jesus films.

However, some of Jesus' declarations in the temple to the Jewish leaders are rather astounding: "I'm throwing away the law. I have a new law and a new hope . . . I'm the end of the old law and the beginning of the new one . . . I'm the saint of blasphemy . . . God is not an Israelite." And during the fantasy sequence, which includes the burning of Jerusalem by the Romans in 70 c.e., Judas upbraids Jesus for not having kept their bargain by Jesus' having forsaken the cross. Judas says: "He was going to be the new covenant; now there's no more Israel. . . . " Therefore, the film ironically anticipates the time when Judaism and Christianity go their separate ways.

THE RESPONSE: **Protest Born Again**

When *The Last Temptation of Christ*, R-rating, opened in selected cities on August 12, 1988, a pattern appeared that would repeat itself in other towns with theater operators willing to show the film. Local police often separated those attending from resident protesters who held Bibles and placards, and who prayed and sang. The protests had an impact. The protests and the continued calls for boycott reduced the number of theaters in which the film was screened nationwide and possibly made the film into a box office loser, at least according to the leaders of the boycott.[9] Even when the film was released in video format the next summer, there were video chains and local stores that refused to stock it.[10]

Throughout the days of controversy, Scorsese submitted himself to a number of self-explanatory and promotional interviews.[11] Among the interviewers was Richard Corliss for *Film Comment* (September-October 1988):

Corliss: Is this Jesus God, or a man who thinks he's God?

Soresese: He's God. He's not deluded. I think Kazantzakis thought that, I think the movie says that, and I know that I believe that . . .

Here in his conversation with Richard Corliss, and elsewhere, Scorsese identified himself as a believer and defended the film as an expression of faith, however unconventional its portrayal of Jesus. Scorsese discovered an admirer in Corliss who, in a brief review in *Time* (15 August 1988), had concluded that "those willing to accompany Scorsese on his dangerous ride through the Gospels may believe that he has created his masterpiece."

Apart from Corliss, few reviewers in the secular press thought that Scorsese had created a masterpiece. Although Janet Maslin in *The New York Times* (12 August 1988) spoke about "this handsome film" and described Scorsese as "perhaps the most innately religious of major American filmmakers," few others responded with such appreciation. By way of sharp contrast, Terrence Rafferty in *The New Yorker* (5 September 1988) reduced the movie to the level of "an honorable mistake." John Simon in the *National Review* (16 September 1988) dismissed it as "a perfectly excruciating 156-minute film." Both Rafferty and Simon made it quite clear that their negative judgments were based on *cinematic*, not *religious*, criteria.

Among the weaknesses of the film noted by many reviewers was the dialogue, both written and spoken. The turn of phrase and inflection often seemed to be that heard on the streets of New York City—at least the words on the lips of Jesus, his followers, and their Jewish contemporaries. For intentional contrast, the Romans and Satan spoke with British accents.

Willem Dafoe's performance as Jesus generally received commendation, but often in cutesy expressions so characteristic of film critics. Terrence Rafferty said, "Willem Dafoe, working hard, plays Jesus about as well as any non-lunatic could." Not to be up-phrased, John Simon observed and asked: "Willem Dafoe, if you like your Jesus as a Zen hippie, is good enough, and very nice-looking, and wouldn't you think that the Son of God would have better teeth?"

The assessment of Scorsese's *The Last Temptation* was perhaps even more negative in the religious press than in the secular. This might have been expected in periodicals representing a conservative, or evangelical, Christian point of view; but it was no less so in liberally inclined Protestant publications. David Neff in an editorial for the evangelical *Christianity Today* (7 October 1988) and James M. Wall in an editorial in the traditionally liberal *The Christian Century* (17–24 August 1988), agreed that the film had failed in its presentation of the Jesus story, but they differed on how it had failed.

Neff considers the film at the obvious level of its deviation from, and distortion of, the New Testament portrayal of Jesus. He documents many of the differences between "the Jesus of history and faith" reported in the gospels and the "symbolic Jesus" created by Kazantzakis and Scorsese in their own images. More substantively, Neff identifies the sharp dualism between the flesh and the spirit—which condemns the flesh but exalts the spirit—as "the most dangerous and most deeply misleading thing about this film." Consequently, as the headline over the editorial declared: "'The Last Temptation' ironically fails in its central purpose—to affirm the humanity of Jesus."

Wall also considered the film a failure at the obvious level of its relation to the New Testament portrayal of Jesus. But, to him, the film fails not because it deviates from the gospels but because it follows the gospels too closely—particularly in its presentation of familiar events in the middle section. He says that the film "presents biblical material with the literal-mindedness of a fundamentalist preacher from Oklahoma." More substantively, Wall condemns the film not for having a dangerous or misleading theological viewpoint but for having *no* theological viewpoint. He declares that

the picture is so utterly lacking any serious theological vision that all the audience hears is a mishmash of words gleaned from popular culture's assumptions about the man called Jesus—references to love, kingdom, power, sin, guilt, anger, forgiveness, not to mention that constant, most oppressive of all forces, the one who makes ultimate demands, God himself.

Wall also complains that the film ended with "no resurrection" so that the headline over his editorial carried double meaning: "'The Last Temptation': A Lifeless Jesus."[12]

In their analysis of *The Last Temptation*, David Neff and James M. Wall each adopted stances that might be expected of the other. Writing for a conservative constituency that expressed protest against a Jesus portrayed too humanly as a sexual being, Neff criticized the film for portraying Jesus as not human enough. Having criticized the film from a liberal viewpoint for being too literal, Wall turned around and objected to its not being literal enough by its omission of the resurrection of Jesus.

Roman Catholic reviewers of Scorsese's film also recognized its *theological* as well as its *artistic* weaknesses. Nonetheless, they were often quick to deny that the film by their fellow Catholic was in any way blasphemous.

In *America* (27 August 1988), Richard A. Blake, S.J. spoke of the production as "this dull, low-budget, pretentious little film" and explored two problematic areas of Christology as presented in the film: the depiction of Jesus as a sexual being, and the presentation of Jesus with a developing awareness of himself and his mission. Blake suggests that anyone taking offense at the notion of Jesus' experiencing sexual temptation often stems as much from that person's own attitude about sex as a reverence for Jesus. Personally, he expressed greater reservation about the way the film dealt with the emerging self-consciousness of Jesus since "the Schrader-Scorsese Christ is not a man heroically searching for His destiny but a tormented, neurotic blunderer who lets circumstances dictate His next step." Like the Protestant James M. Wall, the Catholic Richard A. Blake also observed that "the film suffers cinematically by its own fundamentalistic presentation of the Gospel."[13]

Michael Morris, O.P., wrote about *The Last Temptation* for *American Film* (October 1988). He identified several moments and sayings in the film as being "theological wacko." These included both the intimation that Jesus' self-understanding of himself and his mission not only developed but worked against his divine call and Jesus' self-assertions, implying that he was a sinner. Nonetheless, in considering Scorsese's cinematic portrayal within the overall tradition of Jesus films, Morris concluded:

> More than any other film of its type, Scorsese's 'Last Temptation' measures the magnanimity of Christ's sacrifice in terms of moral choices. This

above all is the value of the film, and for that one can tolerate its theological deficiencies.

In a more popular vein, Father Henry Fehren in *U. S. Catholic* (December 1988), published a loud "Thank You, Martin Scorsese." He thanked Scorsese for daring to portray Jesus as one who was tempted and for reintroducing the notions of temptation and sin for discussion in the church. Fehren did not defend nor critique Scorsese's *The Last Temptation* in terms of particulars; but he did respond to a full-page newspaper advertisement headlined "Public Blasphemy!" taken out by those protesting the film. Fehren responded with a question and an answer: "Who protests money-grabbing, Bible-thumping TV evangelists whose vocal volume increases as their theology decreases, whose sweating, prancing, whooping, and hollering help to cover up their biblical ignorance? They are the blasphemers." The image of the contemporary evangelist conjured up by Fehren's words seems an apt description of Saul—that is, Paul—as portrayed in this Scorsese film about Jesus. Herein, Paul is indeed a huckster on the make.

Although Martin Scorsese and *The Last Temptation* were often defended by Catholic commentators, the film itself did not receive an approval rating from the Catholic Church agency entrusted with evaluating and classifying movies. *The Last Temptation* was given an "O," meaning that the film was judged to be morally offensive.

The Legion of Decency had become the National Catholic Office for Motion Pictures in 1965; and the NCOMP was eventually succeeded in 1980 by the Office for Film and Broadcasting, Department of Communications, the United States Catholic Conference (USCC). Thus, the Catholic Church in this country had not forsaken its long-time commitment to providing moral guidance about films, especially for parents, but without the control it once exercised over filmmaking in this country. The task of evaluating and classifying films continues. The classification system when *The Last Temptation* appeared was built upon the system developed during the decades of the Legion of Decency and the NCOMP. Then the four approval categories were intended to indicate both moral suitability and age appropriateness:

A-I   general patronage
A-II   adults and adolescents
A-III   adults
A-IV   adults, with reservations
O   morally offensive[14]

However, the USCC was succeeded in 2001 by the United States Conference of Catholic Bishops (USCCB), which maintains oversight for the Office of Film and Broadcasting. In 2003, the "A-IV" rating was changed to "L" for "limited adult audience," thereby indicating many Catholics might be troubled by the particular film's content. Shortly after the appearance of Scorsese's *The Last Temptation* (1988), Denys Arcand extended the trajectory of Jesus films with his *Jesus of Montreal* (1989, 1990). This Canadian-produced film received an "R" rating from Hollywood and an "A-IV" rating from the Catholic Church, the equivalent of today's "L."

The Fourteen Stations of the Cross

Both the traditional and the revised passion plays in *Jesus of Montreal* (1989, 1990) use as their framework the so-called Stations of the Cross. The Stations of the Cross represent both a traditional Catholic exercise of Christian piety and the sites where the devotional act is performed.

Central to the devotional act is meditation upon the passion, or suffering of Jesus, at each of the stations erected for that purpose. Each station represents an incident, or stop, along Jesus' way from his condemnation by Pilate to his entombment. The stations, with appropriate carvings or pictures, may be erected within or without a church building; and the worshipper moves pilgrim-like from station to station. The fourteen stations are:

1. Jesus is condemned to death by Pontius Pilate.
2. Jesus is made to carry the cross.
3. Jesus falls for the first time.
4. Jesus meets his mother Mary.
5. Simon of Cyrene is made to carry the cross.
6. Veronica wipes the face of Jesus.
7. Jesus falls for the second time.
8. Jesus speaks to the women of Jerusalem.
9. Jesus falls for the third time.
10. Jesus is stripped and receives gall to drink.
11. Jesus is nailed to the cross.
12. Jesus dies on the cross.
13. The body of Jesus is taken down from the cross.
14. The body of Jesus is laid in the tomb.

JESUS OF MONTREAL: Jesus (Lothaire Bluteau) crucified, with the women beneath the cross (Johanne-Marie Tremblay and Catherine Wilkening).
Source: Film Stills Archive, The Museum of Modern Art

CHAPTER THIRTEEN

1990 | Denys Arcand
Jesus of Montreal

Denys Arcand, a native of Quebec, distinguished himself in the 1970s as a commentator on modern life with a series of controversial socio-political documentaries. He also began making feature films. His 1986 *Le Déclin de l'empire américain* ("The Decline of the American Empire") was nominated for an Academy Award as Best Foreign Language Film. His recent *Les Invasions barbares* ("The Foreign Invasions") not only received a nomination for Best Foreign Language Film for 2003 but an Oscar as well.

His earlier French language *Jésus de Montréal*, with English subtitles, appeared in Canada in 1989 and also received an Academy Award nomination for Best Foreign Language Film. *Jesus of Montreal*, R-rated, was released in the United States with English subtitles in 1990.[1] Arcand both directed and wrote *Jesus of Montreal*, and briefly appears in the film in the role of a judge.[2] Arcand claimed that the idea for the film was sparked by an encounter he had with an actor-friend. The friend explained his having a beard by saying that he was playing the role of Jesus in a passion play staged for tourists at a Roman Catholic basilica, St. Joseph's Oratory, on Mount Royal.[3]

The central character in Arcand's *Jesus of Montreal*, Daniel Coulombe played by Lothaire Bluteau, represents an actor in just such a passion play. Coulombe's antagonist in the film becomes Father Leclerc, the priest responsible for the passion play that has been performed on Mount Royal for decades. Father Leclerc is played by Gilles Pelletier.

Father Leclerc asks Coulombe to rewrite and to restage the traditional passion play, and Coulombe accepts the challenge. He writes a new play and calls together a small company of actors to perform his version of the Jesus story—two male, and two female, in addition to himself. Conflict arises between the company of actors and the church authorities because of the non-traditional nature of the story they narrated and performed. Conflict also arises between the company and the world—Montreal—as Coulombe their leader increasingly internalizes the values of, and acts out, the role of Jesus.

Jesus of Montreal represents still another option in the alternative tradition of Jesus films. Here the ancient story of Jesus is revisualized, but paralleled to—and intersected with—a modern story. The Jesus

195

character in the old story becomes a Christ-figure in the modern world.

Similar to *Jesus Christ Superstar* and *Godspell, Jesus of Montreal* represents a play within a play. But the contemporary setting in those musicals—the Israeli desert for the former, New York City for the latter—simply functioned as frameworks for their imaginative retellings of the Jesus story. For the duration of those musical dramas, the actors no longer had lives in the modern world. Although their participation in the Jesus story may have personally transformed them—as implied by the endings of these films—the viewers were not privileged to see what that transformation subsequently meant in their day-to-day living.

By contrast, in Arcand's film, the viewers see how the actors relate to and interact with each other within their contemporary social environment. Their involvement in the passion play draws them closer to each other and sets them, and Christ, over against their culture. They challenge the worlds of church and state, and of commerce—especially commerce. Very little of contemporary life and popular culture escapes Arcand's satirical commentary. Not the priesthood. Not advertising. Not the entertainment media. Not the pornography industry. Not the court system. Not psychiatry. Not natural science. Not hospitals. Not even the arts, including drama. However, the theater becomes the vehicle for the truth about life and culture in Arcand's film and, presumably, through his film.

Also, *Jesus of Montreal*, like D. W. Griffith's *Intolerance*, parallels the ancient story of Jesus with a later story. Griffith parallels the Judean story with the Modern story of the Boy unjustly accused of murder. But there, the stories intersect in the mind of the viewer, not on the screen where they remain juxtaposed. The Jesus character in the Judean story does not become a Christ-figure in the story set in early twentieth-century America. By contrast, in Arcand's film, the Jesus character in the passion play becomes a Christ-figure in everyday life in late twentieth-century Canada.

As an alternative cinematic approach to the Jesus story, *Jesus of Montreal* bears closest resemblance to another film first released in French, Jules Dassin's *Celui qui doit mourir* (1957), and later in English with dubbing instead of subtitles as *He Who Must Die* (1958).[4] That film—based on a Nikos Kazantzakis novel—also tells how a character chosen to play Jesus in a passion play becomes a Christ-figure in the modern world. There, the setting is a Greek village under Turkish rule. The film narrative shows how the life of Manolios, the shepherd chosen for the Jesus role in the play, becomes Christ-like in his words and deeds—and in his eventual death. In Dassin's film, the viewer never sees the passion play itself enacted by the villager chosen to play

Jesus. However, in Arcand's film, the viewer both sees Coulombe playing Jesus in the passion play and witnesses his transformation into a Christ-figure in the world-at-large.

THE FILM: Montreal and "The Passion on the Mountain"

After Coulombe accepts the invitation by Father Leclerc to rewrite the passion play, he watches a video of the traditional play and undertakes library research for his projected version.

As with the existing play, so Coulombe's version will be staged following the traditional fourteen stations of the cross. Within Catholic liturgical tradition, the fourteen stations represent fourteen incidents that occurred in the experience of Jesus in association with his crucifixion beginning with his condemnation to death by Pontius Pilate and ending with the placement of his body in the tomb. In the film, station one occurs before a statue of Jesus, standing with his hands bound, with an inscription in French on its base: "Jesus Condemned to Death."

Unlike the existing play, Coulombe bases his version of the passion not just on the gospel texts but on what are claimed to be recent historical and archaeological discoveries. In a scene reminiscent of a moment in the Watergate saga *All the President's Men* (1976), when secret information is passed on to investigative news reporters, Coulombe meets in a parking garage with a member of the theology faculty. Coulombe receives from him copies of scholarly articles that allegedly contain new information about what Jesus was really like historically. The viewer later sees pages containing diagrams and pictures related to the practice of crucifixion.[5]

Arcand devotes some twenty to thirty minutes of the film to showing the actors both rehearsing and performing the resulting script. The viewer hears the narration as recited by members of the cast. The viewer moves with the cast and the audience from station to station, at night, with the assistance of a security guard with flashlight. Based on these vignettes, the Jesus story as presented can be at least partially reconstructed; the viewer sees only selected portions, not the entire play.

That story—"the most famous of all"—is introduced with words more characteristic of academic rather than devotional discourse:

> The story of the Jewish prophet Yeshu Ben Panthera, whom we all call Jesus. Historians of the day—Tacitus, Suetonius, Pliny, Flavius Josephus—mention him only in passing. What we know was pieced together by his disciples a century later. Disciples lie; they embellish. We don't know where he was born, or his age when he died. Some say

24, others 50. But we know that on April 7 in year 30 . . . or April 27 in
year 31 . . . or April 3 in year 33 . . . he appeared before the fifth Roman
procurator of Judea . . . Pontius Pilate. [6]

With that cue and the limited cast, Jesus (Coulombe) is brought
before Pilate by two guards (the women). In the midst of a conversation with Jesus, and in response to the urging of an unidentified but
obvious Caiaphas figure (one of the men), Pilate (the other man) does
condemn Jesus to die by crucifixion before the blindfolded statue of
the condemned Jesus.

The spoken narrative marking the transition from the first to the
second station of the cross also begins with a statement about the limited evidence for the historical Jesus but continues with emphasis on
Jesus' Jewishness, an explanation of his name "Ben Panthera," and
concludes with the recognition of his wonder-working:

> Our knowledge of Jesus is so sketchy some claim he never existed.
> Paradoxically, Jesus wasn't Christian but Jewish. He was circumcised
> and observed Jewish law. The destiny of Israel obsessed him. Like us,
> he thought his historical era was more important than any other. And
> that the end was nigh . . . [7]
>
> . . . The Jews claimed Christ was a false prophet, born of fornication.
> They called him Yeshu ben Panthera 'the son of Panthera.' We've dis-
> covered an order to transfer a soldier from Capernaum in 6 a.d. His
> name was Panthera. . . . [8]
>
> . . . Jesus was also a magician. He was said to have grown up in Egypt,
> the cradle of magic. His miracle were more popular than his sermons.[9]

This concluding identification of Jesus as a magician follows comment about how the ancient worldview differs from the modern
understanding of the universe and how the ancient world was filled
with those who practiced the magical arts—such as Judas the Galilean,
Theudas, and Simon (mentioned in the Book of Acts).

This identification of Jesus as magician transforms this enacted
story of Jesus into more than just a passion play based on the traditional stations of the cross. The actors—presumably at the next station—proceed to act out several of Jesus' "mighty works" from the
gospels. Jesus climbs out of a boat and walks on the water (Mark,
Matt, John) after which Peter tries a similar walk and sinks (Matt).
Jesus then heals an unnamed blind person (any gospel) and raises a
presumably dead person with the words, *"Talitha cumi"* (Mark).
Carrying a basket of bread loaves, Jesus distributes individual loaves
to members of the audience standing about. Many of his words are
taken from the Sermon on the Mount (Matt), and others from the parable of the great banquet (Luke).

This portion of the play ends with a scene based on the familiar conversation between Jesus and his disciples in response to the question: "Who do people say I am?" (synoptics) After the conversation, Jesus stands; and, suddenly, two robed figures take him into custody.

As the audience moves to another station, where Jesus has been secured naked to a post and receives lashes on his back, a lengthy narration begins detailing the history of the practice of crucifixion. Specific examples of mass crucifixions are cited from the time of the Persians through the reign of the Hasmonean King Alexander of Judea, to the Roman period and the quelling of the Spartacus-led slave revolt.

During the narration, Jesus is transferred from the place of flogging to the place of crucifixion. In accordance with acts traditionally associated with separate stations, Jesus is made to carry his cross, stripped of his garments, nailed to the cross, and dies on the cross. The only word uttered by him is an abbreviated: " . . . forsaken . . . " (Mark and Matt). With the charges on a wooden placard hanging by a cord around his neck, Jesus himself hangs on the cross, with his back to the city of Montreal below.

The visual presentation of these acts associated with the crucifixion of Jesus does not attempt to reproduce images from the artistic tradition, but is handled in accordance with the historical knowledge about how the Romans actually crucified people. Jesus bears only the crosspiece, not the upright, to which his arms have already been lashed. Once stripped, he is elevated naked on the cross and positioned with legs contorted in accordance with the diagram of the crucified man seen in the scholarly article given to Coulombe in the parking garage.

The crowds now receive the direction to proceed to the "last station"; and they proceed down steep steps into a large underground, tomb-like space where three of the actors sit in white robes. The somber narration begins with these words:

> He'd been long dead. Five years. Perhaps ten. His disciples had scattered, disappointed, bitter, and desperate. . . .

The extensive action and the dialogue during the last scene involve an acting-out of the origins of belief in the resurrection. There are stylized reminiscences of the gospel accounts, especially the appearance to Mary Magdalene in the garden outside the tomb (John) and the appearance to the two followers on the road to Emmaus (Luke).

Suddenly, a Mary Magdalene-like figure runs toward the camera announcing: "I have seen him!" The immediate disbelief of the two who receive the report is overcome when they encounter a robed figure with a face hidden from the viewer. The mysterious figure breaks bread with the two. Then one says: "Lord. It's you. It's you." The narration begins anew and becomes an exhortation addressed directly to those gathered:

> Slowly people were convinced. He had changed. No one recognized him at first. But they all came to believe he was there. Except Peter and John, the disciples were new: Paul, the Pharisee, Barnaby, Stephen, and foreigners, Greeks and Romans. They were ready to die for their convictions. They too were beheaded, crucified, stoned. They were steadfast: Jesus awaited them in his kingdom. They personified hope, the most irrational and unyielding of emotions. Mysterious hope that makes life bearable lost in a bewildering universe. You must find your own path to salvation. No one can help you. Look to yourself with humility and courage. . . .

The play concludes when the four members of the cast mount the steps leading out of the underground chamber and bid farewell:

> Love one another. Seek salvation within yourselves. Peace be with you and your spirit.

Amidst applause, the Jesus figure descends the steps and joins the rest of the cast. Now it is clear: the figure taken to be the resurrected Jesus was not Jesus! In the film, at least in part, belief in the resurrection arose as the result of mistaken identity.

This mistaken identity explanation for the resurrection finds some biblical support in John 20:11–18. In this passage, Mary Magdalene—outside the empty tomb—meets a man whom she takes to be the gardener only to learn that it was actually the resurrected Jesus. According to the mistaken identity view, Mary was initially correct. It was the gardener, not Jesus! This explanation for resurrection belief has, on occasion, expressed itself in life-of-Jesus literature.[10]

Little wonder that Father Leclerc and his fellow priests were disturbed by, and eventually banned, this new version of "The Passion on the Mountain." Daniel Coulombe had used historical findings to "demythologize" the entire Jesus story.[11]

Jesus' conception and birth had been demythologized. He was not the offspring of a virgin, but the illegitimate son of a Roman soldier. Jesus' miracle-working had been demythologized. Although he was a magician within the context of the ancient world, his miraculous deeds—even as observed—are claimed to be incomprehensible to the modern mind. Jesus' death on the cross has been demythologized. With no one attributing saving significance to the crucifixion, he dies more as martyr than savior. Jesus' resurrection has been demythologized. Although the way in which all came to believe in the resurrection remains vague, that belief originated—in part—from the mistaken identity of someone thought to be Jesus. Therefore, in *Jesus of Montreal*, the old, old story of Jesus has been subjected to a historical critique.

Furthermore, *Jesus of Montreal*—like *The Last Temptation of Christ*—sharply raises the question of the relationship between the Christ of faith and the Jesus of history. In Scorsese's film, we see Paul the Apostle defending his "gospel" by putting forth the argument that belief in Jesus as the Christ is justified on the basis of how it meets human need, even if that belief rests on a lie. Here, in *Jesus of Montreal*, Father Leclerc articulates a similar point of view in an encounter with Daniel Coulombe in the church. Leclerc—holding up a discarded walking stick—says that those who come to church in their brokenness "don't care about the latest archaeological finds in the Middle East. They want to hear that Jesus loves them and awaits them." But the Jesus of Leclerc and the church differs markedly from the Jesus portrayed in the passion play, and increasingly embodied by Coulombe in the midst of his own disciples.

THE PORTRAYAL: Jesus as Prophet and Apocalyptist

In *Jesus of Montreal*, the questions of Jesus' identity and message are addressed in two scenes in the passion play itself: the scene of Jesus before Pontius Pilate; and the scene involving a conversation between Jesus and his disciples.

In the one scene, Jesus stands before Pontius Pilate. Pilate sits in judgment with a book open before him. Jesus refuses to answer directly the question of whether he is a member of a sect or just another prophet. But he does respond to Pilate's claim that he has been preaching about the founding of a kingdom with the explanation that such a kingdom is not of this earth (John 18:36). Jesus also denies that he has been preaching against Caesar and Rome. When asked further by Pilate about his teaching, Jesus answers succinctly: "Greater love hath no man than to offer his life for friends" (John 15:13). This human love is repeatedly underscored as the center of Jesus' message in the play, in the narration accompanying the play, and elsewhere in the film.

In the other scene, Jesus sits with his followers and asks: "Who do people say I am?" Then: "Who do you say I am?" Presumably it is Peter who replies: "You're Christ, the Messiah." But then Jesus explicitly tells them not to call him the Christ because, "I am the Son of man" (a declaration implied, not stated, in the gospels). Although Jesus then refuses to say by whose authority he is here, his self-designation as "the Son of man" seems appropriate for one whose message centers in human love among all people.

However, the Jesus of Montreal—both as the figure played by

Coulombe in the play and as embodied by Coulombe in the urban world around him—also functions as a social critic. But Arcand's Jesus differs somewhat from the Jesus whom he most closely resembles, the Jesus in Pier Paolo Pasolini's *The Gospel According to St. Matthew.*

In that film, Jesus also delivered a social critique. Both openly and more subtly, he pronounced judgment on the Jewish religious leaders of his own day and was used by Pasolini to subvert the authority of the Catholic hierarchy in our day. Pasolini's Jesus was a prophet—but prophet and sage. Similarly, Arcand's Jesus stands over against, and condemns, the values and pretensions of religious leaders and the society around him—ancient and modern. But this Jesus of Montreal, through Coulombe, also calls down judgment on the whole modern world. Arcand's Jesus is also a prophet—but prophet and apocalyptist.

The introductory line of the narration that introduces the passion play identifies Jesus as "the Jewish prophet Yeshu Ben Panthera." The forthrightness of Jesus' prophetic activity is reflected in the words of the Caiaphas-figure and those of Pilate at the very outset of the play. Although Pilate considers Jesus to be "harmless," the Jewish leader calls him "a menace." Caiaphas documents for Pilate the social disruption created by Jesus' activity.

JESUS OF MONTREAL: Daniel Coulombe (Lothaire Bluteau), the actor who plays Jesus in the passion play, talks with Father LeClerc (Gilles Pelletier). Source: Cinema Collectors

Allegedly, Jesus has spoken against the priests. He has attracted crowds. He has disciples. He has caused riots in the temple. Pilate gives in to Caiaphas' request that Jesus be crucified in accordance with Caiaphas' observation that "it's better to sacrifice one man" (John 11:50). Pontius Pilate then presents his own catalog of Jesus' enemies. Jesus has been disowned by his family. He has been cast out by his townspeople at Nazareth. He has outraged the Jerusalem establishment. Jesus' own explanation for his having aroused such opposition is quite simple: "They hate me for no reason. Simply because I revealed the truth" (John 18:37).

In *Jesus of Montreal,* the experience of Coulombe as Jesus in the play parallels and then merges with his experiences in the sanctimonious world of the church and the fashionable world of late twentieth- century Montreal.

The parallels between the story of Coulombe and the traditional story of Jesus are obvious to those who know the latter. Even before the title frame and opening credits, there is an allusion to the relationship between John the Baptist and Jesus in the interaction between a fellow actor and Coulombe. After the credits, Coulombe mirrors the gospel account of Jesus' call of disciples. He makes his way from a soup kitchen, to a recording studio, to a filmed scientific presentation of the creation and demise of the universe, to an outdoor shooting of an advertisement promoting perfume in order to find actors for his play. The performance of "The Passion on the Mountain" leads to a scene involving an audition for a singing and dancing beer commercial in which Coulombe acts out the cleansing of the temple. For love's sake, he overturns tables, smashes videotaping hardware, and drives out the modern moneychangers. The popularity of the passion play leads to another scene in which Coulombe, in a skyscraper, is confronted by the temptation of inheriting the kingdoms of the world, or at least the city, if he would only sign a contract with an agent.

As Coulombe's story unfolds, it becomes obvious that his experience with Father Leclerc and the priestly authorities in Montreal parallels the experience of Jesus with the priestly authorities in Jerusalem. In another glimpse of the passion play in progress, the film shows Coulombe as Jesus mouthing words adapted from the "woes" against hypocrites in the gospels (Matthew 23). As he speaks, he looks directly into the faces of Father Leclerc and two other priests identified by their clerical collars. Nothing subtle here: "Do not be called Rabbi, or Reverend Father, or Your Grace, or Your Eminence. . . . "

Coulombe's story and the Jesus story merge at the point of his final, but unauthorized, performance as Jesus. The priests summon the police to halt the play. A riot breaks out as the spectators object. In the midst of the ensuing disturbance, Coulombe suffers what will prove to be a fatal injury. The cross of Jesus becomes the cross of Coulombe.

Coulombe/Jesus does not die instantly. Rushed to the hospital, unconscious in an ambulance, he is accompanied by the two women in his acting company. That same evening, he leaves the hospital— with the women—and descends an escalator to a subway platform. Now he and Jesus are one. Having reflected on his being forsaken and the unhappiness of his contemporaries, Coulombe/Jesus begins verbalizing an adaptation of the so-called apocalyptic discourse in Mark 13. The adaptation incorporates many of the key phrases from this declaration of doom, including:

> All these buildings, these great structures, not a stone will be left some day . . . the abomination of desolation . . . If anyone says, 'Christ is here,' or 'There,' believe it not . . . The powers of the heavens shall be shaken. You know not when. Not the day, nor the hour. You know not when the judgment. Watch!

The discourse on the lips of Jesus in Mark 13 appears to be apocalyptic in the sense of a proclamation about the end-of-the-world and the second-coming of Jesus in glory as "the Son of man." But, as with other dimensions of Jesus' story, so here on the lips of Coulombe/ Jesus the traditional expectation of a so-called second-coming has been demythologized. The reference in Mark 13 to a future coming of "the Son of man" has here been omitted, so that the discourse becomes a prophetic condemnation of this urbanized and commercialized world. As disclosed in the passion play, the "Jesus of Montreal" was "the Son of man" not in the future but in the present, in terms of his basic humanity as one who loves and suffers.

Arcand's film works on many levels. There is about it much playfulness as well as seriousness. Now, two aspects of the film become clearer. First, just before this apocalyptic speech from Mark 13, Coulombe/Jesus had been treated for his injury at St. Mark's hospital. When he collapses on the subway platform after his speech, he does not return to St. Mark's but is taken to a Jewish hospital. Therefore, as a Jesus figure he will die among his own, even as he will—in some sense—experience resurrection.

Secondly, the speech in Mark 13 as adapted here contains allusions to the apocalyptic Book of Daniel. Coulombe's first name, Daniel, in Hebrew means, "My judge [is] God." Daniel represents an appropriate name for a prophet whose final declaration relies on Mark 13 and the Book of Daniel.

However, beyond the name "Daniel," there seems to be little of God in the film. The film has about it a sense of the God-forsakenness, or the absurdity, of modern life. Lines from Dostoyevsky's *The Brothers Karamazov* and the soliloquy from *Hamlet* make their appearance in the film. Suicide receives more than passing comment. Given the absence of transcendent meaning in life, seemingly the best one can do is to follow Coulombe/Jesus in creating a small, caring, interdependent community. But even here, the film leaves viewers with uncertainty about the future of the community without the physical presence of its leader.

However, Arcand tells his story about Jesus of Montreal by using a framing device that retains some continuity with church tradition. Near the beginning, of the film, two young women are shown singing Pergolisi's "Stabat Mater" ("Sorrowful Mother") as they practice with the choir in the basilica accompanied by the organ. At the conclusion of the film, the same two women are singing the same piece in the subway using a boom box.

THE RESPONSE: A Prize Winner

Denys Arcand's *Jesus of Montreal* won the Jury Prize at the Cannes International Film Festival in 1989. The film also won the Golden Globe as Best Foreign Language Film and, as already noted, was also nominated for an Academy Award as Best Foreign Language Film. The film received twelve 1989 Genie awards, the Canadian counterpart to the Oscars, including the awards for Best Picture, Best Director, and Best Actor.

Writing for *Macleans,* the Canadian weekly magazine (29 May 1989 and 18 September 1989), Brian D. Johnson lavished praise on the film, both upon its showing at Cannes and its commercial release in Canada. He concludes his review on the latter occasion with appropriate recognition of how the Jesus story has been used:

> Arcand reinterprets Christianity with agnostic wit. Although the director penetrates to the heart of the Gospel, his hero remains a secular savior. Even for an audience of hardened skeptics, 'Jesus' suggests that where religion has failed, art may yet offer salvation.

Jesus of Montreal opened in New York City at the Paris theater in May, 1990. Its distribution in the United States was limited primarily to larger urban areas, academic communities, and art movie houses. The reviews in much of the secular press were generally positive, although New York film critics seemed less enthusiastic than their counterparts elsewhere.

Caryn James of *The New York Times* (25 May 1990) states what, in her judgment, was required of the film and evaluates it accordingly: "Mr. Arcand needs to balance satire and seriousness with the greatest daring and delicacy. And for the first hour, before it gives in to leaden, self-conscious Christ imagery, 'Jesus of Montreal' succeeds." In other words, the film was most successful while focusing on the Jesus story and the initial presentation of the passion play and less successful as more parallels were drawn between the life of Jesus and the life of

Daniel Coulombe. She found the correlation between Jesus' cleansing
of the temple and Coulombe's disruption of the audition for a beer
commercial, for example, to be "exceptionally unconvincing."

Georgia Brown of the *Village Voice* (29 May 1990) expresses a similar reservation about the temple scene and an even stronger reservation about the "secular miracle Arcand has in store for the resurrection
. . . " She concludes:

> Coulombe's contemporary Jesus isn't my cup of tea. A cool, rational,
> flagrantly sane director, Arcand doesn't mean his hero to be a savior,
> but merely a dedicated, and thwarted, man of the theater who unpre-
> tentiously carries his integrity with him. Rather than representing the
> new Jesus, he's just one more martyr to capitalist crassness. Praising a
> film as a liberal's vision of grace probably sounds fatally dismissive,
> though I mean it half as a compliment.

Sheila Benson, in the *Los Angeles Times* (1 June 1990) and Jay Carr,
in *The Boston Globe* (8 June 1990), wrote more appreciative reviews.
Neither commented negatively on the parody of the temple cleansing.
Each liked the treatment of the resurrection, Benson calling it "ingen-
ious," Carr "bold." Both observe that the descent of Daniel Coulombe
into the subway, between his crucifixion and resurrection, suggests a
descent into hell. However, Carr views the film and its message as
overly simplistic:

> "Jesus of Montreal" is filled with powerful images and affecting acting,
> but betrays little awareness of the problematic nature of human exis-
> tence. Morally, it's all black and white—in short, the very sort of depic-
> tion of the Stations of the Cross it maintains needs enlarging.

Reviews of Arcand's *Jesus of Montreal* often included comparisons
with Scorsese's *The Last Temptation of Christ* that had so recently created a public stir. Thomas O'Brien, a contributor and former film critic
of the Catholic publication *Commonweal*, used the release of Arcand's
film in this country as an occasion for an article in the Jesuit journal
America (26 May 1990). O'Brien considered *Jesus of Montreal* not only
in relation to *Last Temptation* and other biblical epics but in relation to
recent movies—such as *Agnes of God* (1985)—that had treated
Catholicism and Christianity so badly by what he calls their "ironic
assault on religion." Although O'Brien does not ignore the *cinematic*
and *theological* failings of either *Jesus of Montreal* or *Last Temptation*, he
does admire both films for what he calls their "intelligent sincerity."
The cinematic portrayals of Jesus by Denys Arcand and Martin
Scorsese, he writes,

> . . . are valuable precisely because of their lack of dogma: Gone are the
> clichés of sentimental reverence and the (now) equally foregone clichés

of irony. They at least make people think about eternal issues in ways that hyper-pious films do not encourage or that the contemporary cult of irony forbids.

This explanation by Thomas O'Brien of what he meant by the phrase "intelligent sincerity" serves as an appropriate way to conclude our review of those films from the first century of Jesus at the movies. O'Brien has correctly observed that much of the first hundred years of Jesus in film reflected a concern for dogma, reverence, and piety. He holds forth the hope that the Jesus films of the next century will challenge viewers to think about, and come to terms with, eternal issues.

The Jesus-story films that have already appeared at the beginning of the second hundred years may not have fulfilled in every respect the hope that viewers be challenged. But already there has been considerable diversity. The made-for-television *The Miracle Maker* (2000), extends the alternative trajectory by bringing an animated Jesus to the screen.[12] Another film named *Jesus* (2000), also made-for-television, has taken its place in the harmonizing trajectory.[13] *The Gospel of John* (2003) has become another representative of the alternative approach that bases its script on a single gospel.[14] And, more recently, the film with which we conclude our film-by-film survey, became a cinematic and cultural event that has challenged many to reflect on the meaning of the Jesus story: Mel Gibson's *The Passion of the Christ* (2004).

THE PASSION: Jesus (James Caviezel). Source: Jerry Ohlinger's Movie
Material Store

CHAPTER FOURTEEN

2004 | Mel Gibson
The Passion of the Christ

In the more than one hundred years of Jesus cinema, probably no maker of a Jesus film has used the medium to express his own theological vision and religious commitment with greater verve than Mel Gibson. This statement does not detract from the contributions of Gibson's predecessors in the ever-lengthening tradition of Jesus-story films, but it does underscore how *The Passion of the Christ* was very much Gibson's movie from its conceptualization, through its production and varied controversies, to its public release in the United States, on Ash Wednesday, February 25, 2004.[1]

Gibson's own company, Icon Productions, produced the film. He financed the movie with twenty-five million dollars of his own money. He co-wrote the screenplay with Benedict Fitzgerald. He directed the film. He invited a fellow Catholic, James Caviezel, to play Jesus. Gibson did everything short of starring in the film himself, although his hand does appear on-screen holding the nail hammered through Jesus' left hand into the cross. Perhaps Gibson's participation in the crucifixion dramatizes his claim that the responsibility for Jesus' death falls upon all, including himself.

Gibson, of course, had put himself in the position to make *The Passion* through a distinguished and varied career first as an actor and in recent years as a filmmaker. His acting career carried him from playing the hero in the *Mad Max* movies (1979, 1981, 1885) to a role as a not-quite-right cop in the *Lethal Weapon* series (1987, 1989, 1992, 1998). But it was *Braveheart* (1995), the story of the thirteenth-century Scottish rebel William Wallace, that clearly established Gibson as a major force in Hollywood. *Braveheart* film garnered five Oscars, including Best Picture. Gibson received an Oscar for Best Director, and he starred in the title role. Nonetheless, Gibson was unable to secure the services of a major studio to distribute *The Passion*. Newmarket Films signed on as the distributor for the movie.

A crisis in Gibson's life led him to make *The Passion*—a crisis to which he often referred in the months before the film's release. Some years earlier, in his mid-thirties, already having tasted fame and fortune, Gibson experienced a despair and desperation that led him to rediscover the Catholicism on which he had been nurtured in his early years. As Gibson described it, in various words, he had used the

209

wounds of Jesus to heal his own wounds. Thus he had been meditating on the passion of the Christ for twelve years. The Catholicism he rediscovered was traditionalist Catholicism, a sectarian movement that emerged in the 1960s in reaction against many of the reforms of Vatican II and in favor of retaining such Catholic traditions as the Latin mass.

The making of *The Passion* involved Gibson's traveling to Italy, in the summer of 2002, to prepare for the production of the film. He selected Matera, in southern Italy, as the site for filming the exterior scenes. Forty years earlier Pier Paolo Pasolini had also used this location for shooting *The Gospel According to St, Matthew* (1964, 1966). The interior scenes of *The Passion* were filmed in Rome at the Cinecittà Studios.[2]

With the exception of James Caviezel as Jesus, the cast consisted primarily of European actors largely unknown to an American audience: Mattia Sbragia, an Italian, as Caiaphas; Hristo Naumov Shopov, a Bulgarian, as Pontius Pilate; and Maia Morgenstern, a Romanian, as Mary the mother of Jesus. A more familiar face, Monica Bellucci from *The Matrix Reloaded* (2003) and *The Matrix Revolutions* (2003), was chosen to play Mary Magdalene. The casting call for five hundred or so extras went out in September. According to the locals, the three main complaints of the extras—during the five-week shoot in Matera—pertained to low temperatures, lunch consisting of only one sandwich and one drink, and toilets at too great a distance.

That Mel Gibson was preparing to make a Jesus film began to come to public notice in the summer of 2002.[3] Among the announced details were the film's working title, *The Passion*, and the intention to have the players speak in the ancient languages of Latin and Aramaic, without benefit of subtitles. Along the way, of course, the title was extended to *The Passion of the Christ* and subtitles were added. Gibson's decision to use Latin, not Greek, can be viewed as one of the ways he "Catholicized" his Jesus story. Latin became the liturgical language of the Roman Catholic Church whereas Greek had been the international language of the eastern Mediterranean and the original language of the New Testament documents.

That *The Passion* engendered considerable public controversy even before its public release should have surprised no one.[4] A persistent concern associated with Jesus films has been their possible reflection of anti-Semitic themes. As we have seen, filmmakers over the years have adopted various strategies to deflect the charge, or avoid the substance, of anti-Semitism.[5]

Historically, the passion narratives in the gospels and the passion plays based on the gospels contributed to the creation and perpetuation of an anti-Semitism that considered Jews collectively responsible for the death of Jesus. In 1965, at Vatican II, the Roman Catholic Church repudiated this notion; and the United States Bishops, in 1988, issued guidelines for dramatizing the passion.

Thus Gibson's film, *The Passion*, by its very title and focus, called attention to itself and invited careful scrutiny by those committed to guarding against public expressions of anti-Semitism. Concern began to be expressed about how the film would portray the Jewish leaders and Jewish crowds and whether the film would include the words on the lips of the crowd gathered before Pilate: "His blood be on us and on our children" (Matt 27:25). At the center of the public disputation were the Anti-Defamation League, its leader Abraham Foxman, and a group of nine scholars—Catholic and Jewish—with longstanding interest in promoting Christian-Jewish understanding.[6]

Gibson himself seemed caught between the historic association of the passion story with anti-Semitism and his own association with traditionalist Catholicism that had resisted many of the reforms of Vatican II. He reached out for support to those who might find congenial his cinematic Jesus story with its concentration on the suffering and death of Jesus. For them special advance screenings were arranged.

The Gospel According to St. Matthew (1964, 1966) had been dedicated to Pope John XXIII. *Jesus of Nazareth* (1977) received effusive praise from Pope Paul VI the week before its television premier. Reports were published that Pope John Paul II had also seen an advance screening of *The Passion* and seemingly approved the film with the enigmatic words, "It is as it was."[7] But there were denials about the accuracy of the reports. What remained for the film was, at last, an opportunity for the general public to see what Mel Gibson had wrought.

THE FILM: Two Hours of Pain that Seem Like Twelve

Mel Gibson's two-hour film focuses on the last twelve hours of Jesus' life as narrated in the four canonical gospels (Mark 14-15; Matthew 26-27; Luke 22-23; and John 18-19). These passion narratives represent that segment of the Jesus story where all four gospels are in closest agreement—at least in terms of sequence of main events. However, even here, the four gospels offer varying perspectives and often provide different details of Jesus' last hours.

In spite of Gibson's repeated claims about the film's adherence to the gospel texts, often expressed in terms of historical accuracy, he as the director and as co-author of the screenplay had to make decisions throughout the filmmaking process. He had to decide what to include, what to omit, what to add, and how to visualize. This is indeed Gibson's movie, his version of the passion, his view of the Christ.

Among the influences that have shaped Gibson's cinematic retelling of the passion are traditional devotional practices of Roman Catholicism. First, Gibson structures his film around the fourteen Stations of the Cross, which are also presupposed by the passion play within *Jesus of Montreal* (1989, 1990). Second, he is influenced by the praying of the Rosary and the five Sorrowful Mysteries, which include Jesus' agony in the garden, his scourging at the pillar, his being crowned with thorns, his carrying the cross, and his crucifixion. Finally, he is influenced by the Good Friday meditations on the seven Last Words of Jesus from the cross, all of which are included in *The Passion*.

Mel Gibson also acknowledges his dependence upon the mystical visions of Anne Catherine Emmerich, an Augustinian nun (1774–1824), whose experiences appeared in print in 1833. Available in English under the title *The Dolorous Passion of Our Lord Jesus Christ*, this imaginative work contains words and scenes that find their way into the movie script.[8] More than this, Emmerich's account of Jesus' last hours reflects a strong sense of Satanic presence and demonic influence, especially among and upon the Jews collectively; and she spares no words in describing in gory detail the tortured sufferings of Jesus. Nonetheless, whatever other influences may have played upon him, Gibson follows the principal story line that runs through the four canonical passion narratives. Thus his movie extends the harmonizing trajectory of Jesus-story films.

The Passion of the Christ opens in the eerie, even ghoulish, darkness with the camera peering through gnarled tree branches that partially conceal and partially disclose an unidentified figure standing and praying audibly with his back to the viewer. The place is Gethsemane; the man, Jesus. During this beginning sequence that culminates in Jesus' arrest, the camera periodically cuts away to a full moon overhead—lunar shots rivaled in the cinematic tradition only in *The Greatest Story Ever Told* (1965). Whereas the enormous moon in the latter film lights Jesus' arduous climb up the mount of temptation where he meets Satan in the form of a "dark hermit," here in *The Passion* the moon serves as an important chronological marker in the development of the story. The full moon indicates that the events transpiring occur on Passover eve, that the last supper presupposed by these events was a Passover meal, and that the coming crucifixion of Jesus will occur on Passover day.

Already Gibson has had to choose between the Passover dating of these events as reported in the synoptic gospels in contradistinction to the dating in John, where Jesus reportedly dies on the day of preparation of the Passover (John 19:14). A minor point, one might say, except that later in the movie, Caiaphas and his fellow priests follow the cross-bearing Jesus out to Golgotha on the day of Passover itself, hanging around and awaiting his death. Such activities by priests on a holy festival day would have been historically improbable.

That Gibson has placed all narrative events in the film on Passover is confirmed in a scene, not from the gospels. As Jesus is being taken into custody, Mary his mother—in the presence of Mary Magdalene—is suddenly awakened by words from the Passover liturgy: "Why is this night different from every other night?" The two women are soon joined by the disciple John, who has fled the scene of Jesus' arrest.

This opening sequence in Gethsemane incorporates several episodes from the gospels: how Peter, James, and John fall asleep (synoptics); a collateral scene whereby Judas seeks out priests to betray Jesus (synoptics) for thirty pieces of silver (Matt); Jesus' boldness in identifying himself to the arresting party (John) followed by Judas' kiss (synoptics); the severing of the ear of the high priest's servant by an armed disciple (four gospels) identified by the names Malchus and Peter (John); and Jesus' subsequent healing of the ear (Luke).

This opening sequence in Gethsemane also introduces the viewer to a character whose haunting presence will recur throughout the film. Satan, played by Rosalinda Celentano, appears in the guise of an androgynous figure with a telling gaze. As Jesus prays in the garden, Satan tempts him by asking: "Do you really believe one man can carry this burden? . . . " (based on Emmerich). When Satan sends a snake slithering toward Jesus, Jesus stomps the creature underfoot (allusion to Gen 3:15)—with a sudden move likely to evoke, if not applause, a startled gasp from the viewers.

After this dramatic beginning, Gibson unfolds his Jesus story by having Jesus taken under heavy guard that very evening to the Jewish authorities. The physical battering of Jesus begins, in a scene without any basis in the gospels. Knocked over a wall, in a scene that antici-pates the suicide of Judas and features a fleeting glimpse of a were-wolf-like phantasm, Jesus arrives before the authorities with one eye swollen shut from his abuse. Here Caiaphas and the Sanhedrin con-duct what appear to be formal legal proceedings.

The four gospels have again forced Gibson to make a narrative decision. Although all four have Jesus taken to the Jewish authorities that evening, only Mark and Matthew report proceedings that resem-ble a formal trial. Only Mark, as in the film, has Jesus respond to the high priest's question about his messiahship with a forthright acknowledgement: "I am. . . . " (Mark 14:62). Caiaphas tears his clothes, followed by cries of blasphemy and the declaration that Jesus deserves to die. Cries of dissent from some present at the proceedings (Nicodemus? Joseph of Arimathea?) indicate one way that Gibson avoids the impression that all present were against Jesus and thus guards against possible anti-Semitism. Within this setting of Jesus' trial before the Sanhedrin, the viewers experience the first of many flashbacks that provide glimpses into Jesus' life prior to his passion.

During Jesus' trial before the Jewish authorities and its immediate aftermath, tight editing enables the viewers to observe different centers of action with varied relations to the gospel texts. These include: the two Marys and John moving among the crowds (not in the gospels); Peter's threefold denial (four gospels); Jesus' hanging by chains in a subterranean cell while his mother presses her face to the floor above (Emmerich); and the initial appearances of Pilate and his nettlesome wife (the latter based on Matt). Here too are: Judas' failed attempt to return the blood-money (Matt); his being hounded by young lads who are transformed—at least in his imagination—into devils (based on Emmerich); and his suicide by hanging the next morning (Matt).

After his appearance before Caiaphas and the Jewish authorities, Jesus is taken by them before the Roman governor Pontius Pilate. When urged to take care of him under their own law, the Jewish leaders declare that it is unlawful for them to condemn a man to death (only John 18:31). Among the political charges they subsequently bring against Jesus are his inciting the people, his forbidding payment of tribute to Rome, and his claiming to be the messiah, a king (specifically Luke 13:2).

Now the tussle between the Jewish leaders and the Roman governor begins. Caiaphas and his fellow priest become the bullies urging Jesus' crucifixion. Pilate becomes the bullied, a characterization of Pilate contradicted by what is known about his ruthlessness in non-biblical sources (Josephus) and even in the gospels (Luke 13:1-5). The claims of anti-Judaism or anti-Semitism against *The Passion* lie primarily in the negative characterization of the Jewish authorities, on the one hand, and the sensitivity of Pontius Pilate and his wife, on the other. Support for these claims also stems from the way Satan seemingly holds sway over those Jews seeking Jesus' death (see John 8:44)

Pilate takes Jesus into his private chamber where they exchange, in the midst of their conversation, two of the most frequently cited sayings in Jesus cinema: Jesus' declaration: "My kingdom is not of this world" (John 18:36); and Pilate's question: "What is truth?" (John 18:38). Pilate publicly declares that he has found no fault in Jesus. He tries to avoid sending Jesus to the cross by referring Jesus as a Galilean to Herod Antipas for judgment (only Luke). When Herod too finds no fault in Jesus, Pilate turns to the stated custom by which he releases a prisoner annually at Passover: Jesus or Barabbas? By public demand, Barabbas is released (four gospels). Caiaphas immediately urges that Jesus be crucified, but Pilate refuses and delivers him over to Roman soldiers with the stated intention of having Jesus given a proper scourging before being released.

The cinematic characterizations of Herod and Barabbas as buffoons, each in his own distinctive way, provide comic relief before Jesus' calculated torture really commences. The persona of Herod recalls his portrayal in both film versions of *Jesus Christ Superstar* (1973 and 2000). However, neither the staged musical nor the film includes a Barabbas character.

The torture of Jesus while manacled to a stone pillar, prolonged and graphic, with various instruments, takes its point of departure from words in the passion accounts variously translated as "scourged," "flogged," or "whipped" (Mark 15:15; Matt 27:26; John 19:1). Jesus, as though to say, "Bring it on," declares, "My heart is ready, Father." The camera moves from the gleeful faces of the sadistic Roman legionnaires to the flayed back of Jesus. Mary his mother, Mary Magdalene, and John witness the blows, one by one, that eventually become audibly incalculable. Satan moves among those gathered carrying in her arms a deformed baby, perhaps a parody of the relationship between Mary and her son.

When Jesus is unleashed from the whipping post, the camera work and music transform the scene into a macabre ballet as he is dragged away leaving a trail through his own blood. Then Pilate's wife suddenly appears. In a sympathetic gesture, she offers towels to the Marys, with which they wipe up the blood gathered in pools on the pavement (from Emmerich). Meanwhile the soldiers force a crown of thorns onto Jesus' head, put a reed in his hand, and mock him as "king of the Jews" (four gospels).

Returned to Pilate, Jesus must still be dealt with. In a rare moment in Jesus cinema, the viewers hear Jesus presented to the crowds with the familiar Latin phrase, "Ecce homo" (John 19:5). When Pilate reminds Jesus that he as governor has the power to release or to crucify, Jesus informs Pilate that his power as governor comes from above and the greater sin belongs to the one who delivered him over to him, namely Caiaphas (John 19:10-11). Subsequently, Pilate washes his hands of the matter (Matt). He orders Abednader the centurion to do with Jesus as his antagonists wish. To the cross Jesus goes.

The assembled execution party heads toward Golgotha, the place of crucifixion outside the city walls. Jesus carries the entire cross—a Latin cross—while the two other condemned men bear only the crosspieces. Mary the mother, Mary Magdalene, and John dash through side streets and alleys trying to get through to see Jesus. There is a touching moment when Jesus and his mother make eye contact and another when she finally advances to his side saying, "I'm here" (similar moment in Emmerich). Jesus responds with words that find their basis in the Book of Revelation: "See, I make all things new" (21:5). A young woman also steps forward to offer Jesus water and helps him wipe his face (a moment recalling the post-gospel tradition of Veronica that becomes one of the Stations of the Cross).

Jesus falls repeatedly (many more than the three falls included in the traditional Stations of the Cross, but consistent with Emmerich). Jesus' abuse by the soldiers continues as they whip him virtually every step of the way. Finally, a hulk of a man, Simon of Cyrene, is conscripted by a Roman soldier to assist Jesus in carrying the cross. Again Gibson has made a decision in relation to the gospel narratives. The assistance of Simon appears in the three synoptic gospels, not John (another episode that becomes a Station of the Cross). In the film, Simon encourages Jesus with the words, "Almost there." Gibson's sympathetic development of this character—called "Jew" by one of the Roman soldiers—becomes another way that Gibson defends himself against the accusation of his being anti-Jewish.

On Golgotha, the Roman soldiers undertake the wretched task of fixing Jesus to the cross. Once raised into place, the image of Jesus fixed to the cross recalls more the iconographic tradition of Catholic crucifixes than the historical verisimilitude reflected in recent Jesus-story films such as *The Last Temptation of Christ* (1988) and *Jesus of Montreal* (1989, 1990). In the latter films, Jesus has been stripped naked, his body contorted, and the arms secured with nails through the wrists or lashed with ropes.

Certainly it cannot be said that Gibson was simply trying to create a pretty picture. The attack of the bird that plucks out the eye of the unrepentant victim on the adjacent cross captures the documented horror of crucifixion as a means of execution. However, Gibson does not follow the iconographic tradition of posting on the cross the letters INRI (for the Latin, "Jesus of Nazareth King of the Jews"). Neither does he follow the gospel-based tradition of rendering the charge against Jesus in the three languages of Hebrew, Latin, and Greek (John 19:20). The plaque in this film contains Hebrew and Latin, but not Greek.

The harmonizing nature of the film is evident in its inclusion of all seven of Jesus' words on the cross as presented in the four gospels (Luke 23:34; Luke 23:43; John 19:26-27; John 19:28; Mark 15:34 = Matt 27:46; John 19:30; and Luke 23:46). Caiaphas and his fellow priests continue to mock Jesus. When Jesus utters his first word, "Father forgive them . . . ," the penitent victim on the neighboring cross tells Caiaphas, "He prays for you" (not in gospels). This is another of Gibson's gestures that mitigates against the claim that Jews remain responsible for the death of Jesus.

Jesus' own blood, of course, continues to flow. When Mary the mother kisses Jesus' feet, blood is smeared on her mouth and face. After the soldiers break the legs of Jesus' crucified companions and one of them pierces Jesus side with a spear, blood and water spurt forth all over the soldier (based on John). No Roman soldier beneath the cross (contrary to the synoptics) confesses that the Jesus is the Son of God (Mark and Matt) or innocent (Luke).

When Jesus dies, heaven sheds one gigantic tear and the earth quakes. But not even Mel Gibson can one-up Cecil B. DeMille, whose earthquake in *The King of Kings* (1927) momentarily turns that film into a disaster movie. Nonetheless, the shaking of the foundations in the Gibson film does not simply split the curtain of the temple (synoptics) but the temple itself. In a brilliant overhead shot, with the camera pulling away, Satan looks heavenward and cries out in defiance and defeat in response to what has transpired this day, seemingly from the depths of Golgotha, perhaps from the very pit of hell.

Jesus' body is removed from the cross with the assistance of two Roman solders and a priest (Joseph of Arimathea?). The inclusion of the soldiers and priest in this scene suggests that Romans and Jews, anonymous to the viewer, are capable of tender mercies. Mary cradles Jesus in her arms in the traditional pose of the *Pietá* and stares into the camera, and thus at the viewers, with a benumbed and grieving stare. The passion of the Christ has ended. So does the film, shortly thereafter, with only the slightest but unmistakable recognition that the passion heralds a beginning.

Scholarly lives of Jesus inescapably deal with historical issues related to the passion narratives. In recent years, two important works by Roman Catholic scholars have focused specifically on the passion narratives themselves: Raymond Brown, *The Death of the Messiah* (1994); and John Dominic Crossan, *Who Killed Jesus?* (1995). Although different in many ways, both works demonstrate how difficult it is to move from the textual evidence to historical conclusions.

THE PORTRAYAL: Jesus as Blood Sacrifice

The Passion of the Christ opens with words from Isaiah 53 spread across the screen:

He was wounded for our transgressions,
  he was crushed for our iniquities;
    by his wounds we are healed.

Gibson clearly believes that Jesus' passion occurs in fulfillment of this passage. Jesus himself embodies the vicarious role of the "suffering servant." Interestingly, two other films—two very different films—also explicitly identify Jesus as the "suffering servant" by having characters on the screen cite words from Isaiah 53.

In *Jesus of Nazareth* (1977), as Jesus hangs on the cross, Nicodemus—one of the good guys—gazes upon him and audibly utters to himself words from Isaiah 53, "He was despised and rejected by men . . . ." In *The Last Temptation* (1988), in an intimate conversation with his faithful compatriot Judas, Jesus shares a vision of the prophet Isaiah who had pointed to a scroll containing words from Isaiah 53, "He has borne our faults . . . ." In these two films, Jesus' obedience to his Father's will unto death seem to be a full and sufficient sacrifice. But in *The Passion*, the greater the physical pain, the more blood shed, the greater the sacrifice, so it appears. Jesus' prolonged battering transforms him into a bloody sacrifice—a blood sacrifice.[9]

Like the authors of the four gospels themselves, filmmakers Franco Zeffirelli and Martin Scorsese place the death of Jesus within the broader context of his life. Unlike *Jesus of Nazareth* and *The Last Temptation*, *The Passion* focuses narrowly on the final hours of Jesus life. However, Gibson also places Jesus' death within the context of Jesus' life, both through dialogue among the participants in the events of those last hours and, more especially, through the use of flashbacks. These flashbacks cut into the narrative at appropriate moments thereby suggesting that the flashbacks may represent Jesus' memories triggered by current happenings.

When Jesus arrives at the site of his trial before the Jewish leaders, a carpenter appears working in wood. The initial flashback involves Jesus' crafting a table and playfully interacting with Mary his mother (created out of the reference to Jesus as a carpenter, Mark 6:3).

After Peter denies Jesus, another flashback shows Peter promising to remain faithful (synoptics). After Jesus' interminable scourging and the two Marys receiving towels to wipe up his blood, a flashback shows Jesus washing the disciples feet at the last supper and promising that the Father will send a "Helper" (the Paraclete, or Spirit) to teach them (John). While Roman soldiers mock Jesus as king, another flashback shows Jesus delivering the adulterous woman from her accusers (John). The film script identifies Mary Magdalene as this woman (although this identification comes from church tradition, not the gospel texts).

When Jesus is returned to Pilate, just before Pilate washes his hands of any responsibility, a flashback to the last supper shows the disciples washing their hands in preparation for the meal. After Jesus has been delivered over for crucifixion and exits the city gate bearing the cross in humiliation, a flashback recalls Jesus' so-called triumphant entry into the city on an ass earlier that same week (four gospels). As previously noted, Jesus repeatedly falls as he makes his way toward the place of execution. As Mary rushes to her son's side, another flashback recalls a moment when she picked up Jesus after a fall as a young child (not in the gospels).

Jesus arrives atop Golgotha with the assistance and encouragement of Simon of Cyrene. This mount occasions a flashback to the mount on which gave Jesus gave admonitions to love enemies and to pray for persecutors (specifically Matt). As the crucifixion proceeds, flashbacks occur at briefer intervals. Most have as their setting the last supper. Jesus speaks of himself as the good shepherd who lays down his life for the sheep (John). Breaking bread, Jesus declares the bread to be his body (synoptics). He notes that greater love has no one than to lay down his life for his friends (John). He commands his followers to love one another as he has loved them (John). He again speaks about himself as the way, the truth, and the life and observes that no one comes to the Father except through him (John). Pouring wine, he declares this to be his blood of the new covenant (synoptics).

The dialogue throughout the film also establishes a broader context for the passion. It discloses that Jesus in the eyes of his contemporaries is a Galilean from Nazareth. Jesus is the son of a carpenter, although Joseph is neither mentioned by name nor seen. He is a beggar, a prophet, and a practitioner of magic who heals the sick and casts out devils. He also claimed to be the bread of life who invited his hearers to eat his flesh and drink his blood. And Jesus spoke about destroying the temple and rebuilding it in three days.

How does Gibson's placement of Jesus' death within the framework of his life enlarge upon the portrayal we see of Jesus on the screen as a blood sacrifice? Very little, if for no other reason that whatever words are spoken by him or about him are drowned in the flood of bloody images that fill the screen. We learn that he was, in the eyes of his antagonists, a healer and exorcist, and in the ears of his disciples an advocate of love and forgiveness. To those who witness the events of the last twelve hours of his life, he is simply a willing victim.

Although Gibson harmonizes the four passion narratives and can use an occasional saying from the synoptics in the flashbacks, the gospel of John provides him with the theological framework for his Jesus story and serves as the backbone for his narrative. In the film, Jesus is credited with three of the seven "I am" sayings through which Jesus in John identifies himself as the one from God: "I am the bread of life" (John 6:35); "I am the good shepherd" (John 10:11); "I am the way, and the truth, and the life" (John 14:6). Based on the film, no viewer would learn that the three synoptic writers of Matthew, Mark, and Luke consider the parable to be Jesus' most characteristic form of speech and that Jesus' overriding message was not about himself but about "the kingdom of God." Indeed, Jesus' one mention of "kingdom" in the film comes from the fourth gospel when he says to Pilate, "My kingdom is not of this world" (John 18:36).

Gibson's preference for the gospel of John is understandable given, among other factors, his conviction that the gospel represents an eyewitness account. In the film, John himself does witness the passion, front and center, alongside Mary the mother and Mary Magdalene.

RESPONSE: A Hollywood Phenomenon

On Ash Wednesday, February 25, 2004, Mel Gibson's *The Passion of the Christ*, opened in 3,006 theaters on 4,643 screens, with an "R" classification for "graphic violence."[10] Seemingly, few theater managers and few moviegoers chose to give up this Jesus film for Lent. *The Passion* had a strong opening at the box office. The film nearly recovered its $25 million production costs by the end of opening day, with receipts of more than $125 million by the conclusion of the first weekend, and earnings of more than $350 million by the end of Easter Sunday. By mid-May, *The Passion* had opened in more than sixty countries around the world and taken its place among the highest grossing movies of all time. This personal film that grew out of Mel Gibson's imagination, labors, and initial financing had become a Hollywood phenomenon on a global scale.[11]

The shrewd marketing of *The Passion* prior to its release had ensured its financial success.[12] Icon Productions and New Market Films had created core support for this very traditional Catholic portrayal of Jesus among evangelical Protestants. Advance screenings were held in mega-churches before selected audiences; and church leaders became convinced that the film afforded unparalleled Easter time opportunities for bringing people to Christ. *Passion* packs that included a DVD containing film trailers, interviews with Mel Gibson and James Caviezel, and tips and resources for incorporating the film into the outreach program of churches were made available. Although the use of a DVD represents new technology, the potential for using commercial films for evangelistic purposes and many of the recent advertising techniques have been around since such early Jesus films as *The Passion Play of Oberammergau* (1898) and, especially, *From the Manger to the Cross* (1912).

However, awareness of *The Passion* had come to extend well beyond church circles. The media—print and electronic, secular and religious—had been tracking *The Passion* for over a year before its release. Gibson himself gave important interviews along the way, with Bill O'Reilly, Fox News (21 January 2003), Raymond Arroyo, EWTN (14

March 2003), and Diane Sawyer, ABC (16 February 2004). *Time,* the weekly news magazine, periodically apprised its readers of the Gibson film with features bearing such headlines as "The Passion of Mel" (27 January 2003) and "The Last Vexation of Mel" (1 September 2003), which imply that the film was all about Mel, not Jesus.

But faces of Jesus did appear on the covers of three widely circulated news magazines accompanied by cover stories whose approaches complemented each other. *Newsweek* (16 February 2004) displayed a photograph of James Caviezel as Jesus. Inside, Jon Meacham considered the question, "Who Really Killed Jesus?" Although not without broader implications for Christian theology and the issue of anti-Semitism, Meacham grounded his response in what can be known historically. Rembrandt's "Head of Christ" adorned the cover of *U. S. News and World Report* (8 March 2004). The article by Jay Tolson and Linda Kulman entitled "The Real Jesus" recounted how the Jewishness of Jesus was obscured and lost by the emerging church only to be rediscovered and emphasized in recent decades by Christian and Jewish scholars. *Time* (12 April 2004) had on its cover the picture of "Christ Carrying the Cross" by Andrea Solario. David Van Biema addressed the question, "Why Did Jesus Die?" He explored ways Christian theology has answered this question with various theories about how Jesus' death effected at-one-ment between God and humans.

Among those who rightly had been apprehensive about *The Passion's* potential for arousing anti-Jewish violence and damaging relations between Christians and Jews was Paula Fredriksen, a biblical scholar at Boston University. However, she came to see that Gibson's film offered "a priceless opportunity for public education" and "a teachable moment."[13] The popular news magazines mentioned above, through their cover stories, certainly actualized the opportunity and seized the moment.

However, *The Passion* itself had been discussed so widely before its public release little else could be said. Indeed, the issues about the film remained much the same: the reinforcement of longstanding Jewish stereotypes and anti-Jewish views; the use of graphic and grotesque violence; and the theology communicated through story and image. Nonetheless, a significant shift had occurred. Before the public opening, there had been only privileged viewers; but now access to the film could be purchased by anyone with the price of a theater ticket. From among these new viewers came many testimonies to the film's experiential power and meaning.

What was the critical assessment of *The Passion*? In the secular media? In the religious media? In Catholic, or Protestant, or Jewish publications?

The spectrum of responses in the secular press can be epitomized by the divergent views of two syndicated political columnists. Cal Thomas in the [Greensboro, NC] *News & Record* (6 August 2003), a privileged viewer himself several months earlier, lavished praise on the film by declaring that it represents "the most beautiful, profound, accurate, disturbing, realistic, and bloody depiction of the well-known story that has ever been filmed." He concluded, "I doubt that a better film about Jesus could be made." By contrast, William Safire also in the [Greensboro, NC] *News & Record* (2 March 2004) called the film "the bloodiest, most brutal example of sustained sadism ever presented on the screen." He concluded, "The richness of Scripture is in its openness to interpretation answering humanity's current spiritual needs. That's where Gibson's medieval version of the suffering of Jesus, reveling in savagery to provoke outrage and cast blame, fails Christian and Jew today."

On their television show, film critics Roger Ebert and Richard Roeper gave *The Passion* "two thumbs way up" and called it "a great film," as reported in *Chicago Sun-Times* (22 February 2004). Other critics were less enthusiastic about *The Passion*, although they recognized that the film expressed Gibson's own faith convictions.

Joe Morgenstern, in *The Wall Street Journal* (27 February 2004), said that he found himself "stunned, then horrified, then defensively benumbed, by a level of violence that would, in another genre, be branded as pornographic." He observed how Gibson himself was "overwhelmed by his obsession with physical suffering to the exclusion of social, political, and metaphysical context." Citing Gibson's body of cinematic work, Morgenstern wondered: "Was the young actor drawn to violent roles by what now seems to be his dark, Manichean vision of life on earth?"

Ty Burr began his review in *The Boston Globe* (24 February 2004) with his conclusions: "It is, when all is said and done, only a movie. A profoundly medieval movie, yes. Brutal almost beyond powers of description, yes. More obsessed with capturing every drop of martyr's blood and sacred gobbet of flesh than any message of Christian love, yes." But Burr continued by suggesting that these traits made the film a "success" because it "seems to be exactly the movie Mel Gibson wanted to make as an abiding profession of his traditionalist Catholic faith."

A. O. Scott, in *The New York Times* (25 February 2004) claimed that "Mr. Gibson has constructed an unnerving and painful spectacle that is also, in the end, a depressing one. It is disheartening to see a film made with evident and abundant religious conviction that is at the same time so utterly lacking in grace."

Perhaps the most devastating and dismissive critique of *The Passion* came from David Denby in *The New Yorker* magazine (1 March 2004).

His review bore the singular title, "NAILED." He affirmed Gibson's freedom "to skip over the incomparable glories of Jesus' temperament and to devote himself, as he does, to Jesus' pain and martyrdom in the last twelve hours of his life." But Denby then declared that he was "equally free to say that the movie Gibson has made from his personal obsessions is a sickening death trip, a grimly unilluminating procession of treachery, beatings, blood and agony—and to say so without indulging in 'anti-Christian sentiment' (Gibson's term for what his critics are spreading)."

The Roman Catholic Church, in the United States, has formally passed judgment on individual films since the earliest decades of cinema. The U. S. Conference of Catholic Bishops (USCCB), through the Office for Film & Broadcasting (OFB), assigned *The Passion* an A-III (adults) rating and posted its official review on its Web site.[14]

The USCCB review referred to the movie as "a deeply personal work of devotional art—a moving Stations of the Cross, so to speak." However, the film did not escape criticism. The observation was made that although "the Passion is the central event in the history of salvation, the 'how' of Christ's death is lingered on at the expense of the 'why.'" Details in the film were cited to support the claim that "the Jewish people are at no time blamed collectively for Jesus' death" and that "Gibson's film suggests that all humanity shares culpability for the crucifixion, a theological stance established by the movie's opening quotation from Isaiah which explains that Christ was 'crushed for our transgressions.'" The review called upon Catholics to remember the teachings of the Vatican II statement *Nostre Aetate*.

The Bishops also authorized the release of a resource book containing documents and excerpts about the Church's teaching pertinent to the issues raised by *The Passion*. The volume bore the title, *The Bible, the Jews, and the Death of Jesus: A Collection of Catholic Documents.*[15]

America, a national Catholic weekly, among its many reports on the Gibson movie, published two reviews of *The Passion*: "Palestinian Braveheart" (23 February 2004) by Lloyd Baugh, S.J. and "Mel O'Drama: *The Passion of the Christ*" (15 March 2004) by Richard Blake, S.J. Baugh considered the Gibson film within the context of the hundred-year tradition of films about Jesus. He undertook a careful comparison between Gibson's *The Passion of the Christ* and Pasolini's *The Gospel According to St. Matthew* and concluded that the Pasolini movie remains "the greatest of the Jesus-films." Blake examined the Gibson film within the context of the often controversial and varied events that took place before the film's release to the general public. Like other critics, he expressed dismay that in the film "Jesus becomes a pure victim of forces determined to destroy him for reasons that remain murky." He also noted that Gibson himself "shows an almost sadomasochistic fascination with physical pain."

As noted, evangelical Protestants in the United States provided much support for *The Passion* as it made its way from filming in Italy to public viewing in this country.

As David Neff, the editor of the evangelical periodical *Christianity Today* (March 2004) explained, "The evangelical enthusiasm . . . may seem a little surprising, in that the movie was shaped from start to finish by a devout Roman Catholic and by an almost medieval Catholic vision." He continued, "But evangelicals have not found that a problem because, overall, the theology of the film articulates very powerful themes that have been important to all classical Christians."[16] Among these themes, of course, is that of Jesus' obedient death as an atoning sacrifice for the sins of humankind.

The enthusiasm for this film among many Protestants becomes apparent when one peruses the *Christianity Today* Web site and discovers the vast amount of information and the number of links related to Gibson and his film. The review of the film posted there and published in the periodical bears the title, "Lethal Suffering: *The Passion* underlines Christ's humanity like no film before," *Christianity Today* (March 2004) by Peter T. Chattaway. The title identified where Chattaway discovered the film's strength. But his enthusiasm for the film had its limits. He observed how "Gibson often goes beyond the text" and "how much artistic license it takes with its source material." He concluded that Gibson's film remained "somewhat unsatisfying" because "it never gets beyond its raw and prolonged depiction of human and demonic cruelty."

The Christian Century, the ecumenical weekly edited by John M. Buchanan and James Wall, included among its written responses to the film a feature article by Matthew Myer Boulton, "The Problem with *The Passion*" (23 March 2004). Boulton immediately repeated what had become a litany among reviewers, "Most moviegoers will never see a more violent movie than this one (that it is rated 'R' and not 'NC-17' is indefensible), with its sadistic soldiers and pools of blood." He explored the two concerns central to the discussion of the film from the outset—"anti-Judaism and excessive violence." He did this to get at the problem of the film, as he saw it, which was theological: "The trouble with *The Passion* is that it proclaims a *Braveheart* Christianity. The Christ of the New Testament, by contrast, has a heart not so much brave as broken—'broken for you,' Christians recall."

Perhaps the expressed concern that *The Passion* would jeopardize Jewish-Christian dialogue was not realized, as evidenced by two articles occasioned by the film. *Tikkun*, a magazine edited by Rabbi Michael Lerner, published an article by Catholic biblical scholar John Dominic Crossan (March-April 2004). Crossan carefully exposed the "roots" of anti-Semitism in the gospels and considered the peculiar problems related to transforming the multiple gospels into a passion play or a passion movie.[17]

Commonweal, a journal edited by lay Catholics, published an issue with this question on the cover, "What's Wrong with *The Passion*?" (7 May 2004). Rabbi Irving Greenberg, president of Jewish Life Network / Steinhardt Foundation and former chair of the United States Holocaust Memorial Council, contributed the lead article. Within the context of his critique of the Gibson film, Greenberg declared that "the failure of the U.S. Bishops to condemn the film was disappointing." He also took issue with particulars in the official USCCB review. Greenberg said, "By calling *The Passion* 'a deeply personal work of devotional art . . . ,' the conference sanitized the film." More pointedly, "The review's statement that 'concerning the issue of anti-Semitism . . . Jewish people are at no time blamed collectively for Jesus' death' is wrong."

In the same issue of *Commonweal*, Donald Senior, C.P., a New Testament scholar and member of the Pontifical Biblical Commission offered a thoughtful response to Greenberg's far-ranging essay. Senior said, "I do not believe that the bishops' 'silence' about the film should be interpreted as condoning its potential negative impact." Furthermore, "I think the bishop's decision to distribute nationwide a printed compendium of strong and consistent Catholic teaching condemning anti-Semitism, including guidelines for interpretation of the Passion, *is* an appropriate and serious response." So, in spite of differences in the assessment of the film, Jews and Christians continue the conversation.

Mel Gibson's *The Passion of the Christ* (2004) represents the most recent film about Jesus. With this film, we conclude our survey of individual Jesus movies. As the varied and many-leveled response indicates, this movie has not only taken its place in the tradition of Jesus-story films but has earned for itself a place in the history of Hollywood. Based on past experience, the viewers of this film and the readers of this book are left with a certainty: the cinematic Jesus will come again.

Carl Th. Dreyer (d. 1968), Danish film-master, whose own scripted Jesus film never reached production. Source: Film Stills Archive, The Museum of Modern Art

The Cinematic Jesus
Retrospect and Prospect

Cinema has come a long way since the first paying audiences viewed silent moving images in Paris and New York City in the mid-1890s. Throughout movie history, the Jesus-story film has played an important role with both its harmonizing and its alternative trajectories. After a hundred years, cinema remains a relatively young entertainment and artistic medium. As cinema enters its second century, the tradition of Jesus story-films has already extended itself in by works that project Jesus on the screen in new and controversial ways.

The First Hundred Years in Retrospect

The extent to which the Jesus-story film has fulfilled its promise to date can be assessed by recalling the four dimensions of the so-called problem of the cinematic Jesus: the *artistic*, the *literary*, the *historical*, and the *theological*.

First, the *artistic* dimension. Both the harmonizing and the alternative subtypes of Jesus films were represented early in their developments by movies that used the gospels in rather static and one-dimensional ways. *From the Manger to the Cross* (1912) based its screenplay on all four gospels and included scenes from throughout the life of Jesus. The film had the character of a pageant illustrating, instead of developing, the story of Jesus. *Intolerance* (1916) also included scenes based on the synoptic gospels and John, but the choice of scenes from the life of Jesus was even more selective. The few scenes that constituted the Judean story were used simply to illustrate the overall theme of the movie. The theme of "intolerance" was dramatized in greater depth and more interestingly in the three other stories.

With the harmonizing *The King of Kings* (1927), such alternative films as *Ben-Hur* (1925, 1959), and the harmonizing *King of Kings* (1961), the Jesus story certainly "came to life" on the screen. This was achieved in no small measure by the "big scene" and the "big sequence": a banquet in the house of Mary Magdalene and an earthquake during the crucifixion of Jesus; a cruel sea battle and a furious chariot race, both featuring the title character with the given name of

227

Judah; the Roman capture of Jerusalem and a massive zealot uprising in Jerusalem.

Films along the harmonizing and the alternative trajectories often tried to maintain the viewer's interest by developing subplots involving known gospel characters. From DeMille's *The King of Kings* (1927) through *Jesus Christ Superstar* (1973) to *The Last Temptation of Christ* (1988), Judas and Mary Magdalene variously came to the fore in intriguing ways. Bronston's *King of Kings* (1961) also highlighted the interplay among characters known from the traditional gospels. Judas and Barabbas became zealots who pitted themselves against Pilate, Caiaphas, and Herod Antipas, the defenders of the established order. However, the film also introduced the Roman centurion named Lucius, unknown to the gospels, whose presence spanned the duration of Jesus' life.

The Greatest Story Every Told (1965) and *Jesus of Nazareth* (1977) concentrated more sharply on the Jesus character. Nonetheless, the former film offered a very imaginative treatment of the familiar Lazarus and introduced characters not mentioned by name in the gospels, including Uriah the cripple and Old Aram the blind. The latter movie amplified the roles of Nicodemus and Joseph of Arimathea and created an otherwise unknown character called Zerah in order to expand the presentation of the inner workings of the Sanhedrin.

Jesus Christ Superstar (1973) and *Godspell* (1973) invigorated the Jesus story through the use of music, dance, and scenery—the Judean desert and New York City, respectively. *The Gospel According to St. Matthew* (1964, 1966) gave life to a static script through the use of the camera, black and white film, non-professional actors, and a stark setting. By comparison, *Jesus* (1979)—based on the gospel of Luke—was cinematically little more than a faithful illustration of that gospel. The same can be said, even more so, about *The Gospel of John* (2003) that follows word-for-word the text of a particular translation.

Life of Brian (1979) used the Jesus story as a point of departure for a comedic romp that recalls that story and its varied cinematic adaptations. *Jesus of Montreal* (1989, 1990) parallels a non-conventional interpretation of the Jesus story by modern-day actors with a satirical look at modern life through the daily lives of those same actors. *Jesus Christ Superstar* (1973), based on the popular rock opera of the same name, became a cinematic remake also as *Jesus Christ Superstar* (2000). But the film *Jesus* (1979) bears little resemblance to the more recent film called *Jesus* (2000). *The Miracle Maker* (2000) literally animated the Jesus story and highlighted the role of Tamar, the name given to Jairus' daughter.

The Passion of the Christ (2004) returns Jesus cinema to its dramatic and literary beginnings—the passion play. The film narrates the Jesus story not only in accordance with gospel texts but devotional tradition. The depiction of graphic and sustained violence inflicted on Jesus has no precedent in the cinematic tradition of Jesus films. Although Jesus remains front and center, he is accompanied every step of the bloody way by Mary his mother, Mary Magdalene, and John his beloved disciple. The camera, with its close-ups enlarged on the big screen, draws the viewer into the horrible events as they unfold.

Whatever the varying degrees of success among these films for bringing the Jesus story to life in engaging ways, the films most successful thus far *as films*—based on their recognition by filmmaking professionals— were *Ben-Hur* (1959) and *Jesus of Montreal* (1989, 1990). *Ben-Hur* received a then record-establishing eleven Oscars. *Jesus of Montreal* won twelve Genies and an Oscar nomination. The films receiving the most favorable responses by religious organizations, and by film critics representing religious periodicals, were probably *The Gospel According to St. Matthew* (1964, 1966) and *Jesus of Nazareth* (1977). If success means strong openings at the box office, then *The Passion of the Christ* (2004) has become the most successful of all Jesus films.

Secondly, the *literary* dimension. The earliest films in the harmonizing trajectory selected and juxtaposed sayings of, and stories about, Jesus from both the synoptic gospels of Matthew, Mark, Luke, and the Gospel of John in seemingly willy-nilly fashion. In *The King of Kings* (1927), *King of Kings* (1961) and *The Greatest Story Ever Told* (1965), this combining of material from the synoptics and John led to the portrayal of a Jesus at psychological odds with himself and with *no* development in his character. Sometimes, even in the same speech, Jesus spoke both in cryptic terms about the "kingdom" and then more openly about himself with sayings beginning with "I am. . . . "

By contrast to its expansive predecessors, Zeffirelli's *Jesus of Nazareth* (1977) became the finest expression along the harmonizing trajectory of Jesus films. *Jesus of Nazareth* achieved its dramatic coherence by the skillful manner in which it combined the varying synoptic and Johannine characterizations of Jesus into one dramatically convincing figure. The synoptic episode of Peter's confession at Caesarea Philippi became the point at which Jesus on the screen shifted from the reticence characteristic of the synoptic portrayal to the openness of the Johannine portrayal. Although the title figure in *Jesus of Nazareth* performs abundant miracles, the true "miracle" of the film is the harmonized screenplay.

Other films belonging to the alternative trajectory addressed the problem of dramatic coherence by bringing to the screen the story of Jesus as narrated in a single gospel. Such was the approach in *The Gospel According to St. Matthew* (1964, 1966). Heyman's *Jesus* (1979) represented a cinematic version of Luke. More recently, *The Gospel of John*

(2003) followed the text of the fourth gospel. The musical *Godspell* (1973) also claimed to be based on Matthew, but actually borrowed thematic material from all the synoptic gospels. Nonetheless, *Godspell* did resolve the problem of dramatic coherence by presenting a version of the Jesus story based on the synoptics to the exclusion of John.

Thirdly, the *historical* dimension. Films particularly in the harmonizing trajectory have always aimed for a certain historical verisimilitude, or likeness, in their cinematic treatments of the Jesus story. *From the Manger to the Cross* (1912) was actually shot on location in Palestine, although the buildings on the traditional sites visible in the film represent post-biblical constructions. In *The King of Kings* (1927), the *block script* of the Hebrew language often appears— in the sand as Jesus writes, on the headdress of Caiaphas, and on the placard fixed to the cross. Both *King of Kings* (1961) and *The Greatest Story Ever Told* (1965) incorporate into their stories incidents based on the writings of the Jewish historian Josephus in order to show the oppressive nature of Roman rule with its corresponding civil unrest. *Jesus of Nazareth* (1977) too reflects great historical sensitivity by its repeated depiction of the religious ceremonies and worship characteristic of first-century Judaism, thereby underscoring the Jewishness of Jesus and his story. One of the signature features of *The Passion* (2004) is its use of the ancient languages of Aramaic and Latin throughout, with subtitles in English or other modern languages.

Films in the alternative tradition also exhibit an interest in historical verisimilitude. *Life of Brian* (1979) not only associates Latin with the Roman occupation forces but includes a humorous scene where Brian receives a lesson in Latin grammar from a soldier. *Jesus* (1979) exhibits historical sensitivity in its attempt to depict accurately the cultural setting for the Jesus story—clothing and food, customs and architecture. Moreover, this film makes a claim for the overall historical accuracy of its depiction of Jesus, what he does and what he says, by describing itself as a "documentary." *The Miracle Maker* (2000), as noted by the geographical place name "Sepphoris" on the screen, begins its Jesus story in that rebuilt Galilean town where Jesus historians have often claimed Jesus may have used his skills as a carpenter or as a stonemason.

However, the forthright acknowledgement that Jesus himself constitutes a historical problem also appears in the alternative trajectory: *The Last Temptation of Christ* (1988) and *Jesus of Montreal* (1989, 1990). These films represent distinctive cinematic explorations of the Jesus story. Both films, on the screen and in their respective stories, explicitly raise the so-called problem of the historical Jesus—the problem of the relationship between Jesus as confessed to be the Christ by the church and Jesus as he lived and died in first-century Roman Palestine.

In *The Last Temptation of Christ* (1988), the historical problem is articulated by Paul in a face-to-face encounter with Jesus during the
dream-fantasy as Jesus hangs dying on the cross. In *Jesus of Montreal*
(1989, 1990), various aspects of the historical problem are shared by
the actor-narrator with the audience during the performance of "The
Passion on the Mountain." Claims are made that this recently commissioned passion play rests on more accurate historical information
than its dramatic predecessor. The historical problem is also noted by
Father Leclerc in a verbal exchange with Coulombe in the sanctuary
of the shrine. Both Paul in *The Last Temptation* and Father Leclerc in
Jesus of Montreal provocatively claim that what matters about the Jesus
story is not its historicity but whether it meets the needs of people.
Furthermore, both *The Last Temptation* and *Jesus of Montreal* break with
the visual artistic tradition in their staging of the crucifixion. Both
films follow more recent scholarly reconstructions of "how" crucifixion was carried out by showing Jesus fixed to the cross with his body
stripped naked and contorted.

Fourthly, the *theological* dimension. The cinematic Jesus has
appeared in nearly as many guises as the Jesus of culture and the Jesus
of history—as described by Jaroslav Pelikan in *Jesus Through the
Centuries* (1985), and as reconstructed by countless theologians and
scholars.

On the screen, Jesus has appeared as a man of good deeds, *From the
Manger to the Cross* (1912). He has appeared as victim, *Intolerance*
(1916), and as healer, *The King of Kings* (1927). He has also appeared as
crucified redeemer, *Ben-Hur* (1959) and as messiah of peace, *King of
Kings* (1961). In more contemporary idiom, he has appeared as "superstar," *Jesus Christ Superstar*, and as "hippie," *Godspell* (both 1973).

But to return to more traditional characterizations, Jesus has also
appeared as the incarnate Word, *The Greatest Story Ever Told* (1965), as
suffering-servant messiah, *Jesus of Nazareth* (1977), and as *the* unique
person, *Jesus* (1979). Contrary to these traditional portrayals, Jesus
has also appeared as reluctant messiah, *The Last Temptation of Christ*
(1988).

In *The Passion* (2004), based on the text from Isaiah 53 with which
the film opens, Jesus bears the marks of the suffering servant; and he
makes claims to be the incarnate Word, based on the periodic flashbacks with their "I am" sayings from the gospel of John. But the unre-
lenting emphasis on Jesus' physical suffering and his flagellated flesh,
transforms him into a blood sacrifice.

Two films initially released in non-English language versions, *The
Gospel According to St. Matthew* (1964, 1966) and *Jesus of Montreal* (1989,
1990), cast Jesus in the role of prophet. But there are differences. The
former portrays Jesus as what has been called prophet and sage; the
latter, prophet and apocalyptist. *Jesus of Montreal* cites the passage

known as the Marcan—or synoptic—apocalypse (Mark 13) in which Jesus answers the disciples' questions about the "when" of the end of the world. But in this film, the apocalyptic words are not placed on the lips of Coulombe in his role as Jesus, but Coulombe as the actor who plays Jesus.

Remarkably, but understandably, not a single Jesus-story film portrays Jesus as one who expects the end of the world in his own lifetime. Such a characterization of Jesus became common in scholarly circles in the last century through the research and writings of Albert Schweitzer, especially his *The Quest of the Historical Jesus* (1906). The cinematic portrayal of Jesus as one who believed the end of the world to be imminent in his own day would leave the film viewer with the question of how Jesus could have so miscalculated the time of the end. Instead, as we have seen, more than a few Jesus films bridge the time gap between Jesus' day and our day by concluding their cinematic presentations with the saying of the resurrected Jesus with which the gospel of Matthew ends: " . . . I am with you to the end of the age" (28:20).

A Legacy of Controversy

Precisely because the Jesus story represents the story so central for western culture and faith, the cinematic appropriation of that story has involved controversy, public as well as private, ecclesiastical as well as personal. But the projection of Jesus on the screen has not only challenged but also clarified values for those with commitments to him and his story.

The first hundred years of cinema began with an uncertainty among many Christians and Christian churches about the appropriateness of even putting Jesus on the screen. By the end of the 1920s, the question had become not, "Should we?"but, "How reverently does this film treat the Jesus story?" Cecil B. DeMille's silent classic *The King of Kings* (1927) certainly tempered spectacle with reverence.

From the 1930s through the 1960s, reverence for the Jesus story was ensured by a system of self-censorship that involved the film industry and the Catholic Church—the former through the Production Code and the Production Code Administration, the latter through the Legion of Decency. The Legion developed a system for rating films that brought great pressure on filmmakers to avoid a negative classification—particularly the dreaded "C," for condemned.   The 1950s and early 1960s represented the age of Jesus spectaculars—films with sizable budgets, made for wide screens, and with longer running times. The alternative and then the harmonizing approaches to the Jesus story appeared in such productions as *Quo Vadis* (1951), *The Robe* (1953), *Ben-Hur* (1959), *King of Kings* (1961), and *The Greatest Story Ever Told* (1965).

After the gradual erosion of the system of self-censorship that had controlled the film industry for three decades, that system finally collapsed. In 1965, the Legion of Decency became the National Catholic Office for Motion Pictures and gradually refocused its efforts away from condemnation and more toward education. The evaluation of films by the Catholic Church became the responsibility of the United States Catholic Conference (USCC) through the Office for Film and Broadcasting (OFB). The USCC had considerably less power than its predecessors and a more diverse classification system. Since 2001, the OFB has been under the oversight of the United States Conference of Catholic Bishops (USCCB). The current USCCB rating system is as follows: A-I, A-II, A-III, L, and O. In 1968, the Motion Picture Association of America replaced the Production Code with an age-based classification system of its own. This MPAA rating system continues, with occasional adjustments, into our day: G, PG, PG-13, R, and NC-17.

The demise in the 1960s of the long-standing self-censorship system opened the way for greater diversity in filmmaking, generally, and in the making of Jesus films, in particular. The gritty, black-and-white film by Pier Paolo Pasolini, *The Gospel According to St. Matthew* (1964, 1966) heralded this diversity. Cinematic presentations of the Jesus story that would have had difficulty reaching the screen a decade earlier soon followed: *Jesus Christ Superstar* and *Godspell* (both 1973), based on staged musicals; *Greaser's Palace* (1972) and *Monty Python's Life of Brian* (1979), very different but intended to be humorous takes on the sacred story; and *The Passover Plot* (1976), with its suggestion that Jesus sought to perpetrate fraud. More recently, Jesus has moved from the pages of a controversial novel to the screen, in *The Last Temptation of Christ* (1988), and appeared in an equally controversial play within a play, in *Jesus of Montreal* (1989, 1990). By the end of the first hundred years of Jesus at the movies, the question had seemingly become not "How reverently does this film treat the Jesus story?" but "How far can we take it?"

How far Mel Gibson has taken it with *The Passion* (2004) now belongs to the public record, although that record remains open because the film's release has been so recent. How the film initially performed at the box office is abundantly clear. Film reviews are in from both the religious and the secular media. But the film industry itself has not yet had the opportunity to pass judgment, with its annual awards. How the film will stand the test of time, only time will tell.

Over the past century, formal responses to Jesus films by religious leaders, organizations, and publications have served to disclose their own basic commitments. The religious responses to the Jesus films cited in our study lead to a few general observations.

Representatives of mainline, or liberal, Protestantism often evaluated Jesus films, and Jesus as portrayed in those films, on the basis of the film's social relevance and Jesus' humanness. Representatives of evangelical, or conservative, Protestantism were more concerned with the faithfulness of Jesus films to the biblical text and to Jesus' divinity. As attested by the very noisy public controversies related to the releases of such dissimilar films as *Jesus of Nazareth* (1977), *Life of Brian* (1979), and *The Last Temptation of Christ* (1988), conservative Protestants have been more willing in recent years to take to the mail, to the airwaves, and even to the streets to prevent the making and the showing of Jesus films that violate their own theological sensibilities.

Catholic reaction to Jesus films, at least by reviewers in Catholic publications, has reflected less concern for either social relevance or biblical faithfulness. Catholic reviewers seemed more comfortable than Protestants with Jesus on the screen as image—however provocative that moving image may have been. Reflected here, no doubt, is Catholicism's traditional appreciation for the sacred image of Jesus and his story. Perhaps it was the implicit power of Jesus as sacred image, whatever other factors were involved, that has led filmmakers of Catholic heritage to translate the Jesus story into celluloid in recent decades, including Pier Paolo Pasolini, Franco Zeffirelli, Martin Scorsese, Denys Arcand, and now Mel Gibson.

As we have observed, one of the striking features about the responses to *The Passion* has been the way in which those conservative Protestant constituencies most willing to protest against certain Jesus films in the last half of the twentieth century found themselves to be strong promoters of a film by a traditionalist Catholic. The focus of this film on the death of Jesus, enabled many Protestants and Catholics to find common cause within a broader cultural context that that has become increasingly polarized in the United States religiously, economically, and politically.

By contrast to these varying Christian appraisals of the cinematic Jesus, the history of Jesus in film has also been a history of ongoing Jewish vigilance against anti-Semitism. Many Christians too have come to share a similar alertness. Thus the cinematic treatment of the Jesus story has exhibited increased sensitivity by filmmakers to the Jewishness of the story itself. Strikingly, two late twentieth-century Jesus films that communicate in straightforward fashion the traditional Christian claims about Jesus as the Christ, the Son of God, leave no doubt that Jesus himself was a Jew. These films are *Jesus of Nazareth* (1977) and *Jesus* (1979). For whatever reasons, Mel Gibson seemed unaware of the questions that would be posed and the depth of feelings that would be aroused by his passion project.

Of such has been the cinematic Jesus in retrospect. But the cinematic Jesus has not only a past. He has a future. To that future we now turn.

The Beginning of the Second Hundred Years

While the harmonizing tradition of Jesus cinema moved toward greater dramatic coherence, the alternative tradition moved toward greater recognition of the problem of the historical Jesus and a concern not just for verisimilitude but for historicity. However, to date, no filmmaker has created a Jesus-story film that *explicitly* claims to base its characterization of Jesus on the historical conclusions of life-of-Jesus research as synthesized by the filmmaker. Therefore, whatever the future may be for the cinematic Jesus, there is a niche for such a film.

Of course, the ongoing quest of the historical Jesus continues to demonstrate that there is *no one way* to reconstruct Jesus' life historically. Even historians tend to make Jesus over in their own images. But historians do not have the same freedom of imagination as artists. Historians supposedly practice their craft within the bounds of historical reason. Based on the evaluation of literary and physical evidence, they draw conclusions with greater or lesser degrees of probability. A filmmaker could commit himself, or herself, to making a film that expresses artistic imagination, but an imagination disciplined by historical inquiry and historical possibility.

In spite of its own historical sensitivity in some areas, Martin Scorsese's *The Last Temptation of Christ* (1988) was prefaced by these words that referred to the Kazantzakis novel of the same name:

This film is not based upon the gospels
but upon the fictional exploration
of the eternal spiritual conflict.

A film based on the conclusions of historical research could open with a statement something like this:

This film is based upon the gospels
but represents one historical exploration
of the eternal spiritual quest.

A film artist whose own historical exploration of the Jesus story never reached the screen was the highly acclaimed Danish director Carl Th. Dreyer. His films were highly introspective in nature with religious themes and subject matter. Among his most acclaimed works are: *The Passion of Joan of Arc* (*La Passion de Jeanne d'Arc*, 1928, French); *Vampire* (*Vampyr*, 1932, German); *The Day of Wrath* (*Vredens Dag*, 1943, Danish); *The Word* (*Ordet*, 1955, Danish); and, his last film, *Gertrud* (1964, Danish).[1]

Dreyer grew up as an adopted child in a strict Lutheran home and began his life of work as a journalist, before turning to cinema. His second film, *Leaves from Satan's Notebook* (*Blade Af Satans Bog*, 1921), consciously imitated D. W. Griffith's monumental *Intolerance* (1916) by telling four stories, from four different historical periods, but in chronological order. The first story involved the relationship between Jesus and Judas whereas the subsequent stories centered around the Spanish Inquisition, the French Revolution, and events in Finland related to the Russian Revolution.

It was only after Dreyer had finished his film on Joan of Arc, in the late 1920s, that he began thinking about the gospels as material for a fully developed movie about Jesus.[2] Then, when the Germans occupied his native Denmark in the spring of 1940, Dreyer suddenly realized the parallel between the experience of his own people under Nazi oppression and the Jews under Roman occupation.

After the war—in June 1949—Dreyer entered into a contract with Blevins Davis, an American theater producer, to write a scenario on the life of Jesus for a film that Dreyer would bring to the screen. The two had met when Blevins was in Denmark for the staging of his stage production of *Hamlet* at Kronborg castle in Elsinore. Later that very summer, Dreyer made a trip to Palestine to begin serious research for his Jesus film. Returning to Denmark in August, Dreyer then traveled to the United States for further research and writing—at the New York Public Library, and subsequently at Davis' farm in Missouri.

It was during this period of residence in the United States that Dreyer discovered a historical work by the Jewish scholar Solomon Zeitlin, a longtime member of the faculty at Dropsie College, in Philadelphia. The title of Zeitlin's work (first published in 1942) was *Who Crucified Jesus?* As had Zeitlin, so Dreyer wanted not only to "let Jesus be represented as a Jew" but "to refute the accusation against the Jews for having murdered Jesus."[3]

Dreyer even met with Zeitlin and discussed his then-completed manuscript for his Jesus-story film. The filmmaker and the historian, according to Dreyer's recollection, agreed on every point except one: the character of Caiaphas, the high priest. Dreyer argued that Caiaphas was a well-meaning "politician" who acted in what he thought was the best interest of his people. But Zeitlin understood Caiaphas to be a "quisling," or turncoat, who had sold out to the Romans.

The scenario for Dreyer's Jesus-story film found its way into print after his death.[4] However, the film itself was never made. Sixteen years of correspondence between Dreyer and Davis, some 256 letters and telegrams, has also been published.[5] These communications indicate that Blevins—for whatever reasons—never secured the promised financial backing for the project.

However, throughout Dreyer's prolonged wait for the signal from

Blevins that production could begin, Dreyer maintained a state of readiness. In the mid-1950s, he even shipped his research materials to Israel; but the uncertainties of Middle Eastern politics prevented his joining them. He studied the Hebrew language from the son of the chief rabbi of Copenhagen. He became determined to shoot the film in Israel and to cast Jews in the roles of Jesus and his disciples.

Furthermore, Dreyer made overtures toward representatives of Hollywood studios, within the framework of what he considered at the time to be his contractual obligation to Davis. These inquiries elicited the repeated response that the studios already had commitments to other Bible-based films—among them, Bronston's *King of Kings* (1961) and Stevens' *The Greatest Story Ever Told* (1965).

Finally, in 1967, the Danish Film Foundation offered a sum of money equal to a half-million dollars to any Danish film company that would undertake the making of Dreyer's Jesus film—although Dreyer had projected the cost would run between three and five million. Then, RAI, the Italian television company, also expressed an interest in filming Dreyer's screenplay. Shortly thereafter, at age 79, he died, on March 20, 1968.

The year after Dreyer's death, shipping crates containing his varied research materials were discovered in a warehouse in Jerusalem where they had rested unclaimed for more than a decade.[6] Within a decade of Dreyer's death, RAI the Italian television company would collaborate with ATV, the British commercial company, and bring forth Zeffirelli's *Jesus of Nazareth* (1977).

Another filmmaker whose historical exploration of the Jesus story remains in progress is the Dutch director Paul Verhoeven. Verhoeven began his cinematic career in the Netherlands. His early film *Turkish Delight* (*Turks Fruit*, 1972, Dutch) received a 1973 Academy Award nomination for Best Foreign Language Film.[7] Since moving to the United States to direct *Robocop* (1987), he has directed *Total Recall* (1990), *Basic Instinct* (1992), *Showgirls* (1995), *Starship Troopers* (1997), and *Hollow Man* (2000)[8]

Verhoeven grew up without considering himself to be in any way a Christian. But even before earning a Ph.D. degree in mathematics from the University of Leiden, he had become fascinated with the figure of Jesus.[9] Having lived as a child through the Nazi occupation of his homeland, Verhoeven—like Carl Th. Dreyer before him—came to see similarities between that modern situation and the plight of the Jews under Roman rule.

Therefore, it is not completely surprising that in the spring of 1988, just before the public controversy over the release of Scorsese's *The Last Temptation*, Verhoeven asked a group of scholars to assist him in clarifying his understanding of Jesus so that he could develop a treat-

ment for a screenplay. The scholarly group approached by Verhoeven
was the Jesus Seminar. Sponsored by the Westar Institute, under the
leadership of Robert W. Funk, the Jesus Seminar had been meeting
twice annually since 1985.[10]

At that Jesus Seminar meeting in Sonoma, California, in the spring
of 1988, Verhoeven presented his initial plans for a film about Jesus.
He distributed a seventeen page document that he had written, with
the working title, "Christ the Man: Backgrounds for an action-script."
The contents of this document with its attached bibliography, as well
as his repartee, indicated that he was thoroughly conversant with the
scholarly literature on the historical Jesus. From that occasion on,
Verhoeven became an active member of the Jesus Seminar; and the
Seminar became the advisory body to Verhoeven for his film project.
Since then, he has met and interacted regularly with the Seminar at its
four-day sessions, twice each year.

A Cinema Seminar met co-laterally with the Jesus Seminar with sessions devoted specifically to Verhoeven's prospective film. Some sessions centered around papers by members of the Seminar prepared at
Verhoeven's request. At the 1989 fall meeting at the University of
Toronto, four different scenarios were prepared taking into account
the events of Jesus' last week. Also, four cameo essays were presented
centering around different visual aspects of this period in Jesus' life—
asses in first-century Palestine, the Jerusalem temple, meal customs in
first-century Palestine, and Roman trial procedure.[11]

Other sessions centered around papers written by Verhoeven to
elicit critical reaction by members of the Seminar. For the 1990 fall
meeting at Xavier University in Cincinnati, he outlined what he considered to be key elements of the dramatic structure of his Jesus film.
That structure extended from Jesus' coming of age in Nazareth, in a
household consisting of his mother Mary and his siblings, to his crucifixion outside Jerusalem upon the order of Pontius Pilate.[12]

Over the course of nearly seventeen years of give-and-take,
Verhoeven's working title as well as his ideas have developed. By the
1994 fall meeting, in Santa Rosa, California, his twenty-three page scenario bore the title "Fully Human"; and, a year later at the 1995 fall
meeting, his nine page presentation was labeled "Ecce Homo:
Dramatic structure of the movie." Of ongoing concern for Verhoeven,
for example, has been the issue of Jesus' relationship to John the
Baptist: how Jesus was baptized by and influenced by John, but how
he later declared his independence from John. In "Ecce Homo," Jesus'
theological independence comes, in the desert, from "a major transformation of his thinking" whereby "the revengeful God disappeared
and 'Abba' emerged, the merciful father." More recently, for the fall
2002 meeting, in Santa Rosa, California, Verhoeven distributed a "Film
Project Report," that consisted of another narrative sketch of Jesus'

activities. His paper included the observation that Jesus' most important parables seemed to him to be the parables of the Prodigal Son and
the Good Samaritan. At the fall 2003 meeting, also in Santa Rosa, he
presented exegeses and interpretations of selected gospel texts.

The makers of virtually all Jesus films over the past century have
had religious advisors. Verhoeven's turn to the Jesus Seminar for help
says much about the nature of his project. Earlier filmmakers sought
advice from representatives of confessional religious communities and
organizations—Protestant, Catholic, and Jewish. Although most participants in the Jesus Seminar have loyalties to church or synagogue,
the Fellows of the Jesus Seminar are bound by common scholarly
interests. Most Fellows serve on faculties at colleges and universities,
at state-sponsored and church-affiliated institutions.

Furthermore, the common goal of the Jesus Seminar at its inception
had not been theological but historical. The agenda of the Seminar
involved studying all known sayings of Jesus and stories about Jesus
from the ancient world in order to determine—using established liter-
ary-historical criteria—the degree of historical probability for Jesus'
actually having said a particular saying or having performed a specific act.

By associating himself with the Seminar, Verhoeven committed
himself to exercise his artistic imagination within the framework of
historical reason. This does not mean that Verhoeven committed himself to bring the Jesus Seminar's collective understanding of Jesus to
the screen. This will be his film. Just as the Seminar has challenged
him to think historically, so he has pushed the members of the Seminar
to think imaginatively about their historical conclusions.

When notices of Verhoeven's project first began to appear in the
media, the magazine *Newsweek* (15 August 1988) accurately reported
about his film-in-the-making: "It's described as a realistic look at the
historical Jesus."[13] Shortly thereafter, in an interview, Verhoeven
responded thusly to a question about his proposed film:

> My film will be historical, whatever that is. History is partly under a
> veil there. I think it will be more rough and crude, more realistic, than
> [Nicholas] Ray and [George] Stevens, although there are things in Ray's
> movie I like.[14]

Because of the sexual as well as violent content of his movies,
Verhoeven was asked in the same interview about Jesus' sexuality. He
replied:

> If you insist on Jesus' sex life, I think you're making a big mistake. I
> don't think Jesus at this point in his life—we're talking about his last
> couple of years—was interested in sex. I think he had something really
> different in mind.[15]

The future of the tradition of Jesus-story films, of course, does not depend upon Paul Verhoeven any more than it depended upon Carl Th. Dreyer, or any other single filmmaker. If Verhoeven's film eventually makes it to the screen, what he thinks Jesus had in mind will become public. If his Jesus film appears, that film may well fill that hitherto unoccupied niche in the ongoing tradition of Jesus at the movies: a film that *explicitly* claims to base its characterization of Jesus on the results of life-of-Jesus research.

Meanwhile, the second hundred years of Jesus cinema has begun. If the films released to date are harbingers of the future, Jesus films will continue along harmonizing and alternative trajectories and will reflect considerable diversity. Stanislav Sokolav's and Derek Hayes' *The Miracle Maker* (2000) uses 3D animation to tell the Jesus story with a focus on the daughter of Jairus, named Tamar, whom Jesus healed. Gale Edwards' *Jesus Christ Superstar* (2000), a cinematic remake of the rock opera, again brings a singing Jesus to the screen. Philip Savile's *The Gospel of John* (2003) follows a cinematic approach taken by other movies in relation to the gospels by filming the Jesus story from a single gospel. However, two other Jesus films signal a return to the cinematic harmony. Both Roger Young's made-for-television miniseries, *Jesus* (2000), and Mel Gibson's more recent presentation of Jesus' final hours, *The Passion of the Christ* (2004), draw upon all four gospels for their respective stories.

Checklist of
Jesus-story Films

This chart lists in chronological order the principal Jesus-story films discussed in this guide to the history of Jesus in film. Under the headings of [1] Infancy, [2] Ministry, and [3] Passion are listed a few of the most recognizable events and dimensions of Jesus' life that are attested in one, or more, of the four gospels.

The marks on the chart identify the films in which particular events and dimensions are portrayed, so that, at a glance, the viewer can make at least a twofold determination.

First, the viewer can see the overall shape of a particular film's story about Jesus. Does a film begin with the infancy? Only with the baptism by John and the temptation by Satan? Or with the entry into Jerusalem a week before the crucifixion? Does a film end with the crucifixion? With events related to the resurrection such as the discovery of the empty tomb and the appearances of the resurrected Jesus? Or the ascension into heaven? However, on occasion, an event early in Jesus' ministry—according to the gospels—has been relocated in the film to a later moment in his ministry. For example, in *The King of Kings* (1927), the "temptation by Satan" occurs not in the wilderness *before* Jesus' public activity but in Jerusalem *after* Judas has acclaimed him as "our king."

Secondly, the chart enables the viewer to identify those films that include a particular event or dimension related to Jesus' life. Which films bring to the screen the Sermon on the Mount? The cleansing of the temple? Jesus' carrying the cross alone, without the assistance of Simon of Cyrene? "Kingdom" parable(s), from the synoptics? "I am" saying(s), from John?

The chart identifies only those events or dimensions that are dramatized on the screen. Events are *not* marked if they are only verbally acknowledged by the narrator or a character in a film.

For example, in the column under *Ben-Hur* (1959), the category "last word(s) on cross" remains unmarked because in the film we hear Judah tell Esther that he heard Jesus say, "Father, forgive. . . . "; we do not hear Jesus speak the words himself. Also, for *King of Kings* (1961), the categories of "walking on water" and "feeding of multitudes" remain unmarked because these natural wonders have been reported

241

verbally by Lucius to Pontius Pilate rather than shown on screen. Still again, *Jesus Christ Superstar* (1973), after the fashion of a passion play, confines its on-screen story to events related to Jesus' last week—with the exception of a stylized scene depicting Jesus as healer and exorcist. The lyrics of the songs contain many allusions to recognizable events in Jesus' life before that last week—such as Jesus' baptism by John. However, the category of "baptism by John" appears unmarked since the viewer does not see the baptism itself.

Neither are events marked on the chart if they have been symbolically enacted in a story parallel to the Jesus story. For example, in the column under *Jesus of Montreal* (1990), the category "cleansing of temple" remains unmarked because the incident occurred in the life of

	Manger to Cross 1912	Intolerance 1916	The King of Kings 1927	Ben-Hur 1959	King of Kings 1961	Greatest Story 1965	Gospel of Matthew 1966	Superstar 1973	Godspell 1973	Jesus of Nazareth 1977	Life of Brian 1979	Jesus 1979	Last Temptation 1988	Jesus of Montreal 1990	The Passion 2004
1. Infancy															
visit of wise men	✓		✓	✓	✓	✓				✓	✓				
visit of shepherds	✓		✓	✓	✓					✓		✓			
to Jerusalem at age 12	✓									✓		✓			
2. Ministry															
baptism by John					✓	✓	✓			✓	✓		✓	✓	
temptation by Satan				✓	✓	✓	✓	✓		✓			✓	✓	
call of disciples	✓				✓	✓	✓	✓		✓		✓	✓	✓	
Sermon on the Mount				✓	✓	✓	✓			✓	✓		✓	✓	✓
Lord's Prayer					✓	✓	✓			✓		✓			
dance of Salome					✓	✓	✓			✓					
execution of John					✓	✓	✓			✓					
rejection at Nazareth					✓	✓				✓	✓		✓		
confession of Peter					✓	✓				✓	✓			✓	
rich young ruler					✓	✓				✓	✓				
water into wine	✓	✓								✓			✓		
feeding of multitudes							✓			✓		✓		✓	
walking on water	✓						✓							✓	
woman in adultery	✓	✓	✓		✓	✓				✓			✓		✓
raising of Lazarus	✓		✓				✓			✓			✓		
healing(s)	✓		✓	✓	✓	✓	✓	✓		✓		✓	✓	✓	✓
exorcism(s)			✓	✓			✓	✓	✓	✓		✓	✓		
"kingdom" parable(s)					✓		✓		✓	✓		✓	✓	✓	
"I am" saying(s)			✓		✓	✓				✓			✓		✓

Daniel Coulombe the actor when he was not playing Jesus in the passion play.

Also, notice how few of the gospel-attested events from the life of Jesus are marked in the column below *Godspell* (1973). This stems from the stylized nature of the entire film as well as the film's extensive dependence on the "kingdom" parables for its script. Jesus and his troupe spend much of their time playfully performing parables as they travel about New York City.

More recently, the conclusion of *The Passion* (2004) clearly indicates that Jesus was entombed and resurrected. However, the film shows neither the discovery of the empty tomb nor the post-resurrection appearances. Thus the chart has no marks beside these categories.

3. Passion

Event	Manger to Cross 1912	Intolerance 1916	The King of Kings 1927	Ben-Hur 1959	King of Kings 1961	Greatest Story 1965	Gospel of Matthew 1966	Superstar 1973	Godspell 1973	Jesus of Nazareth 1977	Life of Brian 1979	Jesus 1979	Last Temptation 1988	Jesus of Montreal 1990	The Passion 2004
entry on ass	✓				✓	✓	✓	✓		✓	✓	✓	✓		✓
cleansing of temple	✓		✓			✓	✓	✓		✓		✓	✓		
betrayal of Judas	✓		✓		✓	✓	✓	✓		✓		✓	✓		✓
Last Supper	✓		✓		✓	✓	✓	✓		✓		✓	✓		✓
bread and wine	✓		✓		✓	✓	✓	✓	✓	✓		✓	✓		✓
footwashing	✓														✓
prayer in Gethsemane	✓		✓		✓	✓	✓	✓	✓	✓		✓	✓	✓	✓
denial of Peter	✓		✓		✓	✓	✓	✓		✓		✓			✓
suicide of Judas	✓		✓		✓	✓	✓	✓		✓	✓	✓			✓
before Caiaphas			✓			✓	✓	✓		✓		✓		✓	✓
before Pontius Pilate	✓	✓	✓	✓	✓	✓	✓	✓		✓		✓	✓	✓	✓
before Herod Antipas	✓					✓	✓	✓				✓			✓
scourging	✓		✓		✓	✓	✓	✓		✓		✓	✓	✓	✓
release of Barabbas			✓		✓	✓	✓	✓		✓		✓			✓
way to cross	✓	✓	✓	✓	✓	✓	✓	✓		✓		✓	✓	✓	✓
Simon of Cyrene assists	✓	✓	✓	✓	✓	✓	✓					✓			✓
crucifixion (execution)	✓	✓	✓	✓	✓	✓	✓	✓	✓	✓		✓	✓	✓	✓
last word(s) on cross	✓		✓		✓	✓	✓	✓	✓	✓		✓	✓	✓	✓
death	✓	✓	✓	✓	✓	✓	✓	✓	✓	✓		✓	✓	✓	✓
confession of centurion			✓			✓	✓					✓			
removal of body						✓		✓				✓			✓
burial in tomb						✓	✓	✓				✓			
empty tomb					✓	✓	✓			✓		✓			
resurrection appearances			✓		✓	✓	✓			✓		✓		✓	
ascension			✓				✓					✓			

Jesus-story Films
and Christ-figure Films

Just as biblical scholarship has made a distinction between the Jesus of history and the Christ of faith, so film study—in various ways—has made a distinction between the cinematic Jesus and the cinematic Christ. This guide to Jesus in film has focused on Jesus-story films thereby limiting itself to a consideration of the cinematic Jesus. The films analyzed have retold the story of Jesus, as narrated in the four gospels, with an actor playing the part of Jesus himself.

However, there has flourished alongside the tradition of Jesus-story films a tradition of Christ-figure films. Christ-figure films tell stories in which characters, events, or details substantially recall, or resemble, the story of Jesus. The character whose life—and death—resembles Jesus' experience represents the cinematic Christ.

Cinematic Christs, or Christ figures, have been identified in films representing most movie genres, or types: drama and action, western and comedy, historical epic and science fiction. Understandably, Christian priests—or preachers—and Jewish characters lend themselves to be projected as Christ figures. All Christians are called upon to imitate Christ in their living; and priests, with their clerical attire, are easily identifiable as persons with commitments to Jesus as the Christ. Since Jesus was a Jew, a persecuted Jew, contemporary Jewish characters have sometimes been portrayed as embodying suffering similar to his. Social misfits, alienated individuals, also lend themselves to be portrayed as Christ figures. Among such outcasts have been inmates of prisons and other kinds of asylums.

CINEMATIC CHRISTS: Explicit and Implicit

Two decades ago, Neil P. Hurley published a seminal essay, "Cinematic Transfigurations of Jesus," in a symposium on *Religion in Film* (1982). What we are calling Christ-figure films, Hurley called "cinematic transfigurations of Jesus." As of the date of his writing, Hurley claimed to have discovered more than sixty examples of such films.

Hurley further proposed that his broad category "cinematic transfigurations of Jesus" be further divided into two cinematic subtypes:

245

the Jesus transfiguration, narrowly defined, on the one hand; and the Christ figure, on the other.

According to Hurley, a Jesus transfiguration film has secular traditions as subtexts and projects a more humanistic—or even atheistic—Jesus *persona*. For examples: John Sturges' *The Old Man and the Sea* (1958), based on the Ernest Hemingway novel, and Ken Russell's *Tommy* (1975), an adaptation of The Who's best-selling rock opera. By contrast, a Christ-figure film is faith-inspired and gives expression to such traditional Christian notions as messiahship, divinity, and resurrection. For example: Robert Bresson's *Diary of a Country Priest* (1951, English) and Alfred Hitchcock's *I Confess* (1953).

However, Hurley's subcategories of Jesus transfiguration and Christ figure are admittedly ideological in the sense of being determined by the ideas and values projected by the film and the film's protagonist. That is, the subtype represented by a particular cinematic transfiguration of Jesus depends upon the extent to which that particular film is "not Christian" or "Christian." Hurley's delineation of subcategories leaves too much to the ideology, or the theology, of the viewer. A different way to define the categories of Christ-figure films would be to do so *not* in ideological but in formal terms.

According to the categories suggested here, and contrary to Hurley, a Christ-figure film tells a story which recalls the Jesus story—whatever the "intention" of the filmmaker, and whatever the "message" of the film. *How* the maker of a Christ-figure film has used the Jesus story determines the kind of subtype it represents: *an explicit* Christ-figure film or an *implicit* Christ-figure film.

Some Christ-figure films have a character who *explicitly* identifies himself (or herself) with Jesus, or with a particular dimension of the Jesus story. Sometimes, these films revolve around a specific gospel text that is actually cited—verbally or visually—within the story itself.

No twentieth-century filmmaker drew more extensively on theological and biblical themes than the Swedish pastor's son Ingmar Bergman. Central to his body of work is the trilogy *Through a Glass Darkly* (1962, English) *Winter Light* (1963, English) and *The Silence* (1964, English). The middle film, *Winter Light,* represents a dramatic snapshot in the life of Tomas Ericsson, the pastor of two small churches in rural Sweden. All the action—mainly talk—occurs within a three hour period on a Sunday afternoon, bracketed by a midday service in one church and vespers in the other. The film visually, thematically, and verbally represents a profound commentary on Jesus' word on the cross: "My God, my God, why have you abandoned Me?" (Mark 15:34 and Matt 27:46). Like Jesus on the cross, "doubting" Tomas experiences the silence of God. However, it is Algot Frovik, the sexton, who expounds on the meaning of these words and the nature of Jesus' suffering with a profundity seldom heard in church homilies on the passion. The sexton's analysis also provides an alternative to the cinematic interpretation displayed in Mel Gibson's *The Passion (2004)*.

Perhaps the least likely place to discover a cinematic Christ would be in a comedy starring the late Peter Sellers. However, the Boulting Brothers Production, *Heavens Above!* (1963) represents such a film. Malcolm Muggeridge receives credit for the idea underlying the screenplay by Frank Harvey and John Boulting. Sellers plays the role of the Rev. John Smallwood, an Anglican priest mistakenly appointed vicar of Holy Trinity Church in the small English town of Orbiston Parva. The economy of the village thrives thanks to the wealthy Despard family whose company manufactures a trinitarian pill—a sedative, a pepper-upper, and a laxative, all in one. The film satirically shows what happens when Jesus' teaching on wealth is taken literally. Jesus' injunction to the so-called rich, young ruler constitutes the text of the film; and the viewer sees these words highlighted in an open Bible: "If you would be perfect, go, sell what you possess and give to the poor . . . " (Matt 19:21).

Like Ingmar Bergman, Luis Buñuel was a filmmaker who often turned to the Jesus story for thematic materials, although often with a more obvious assault on Christianity itself—as seen in his *Viridiana* (1962, English), with its outrageous parody of the Last Supper, and in his *Simon of the Desert* (1969, English), about the fifth-century monk who lived atop a thirty-foot pillar. Buñuel's *Nazarin* (1961, English), based on the 1895 novel by the Spanish novelist Benito Pérez Galdós, tells a superbly moving story—relocated in Mexico—of a Catholic priest who takes seriously Jesus' identification with the poor and social outcasts, particularly women. In many ways, Nazarin's activity and experience recapitulates that of Jesus as narrated in the synoptic gospels. Like the Rev. John Smallwood in *Heavens Above!*, the priest encounters the ongoing hostility of the "real" world.

In John Frankenheimer's *The Fixer* (1968), the *explicit* Christ figure appears in the personage of Yakov Bok, a Jewish fixer, or carpenter. The movie brings to the screen the 1966 novel of the same title by Bernard Malamud that was, in turn, based on a historical incident in turn-of-the-century Czarist Russia. In the film, Bok receives direction for his life primarily by reading the writings of the Jewish philosopher Baruch Spinoza. However, as a Jew, he becomes the object of blood-libel—the false accusation that he had killed a Christian child to obtain blood for religious purposes. During his imprisonment, Bok identifies personally with the suffering of *the* Jewish carpenter of ages past by reading the story of Jesus in the New Testament given to him by his captors. As Bok later tells the jailer: "I understand something.

He who hates a Jew, or any other man, hates Jesus. To be anti-Semitic you've first got to be anti-Christian. It's in the book."

There are also films in which a character does more than just identify himself (or herself) with the Jesus story. Here, a character understands himself *to be* the Christ. A notable example of such a "Christomaniac" appears in Peter Medak's *The Ruling Class* (1972), starring Peter O'Toole as Jack, the fourteenth Earl of Gurney, a performance that earned O'Toole an Academy Award Nomination for Best Actor. A biting satire on British society, including the church, the film has Jack—at a farcical moment—express his self-understanding with a telling declaration from the gospels: "I am the resurrection and the life" (John 11:25).

In addition to *explicit* Christ-figure films, and they are many, there are also *implicit* Christ-figure films. Here, the central characters do not understand themselves to be acting out the Jesus story, but rather the filmmaker uses images that lead the viewer to make the identification.

Stuart Rosenberg's *Cool Hand Luke* (1967), based on the novel by Donn Pearce, has become one of the most widely recognized and discussed Christ-figure films in American cinema. Paul Newman received an Academy Award nomination for Best Actor for his performance in the title role of Luke; and George Kennedy won an Oscar for Best Supporting Actor as Luke's buddy, Dragline.

The film tells the story of Luke Jackson, a loner and non-conformist who does time for petty theft on a southern prison farm—on the chain-gang. Luke does not survive what proves to be his final escape attempt; but stories about him live on among his fellow inmates after his death. Parallels between this cinematic story and the Jesus story in the gospels abound. Allusions and images are obvious. Luke occasionally calls upon God in moments of despair. He is honored for his exploits by his admirers, and his buddy Dragline remembers him as " . . . ol' Luke . . . some boy . . . cool hand Luke . . . a natural-born world-shaker." The film ends with the camera angled to show a montage of cruciform images—a road intersection, telephone poles, and a torn but mended photograph.

Nonetheless, there is no indication within the story that Luke or his friends view him as a Christ figure. Such an identification occurs through the eyes and in the minds of the viewers.

A more surprising, and subtle, Christ figure appears in Stanley Kubrick's epic *Spartacus* (1960), a film honored with four Academy Awards. Based on a 1951 novel by Howard Fast, and with Kirk Douglas in the title role, the film tells the story of the Thracian slave who led the great revolt against the Romans a century prior to the life and death of Jesus. However, the film opens with a voice-over narration calling attention to the relationship between the Spartacus story and the subsequent Jesus story: "In the last century before the birth of the new faith called Christianity, which was destined to overthrow the pagan tyranny of Rome. . . . " The film concludes with a closeup of Spartacus' face as he hangs on the cross and a distant shot of him as he watches his wife and child ride away to their freedom, in a cart, along the road lined with crucified men.

If *Spartacus* (1960) offers a Christ figure in a story set in the distant past, the Wachoski brothers' science fiction *Matrix* trilogy (1999, 2003, 2003) with its revolutionary technical wizardry presents such a figure in a tale set in the future, sometime around the year 2199. Perhaps Thomas A. Anderson, also known as Neo, becomes the first computer hacker to be called to the redemptive mission of laying down his life to save humanity. Neo and the film recall a plethora of religious traditions and raise a myriad of philosophical questions appropriate for a beyond-post-modern world. However, in the sequence that introduces Neo to the viewer, he is told in an off-handed way, "Hallelujah! You're my savior man, my own personal Jesus Christ." Although Neo only gradually comes to understand and accept his role as the expected one, he arises to fulfill his chosen task of saving humanity in the great cataclysmic war against the machines.

The preceding survey of Christ-figure films simply illustrates, and does not comprehensively represent, how the cinematic Jesus has a counterpart in the cinematic Christ. But even the few films receiving comment lead to an observation. Many, if not most, Christ-figure films are based on novels whose stories already include a Christ figure.

CINEMATIC CHRISTS: Sources from Literature

Whereas Jesus-story films have their antecedents in passion plays and the visual arts, so Christ-figure films have their antecedents in literary fiction. Whereas an understanding of the Bible and the work of biblical scholars can enhance an appreciation of Jesus-story films, so familiarity with literary tradition and the analyses of literary critics can enrich the meaning of Christ-figure films for the viewer.

In fact, Hurley, in his essay on "cinematic transfigurations of Jesus," acknowledges an indebtedness to two literary critics: Robert Detweiler and Theodore Ziolkowski. Detweiler wrote an influential essay, "Christ and the Christ Figure in American Fiction" (1964), and Ziolkowski published a more expansive volume, *Fictional Transfigurations of Jesus* (1972).

Detweiler—as a literary critic with theological training—counters the notion that a literary "Christ figure" must be Jesus the man, or the Christ of faith, in modern dress. To Detweiler, the fiction writer has no obligation to present a Christ figure consistent with Christian teaching or dogma. Therefore, many literary Christ figures embody the values of a skeptical, secular age. Among the Christ figures representing different literary subtypes that he identifies are: Jim Conklin in Stephen Crane's *The Red Badge of Courage* (1895), the title character in Herman Melville's *Billy Budd* (1924, published posthumously), the protagonist in Nathanael West's *Miss Lonelyhearts* (1933), Jim Casey in John Steinbeck's *The Grapes of Wrath* (1939), and Ike McCaslin in William Faulkner's *The Bear* (1942),

Ziolkowski prefers to speak of "fictional transfigurations of Jesus" instead of "Christ figures." He also considers novels containing such transfigurations to belong to that broader category of novels known as "post-figurative." Post-figurative novels have their action "pre- figured" in well-known mythic patterns—whether the pattern of Jesus Christ, Ulysses, the Buddha, or some other ancient figure. The twenty or so literary transfigurations of Jesus discussed by Ziolkowski include: Benito Pérez Galdós' *Nazarín* (1895, Spanish), Hermann Hesse's *Demian* (1919, German), John Steinbeck's *The Grapes of Wrath* (1939), Graham Greene's *The Power and the Glory* (1940), William Faulkner's *A Fable* (1954), and John Barth's *Giles Goat-Boy* (1966).

Any student of film will immediately recognize by their titles that many of the novels discussed by Detweiler and Ziolkowski have been adapted for the screen. Therefore, many literary Christ figures, or fictional transfigurations of Jesus, have become cinematic Christs—but which ones?

With a novel as the source of a screenplay, the filmmaker can make his cinematic Christ more or less explicit, more or less implicit. For example, both Detweiler and Ziolkowski include Steinbeck's *The Grapes of Wrath* as a novel with a Christ figure—the preacher Jim Casey (note the initials, J. C.), who suffers martyrdom for his labor organizing activity. However, nothing in John Ford's 1940 Academy Award-winning movie suggests a correlation between Jim Casey and Jesus Christ. Similarly, narrative clues in Ken Kesey's novel *One Flew Over the Cuckoo's Nest* (1962) suggest that Randle P. McMurphy, the rebellious character who finds himself incarcerated in a mental hospital, is a Christ figure. Most of these clues did not find their way into Milos Forman's 1975 Academy Award-winning film. More recent films adapted from works of fiction, whose central characters have been viewed as Christ figures, include Gabriel Axel's *Babette's Feast* (1987) and Frank Darabont's *The Green Mile* (1999). The former finds its literary base in a story by Isak Dinesen, the latter in the serialized novel by Stephen King.

To conclude: The Jesus story, as narrated in the four gospels, has served as text and subtext for films. Jesus-story films have used the gospels as texts in their cinematic retellings of the old, honored story.

Jesus-story films themselves represent two subtypes: harmonizing and alternative Jesus films. Christ-figure films have used the gospels as subtexts in their cinematic telling of other, usually more recent, stories. Christ-figure films also represent two subtypes: explicit and implicit Christ films.

THE CINEMATIC JESUS: Promise and Problem

1. This volume is now accompanied by its 1997 companion work, *The Illustrated Jesus through the Centuries*. Other recent publications that introduce readers to the immense variety of ways Jesus has been imaged, textually and visually, over the centuries include: Porter, Hayes, and Tombs (eds.), *Images of Christ: Ancient and Modern*; and David F. Ford and Mike Higton (eds.), *Jesus*.

2. Most film histories offer detailed information about the importance of the Lumière brothers and Thomas A. Edison for the origins of cinema. These include the handsomely illustrated tome assembled to commemorate the centennial of cinema: Karney, *Chronicle of the Cinema*.

3. Films produced by the Lumière brothers, Thomas A. Edison, and other film pioneers are available in a five videocassette series: *The Movies Begin* (New York: Kino on Video, 1994).

4. See Musser, "Passions and the Passion Play."

5. *The Bible on Film*, 73.

6. Brief overviews of the earliest portrayals of Jesus in film, although not always in agreement about specifics, include: Kinnard and Davis, *Divine Images*; Holloway, "From 'The Passion Play' to 'Intolerance'"; Schweitzer, *The Biblical Christ in Cinema*; and Butler, *Religion in the Cinema*.

7. Quoted by Ramsaye, "The Saga of Calvary," 373.

8. See Ramsaye, "The Saga of Calvary."

9. A print of the Hollaman film, *The Passion Play of Oberammergau* (1898), is available for screening at the Museum of Modern Art (MOMA) in New York City. The descriptive cards of the film on file there are from the card catalog at the George Eastman House (GEH), Rochester, NY, that also preserves a print.

10. For overviews of recent Jesus scholarship, consult Tatum, *In Quest of Jesus*; Powell, *Jesus as a Figure in History*; Witherington, *The Jesus Quest*; and Borg, *Jesus in Contemporary Scholarship*.

11. For the texts and analyses of these gospels, and more, see Miller, *The Complete Gospels*.

12. For a documentary movie about Jesus in film that covers the first 100 years, through *Jesus of Montreal*, see *Jesus Christ, Movie Star* (Hillside, Merry Hill Road, Bushey, Herts WD2 1DR, England: CTVC, © 1992) color, 52 mins.

CHAPTER ONE: From the Manger to the Cross

1. The first international colloquium of Domitor, the international society for the study of early film, was held in Québec, Canada, June 7–13, 1990. The

theme for the conference was "Religion and Cinema Before 1915." In anticipation of this meeting, prescreenings were held the previous year over three day periods in London, at the National Film Theatre (NFT), March 2–4, 1989, and in New York City, at the Museum of Modern Art (MOMA), June 8–10, 1989. Most, if not all, of the twelve specifically New Testament films scheduled for screening in London, and the eight in New York, dealt with the Jesus story. Both sites exhibited Sidney Olcott's *From the Manger to the Cross* (1912). The papers from this conference have been published in Cosandey, et al., *Une invention du diable?*

2. Campbell and Pitts list thirty-five New Testament films, beginning with 1900 and before 1915, many of which take their thematic material from the Jesus story: *The Bible on Film*, 75–89. In their list, of course, they include *From the Manger to the Cross* (1912) with an extensive annotation that identifies it as "the first important religious film produced by a United States film company."

3. This analysis of *From the Manger to the Cross* presupposes the 1919 release by Vitagraph, preserved in the Library of Congress, Washington, DC, FEB 3781–86; and the print now available in videocassette format: *From the Manger to the Cross* (New York: Kino on Video, 1994) color tinted, silent, music composed and performed by Timothy Howard, 71 min. Available: VHS and DVD.

4. Campbell and Pitts (*The Bible on Film*, 76), among others, identify Sidney Olcott as the director of the 1907 *Ben-Hur*. Only the chariot race sequence from this film has been preserved in the film collection at the Library of Congress, Washington, DC, H102798.

5. For the production credits and brief comment, see Anthony Slide, "From the Manger to the Cross," *MSOC*, SF, 2.461–63; and "From the Manger to the Cross," *AFI Catalog, 1911–1920*, 307; Campbell and Pitts, *The Bible on Film*, 80–82; Kinnard and Davis, *Divine Images*, 21–22.

6. *The Life of Our Saviour Jesus Christ*. This folio-size English edition includes the gospel texts and explanatory notes.

7. Reynolds, "From Palette to the Screen: The Tissot Bible as Sourcebook for 'From the Manger to the Cross.'"

8. In the collection of the Library of Congress, Washington, DC, FGE 3425.

9. For example: Witherington, *Women in the Ministry of Jesus;* Moltmann-Wendel, *The Women Around Jesus*; Corley, *Private Women, Public Meals*; and Corley, *Women and the Historical Jesus*.

10. Bland, *From Manger to Cross*; and Henderson-Bland, *Actor-Soldier-Poet*. Chapters 2–8 in the former volume have been incorporated word-for-word into chapters 2–9 of the latter.

11. *Actor-Soldier-Poet*, 33.

12. Musser, "Passions and the Passion Play," especially 438, 443–44.

13. Cited by Ramsaye, "The Saga of Calvary," 375.

14. *Hollywood Vs. America.*

15. See Musser, "Passions and the Passion Play," especially 449–51; Staiger, "Conclusions and New Beginnings"; and Couvares, "Hollywood, Main Street, and the Church."

16. *Actor-Soldier-Poet*, 70.

17. *Actor-Soldier-Poet*, 71 and 32.

18. Henderson-Bland has included in his *Actor-Soldier-Poet* lengthy quota-

tions from the British press about *From the Manger to the Cross* on the occasions of its releases in 1912, 1922, 1938.

CHAPTER TWO: Intolerance

1. The print presupposed by this analysis is *Intolerance* ([Sandy Hook, CT:] Video Images presents a Video Yesteryear Recording, © 1984) b & w, silent, original organ score by Rosa Rio, 2 videocassettes, 208 mins. The film has also been released in videocassette format in a slightly shorter version: *Intolerance* (New York: Kino on Video, © 1990) color tinted, silent, organ score by Gaylord Carter, 2 videocassettes, 171 mins. In spite of the different running times of these two videocassette versions of *Intolerance,* the Judean story appears to be identical in both. Available: VHS and DVD.

2. For production credits: Anthony Slide, "Intolerance," *MSOC,* SF, 2.570–74; and "Intolerance," *AFI Catalog: 1911–1920,* 458–59; Campbell and Pitts, *The Bible on Film,* 91–93; Kinnard and Davis, *Divine Images,* 22–27.

3. See Addams, *The Spirit of Youth and the City Streets,* especially 75–103; and *Twenty Years at Hull House,* 386–87.

4. For an excellent overview of the WCTU's campaign for movie censorship, consult Parker, "Mothering the Movies: Women Reformers and Popular Culture."

5. *The New York Times,* 22 September 1916. An excerpt from this 45-page pamphlet can be found in Geduld, *Focus on D. W. Griffith,* 43–45.

6. *The New York Times,* 10 May 1916 and 22 October 1916.

7. *Adventures with D. W. Griffith,* 137.

8. Schickel, *D. W. Griffith,* 313.

9. *Variety,* 7 April 1916.

10. Drew, *D. W. Griffith's Intolerance.*

CHAPTER THREE: The King of Kings

1. The version of the film presupposed herein is available in videocassette format: *The King of Kings* (Omaha, Nebraska: Modern Sound Pictures, © 1971) b & w, silent, 115 min. Also: *The King of Kings* (New York: Kino on Video, © 1997) color tinted with Technicolor sequence, silent, original phonophone score, 112 min. For credits and commentary, see Carolyn McIntosh, "The King of Kings," *MSOC,* SF, 2.628–30; "The King of Kings," *AFI Catalog: 1921–1930,* 405–6; Campbell and Pitts, *The Bible on Film,* 105–8; Kinnard and Davis, *Divine Images,* 40–45. Available: VHS.

2. For the opinions of Cecil B. DeMille and many details about the production of *The King of Kings* cited herein, see Hayne, ed., *Autobiography of Cecil B. DeMille,* 274–87.

3. *Autobiography of Cecil B. DeMille,* 279.

4. Campbell and Pitts, *The Bible on Film,* 103.

5. *Autobiography of Cecil B. DeMille,* 280.

6. Based on a 1943 interview with Karl Brown, preserved in the Museum of Modern Art, and cited in Henderson, *D. W. Griffith,* 170.

7. Higham, *Cecil B. DeMille*, 161.

8. Bruce Babington and Peter William Evans consider these three films by DeMille individually to represent one of the three subtypes of the biblical epic: the Christ film, the Old Testament epic, and the Roman/Christian epic (see their *Biblical Epics*). Babington and Evans assign only four of the Jesus-story films we analyze to the Christ film subtype of the biblical epic: DeMille's *The King of Kings* (1927), Bronston's *King of Kings* (1961), Stevens' *The Greatest Story Ever Told* (1965), and Scorsese's *The Last Temptation of Christ* (1988).

9. *Autobiography of Cecil B. DeMille*, 275.

10. For example: Fuller, *Interpreting the Miracles;* Davies, *Jesus the Healer;* and Smith, *Jesus the Magician*.

11. *Autobiography of Cecil B. DeMille*, 277.

12. The story of the film industry and Will Hays has been told many times. But for an excellent, and brief, overview of the churches' roles in these events in the 1920s, see Couvares, "Hollywood, Main Street, and the Church."

13. For a complete list of the "Don'ts and Be Carefuls" see Miller, *Censored Hollywood*, 39–40.

14. *Autobiography of Cecil B. DeMille*, 281.

15. *The Literary Digest*, 21 May 1927.

16. *Autobiography of Cecil B. DeMille*, 282.

17. Giannetti and Eyman, *Flashback: A Brief History of Film*, 78.

18. Available for viewing in the film collection at the Library of Congress, Washington, DC, FCA 0532–35 and FDA 0234–35. For production details, see Campbell and Pitts, *The Bible on Film*, 111–12.

19. *Franco Zeffirelli's JESUS*, 4.

CHAPTER FOUR: Ben-Hur

1. See Forshey, *American Religious and Biblical Spectaculars*.

2. As documented by Campbell and Pitts in *The Bible on Film*, motion pictures that dealt with the Jesus story in a harmonizing way were produced in America from the late 1920s, through the 1930s and 1940s, and into the 1950s. These movies often followed the passion play model. They were not produced by the major commercial studios, but often by smaller commercial companies or religious companies aiming for the church market. Among them was the Rev. James K. Friedrich's Cathedral Films whose *Day of Triumph* (1952) was issued by Century Films to theaters in 1954.

3. For the full text of the Production Code and other primary documents, see Gardner, *The Censorship Papers*.

4. Several recent studies provide detailed histories of the Production Code and the Legion of Decency. Among them: Leff and Simmons, *The Dame in the Kimono;* Skinner, *The Cross and the Cinema;* and Walsh, *Sin and Censorship*.

5. Schweitzer, *The Biblical Christ in Cinema*, 3–4.

6. These four films are available on videocassette; and the analyses of these films herein are based on the following versions: *Quo Vadis* (New York: MGM/UA Home Video, © 1986) color, 2 hrs. 51 mins.; *The Robe* (Farmington Hills, MI: Farmington Video, © 1980) color, 133 mins.; *Barabbas* (Burbank, CA: RCA/Columbia Pictures Home Video, © 1983) color, [144 mins.]; *Ben-Hur*

(New York: MGM/UA Home Video, [n.d.]) color, 206 mins. *Quo Vadis* available: VHS. *The Robe, Ben-Hur*, and *Barabbas* available: VHS and DVD.

7. For production credits and brief commentary on these films, see: Ronald Bowers, "Quo Vadis," *MSOC*, ELF, 1st Series, 3.1411–14; John C. Carlisle, "The Robe," *MSOC*, ELF, 2nd Series, 5.2025–28; Katharine M. Morsberger and Robert E. Morsberger, "Ben-Hur," *MSOC*, ELF, 1st Series, 1.149–54; Campbell and Pitts, *The Bible on Film*, 119–20, 123–24, 137–40, 148–49; Kinnard and Davis, *Divine Images*, 73–79, 84–88, 118–26, 145–52.

8. Babington and Evans, *Biblical Epics*, 177–79.

9. *The Robe* bears kinship with two other Roman/Christian pictures of the 1950s. *Demetrius and the Gladiators* (1954), also produced by Frank Ross in CinemaScope for 20th Century-Fox was an immediate sequel to *The Robe*. It continued the story of Demetrius the Greek slave of Marcellus. *The Big Fisherman* (1959), directed by Frank Borzage, was based on another popular Lloyd C. Douglas novel. "The Big Fisherman" is a nickname for the disciple with the better known nickname of Peter. Both *Demetrius and the Gladiators* and *The Big Fisherman* approach the figure of Jesus in indirect ways.

10. *The New York Times*, 7 October 1962.

11. See Talbert, *Reimarus: Fragments*.

12. Kern identifies the period in Wyler's career from 1956 to 1959 as "Pacifism and the Big Screen Years" in her book *William Wyler*, 36.

13. *The New York Times*, 26 November 1959.

14. For a thoughtful analysis of *Ben-Hur* in its varied literary and cinematic recensions and in relation to New Testament texts, see Kreitzer, "'Ben-Hur': The 'Cup of (Cold) Water' and the 'I Thirst' Saying of Jesus" in his book *The New Testament in Fiction and Film*, 44–66. Kreitzer also devotes chapters to Dino De Laurentiis' *Barabbas* (1962) and to Stanley Kubrick's *Spartacus* (1960).

15. See Apostolos-Cappadona, "The Art of 'Seeing': Classical Paintings and 'Ben-Hur.'"

16. Babington and Evans, *Biblical Epics*, 4–8.

17. These rejoinders by Wyler and Heston are reported in *Variety*, 11 November 1959.

18. Babington and Evans, *Biblical Epics*, 199–202.

19. For example, Winter, *On the Trial of Jesus*, and Wilson, *The Execution of Jesus*.

20. Crossan, *Who Killed Jesus?*

CHAPTER FIVE: King of Kings

1. *Variety*, 22 June 1960.

2. The videocassette version presupposed by this analysis: *King of Kings* (Culver City, CA: MGM/UA Home Video, © 1961) color, 2 videocassettes, 2 hours 50 mins. Available: VHS and DVD.

3. Among sources identifying Bronston's *King of Kings* as a remake: Singer, "Cinema Savior," 45; and Maltin, *Leonard Maltin's Movie and Video Guide 1993*, 655.

4. For production credits and brief commentary: Gregory William Mank, "King of Kings," *MSOC*, ELF, 1st Series, 2.908–910; *AFI Catalog: 1961–1970*,

578–79; Campbell and Pitts, *The Bible on Film*, 145–48; Kinnard and Davis, *Divine Images*, 131–45.

5. For example: Babington and Evans, *Biblical Epics*, 127–38.

6. Ray, *I Was Interrupted*, xlvii.

7. *King of Kings* [souvenir book].

8. Oddly, the synopsis of *King of Kings* in the MSOC does not even list Lucius the centurion as a "principal character" (*MSOC*, ELF, 1st Series, 2.908–10).

9. For the role of Mary Magdalene in the history of church and culture, see Haskins, *Mary Magdalen: Myth and Metaphor*. Haskins has done for Mary Magdalene what Pelikan did for Jesus in his *Jesus Through the Centuries*. Unlike Pelikan, she does discuss—in her final chapter—such relatively recent Jesus films as Zeffirelli's *Jesus of Nazareth* (1977), Scorsese's *The Last Temptation of Christ* (1988), and Arcand's *Jesus of Montreal* (1989, 1990).

10. King, "The Gospel of Mary Magdalene," and *The Gospel of Mary of Magdala: Jesus and the First Woman Apostle*.

11. This comment by Jeffrey Hunter's widow comes from her telephone interview with R. F. Schweitzer: *The Biblical Christ in Cinema*, 131–36.

12. Babington and Evans, *Biblical Epics*, 127. Therefore, they single out the "Son of Man" title as the defining category for the portrayal of Jesus in the Bronston film.

13. Quoted in *America*, 21 October 1961.

14. For letters in response to Walsh's review and her reply to those letters, see *America*, 2 December 1961.

CHAPTER SIX: The Greatest Story Ever Told

1. *The New York Times*, 26 June 1960.

2. *The New York Times*, 4 August 1961.

3. For production credits and brief commentary: *AFI Catalog: 1961–1970*, 430; Campbell and Pitts, *The Bible on Film*, 153–56; Kinnard and Davis, *Divine Images*, 154–62.

4. See Campbell and Pitts, *The Bible on Film*, 185–87. *The Day Christ Died* was first telecast by CBS-TV on March 26, 1980. A print is available for viewing in the collection of the Library of Congress: VBB 1588–90.

5. *Dwight Macdonald on Movies*, 432.

6. Niven, *Carl Sandburg, A Biography*, 685.

7. In Campbell and Pitts, *The Bible on Film*, 153. The version presupposed by this discussion: *The Greatest Story Ever Told* (Culver City, CA: MGM/UA Home Video, © 1990) color, 2 videocassettes, 199 mins. Available: VHS and DVD.

8. Quoted in *Time* magazine, 28 December 1962.

9. Quoted in the feature article by Stang, "'The Greatest Story' in One Man's View."

10. Contrary to Babington and Evans, *Biblical Epics*, 143–48.

11. An article in *Time* magazine (28 December 1962) with appropriate photographs featured Stevens and members of the cast shooting on location in Utah. Therefore, the claim by Campbell and Pitts (*The Bible on Film*, 156) that

the "film was made between October, 1962 and July, 1963" has support over against the statement by Babington and Evans (*Biblical Epics*, 142) that the "film went into production in 1964."

12. Roberto Rossellini's final feature film was a Jesus-story film, *Il messias / The Messiah* (1975). Available: VHS.

13. From an article by Jack Valenti, "The Voluntary Movie Rating System," http://www.mpaa.org/ratings.html; accessed 8 April 1997; no longer available.

14. Shana Alexander, *Life*, 26 February 1965; Kauffmann, *A World on Film*, 28; Macdonald, *Dwight Macdonald on Movies*, 431; Simon, *Private Screenings*, 173; Anonymous, *Newsweek*, 22 February 1965.

CHAPTER SEVEN: The Gospel According to St. Matthew

1. The production credits and summary of *RoGoPaG* are included in Campbell and Pitts, *The Bible on Film*, 150–51.

2. For production credits and brief commentary, see Gordon Walters, "The Gospel According to St. Matthew (Il Vangelo Secondo Matteo)," *MSOC*, FLF, 3.1264–71; *AFI Catalog: 1961–1970*, 421–22; Campbell and Pitts, *The Bible on Film*, 152-53; Kinnard and Davis, *Divine Images*, 162–66.

3. In Campbell and Pitts, *The Bible on Film*, 152. The videocassette version presupposed by this analysis: *The Gospel According to St. Matthew* (New York: Video Dimensions, [n.d.]) b & w, dubbed in English, 125 mins. Also available: *The Gospel According to St. Matthew* ([Sandy Hook, CT:] Video Yesteryear, [n.d.]) b & w, dubbed in English, 134 mins. Available VHS and DVD.

4. *The Christian Century*, 23 December 1964; *The New York Times*, 1 August 1965; *America*, 26 February 1966; *Commonweal*, 6 March 1966.

5. Gordon Walters, "The Gospel According to St. Matthew," *MSOC*, FLF, 3.1264.

6. Perrin, *What Is Redaction Criticism?*

7. For an analysis of the cinematic techniques, see Snyder, "'The Gospel According to St. Matthew': Meta-Cinema and Epical Vision."

8. For Pasolini's reflections on his making of the film, see Stack, *Pasolini on Pasolini*, 77–98.

9. Stack, *Pasolini on Pasolini*, 82.

10. Stack, *Pasolini on Pasolini*, 86.

11. Stack, *Pasolini on Pasolini*, 83.

12. Stack, *Pasolini on Pasolini*, 96.

13. Stack, *Pasolini on Pasolini*, 96.

14. Stack, *Pasolini on Pasolini*, 97.

15. *The New Republic*, 26 March 1966.

16. These words of commendation appear in the brochure distributed with rentals of the movie in 16 mm: "'The Gospel According to St. Matthew': A Guide to the Film," prepared by Thomas P. Allen.

17. *Kiss Kiss Bang Bang*, 133.

18. Brendan Gill, in *The New Yorker*, 5 March 1966; and Hollis Alpert in *Saturday Review*, 26 March 1966.

CHAPTER EIGHT: Superstar / Godspell

1. The videocassette version presupposed by this analysis is *Jesus Christ Superstar* (Universal City, CA: MCA Home Video, © 1986) color, 1 hour 48 mins. Available: VHS and DVD. After the initial commercial showings of *Godspell*, the movie circulated in 16mm film; but, as of 1997, *Godspell* was not immediately made available in videocassette format. Stephen Schwartz, the composer of the music for *Godspell*, granted permission for the use of the song titles and lyrics from the musical. But *Godspell* currently available: VHS and DVD.

2. For the evolution of *Jesus Christ Superstar* from just an idea through the initial recording to its initial staging, see McKnight, "Super Jesus."

3. Interview with Lloyd Webber, *The Christian Century*, 18–25 March 1987.

4. For production credits and brief commentary, see Pat H. Broeske, "Jesus Christ Superstar," *MSOC*, ELF, 2nd Series, 3.1216–19; Campbell and Pitts, *The Bible on Film*, 167–73; Kinnard and Davis, *Divine Images*, 177–82.

5. Cited by Barton, "The Godspell Story," 516–17.

6. Also in Barton, "The Godspell Story."

7. For production credits and brief commentary, see Campbell and Pitts, *The Bible on Film*, 163–66; Kinnard and Davis, *Divine Images*, 177.

8. *The New York Times*, 15 August 1972.

9. Available in Schubert Ogden's 1984 edition of *New Testament & Mythology and Other Basic Writings*, 1–43.

10. For reports of the *Parable* controversy, see *Time*, 24 April 1964; *Newsweek*, 27 April 1964; and *The Christian Century*, 27 May 1964. This brief 22-minute film has recently been released in a fortieth anniversary edition by United Methodist Communications (UMCom). Available: VHS and DVD.

11. In his writings of the 1960s, theologian Harvey Cox also interpreted Jesus as a "hippie." See especially "God and the Hippies," 93–94, 206–10; and *The Feast of Fools*.

12. "Jesus on Stage," 785–86.

13. Forshey, *American Religious and Biblical Spectaculars*, 104.

14. *Jesus Christ Superstar* (2000) is available in VHS and DVD formats.

15 Andrew Lloyd Webber later acknowledged that Martin Sullivan, the Dean of St. Paul's in London, had forewarned Tim Rice and himself—as early as 1968 when *Superstar* was only an idea—that they might be accused of anti-Semitism if they proceeded with plans to translate the Jesus story into a musical (McKnight, "Super Jesus," 104).

16 From an article by Jack Valenti, "The Voluntary Movie Rating System," http://www.mpaa.org/ratings.html; accessed 8 April 1997; no longer available.

17 For production credits of *The Gospel Road* (1973), see Campbell and Pitts, *The Bible on Film*, 166–67; Kinnard and Davis, *Divine Images*, 175–77. This film was released in videocassette format.

18 For production credits of *Greaser's Palace* (1972), see Campbell and Pitts, *The Bible on Film*, 161–62. The film is available for viewing at the Library of Congress in Washington, DC, FCA 9531–33. Also: VHS

19 For production credits of *The Passover Plot* (1976), see Campbell and

Pitts, *The Bible on Film*, 176–77; Kinnard and Davis, *Divine Images*, 183–84. Although not in the film collection of the Library of Congress, Washington, DC, this film was released in videocassette format.

20. A report by Trevor Beeson from London, in *The Christian Century* (27 October 1976), provides an overview of the public discussion about the Thorsen film in Europe. Kinnard and Davis conclude their volume (*Divine Images*, 219) with a paragraph noting that the Thorsen film finally was made under the title *The Return of Jesus Christ* and opened in Copenhagen in the spring of 1992. I have not been able to confirm this nor, therefore, to establish a relationship between the film released as *The Return of Jesus Christ* and Thorsen's intended film of the 1970s.

CHAPTER NINE: Jesus of Nazareth

1. The videocassette version presupposed by this analysis is *Jesus of Nazareth* (Van Nuys, CA: Live Home Video, distributed by the Bridgestone Group, © 1992) color, 3 videocassettes, 382 mins. A print version of the Jesus story in the film was published in the same year as the initial telecast: Barclay, *Jesus of Nazareth*. Available: VHS and DVD.

2. Franco Zeffirelli has reported on the making of the film in two significant volumes: *The Autobiography of Franco Zeffirelli*; and *Franco Zeffirelli's Jesus*. For an interview with Zeffirelli about the film before its debut telecast, see Loney, "The Jesus Marathon."

3. *Franco Zeffirelli's Jesus*, 7.

4. *Franco Zeffirelli's Jesus*, viii.

5. *Autobiography of Franco Zeffirelli*, 275.

6. For production information and credits: Campbell and Pitts, *The Bible on Film*, 177–80; Kinnard and Davis, *Divine Images*, 185–89.

7. *Franco Zeffirelli's Jesus*, 74; *Autobiography of Franco Zeffirelli*, 281.

8. *Autobiography of Franco Zeffirelli*, 281–82.

9. Among those British scholars who dissented from the view that Jesus consciously used Isaiah 53 to define his messiahship was Morna D. Hooker, *Jesus and the Servant*. See the more recent symposium of papers on the subject published in Bellinger and Farmer, *Jesus and the Suffering Servant*, that includes her reaffirmation of her longstanding position.

10. "Messianic Ideas and Their Influence on the Jesus of History."

11. "How Jesus Saw Himself"; also *Jesus and the Victory of God*, esp. 541–611.

12. *Autobiography of Franco Zeffirelli*, 296.

13. *Les Brown's Encyclopedia of Television*, 287.

14. Including *The New York Times*, 1 August 1974; *Birmingham [AL] News*, 1 August 1974.

15. See, for example, the open letter to General Motors by Martin E. Marty, *The Christian Century*, 13 April 1977.

16. The names and affiliations of the "religious technical advisors" appeared in the issue of *TV WEEK* (3 April 1977), distributed in such Sunday papers as the *Greensboro [NC] Daily News* (3 April 1977), on the day the film was first telecast.

CHAPTER TEN: Life of Brian

1. Significant book-length overviews of the career of the Monty Python ensemble have appeared in recent years. These include: Kim "Howard" Johnson, *The first 280 Years of Monty Python* (New York: Thomas Dunn Books / an imprint of St. Martin's Press, 1999); and David Morgan, *Monty Python Speaks! : John Cleese, Terry Gilliam, Eric Idle, Terry Jones, and Michael Palin (and a few friends and collaborators) recount an amazing—and silly—thirty-year spree in television and film in their own words, squire!* (New York: Avon Books, 1999). Also: the videocassette: *Life of Python* (Hollywod, CA: Paramount Studios © 1992, earlier © BBC and Devillier Donegan Enterprises, color, 56 mins.

2. Douglas L. McCall, *Monty Python: A Chronological Listing of the Troupe's Creative Output, and Articles and Reviews about Them, 1969-1989* (Jefferson, NC, and London: McFarland & Company, 1991).

3. *Monty Python Speaks!*, 226.

4. *Monty Python Speaks!*, 238-239.

5. The commentary herein presupposes the videocassette version: *Monty Python's Life of Brian* (Hollywood, CA: Paramount Pictures, ©1990) color, 1 hour 34 mins. The screenplay was included in *Monty Python's The Life of Brian (of Nazareth)* / MONTYPYTHONSSCRAPBOOK (Great Britain: Eyre Methuen, 1979). The published screenplay includes sketches of "Pilate's Wife" and "Otto," which were cut from the film in order to shorten the screening time. The printed screenplay has been consulted for printing bits of dialogue in this analysis, but not followed when there seem to be differences from the video version. Available: VHS and DVD.

6. See Appendix B, "Jesus Story Films and Christ figure films" for the discussion on Christ-figures in films.

7. For a careful viewer-response analysis of *Monty Python's Life of Brian* by a biblical scholar who explores the possible ancient non-biblical sources used for the film, see Philip R. Davies, "Life of Brian Research," *Biblical Studies / Cultural Studies: The Third Sheffield Colloquium*, J. Cheryl Exum and Stephen D. Moore, eds. (JSOT 266; Gender Culture, Theory 7; Sheffield: Sheffield Academic Press, 1998), 400-414.

8. McCall (in *Monty Python*, 70) lists eighteen sketches by name. The DVD (The Criterion Collection) lists nineteen chapters, also with names that vary from those that appear in print. Both these lists have been consulted. But the identifying names for the sketches herein have been formulated for this analysis of the film.

9. Robert Hewison offers an excellent survey and analysis of Monty Python's struggle against censorship of various kinds, which includes a detailed accounting of the responses to *Life of Brian* both in the United States and in the United Kingdom: *Irreverence, scurrility, profanity, vilification, and licentious abuse: Monty Python the Case Against* (New York: Grove Press, 1981), especially 78-95. The overview herein of these events draws heavily upon Hewison's illustrated narrative as well as Robert Sellers' more recent *Always Look on the Bright Side of Life: The Inside Story of Handmade Films* (Metro Publishing, 2003).

10. Cited in McCall, *Monty Python*, 72.

11. Cited in Hewison, *Irreverence*, 86.

12. Clips of this televised debate appear in the video *Jesus Christ, Movie Star* (Hillside, Merry Hill Road, Bushey, Herts.: England CTVC, © 1992) color, 52 mins.

CHAPTER ELEVEN: Jesus

1. *I Just Saw Jesus.*

2. The version presupposed herein appears on videocassette: *Jesus* ([San Clemente, CA]: An Inspirational Films Presentation of a Genesis Project Production, distributed by The JESUS Film Project, Campus Crusade for Christ, [n.d.]) color, 120 mins. Available: VHS and DVD. A print version based on the screenplay of the film, with 32 pages of still photographs, was published in conjunction with the film's initial release: Roddy, *Jesus.* Because of the film's varied use and multiple translations, the film *Jesus* appears in different cuts and lengths. For example, the version used for distribution to households in Alabama, through the Jesus Video Project of America (JVPOA), has on the cassette the title *Jesus: Special Edition* and a listed running time of 83 mins.

3. For production information and credits, see Campbell and Pitts, *The Bible on Film*, 183–84; Kinnard and Davis, *Divine Images*, 195–98.

4. Eshleman, *I Just Saw Jesus*, 50.

5. Eshleman's *I Just Saw Jesus* contains not only information about the making of the film, but reports its initial distribution in the United States and documents its missionary success around the world through the mid-1980s.

6. Hayne, *The Autobiography of Cecil B. DeMille*, 281.

7. *Franco Zeffirelli's Jesus*, ix.

8. Website: http://www.jesusfilm.org/progress/statistics.html; accessed May 15, 2004.

9. For production information and credits of *The Day Christ Died* (1980), see Campbell and Pitts, *The Bible on Film*, 185–86; Kinnard and Davis, *Divine Images*, 201–2. The film is available for viewing at the Library of Congress, Washington, DC, VBB 1588–90.

10. For production information and credits of *In Search of Historic Jesus* (1980), see Campbell and Pitts, *The Bible on Film*, 187–88; Kinnard and Davis, *Divine Images*, 203. The text presupposed by the film has been made available in print: Roddy and Sellier, *In Search of Historic Jesus;* and the film itself has been released in VHS format.

CHAPTER TWELVE: The Last Temptation of Christ

1. Interview with Corliss, "Body . . . and Blood," especially 38–39.

2. The commentary herein presupposes the videocassette version: *The Last Temptation of Christ* (Universal City, CA: MCA Home Video, © 1989) color, 2 hours 43 mins. Available: VHS and DVD.

3. *Christianity Today*, 17 February 1984, 46–47.

4. Corliss, "Body . . . and Blood," 36ff.

5. *Christianity Today*, 4 March 1988 and 15 July 1988, 43 and 51.

6. For production credits and a brief analysis of Scorsese's film, see Janet E. Lorenz, "The Last Temptation of Christ," *Magill's Cinema Annual 1989*, 179–82; Kinnard and Davis, *Divine Images*, 207–12.

7. Babington and Evans consider Scorsese's *The Last Temptation* to represent that sub-genre of the biblical epic known as the Christ film (*Biblical Epics*, 149–68).

8. Talbert, *Reimarus: Fragments*, 153–229.

9. For the ongoing reporting of the controversy with claims that the protest and boycott succeeded, see the varied reports and articles in *Christianity Today*, 16 September 1988, 41–42; 18 November 1988, 68; 7 April 1989, 14; 21 April 1989, 36–37. Also: Medved, *Hollywood Vs. America*, 37–49; and, more recently, Robin Riley, *Film, Faith, and Cultural Conflict: The Case of Martin Scorsese's "The Last Temptation of Christ,"* especially, 11-34.

10. Blockbuster Video and Action Video were among the chains not stocking the movie nationally, as reported in the Greensboro [N.C.] *News & Record*, 17 June 1989.

11. Some of the interviews: *Christianity and Crisis*, 10 October 1988; and *Playboy*, April 1991.

12. For a sampling of the letters about the film received by *The Christian Century*, see the issue dated 12 October 1988.

13. For letters from readers of *America* about the film, see the issues of 24 September 1988 and 1 October 1988. For further comment by Blake, see his "An Autopsy on 'Last Temptation,'" also in *America*, 4 March 1989.

14. Herx, *Family Guide to Movies and Videos*, 2.

CHAPTER THIRTEEN: Jesus of Montreal

1. This analysis presupposes the videocassette version: *Jesus of Montreal* (New York: Orion Home Video, © 1991) color, in French with English subtitles, 119 mins. Available: VHS and DVD.

2. For production credits and a brief analysis of Arcand's film, see Paul Salmon, "Jesus of Montreal (Jésus de Montréal)," *Magill's Cinema Annual 1990*, 201–4; also Kinnard and Davis, *Divine Images*, 212–13.

3. Cunneen, "'Jesus of Montreal': Role is the man is the Son."

4. For a synopsis, consult James Baird, "He Who Must Die," *MSOC*, FLF, 3.1351–55; Kinnard and Davis, *Divine Images*, 107–10. Dassin's film has not been released in videocassette format. However, the film is available for viewing at the Library of Congress, Washington, DC: FGC 0906–12.

5. The diagram of the crucified man briefly seen in the article on the movie screen does correspond to the kind of diagram often seen in scholarly literature in recent years. For example, see Charlesworth, "Jesus and Jehohanan." This article reports on the 1968 discovery, in a cave-tomb north of Jerusalem, of the physical remains of a crucified man whose name had been chiseled on the ossuary: "Jehohanan." Based on this evidence, scholars have debated the exact positioning of the man's body on the cross. In *Jesus of Montreal* (1990), and in *The Last Temptation of Christ* (1988), the twisting of Jesus' nude body and the doubling of his knees on the cross reflect the influence of recent scholarly reconstructions and do not represent traditional poses from the artistic tradition. Also Rousseau and Arav, "Crucifixion," in *Jesus and His World*.

6. That Jesus died during the rule of Pontius Pilate appears indisputable. This means that the crucifixion occurred sometime between 26 and 36 c.e. The differences of opinion about the specific date depend upon a number of factors including how the difference in dating between the synoptics and John is reconciled as well as the dates of Passover in a particular year. John P. Meier, in the most extensive recent examination of the chronology of Jesus' life, concludes that Jesus was probably crucified on the day of preparation for Passover, on Friday April 7, 30 c.e., making him about thirty-seven years of age (*A Marginal Jew*, I.372–433).

7. Certainly one of the pervasive characteristics of Jesus research in recent years has been the emphasis on his Jewishness. Notice the titles of recent works on the historical Jesus by scholars representing Jewish and Christian, Catholic and Protestant, backgrounds. See the trilogy by Vermes: *Jesus the Jew* (1973), *Jesus and the World of Judaism* (1983), and *The Religion of Jesus the Jew* (1993). Also: Sanders, *Jesus and Judaism* (1985); Charlesworth, *Jesus Within Judaism* (1988); Crossan, *The Historical Jesus: The Life of a Jewish Mediterranean Peasant* (1991); Meier, *A Marginal Jew* (1991, 1994, 2001); and Chilton, *Rabbi Jesus* (2000).

8. That there developed in ancient Jewish circles a tradition claiming Jesus to be the illegitimate offspring of a union between Mary and a Roman soldier named Panthera has been known and documented for many years. The tradition is cited in the writing of the third-century church father Origen and attested, in various forms, in the Talmud itself. Recent study of this evidence in relation to the infancy narratives in Matthew and Luke has led at least one scholar to conclude that Jesus was in all likelihood illegitimate and that the gospel narratives represent coverups of this fact. See Schaberg, *The Illegitimacy of Jesus.*

9. The Talmud also dismisses Jesus as something of a magician; and the term "magician" has in recent decades been applied to Jesus as an accurate historical description by Morton Smith, *Jesus the Magician* (1978). However most scholars would prefer to speak of him as a healer and an exorcist: Davies, *Jesus the Healer* (1995) and Twelftree, *Jesus the Exorcist* (1993).

10. For example: Hugh J. Schonfield uses the wrong tomb theory in his convoluted explanation for what happened after the crucifixion of Jesus in his *The Passover Plot* (1966).

11. The category of "demythologizing" comes from the theological program of Rudolf Bultmann. He proposed that the New Testament with its three-story worldview should be demythologized through existential interpretation. Accordingly, the dimensions of the Jesus story to be demythologized included the virgin birth and the miracles understood as interruptions of natural law, the crucifixion understood as vicarious atonement, the resurrection understood as a dead man's coming to life again, and the second coming as a future event in space and time. See his 1941 essay "New Testament and Mythology."

12. Directed by Stanislav Sokolav and Derek Hayes, *The Miracle Maker: The Story of Jesus* premiered in the United States, on ABC-TV, on Easter Sunday, April 23, 2000. The film was produced in Wales and Russia. Set in Palestine, in the year 30, this film—in 3D animation—features the voice of Ralph Fiennes as Jesus. Jesus' relation to Jairus' daughter, healed by him in the synoptics

and named Tamar in the film, provides the narrative framework for this retelling of the Jesus story. Available: VHS and DVD.

13. The made-for-television mini-series *Jesus* was first telecast in the United States over two evenings on NBC in the spring of 2000. Directed by Roger Young and starring Jeremy Sisto in the title role, the film was produced through the initiative of *Lux Vide*, an Italian company, which has overseen the production of a series of Bible-based films for television. Available: VHS and DVD. I have published a detailed analysis of this film elsewhere: W. Barnes Tatum, "*Jesus*: The Mini-Series: CBS, May 14 and 17, 2000," *The Fourth R* 13, 4 (July-August 2000), 3-6. The review can be accessed at Westar Institute's site: www.westarinstitute.org/Periodicals/4R_Articles/Jesus/jesus.html.

14. *The Gospel of John*, now a film with a PG-13 rating, received its public debut at the Toronto Film Festival, in September, 2003, and subsequently shown in selected theaters in Canada and the United States. Directed by Philip Savile, with Christopher Plummer serving as narrator and Henry Ian Cusick as Jesus, the three-hour film was produced by Visual Bible International. Appropriately, the film represents a visualization of the gospel of John, following faithfully the American Bible Society's Good News Translation. Available: VHS and DVD.

CHAPTER FOURTEEN: The Passion of the Christ

1. The commentary herein on *The Passion of the Christ* presupposes the version initially screened in theaters in the United States prior to the film's availability on VHS and DVD scheduled for release on Aug 31, 2004. Particularly helpful in establishing the textual basis for scenes and dialogue in this commentary was the information in the e-book, *The Passion Papers*, available through beliefnet.com and assembled by Darrell Bock and the Beliefnet staff. For a collection of essays about *The Passion*, consult: Kathleen Corley and Robert Webb, eds., *Jesus and Mel Gibson's "The Passion of the Christ": the Film, the Gospels, and the Claims of History*. New York and London: Continuum, 2004.

2. The local authorities in Matera established an unofficial web site out of civic pride and with the intention of attracting tourists to the Sassi di Matera area, a UNESCO World Heritage Site and the location where much of *The Passion* was filmed (www.sassiweb.it; accessed May 12, 2004.) The Web site contains photographs, a detailed chronology, and anecdotes about the weeks Mel Gibson and his crew were in town.

3. Dana Harris and Cathy Dunkley, "Inside Moves," *Daily Variety* (9 August 2002), News, Pg. 5. http://web.lexis-nexis.com/universe; accessed May 13, 2004.

4. The scholarly world was not surprised at the controversy created by the making of *The Passion*. On January 29, 2004, a symposium hosted by Creighton University and the University of Nebraska Omaha convened in Omaha to explore various topics related to the Gibson film. The papers presented were made available in the electronic journals, the *Journal of Religion and Society* (www.creighton.edu/JRS/) and the *Journal of Religion and Film* (www.unomaha.edu/~wwwjrf/). The Society of Biblical Literature, also featured through its online Forum, for the month of March 2004, a series of articles available on the SBL web site: www.sbl-site.org. The Jesus Seminar and its host organiza-

tion the Westar Institute, as advocates for religious literacy, also provided through their Web sites access to a broad range and diverse sources related to *The Passion* (www.westarinstitute.org)

5. For a recent analysis of the portrayal of Jews and Judaism that constituted the key-note address at *The Passion* symposium held at the University of Nebraska Omaha, see Adele Reinhartz, "Passion-ate Moments in the Jesus Film Genre," *Journal of Religion & Society* 6 (2004): 1-10. Available at–http://moses.creighton.edu/JRS/2004/2004.3a.html; accessed February 29, 2004.

6. A helpful overview of the controversy may be found in the following: Peter J. Boyer, "The Jesus War: Mel Gibson's Obsession," *The New Yorker* (15 September 2003): 58-71.

7. "Papal praise for *The Passion*: 'It is as it Was,' John Paul II Says," ZENIT News Service (18 December 2003).

8. *The Dolorous Passion of Our Lord Jesus Christ: From the Meditations of Anne Catherine Emmerich* (Rockford, Ill.: Tan Books and Publishers, 1983).

9. For the importance of blood sacrifice for Mel Gibson, see David Neff, "The Passion of Mel Gibson," *Christianity Today* 48, 3 (March 2004), 35

10. For the numbers on theaters and screens, also see David Neff "The Passion of Mel Gibson," *Christianity Today* (March 2004) at www.christianity-today.com/movies/commentaries/passion-passionofmel.html; posted 02/20/04 and accessed 4/10/2004. The printed edition does not have these specific figures.

11. For the box office receipts for *The Passion*, consult: www.boxoffice-mojo.com; accessed 6/8/2004.

12. For a detailed account of the marketing campaign for *The Passion*, see the article by T. L. Stanley, "Producers keep up passion for 'Passion'," *Advertising Age* (March 22, 2004), 3, 26-27.

13. "Responsibility for Gibson's *Passion of Christ*," *The Responsive Community* 14, 1 (Winter 2003-2004), 59-63.

14. Web site: www.usccb.org/movies/p/thepassionofthechrist.htm; accessed 4/11/2004.

15. *The Bible, the Jews, and the Death of Jesus: A Collection of Catholic Documents* (Washington, D.C.: USCCB, 2004). For an assessment by a Catholic scholar of how the Gibson film measures up, see Philip A. Cunningham, "A Dangerous Fiction: *The Passion of the Christ* and post-conciliar Catholic teaching," *America* (5 April 2004), 8-11.

16. David Neff, "The Passion of Mel Gibson," *Christianity Today* 48, 3 (March 2004), 30.

17. For Crossan's detailed analysis of the passion narratives, see his: *Who Killed Jesus?*

THE CINEMATIC JESUS: Retrospect and Prospect

1. For credits and comment, see: Ira Konigsberg, "Vampyr," *MSOC*, FLF, 7.3248–53; Raymond Carney, "Day of Wrath," *MSOC*, FLF, 2.739–45; Raymond Carney, "Ordet," *MSOC*, FLF, 5.2300–5; and Blake Lucas, "Gertrud," *MSOC*, FLF, 3.1216–19.

2. Skoller, *Dreyer in Double Reflection*, 145.

3. Skoller, *Dreyer in Double Reflection*, 146 and 155.

4. Cornfield, *Carl Theodor Dreyer's Jesus*. David Bordwell, in his article "Passion, Death, and Testament," provided a detailed summary of the script of Dreyer's intended movie when that script was first published.

5. Drouzy and Jørgensen, *Letters about the Jesus Film.*

6. Bordwell, "Passion, Death, and Testament," 60.

7. For credits and comment, see Arjen Uijterlinde, "Turkish Delight," *MSOC*, FLF, 7.3175–79.

8. For credits and comment, see Chon Noriega, "Robocop," *Magill's Cinema Annual 1988*, 303–6; Marc Mancini, "Total Recall," *Magill's Cinema Annual 1991*, 377–80; and Douglas Gomery, "Basic Instinct," *Magill's Cinema Annual 1993*, 49–51.

9. Interview with Donnell Stoneman, film critic for the [Greensboro, NC] *News & Record*, "Paul Verhoeven: Film Maker." The interview was conducted on December 12, 1989, and initially appeared in the [Greensboro, NC] *News and Record*, 14 December 1989.

10. For the results and a brief history of the Jesus Seminar, consult Funk and Hoover, *The Five Gospels*; and Tatum, *John the Baptist and Jesus.*

11. The particulars about these sessions in Toronto have been published in Borg, "Christ the Man: The Toronto Report." The four scenarios were developed by John Dominic Crossan, Richard Horsley, Mahlon Smith, and Marcus Borg. The four cameo essays were prepared by Loren Mack-Fisher, Douglas Oakman, Hal Taussig, and Milfred Smith.

12. For Verhoeven's paper, along with three formal responses, see his "Christ the Man." The three respondents were Roy W. Hoover, Bruce Chilton, and Arthur J. Dewey.

13. Other early notices include: Singer, "Cinema Savior"; Blake, "An Autopsy on 'Last Temptation'; and Medved, "Hollywood vs. Religion."

14. Stoneman, "Paul Verhoeven: Film Maker," 3

15. Stoneman, "Paul Verhoeven: Film Maker," 3f.

Reference Works

The American Film Institute Catalog of Motion Pictures Produced in the United States. [AFI Catalog].
> Feature Films, 1911–1920. 2 vols. Berkeley: University of California Press, 1988.
> Feature Films, 1921–1930. 2 vols. New York and London: R. R. Bowker, 1972.
> Feature Films, 1931–1940. 2 vols. Berkeley: University of California Press, 1993.
> Feature Films, 1961–1970. 2 vols. New York and London: R. R. Bowker, 1976.

Campbell, Richard H., and Michael R. Pitts. *The Bible on Film: A Checklist, 1897–1980.* Metuchen, NJ, and London: Scarecrow Press, 1981.

Kinnard, Roy, and Tim Davis. *Divine Images: A History of Jesus on the Screen.* New York: Carol Publishing Group, A Citadel Press Book, 1992.

Les Brown's Encyclopedia of Television. 3d ed. Detroit and London: Gale Research, 1992.

Magill, Frank N., ed. *Magill's Survey of Cinema. [MSOC].* Englewood, NJ: Salem Press.
> English Language Films [ELF], 1st Series. 4 vols. 1980.
> English Language Films [ELF], 2nd Series. 6 vols. 1981.
> Silent Films [SF]. 3 vols., 1982.
> Foreign Language Films [FLF]. 8 vols. 1985.
> Magill's Cinema Annuals. 1982—.

Monographs

Addams, Jane. *The Spirit of Youth and the City Streets.* New York: Macmillan, 1911. [Original, 1909.]

____. *Twenty Years at Hull House.* New York: Macmillan, 1916. [Original, 1910.]

Allison, Dale C. *Jesus of Nazareth: Millenarian Prophet.* Minneapolis: Fortress, 1998.

Babington, Bruce, and Peter William Evans. *Biblical Epics: Sacred Narrative in the Hollywood Cinema.* Manchester and New York: Manchester University Press, 1993.

Barclay, William. *Jesus of Nazareth.* London and Cleveland: Collins, 1977.

Barton, Bruce. *The Man Nobody Knows.* Indianapolis: Bobbs-Merrill, 1924.

Baugh, S. J., Lloyd, *Imaging the Divine: Jesus and Christ-figures in Film.* Kansas City, MO: Sheed & Ward, 1997.

Bellingham, Jr., William H., and William R. Farmer, eds. *Jesus and the Suffering Servant: Isaiah 53 and Christian Origins.* Harrisburg, PA: Trinity International, 1998.

Bland, Henderson. *From Manger to Cross: The Story of the World-Famous Film of the Life of Jesus.* London: Hodder and Stoughton, 1922. [Same author as R. Henderson-Bland.]

Bishop, Jim. *The Day Christ Died: An Historical Novel.* New York: Harper-Collins, 1995. [Original, 1957.]

Borg, Marcus J. *Jesus: A New Vision.* San Francisco: HarperSanFrancisco, 1987.

____. *Jesus in Contemporary Scholarship.* Valley Forge, PA: Trinity, 1994.

____. *Meeting Jesus Again for the First Time.* San Francisco, HarperSanFrancisco, 1994.

Brown, Karl. *Adventures with D. W. Griffith.* New York: Farrar, Straus, and Giroux, 1973.

Brown, Raymond E. *The Death of the Messiah: From Gethsemane to the Grave.* 2 vols. New York: Doubleday, 1994.

Butler, Ivan. *Religion in the Cinema.* International Film Guide Series. New York: A. S. Barnes, 1969.

Case, Shirley Jackson. *Jesus: A New Biography.* Chicago: University of Chicago Press, 1927.

Charlesworth, James H. *Jesus Within Judaism.* New York: Doubleday, 1988.

Chilton, Bruce. *Rabbi Jesus: An Intimate Biography.* New York: Doubleday, 2000.

Corley, Kathleen, and Robert Webb, eds. *Jesus and Mel Gibson's "The Passion of the Christ": The Film, the Gospels, and the Claims of History.* New York and London: Continuum, 2004.

Corley, Kathleen E. *Private Women, Public Meals: Social Conflict in the Synoptic Tradition.* Peabody, MA: Hendrickson, 1993.

____ . *Women and the Historical Jesus: Feminist Myths of Christian Origins.* Santa Rosa, CA: Polebridge Press, 2002.

Cornfield, Robert, ed. *Carl Theodor Dreyer's Jesus.* New York: Dial, 1972.

Cosandey, Roland, André Gaudreault, and Tom Gunning, eds. *Une invention du diable? Cinéma des premiers temps et religion.* Sainte-Foy: Les Presses de l'Université Laval, 1992.

Couvares, Francis G., ed. *Movie Censorship and American Culture.* Washington and London: Smithsonian Institution Press, 1996.

Cox, Harvey. *Feast of Fools: A Theological Essay on Festivity and Fancy.* Cambridge: Harvard University Press, 1969.

Crossan, John Dominic. *The Historical Jesus: The Life of a Jewish Mediterranean Peasant.* San Francisco: HarperSanFrancisco, 1991.

____. *Jesus: A Revolutionary Biography.* San Francisco: Harper SanFrancisco, 1994.

____. *Who Killed Jesus? Exposing the Roots of Anti-Semitism in the Gospel Story of the Death of Jesus.* San Francisco: HarperSanFrancisco, 1995.

Davies, Stevan L. *Jesus the Healer: Possession, Trance, and the Origins of Christianity.* New York: Continuum, 1995.

Dodd, C. H. *The Founder of Christianity.* New York: Macmillan, 1970.

Drew, William M. *D. W. Griffith's Intolerance: Its Genesis and Its Vision.* Jefferson, NC, and London: MacFarland, 1986.

Drouzy, Martin, and Lisbeth Nannestad Jørgensen, eds. *Letters About the Jesus Film: 16 Years of Correspondence Between Carl Th. Dreyer and Blevins Davis.* Copenhagen: University of Copenhagen, 1989.

Ehrman, Bart D. *Apocalyptic Prophet of the Millenium.* Oxford: Oxford University Press, 1999.

Emmerich, Anne Catherine. *The Dolorous Passion of Our Lord Jesus Christ.* Rockford, IL: Tan Books and Publishers, 1983.

Enslin, Morton. *The Prophet from Nazareth.* New York: McGraw-Hill, 1961.

Eshleman, Paul. *I Just Saw Jesus.* Laguna Niguel, CA: The JESUS Film Project, 1985.

Flannery, Austin, O.P., gen. ed. *Vatican Council II: The Conciliar and Post Conciliar Documents.* New revised edition. Northport, NY: Costello Publishing Company, 1992.

Ford, David F., and Mike Higton, eds. *Jesus.* Oxford Readers. Oxford: Oxford University Pres, 2002.

Forshey, Gerald E. *American Religious and Biblical Spectaculars.* Media and Society Series. Westport, CT, and London: Praeger, 1992.

Fredriksen, Paula. *Jesus of Nazareth: King of the Jews.* New York: Alfred A. Knopf, 1999.

Fuller, Reginald H. *Interpreting the Miracles.* Philadelphia: Westminster, 1963.

Funk, Robert W. *Honest to Jesus: Jesus for a New Millennium.* San Francisco: HarperSanFrancisco, 1996.

Funk, Robert W., Roy W. Hoover, and the Jesus Seminar. *The Five Gospels: The Search for the Authentic Words of Jesus.* New York: Macmillan, A Polebridge Press Book, 1993.

Funk, Robert W., and the Jesus Seminar. *The Acts of Jesus: The Search for the Authentic Deeds of Jesus.* San Francisco: HarperSanFrancisco, A Polebridge Press Book, 1998.

Gardner, Gerald. *The Censorship Papers: Movie Censorship Letters in the Hays Office, 1934–1968.* New York: Dodd, Mead & Company, 1987.

Geduld, Harry M. *Focus on D. W. Griffith.* Englewood Cliffs, NJ: Prentice-Hall, 1971.

Giannetti, Louis, and Scott Eyman. *Flashback: A Brief History of Film.* 2d ed. Englewood Cliffs, NJ: Prentice-Hall, 1991.

Haskins, Susan. *Mary Magdalen: Myth and Metaphor.* New York: Harcourt Brace & Co., 1993.

Hayne, Donald, ed. *The Autobiography of Cecil B. DeMille.* Englewood Cliffs, NJ: Prentice-Hall, 1959.

Henderson, Robert M. *D. W. Griffith: His Life and Work.* New York: Oxford University Press, 1972.

Henderson-Bland, R. *Actor-Soldier-Poet.* London: Heath Cranton, 1939. [Same author as Henderson Bland.]

Herx, Henry, ed. *The Family Guide to Movies and Videos.* Washington, DC: United States Catholic Conference, 1995.

Higham, Charles. *Cecil B. DeMille.* New York: Charles Scribner's Sons, 1973.

Hooker, Morna. *Jesus and the Servant.* London: SPCK, 1959.

Horsley, Richard A. *Jesus and the Spiral of Violence*. Minneapolis: Fortress Press, 1993. [Original, 1987.]

Hunter, A. M. *The Work and Words of Jesus*. Philadelphia: Westminster, 1950.

Jacobs, Lewis. *The Rise of the American Film: A Critical History*. New York: Columbia University, Teachers College Press, 1968.

Jefferson, Thomas. *The Jefferson Bible: The Life and Morals of Jesus of Nazareth*. Boston: Beacon, 1989. [Original, 1820.]

Johnson, Kim "Howard" Johnson, *The First 280 Years of Monty Python*. New York: Thomas Dunn Books, imprint of St. Martin's Press, 1999.

Kael, Pauline. *Kiss Kiss Bang Bang*. Boston and Toronto: Little, Brown, 1965.

Karney, Robyn, ed.-in-chief. *Chronicle of the Cinema*. London-New York-Stuttgart-Moscow: Dorling Kindersley, 1995.

Kauffmann, Stanley. *A World on Film*. New York: Dell, 1966.

Kaylor, R. David. *Jesus the Prophet: His Vision of the Kingdom of God on Earth*. Louisville: Westminster/John Knox, 1994.

Kazantzakis, Nikos. *The Last Temptation of Christ*. Trans. P. A. Bien. New York: Simon and Schuster, 1960. [Greek original, 1955.]

Kern, Sharon. *William Wyler: A Guide to References and Resources*. Boston: G. K. Hall, 1984.

King, Karen. *The Gospel of Mary of Magdala: Jesus and the First Woman Apostle*. Santa Rosa, CA: Polebridge Press, 2003.

King of Kings. Souvenir book. New York: Metro-Goldwyn-Mayer/Samuel Bronston Productions, Inc., 1961.

Kreitzer, Larry J. *The New Testament in Fiction and Film: On Reversing the Hermeneutical Flow*. The Biblical Seminar 17. Sheffield: JSOT Press, 1993.

Leff, Leonard J., and Jerold Simmons. *The Dame in the Kimono: Hollywood, Censorship, and the Production Code from the 1920s to the 1960s*. New York: Grove Weidenfeld, 1990.

Macdonald, Dwight. *Dwight Macdonald on Movies*. Englewood Cliffs, NJ: Prentice Hall, 1969.

Mack, Burton. *The Lost Gospel: The Book of Q and Christian Origins*. San Francisco: HarperSanFrancisco, 1994.

MacLuhan, Marshall. *Understanding Media: The Extensions of Man*. New York: MacGraw-Hill, 1964.

Maltin, Leonard. Ed. *Leonard Maltin's Movie andf Video Guide 1993*. New York: Penguin Books, A Signet Book, 1992,

Manson, T. W. *The Servant-Messiah*. Grand Rapids: Baker Book House, 1977. [Original, 1953.]

Medved, Michael. *Hollywood Vs. America: Popular Culture and the War on Traditional Values*. New York: HarperCollins and Zondervan, 1992.

Meier, John P. *A Marginal Jew*. 3 vols. New York: Doubleday, 1991, 1994, 2001.

Miller, Frank. *Censored Hollywood: Sex, Sin, and Violence on the Screen*. Atlanta: Turner Publishing, 1994.

Miller, Robert J., ed. *The Complete Gospels: Annotated Scholars Version*. Revised and expanded edition. Santa Rosa, CA: Polebridge Press, 1994.

Moltmann-Wendel, Elisabeth. *The Women Around Jesus*. New York: Crossroad, 1997.

MONTYPYTHONSSCRAPBOOK. Great Britain: Eyre Methuen, 1979.

Morgan, David. *Monty Python Speaks!: John Cleese, Terry Gilliam, Eric Idle, Terry Jones, and Michael Palin (and a few friends and collaborators) recount an amazing-and silly-thirty-year spree . . . in their own words, squire!* New York: Avon Books, 1999.

Niven, Penelope. *Carl Sandburg: A Biography.* New York: Charles Scribner's Sons, 1991.

Oursler, Fulton. *The Greatest Story Ever Told.* Garden City, NY: Doubleday, 1949.

Stephen J. Patterson, The God of Jesus: The Historical Jesus and the Search for *Meaning.* Harrisburg, PA, 1998.

Pelikan, Jaroslav, *The Illustrated Jesus Through the Centuries.* New Haven and London: Yale University Press, 1997.

____. *Jesus Through the Centuries: His Place in the History of Culture.* New Haven and London: Yale University Press, 1985.

Perrin, Norman. *What Is Redaction Criticism?* Philadelphia: Fortress Press, 1969.

Porter, Stanley E., Michael A. Hayes, and David Tombs, eds. *Images of Christ: Ancient and Modern.* Roehampton Institute London Papers, 2. Sheffield: Sheffield Academic Press, 1997.

Powell, Mark Allan. *Jesus as a Figure in History: How Modern Historians View the Man from Galilee.* Louisville, KY: Westminster John Knox Press, 1998.

Ray, Nicholas. *I Was Interrupted: Nicholas Ray on Making Movies.* Eds. Susan Ray, and Bernard Eisenschitz, biographical outline. Berkeley: University of California Press, 1993.

Riley, Robin. *Film, Faith, and Cultural Conflict: The Case of Martin Scorsese's The Last Temptation of Christ.* Westport, CT: Praeger, 2003. Westport, CT, and London: Praeger, 2003.

Roddy, Lee. *Jesus.* Clover, SC: Commission Press, 1979.

Roddy, Lee, and Charles E. Sellier, Jr., *In Search of Historic Jesus.* New York: Bantam, 1979.

Rousseau, John J., and Rami Arav. *Jesus & His World: An Archaeological and Cultural Dictionary.* Minneapolis: Fortress Press, 1995.

Sanders, E. P. *The Historical Jesus.* London: Allen Lane, The Penguin Press, 1993.

____. *Jesus and Judaism.* Philadelphia: Fortress Press, 1985.

Schaberg, Jane. *The Illegitimacy of Jesus: A Feminist Theological Interpretation of the Infancy Narratives.* New York: Crossroad, 1990.

Schickel, Richard. *D. W. Griffith: An American Life.* New York: Simon and Schuster, 1984.

Schonfield, Hugh J. *The Passover Plot.* New York: Bernard Geis, 1966.

Schüssler Fiorenza, Elisabeth. *In Memory of Her: A Feminist Theological Reconstruction of Christian Origins.* New York: Crossroad, 1986.

Schweitzer, Albert. *The Quest of the Historical Jesus.* Trans. W. Montgomery. New York: Macmillan, 1968. [German original, 1906.]

Schweitzer, Robert Fred. *The Biblical Christ in Cinema.* Ph.D. dissertation, University of Missouri, 1971. Ann Arbor: University Microfilms International.

Sellers, Robert. *Always Look on the Bright Side of Life*. Metro Publishing, 2003.

Sheldon, Charles M. *In His Steps*. Grand Rapids, MI: Zondervan, 1970. [Original, 1897.]

Simon, John. *Private Screenings*. New York: Berkley, 1971.

Skinner, James M. *The Cross and the Cinema: The Legion of Decency and the National Catholic Office for Motion Pictures, 1933–1970*. Westport, CT and London: Yale University Press, 1996.

Skoller, Donald, ed. *Dreyer in Double Reflection: Translation of Carl Th. Dreyer's Writings About the Film (Om Filmen)*. New York: Da Capo, 1991.

Smith, Morton. *Jesus the Magician*. New York: Harper & Row, 1978.

Stack, Oswald. *Pasolini on Pasolini: Interviews with Oswald Stack*. Bloomington and London: Indiana University Press, 1970.

Stern, Richard C., Clayton N. Jefford, and Gueric Dabona, O.S.B. *Savior on the Silver Screen*. Mahwah, N.J.: Paulist, 1999.

Talbert, Charles H., ed. *Reimarus: Fragments*. Trans. Ralph S. Fraser. Lives of Jesus Series. Philadelphia: Fortress Press, 1970.

Tatum, W. Barnes. *In Quest of* Jesus. Rev. and enl ed.; Nashville: Abingdon, 1999).

_____. *John the Baptist and Jesus: A Report of the Jesus Seminar*. Sonoma, CA: Polebridge Press, 1994.

Taylor, Vincent. *The Life and Ministry of Jesus*. Nashville: Abingdon, 1955.

Tissot, James Joseph Jacques. *The Life of Our Savior Jesus Christ: Three Hundred and Sixty-five Compositions from the Four Gospels*. 3 vols. New York: Werner, 1903.

Twelftree, Graham H. *Jesus the Exorcist*. Tübingen: Mohr, 1993.

United States Conference of Catholic Bishops. *The Bible, The Jews, and the Death of Jesus: A Collection of Catholic Documents*. Washington, DC: Unites States Conference of Catholic Bishops, 2004.

Vermes, Geza. *Jesus the Jew*. London: William Collins Sons, 1973.

_____. *Jesus and the World of Judaism*. London: SCM, 1983.

_____. *The Religion of Jesus the Jew*. Minneapolis: Fortress Press, 1993.

Wallace, General Lew. *Ben-Hur: A Tale of the Christ*. New York: Harper, 1905. [Original, 1880.]

Walsh, Frank. *Sin and Censorship: The Catholic Church and the Motion Picture Industry*. New Haven and London: Yale University Press, 1996.

Walsh, Richard. *Reading the Gospels in the Dark: Portrayals of Jesus in Film*. Harrisburg, Pa.: Trinity, 2003.

Wilson, William R. *The Execution of Jesus: A Judicial, Literary, and Historical Investigation*. New York: Charles Scribner's Sons, 1970.

Winter, Paul. *On the Trial of Jesus*. Berlin: Walter de Gruyter, 1961.

Witherington, III, Ben. *The Christology of Jesus*. Philadelphia: Fortress Press, 1990.

_____. *The Jesus Quest: The Third Search for the Jew of Nazareth*. Downers Grove, IL: InterVarsity, 1995.

_____. *Women in the Ministry of Jesus: A Study of Jesus' Attitudes to Women and Their Roles as Reflected in His Earthly Life*. Cambridge: Cambridge University Press, 1984.

Wright, N. T. *Jesus and the Victory of God*. Minneapolis: Fortress Press, 1996.

Zeffirelli, Franco. *The Autobiography of Franco Zeffirelli*. New York: Weidenfeld & Nicolson, 1986.

____. *Franco Zeffirelli's Jesus: A Spiritual Diary*. Trans. Willis J. Egan, S. J. San Francisco: Harper & Row, 1984. [Italian original, 1977.]

Ziolkowski, Theodore. *Fictional Transfigurations of Jesus*. Princeton: Princeton University Press, 1972.

Articles and Chapters

Allen, Thomas P. "'The Gospel According to St. Matthew,' A Guide to the Film." Mt. Vernon, NY: Macmillan Audion Brandon Films, n.d.

Apostolos-Cappadona, Diane. "The Art of 'Seeing': Classical Paintings and 'Ben-Hur.'" Pp. 104–115 in *Image and Likeness*. Ed. John R. May. New York and Mahwah, NJ: Paulist Press, 1992.

Barton, Joseph. "The Godspell Story." *America* 125 (11 December 1971): 516–17.

Blake, Richard A., S. J. "An Autopsy on 'Last Temptation.'" *America* 160 (4 March 1989), 199–201.

Bordwell, David. "Passion, Death, and Testament: Carl Dreyer's Jesus Film." *Film Comment* 8 (Summer 1972): 59–63.

Borg, Marcus J. "Christ the Man: The Toronto Report." *The Fourth R* 3, 1 (January 1990): 1–5.

Boyer, Peter J. "The Jesus War: Mel Gibson's Obsession," *The New Yorker* (15 September 2003): 58-71.

Bultmann, Rudolf. "New Testament and Mythology." Pp. 1-43 in *New Testament & Mythology and Other Basic Writings*. Ed. and trans. Schubert Ogden. Philadelphia: Fortress Press, 1984. [Original German, 1941.]

Charlesworth, J. H. "Jesus and Jehohanan: An Archaeological Note on Crucifixion." *Expository Times* 84 (Fall 1973): 147–150.

Corliss, Richard. "Body . . . and Blood." *Film Comment* 24 (September-October 1988): 34ff.

Couvares, Francis G. "Hollywood, Main Street, and the Church: Trying to Censor Movies before the Production Code." Pp. 129–158 in *Movie Censorship and American Culture*. Ed. Francis G. Couvares. [See Monographs.]

Cox, Harvey. "God and the Hippies." *Playboy* (January 1968): 93–94, 206–210.

Cunneen, Joseph. "'Jesus of Montreal': Role is the man is the Son." *National Catholic Reporter* 26 (29 June 1990): 19.

Cunningham, Philip A. "A Dangerous Fiction: *The Passion of the Christ* and Post-Conciliar Catholic Teaching," *America* 190, 12 (5 April 2004): 8-11.

Davies, Philip R. "Life of Brian Research." Pp. 400-414 in *Biblical Studies/Cultural Studies: The Third Sheffield Colloquium*. Eds. J. Cheryl Exum and Stephen D. Moore. JSOT 266; Sheffield: Sheffield University Press, 1998.

Detweiler, Robert. "Christ and the Christ Figure in American Fiction." *The Christian Scholar* 47 (Summer 1964): 111–124.

Dunn, J. D. G. "Messianic Ideas and Their Influence on the Jesus of History." Pp. 365–81 in *The Messiah: Developments in Earliest Judaism and Christianity.* Ed. James H. Charlesworth. Minneapolis: Fortress Press, 1992.

Dyke, Carl. " Learning from *The Life of Brian*: Saviors for Seminars." Pp. 229-50 in *Screening Scripture: Intertextual Connections Between Scripture and Film.* Eds. George Achiele and Richard Walsh. Harrisburg: Trinity, 2002.

Fredriksen, Paula. "Responsibility for Gibson's *Passion of Christ.*" *The Responsive Community* 14, 1 (Winter 2003-2004): 59-63.

Hewison, Robert. *Irreverence, scurrility, profanity, vilification, and licentious abuse: Monty Python the Case Against.* New York: Grove, 1981.

Holloway, Ronald. "From the Passion Play to 'Intolerance.'" *Beyond the Image: Approaches to the Religious Dimension in Cinema.* Geneva: World Council of Churches, 1977: 46-59.

Hurley, Neil P. "Cinematic Transfigurations of Jesus." Pp. 61–78 in *Religion in Film.* Eds. John R. May and Michael Bird. Knoxville: University of Tennessee Press, 1982.

Jacobson, Harlan. "You Talkin' to Me?" *Film Comment* 24 (September-October 1988): 32–33.

King, Karen L. "The Gospel of Mary Magdalene." Vol. 2, pp. 601–34 in *Searching the Scriptures: A Feminist Commentary.* 2 vols. Ed. Elisabeth Schüssler Fiorenza. New York: Crossroad, 1993–1994.

Loney, Glenn. "The Jesus Marathon." *The Christian Century* 93 (13 October 1976): 872–75.

Mahan, Jeffrey H. Celluloid Savior: Jesus in the Movies," 6,1 (April 2002): Available online: www.unomaha.edu/~wwwjrf

McCall, Douglas L. *Monty Python: A Chronological Listing of the Troupe's Creative Output and Articles and Reviews About Them, 1969-1989.* Jefferson, NC and London: McFarland, 1991.

McKnight, Gerald. "Super Jesus." *Andrew Lloyd Webber.* New York: St. Martin's, 1984: 104-116.

Medved, Michael. "Hollywood vs. Religion." *Imprimis* 18 (December 1989): 1–4.

Musser, Charles. "Passions and the Passion Play: Theatre, Film, and Religion in America, 1880–1900." *Film History* 5 (December 1993): 419–456. [Reprinted as pp. 43–72 in *Movie Censorship and American Culture.* Ed. Francis G. Couvares. (See Monographs.)]

Neff, David. "The Passion of Mel Gibson." *Christianity Today* 48 (March 2004): 30-35.

Parker, Alison. "Mothering the Movies: Women Reformers and Popular Culture." Pp. 73–96 in *Movie Censorship and American Culture.* Ed. Francis G. Couvares. [See Monographs.]

Ramsaye, Terry. "The Saga of Calvary." *A Million and One Nights: A History of the Motion Picture.* New York: Simon and Schuster, 1926: 366-78.

Reinhartz, Adele. "Jesus in Film: Hollywood Perspectives on the Jewishness of Jesus." *Journal of Religion and Film* 2,2 (October 1998). Available online: www.unomaha.edu/~wwwjrf

_____. "Passion-ate Moments in the Jesus Film Genre." *Journal of Religion and Society* 6 (2004). Available online: www.creighton.edu/JRS

Reynolds, Herbert. "From Palette to the Screen: The Tissot Bible as Sourcebook for 'From Manger to the Cross'." Pp. 275–310 in *Une invention du diable? Cinéma des premiers temps et religion.* Eds. Roland Cosandey, André Gaudreault, and Tom Gunning. [See Monographs.]

Singer, Michael. "Cinema Savior." *Film Comment* 24 (September-October 1988): 44–47.

Snyder, Stephen. *"The Gospel According to St. Matthew*: Meta-Cinema and Epical Vision." *Pier Paolo Pasolini.* Boston: Twayne, 1980: 59-70,

Staiger, Janet. "Conclusions and New Beginnings." Pp. 353–60 in *Une invention du diable? Cinéma des premiers temps et religion.* Eds. Roland Cosandey, Andre Gaudreault, and Tom Gunning. [See Monographs]

Stang, Joanne. "'The Greatest Story' in One Man's View." *New York Times* (14 February 1965): sec. 2, page 1.

Stoneman, Donnell. "Paul Verhoeven: Film Maker." *The Fourth R* 3,1 (January 1990): 2–6.

Tatum, W. Barnes. "Jesus—The Mini-Series: CBS, May 14 and 17, 2000." *The Fourth R* 13,4 (July-August 2000): 3-6. This review is also available online: www.westarinstitute.org/Periodicals/4R_Articles/Jesus/jesus.html

Tatum, W. Barnes, and Henry Black Ingram. "Whence and Whither the Cinematic Jesus?" *Religion in Life* 44 (1975): 470–478.

Verhoeven, Paul. "Christ the Man." *The Fourth R* 4,1 (January 1991): 5–8.

Wright, Elliott. "Jesus on Stage: A Reappraisal." *The Christian Century* 89 (19 July 1972): 785–86.

Wright, N. T. "How Jesus Saw Himself." *Bible Review* 12 (June 1996): 22–29.

Individuals

James D'Arc, DeMille Archives, Harold B. Lee Library, Brigham Young University; Berry Fiess, The JESUS Film Project, Campus Crusade for Christ; Terry Geesken, Film Stills Archive, The Museum of Modern Art; Henry Herx, Office for Film and Broadcasting, Department of Communications, United States Catholic Conference; Roy Kinnard, author of *Divine Images*; Jon Maslansky, Video Yesteryear; Nicholas Mulligan, Kino on Video; Stephen Schwartz and Hope Taylor, Paramuse Artists Associates; Christopher Shannon, George Eastman House; Sandra Smith and Dorothy Shamblen, Modern Sound Pictures; Marcus Greene, [Greensboro, NC] *News & Record.*

Documents

Excerpts from *Vatican Council II: The Conciliar and Post Conciliar Documents, New Revised Edition,* edited by Austin Flannery, O.P., copyright © 1996, Costello Publishing Company, Inc., Northport, NY, are used by permission of the publisher, all rights reserved. No part of these excerpts may be reproduced, stored in a retrieval system, or transmitted in any form or by any means—electronic, mechanical, photo-copying, recording or otherwise, without express permission of Costello Publishing Company.

Periodical Articles and Reviews

Excerpts from *America* with the permission of America Press, Inc., 106 West 56th Street, New York, NY 10019, all rights reserved, © 1961–73: Moira Walsh, review of *Barabbas,* Oct. 6, 1962; Moira Walsh, review of *King of Kings,* Oct. 21, 1961; Moira Walsh, review of *The Greatest Story Ever Told,* Feb. 27, 1965; Moira Walsh, review of *The Gospel According to St. Matthew,* Feb. 26, 1966; Moira Walsh, review of *Jesus Christ Superstar,* Sept. 1, 1973; Moira Walsh, review of *Godspell,* Apr. 21, 1973.

Excerpts from *America* with the permission of America Press, Inc., 106 West 56th Street, New York, NY 10019, all rights reserved, © 1980: John W. Donahue, review of *Jesus,* May 10, 1980.

Excerpts from *America* with the permission of Richard A. Blake, S.J. and America Press, Inc., 106 West 56th Street, New York, NY 10019, all rights reserved, © 1973–88: Richard A. Blake, S.J., review of *Godspell,* Apr. 14, 1973; Richard A. Blake, S.J., review of *Jesus of Nazareth,* Apr. 9, 1977; Richard A.

279

Blake, S.J., review of *The Last Temptation of Christ*, Aug. 27, 1988; Richard A. Blake, S.J., review of *The Passion of the Christ*, Mar. 15, 2004.

Excerpts from *America* with the permission of America Press, Inc., in the absence of Thomas O'Brien, 106 West 56th Street, New York, NY 10019, © 1990: Thomas O'Brien, review of *Jesus of Montreal*, May 26, 1990.

Excerpts courtesy of *America*: a commentary on *Life of Brian*, Sept. 15, 1979.

Excerpts courtesy of *America*: Lloyd Baugh, S.J., review of *The Passion of the Christ*, Feb. 23, 2004.

Excerpts from *American Film:* Michael Morris, O.P., review of *The Last Temptation of Christ*, October 1988.

Excerpts courtesy of *The Boston Globe:* Jay Carr, review of *Jesus of Montreal*, June 8, 1990; Ty Burr, review of *The Passion of the Christ*, Feb, 24, 2004.

Excerpts with the permission of *The Catholic World:* Edward H. Peters, review of *The Greatest Story Ever Told*, April 1965 © Paulist Press.

Excerpts with the permission of *The Christian Century*, copyrighted by The Christian Century Foundation: editorial on *Ben-Hur*, Oct. 28, 1959, © 1959; Martin E. Marty, review of *Ben-Hur*, Jan. 13, 1960, © 1960; Tom F. Driver, review of *King of Kings*, Nov. 11, 1961, © 1961; Fred Myers, on *The Greatest Story Ever Told*, Apr. 21, 1965, © 1965; Martin E. Marty, review of *The Gospel According to St. Matthew*, Dec. 23, 1964, © 1964; Robert J. Nelson, review of *The Gospel According to St. Matthew*, Mar. 16, 1966, © 1966; Elliott Wright, "Jesus on Stage: A Reappraisal" [On *Jesus Christ Superstar and Godspell*], July 19, 1972, © 1972; James M. Wall, review of *Jesus Christ Superstar*, June 27, 1973, © 1973; Rabbi Marc Tanenbaum, reader's response, *Jesus Christ Superstar*, Sept. 5, 1973, © 1973; interview, with Andrew Lloyd Webber on *Jesus Christ Superstar*, Mar. 18–25, 1987, © 1987; Charles P. Henderson, review of *Jesus of Nazareth*, Apr. 20, 1977, © 1977; James M. Wall, editorial on *The Last Temptation of Christ*, Aug. 17–24, 1988, © 1988; Matthew Myer Boulton, review of *The Passion of the Christ*, Mar. 23, 2004 © 2004.

Excerpts with the permission of *Christianity Today*: Cheryl Forbes, *Jesus Christ Superstar*, Oct. 12, 1973; Cheryl Forbes, review of *Godspell*, Apr. 10, 1973; editorial, on *Jesus of Nazareth*, Apr. 15, 1977; Cheryl Forbes, review of *Jesus of Nazareth*, May 20, 1977; Thomas Trumbull Howard, review of *Jesus*, Dec. 21, 1979; David Neff, editorial on *The Last Temptation of Christ*, Oct. 7, 1988; Harvie Conn, commentary on *Life of Brian*, Nov 16, 1979; David Neff, article on *The Passion of the Christ*, March 2004; Peter T. Chattaway, review of *The Passion of the Christ*, March 2004.

Excerpts with the permission of *Commonweal:* Philip T. Hartung, review of *Barabbas*, Nov. 9, 1962; Philip T. Hartung, review of *The Greatest Story Ever Told*, Mar. 12, 1965; Philip T. Hartung, review of *The Gospel According to St. Matthew*, Mar. 6, 1966; articles "Anti-Semitism in *The Passion*" by Rabbi Irving Greenberg and "Blame the Gospels?" by Donald Senior, C.P., issue of May 7, 2004.

Excerpts courtesy of *Esquire Magazine* and the Hearst Corporation: Dwight Macdonald, review of *Ben-Hur*, March 1960; Dwight Macdonald, review of *King of Kings*, March 1962.

Excerpts with the permission of *Film Comment:* Harlan Jacobson, "You Talkin' to Me?" pp. 32–33. [On *The Last Temptation of Christ*], September-

October 1988; Richard Corliss, "Body . . . And Blood," pp. 34f. [On *The Last Temptation of Christ*], September-October 1988.

Excerpts courtesy of *The Los Angeles Times::* Sheila Benson, review of *Jesus of Montreal*, June 1, 1990.

Excerpts with the permission of *Macleans*: Lawrence O'Toole, review of *Life of Brian*, Sept. 10, 1979; Brian D. Johnson, review of *Jesus of Montreal*, May 29, 1989; Brian D. Johnson, another review of *Jesus of Montreal*, September 18, 1989.

Excerpts with the permission of *The Nation:* Robert Hatch, review of *The Greatest Story Ever Told*, Mar. 1, 1965 (FILM REVIEWS); Robert Hatch, review of *The Gospel According to St. Matthew*, Mar. 7, 1966 (FILM REVIEWS).

Excerpts with the permission of *National Catholic Reporter:* Michael O. Garvey, "What Does a Man Who Is Also God Look Like" [On *The Last Temptation of Christ*], June 29, 1990.

Reprinted by permission of *National Review*, Inc., 215 Lexington Avenue, New York, NY 10016: John Simon, review of *The Last Temptation of Christ*, September 1988, © 1988.

Excerpts with the permission of *The New Republic:* Gilbert Seldes, review of *The King of Kings*, 4 May 1927; Stanley Kauffmann, review of *The Gospel According to St. Matthew*, 26 March 1966, review of *Godspell*, 12 May 1973; Stanley Kauffmann, review of *Life of Brian*, Sept, 22, 1979.

Excerpts from *Newsweek* with the permission of Newsweek, Inc., all rights reserved: review of *Ben-Hur*, Nov. 30, 1959, © 1959; review of *King of Kings*, Oct. 30, 1961, © 1961; review of *The Greatest Story Ever Told*, Feb. 22, 1965, © 1965; review of *The Gospel According to St. Matthew*, Feb. 28, 1966, © 1966; review of *Jesus Christ Superstar*, July 9, 1973, © 1973; review of *Godspell*, Apr. 9, 1973, © 1973; Harry F. Waters, review of *Jesus of Nazareth*, Apr. 4, 1977, © 1977; David Ansen, review of *Life of Brian*. Sept. 3, 1979, © 1979.

Excerpts with the permission of *The New York Times*, copyrights held by the New York Times Company: Mordaunt Hall, review of *The King of Kings*, Apr. 20, 1927, © 1965; Bosley Crowther, review of *Quo Vadis*, Nov. 9, 1951, © 1951; Bosley Crowther, review of *The Robe*, Sept. 27, 1953, © 1953; Joanne Stang, feature on *The Greatest Story Ever Told*, Feb. 14, 1965, © 1965; Bosley Crowther, review of *The Greatest Story Ever Told*, Feb. 16, 1965, © 1965; Bosley Crowther, review of *The Gospel According to St. Matthew*, Feb. 18, 1966, © 1966; Vincent Canby, review of *Godspell*, Mar. 22, 1973, © 1973; Vincent Canby, review of *Life of Brian*, Aug. 17, 1979, © 1979; Vincent Canby, article on *Life of Brian*, Sept. 30, 1979, © 1979; Janet Maslin, review of *The Last Temptation of Christ*, Aug. 12, 1988, © 1988; Caryn James, review of *Jesus of Montreal*, May 25, 1990, © 1990; A. O. Scott, review of *The Passion of the Christ*, Feb. 25, 2004, © 2004; column by William Safire on *The Passion of the Christ*, © 2004, published Mar. 1, 2004, syndicated in [Greensboro, NC] *News & Record*, Mar. 2, 2004.

Excerpts with the permission of *The New Yorker Magazine*, Inc., all rights reserved: Brendan Gill, review of *King of Kings*, Oct. 21, 1961, © 1961; Brendan Gill, review of *The Greatest Story Ever Told*, © 1965 Feb. 20, 1965, © 1965; Penelope Gilliatt, review of *Godspell*, April 7, 1973, © 1973; and by courtesy of *The New Yorker*, David Denby review of *The Passion of the Christ*, Mar. 1, 2004, © 2004; Anthony Lane, review of *Life of Brian*, May 3, 2004, © 2004.